ACCA

X A M   P R A C T I C E   K I T

DIPLOMA IN INTERNATIONAL FINANCIAL REPORTING

BPP Learning Media is an **ACCA Content Partner** for the DipIFR qualification. This means we work closely with ACCA to ensure our products fully prepare you for your DipIFR exams.

In this Exam Practice Kit, which has been reviewed by the **DipIFR examining team**:

- We discuss the **best strategies** for revising and taking your DipIFR exam

- We show you how to be **well prepared** for your exam

- We give you **lots of great guidance** on tackling questions

- We provide you with **three** mock exams including the **June 2023** and **December 2023** exams

Our **Passcards** also support this qualification.

FOR EXAMS IN DECEMBER 2024 AND JUNE 2025

First edition 2004
Seventeenth edition 2024

ISBN 9781 0355 1471 7
(previous ISBN 9781 0355 0678 1)
e-ISBN 9781 0355 1474 8

British Library Cataloguing-in-Publication Data
A catalogue record for this book
is available from the British Library

Published by
BPP Learning Media Ltd
BPP House, Aldine Place
London W12 8AA

learningmedia.bpp.com

Printed in the United Kingdom

Your learning materials, published by BPP Learning Media Ltd, are printed on paper obtained from traceable, sustainable sources.

Contents

Review form

Using your BPP Learning Media products

This Exam Practice Kit gives you the question practice and guidance you need in the exam.

As an ACCA **Approved Content Partner**, BPP Learning Media gives you the **opportunity** to use revision materials reviewed by the ACCA examining team. By incorporating the examining team's comments and suggestions regarding the depth and breadth of syllabus coverage, the BPP Learning Media Exam Practice Kit provides excellent, **ACCA-approved** support for your studies.

These materials are reviewed by the ACCA examining team. The objective of the review is to ensure that the material properly covers the syllabus and study guide outcomes, used by the examining team in setting the exams, in the appropriate breadth and depth. The review does not ensure that every eventuality, combination or application of examinable topics is addressed by the ACCA Approved Content. Nor does the review comprise a detailed technical check of the content as the Approved Content Provider has its own quality assurance processes in place in this respect.

Our other products can also help you pass:

- The **Study Text** outlines the content of the qualification, the necessary skills the examining team expect you to demonstrate and any assumed prior knowledge and is completely focused on helping you pass the exam.

- **Passcards** provide you with clear topic summaries and exam tips.

You can purchase these products by visiting learningmedia.bpp.com

Question and Answer checklist/index

The headings in this index indicate the main topics of questions, but questions often cover several different topics. Questions that include an ethics element are marked with an asterisk (*).

BPP LEARNING MEDIA

Effective revision

What you must remember

Effective use of time as you approach the exam is very important. You must remember to:

- Believe in yourself
- Use time sensibly

Believe in yourself

Are you cultivating the right attitude of mind? There is absolutely no reason why you should not pass this **exam** if you adopt the correct approach.

- **Be confident** – you've passed exams before, you can pass them again
- **Be calm** – plenty of adrenaline but no panicking
- **Be focused** – commit yourself to passing the exam

Use time sensibly

1   **How much study time do you have?** Remember that you must **eat**, **sleep**, and of course, **relax**.

2   **How will you split that available time between each subject?** A **revision timetable**, covering **what** and **how** you will revise, will help you organise your revision thoroughly.

3   **What is your learning style?** AM/PM? Little and often/long sessions? Evenings/weekends?

4   **Do you have quality study time?** Unplug the phone. Let everybody know that you're studying and shouldn't be disturbed.

5   **Are you taking regular breaks?** Most people absorb more if they do not attempt to study for long uninterrupted periods of time. A five minute break every hour (to make coffee, watch the news headlines) can make all the difference.

6   **Are you rewarding yourself for your hard work?** Are you leading a **healthy lifestyle?**

What to revise

Key topics

You need to spend most time on, and practise full questions on, **key topics**.

Key topics

- Recur regularly
- Underpin whole exam
- Discussed currently in press
- Covered in recent articles by examining team
- Shown as high priority in study material

Difficult areas

You may also still find certain areas of the syllabus difficult.

> Difficult areas
>
> - Areas that are not relevant to your work
> - Subjects you highlighted as difficult when taking notes
> - Topics that gave you problems when you answered questions or reviewed the material

DON'T let these areas get you down; instead do something about them.

- Build up your knowledge by **quick tests** such as the quick quizzes in your BPP Learning Media Study Text.

- Work carefully through **numerical examples** and **questions** in the BPP Study Text for exams in December 2024 and June 2025, and refer back to the Study Text if you struggle with computations in the Exam Practice Kit.

- **Note down weaknesses** that your answers to questions contained; you are less likely to make the same mistakes if you highlight where you went wrong.

Breadth of revision

Make sure your revision has sufficient **breadth**. Given that all questions are compulsory, you need to be prepared for anything. There are also regular questions on what you may consider to be peripheral areas, eg IAS 41 *Agriculture*, IFRS 6 *Exploration for and Evaluation of Mineral Resources*, so you must know the entire syllabus.

DipIFR

In this exam, do not spend all your revision practising the numerical techniques. Past exams include computational and discursive elements.

How to revise

There are four main ways that you can revise a topic area.

- Write it!
- Read it!
- Teach it!
- Do it!

Write it!

The Study Text is too bulky for revision. You need a slimmed down set of notes that summarise the key points. Writing important points down will help you recall them, particularly if your notes are presented in a way that makes it easy for you to remember them.

Read it!

You should read your notes actively, testing yourself by doing quick quizzes or Exam Practice Kit questions while you are reading.

Teach it!

Exams require you to show your understanding. Teaching what you are revising to another person helps you practise explaining topics. Teaching someone who will challenge your understanding, someone for example who will be taking the same exam as you, can help both of you.

Do it!

Remember that you are revising in order to be able to answer questions in the exam. Answering questions will help you practise **technique** and **discipline**, which the examining team emphasise over and over again can be crucial in passing or failing exams.

1   The more exam-standard questions you do, the more likely you are to pass the exam. Please remember that the DipIFR exam is a computer-based exam (CBE) and the more you can incorporate question practice in the ACCA CBE software into your preparation, the better.

2   You should produce **full answers** under **timed conditions**, and don't cheat by looking at the answer! If you are struggling, look back at your notes or the BPP Study Text; also read the guidance attached to certain questions and the questions with analysis. Produce answer plans if you are running short of time.

3   ACCA have provided a provided access to the Specimen Exam in the CBE software. You should allow time to practise answering this mock exam in full in order to become familiar with the CBE functionality.

4   Always read the **guidance** in the answers. It's there to help you, and will show you which points in the answer are the most important. In particular, see how you could have gained **easy marks** on the question. Also study carefully the guidance accompanying the answers to the questions with analysis, and the commentary provided with the student answers.

5   **Don't get despondent** if you didn't do very well. Be sure to try another question that covers the same subject.

The exam

Format of the exam

DipIFR is a computer-based exam (CBE). The duration of the exam is 3 hours and 15 minutes. The exam contains four 25-mark questions and all questions are compulsory. Most questions will contain a mix of computational and discursive elements.

Question one will involve the preparation of one or more of the consolidated financial statements that are examinable within the syllabus. This question will often include issues that will need to be addressed prior to performing the consolidation procedures. Generally these issues will relate to the financial statements of the parent prior to their consolidation. Note that from the June 2023 exam, the spreadsheet response option for Question 1 will be pre-populated with the financial statements provided in Exhibit 1 of the question. More information is available on the ACCA website:

https://www.accaglobal.com/content/dam/acca/global/PDF-students/ifr/ifrint/6328_DipIFR-spreadsheet-response-v2.pdf

Question 2 will often be related to a scenario in which questions arise regarding the appropriate accounting treatment and/or disclosure of a range of issues. In this question candidates may be asked to comment on management's chosen accounting treatment and determine a more appropriate one, based on circumstances described in the question. This question will also contain an ethical and professional component related to the accounting treatment that is being examined. The ethical aspect of question two will have a mark ceiling of 5 marks.

Question 3 will usually focus more specifically on the requirements of one specific IFRS® Accounting Standard. This question will typically contain a mixture of explanation of the principles underpinning the standard and practical application of those principles.

Question 4 will usually consist of a scenario in which the candidate is given a series of queries from a superior relating to the financial statements. The requirement will usually be to answer each query. The queries will normally be independent of each other. It will be rare for the queries in question four to require a numerical answer.

Some IFRS Accounting Standards are very detailed and complex. In the DipIFR exam candidates need to be aware of the principles and key elements of these Standards. Candidates will also be expected to have an appreciation of the background and need for international financial reporting standards and issues related to harmonisation of accounting in a global context.

Finally the syllabus contains outcomes relating to the demonstration of appropriate digital and employability skills in preparing for and taking the DipIFR examination. This includes being able to interact with different question item types, including the prepopulated spreadsheet in Question 1, manage information presented in digital format and being able to use the relevant functionality and technology to prepare and present response options in a professional manner. These skills are specifically developed by practicing and preparing for the DipIFR exam, using the learning support content for CBEs available via the ACCA website and will need to be demonstrated during the live exam.

The overall pass mark for the Diploma in International Financial Reporting is 50%.

Examinable documents

ACCA has an annual cut off rule when deciding what comprises an examinable document which could be used as part of an exam. Knowledge of new examinable regulations issued by 1 September will be required in examination sessions being held in the following calendar year. Documents may be examinable even if the effective date is in the future.

The Study Guide provides more detailed guidance on the depth and level at which the examinable documents will be examined. Examinable documents are listed in the study support resources section of ACCA's website.

Analysis of past exams

The analysis below shows the elements of the syllabus that have been examined under the current syllabus for the past five years.

Covered in Text chapter		Dec 23	Jun 23	Dec 22	Jun 22	Dec 21	Jun 21	Dec 20	Sep 20*	Dec 19	Jun 19
	International sources of authority										
1	The regulatory framework and ethics	✓	✓	✓	✓	✓		✓			
2	The *Conceptual Framework*					✓					
	Elements of financial statements										
3	Revenue		✓	✓	✓			✓		✓	
4 and 5	Accounting for tangible non-current assets and other comprehensive income Impairment of assets	✓	✓	✓	✓			✓	✓	✓	✓
6	Accounting for leases					✓	✓		✓		✓
7	Intangible assets and goodwill		✓								
8	Provisions, contingent liabilities and contingent assets		✓							✓	✓
9	Employee benefits	✓			✓	✓		✓		✓	
10	Financial instruments	✓	✓	✓	✓	✓	✓		✓	✓	✓
11	Accounting for taxation	✓			✓	✓			✓		
12	Foreign currency translation			✓			✓				✓
13	Other assets: Agriculture, mineral resources and inventories	✓		✓			✓	✓	✓	✓	
14	Share-based payment				✓			✓	✓		✓
	Presentation of financial statements and additional disclosures										
15	Presentation of published financial statements		✓		✓					✓	
16	Reporting financial performance	✓		✓		✓	✓	✓		✓	
17	Earnings per share	✓					✓			✓	
18	Related party disclosures and segment reporting		✓		✓	✓			✓		
19	Reporting for small and medium-sized entities		✓				✓				
	Preparation of external financial reports for combined entities and joint arrangements										
20	Constitution of a group		✓		✓		✓			✓	✓
21	The consolidated statement of financial position	✓		✓	✓		✓	✓		✓	
22	The consolidated statement of profit or loss		✓			✓			✓		✓
23	Accounting for associates	✓		✓			✓				✓
24	Accounting for joint arrangements		✓							✓	

* Exam was held in September 2020 rather than June 2020 due to Covid-19.

Exam success skills

Passing the DipIFR exam requires more than applying syllabus knowledge; it also requires the development of excellent exam technique through question practice. We consider the following six skills to be vital for exam success.

Exam success skill 1: Managing information

Questions in the exam will present you with a lot of information. The skill is how you handle this information to make the best use of your time. The key is determining how you will approach the exam and then actively reading the questions.

Advice on developing this skill

To avoid being overwhelmed by the quantity of information provided, you must take an active approach to reading each question.

Active reading means focussing on the question's requirement first, highlighting key verbs such as 'prepare', 'comment', 'explain', 'discuss', to ensure you answer the question properly. Then read the rest of the question, and as you now have an understanding of what the question requires you to do, you can highlight important and relevant information, and use the scratchpad within the exam software to make notes of any relevant technical information you think you will need.

The highlighter tool provided in the toolbar at the top of the exam screen offers a range of colours:

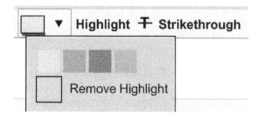

This allows you to choose **different colours to highlight different aspects to a question**. For example, if a question asked you to discuss the pros and cons of an issue then you could choose a different colour for highlighting pros and cons within the relevant section of a question.

The **strikethrough function** allows you to delete areas of a question that you have dealt with – this can be useful in managing information if you are dealing with numerical questions because it can allow you to ensure that all numerical areas have been accounted for in your answer.

You can **resize windows** within the exam by clicking and dragging on the bottom right-hand corner of the window.

This functionality allows you to **display a number of windows at the same time**, so this could allow you review:

- The question requirements and the exhibit relating to that requirement, at the same time; or
- The window containing your answer (whether a word processing or spreadsheet document) and the exhibit relating to that requirement, at the same time.

Exam success skill 2: Correct interpretation of the requirements

The active verb used often dictates the approach that written answers should take (eg 'explain', 'discuss', 'evaluate'). It is important you identify and use the verb to define your approach. The **correct interpretation of the requirements** skill means correctly producing only what is being asked for by a requirement. Anything not required will not earn marks.

Advice on developing this skill

This skill can be developed by analysing question requirements and applying this process:

Step 1	**Read the requirement** Firstly, read the requirement a couple of times slowly and carefully and highlight the active verbs. Use the active verbs to define what you plan to do. Make sure you identify any sub-requirements. You may find it useful to begin by **copying the requirements into your chosen response option** (eg word processor), in order to form the basis of your answer plan. See Exam success skill 3: Answer planning below.
Step 2	**Read the rest of the question** By reading the requirement first, you will have an idea of what you are looking out for as you read through the scenario and exhibits. This is a great time saver and means you don't end up having to read the whole question in full twice. You should do this in an active way – see Exam success skill 1: Managing information.
Step 3	**Read the requirement again** Read the requirements again to remind yourself of the exact wording before starting your answer. This will capture any misinterpretation of the requirements or any requirements missed entirely.

It is particularly important to pay attention to any dates you are given in requirements. This is especially the case when, for example, discussing an accounting treatment up to a particular date. No marks will be awarded for discussing the treatment at a different date than that asked for in the requirement.

Exam success skill 3: Answer planning: Priorities, structure and logic

This skill requires the planning of the key aspects of an answer which accurately and completely responds to the requirement.

Advice on developing this skill

Everyone will have a preferred style for an answer plan. For example, it may be to use the scratch pad to draw up a mind map or bullet-pointed lists. However, a time-saving approach in a CBE is to **plan your answer directly in your chosen response option** (eg word processor) and then fill out the detail of the plan with your answer. This will save you time spent on creating a separate plan in the scratchpad and then typing up your answer separately – though you could copy and paste between the scratchpad and response option if you wanted to do so.

The easiest way to start your answer plan is to **copy the question requirements to your chosen response option** (eg word processor). This will allow you to ensure that your answer plan addresses all parts of the question requirements. Then, as you **read through the exhibits, you can copy and paste any relevant information into your chosen response option** under the relevant requirement. This approach also has the advantage of making sure your answer is applied to the scenario given.

Copying and pasting simply involves selecting the relevant information and either right clicking to access the copy and paste functions, or alternatively using Ctrl-C to copy and Ctrl-V to paste.

Exam success skill 4: Efficient numerical analysis

This skill aims to maximise the marks awarded by making clear to the marker the process of arriving at your answer. This is achieved by laying out an answer such that, even if you make a few errors, you can still score subsequent marks for follow-on calculations. It is vital that you do not lose marks purely because the marker cannot follow what you have done.

Advice on developing this skill

This skill can be developed by applying the following process:

Step 1	**Use a standard proforma working where relevant** If answers can be laid out in a standard proforma then always plan to do so. This will help the marker to understand your working and allocate the marks easily. It will also help you to work through the figures in a methodical and time-efficient way.
Step 2	**Show your workings** Keep your workings as clear and simple as possible and ensure they are cross-referenced to the main part of your answer. Where it helps, provide brief narrative explanations to help the marker understand the steps in the calculation. This means that if a mistake is made you do not lose any subsequent marks for follow-on calculations.
Step 3	**Keep moving!** It is important to remember that, in an exam situation, it is difficult to get every number 100% correct. The key is therefore ensuring you do not spend too long on any single calculation. If you are struggling with a solution then make a sensible assumption, state it and move on.

In the CBE, you can use the spreadsheet to prepare calculations, if you wish. If you do so, you can make use of formulas to help with calculations, instead of using a calculator. For example, the 'sum' function: =SUM(A1:10) would add all the numbers in spreadsheet cells A1 to A10. You can use the symbol ^ to calculate a number 'to the power of…', eg =1.10^2 calculates 1.10 squared – this is very useful if you need to perform a discounting calculation.

If you use the spreadsheet for calculations, make sure the spreadsheet cell includes your formula and not just the final answer, so that the marker can see what you have done and can award follow-on marks even if you have made a mistake earlier in the calculation.

If you do decide to use a calculator instead, don't just put the final answer into a cell without including your workings – make sure you type up your workings as well and cross refer to them in your final answer.

Exam success skill 5: Effective writing and presentation

Narrative answers should be presented so that the marker can clearly see the points you are making, presented in the format specified in the question. The skill is to provide efficient narrative answers with sufficient breadth of points that answer the question, in the right depth, in the time available.

Advice on developing this skill

Step 1	**Use headings**
	Using the headings and sub-headings from your answer plan will give your answer structure, order and logic. This will ensure your answer links back to the requirement and is clearly signposted, making it easier for the marker to understand the different points you are making. Underlining or making your headings bold will also help the marker.
Step 2	**Type your answer in short, but full, sentences**
	Use short, punchy sentences with the aim that every sentence should say something different and generate marks. Type in full sentences, ensuring your style is professional.
Step 3	**Do your calculations first and explanation second**
	Questions sometimes ask for an explanation with supporting calculations. The best approach is to prepare the calculation first but present it on the bottom half of the page of your answer. Then add the explanation before the calculation. Performing the calculation first should enable you to explain what you have done.
	In the CBE, this is easy to do – prepare your calculation, then type up your answer above it. If you wish, you can use the word processor to type up narrative discussion and the spreadsheet to prepare any calculations. If you do so, make sure you clearly cross reference to your calculation so the marker can follow what you have done. See Exam success skill 4: Efficient numerical analysis.

Exam success skill 6: Good time management

This skill means planning your time across all the requirements so that all tasks have been attempted at the end of the 3 hours 15 minutes available and actively checking on time during your exam. This is so that you can flex your approach and prioritise requirements which, in your judgement, will generate the maximum marks in the available time remaining.

Advice on developing this skill

The exam is 3 hours 15 minutes long, which translates to 1.95 minutes per mark. Therefore a 10-mark requirement should be allocated a maximum of 20 minutes to complete your answer before you move on to the next task. At the beginning of a question, work out the amount of time you should be spending on each requirement and type the time allocation next to the requirements in your answer plan. If you take the approach of spending 10–15 minutes reading and planning at the start of the exam, adjust the time allocated to each question accordingly; eg if you allocate 15 minutes to reading, then you will have 3 hours remaining, which is 1.8 minutes per mark.

Keep an eye on the clock

Aim to attempt all requirements, but be ready to be ruthless and move on if your answer is not going as planned. The challenge for many is sticking to planned timings. Be aware this is difficult to achieve in the early stages of your studies and be ready to let this skill develop over time.

If you find yourself running short on time and know that a full answer is not possible in the time you have, consider recreating your plan in overview form and then add key terms and details as time allows. If you have done your planning directly in your chosen response option, this should be straightforward to do if you are short of time. Remember, some marks may be available, for example, simply stating a conclusion which you don't have time to justify in full.

Approaching a computer-based exam (CBE)

DipIFR is examined using a CBE. You need to make sure that you know how to use the CBE software so that you are fully prepared for your exam.

It is very important for you to become familiar with the CBE software. On the ACCA website, there are various CBE resources which you should ensure you access before attempting your DipIFR exam. In particular, you should attempt the DipIFR Specimen exam in the CBE practice software, available here:

https://www.accaglobal.com/uk/en/student/exam-support-resources/dipifr-study-resources/cbe-specimen-exam.html

You should also access the past exams available in the practice software here:
https://www.accaglobal.com/gb/en/student/exam-support-resources/dipifr-study-resources/past-examinations.html#

You should familiarise yourself with the prepopulated spreadsheets used in Question 1:

https://www.accaglobal.com/content/dam/acca/global/PDF-students/ifr/ifrint/6328_DipIFR-spreadsheet-response-v2.pdf

---

In this section, we will explore how to use the CBE software using syllabus section E: **Employability and technology skills** as a framework. We will also refer to the exam success skills covered in the previous section.

Syllabus learning outcome E1. Use computer technology to efficiently access and manipulate relevant information

CBE tools can be used to support the exam success skill of managing information (exam success skill 1).

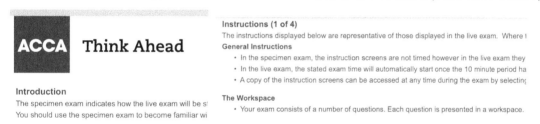

The first thing you will see when you open a CBE is an introduction followed by a series of instructions on how to use the CBE software. On the ACCA website, there is a document which explains the differences in functionality between the CBE specimen and the live exam: https://www.accaglobal.com/uk/en/student/exam-support-resources/dipifr-study-resources/cbe-specimen-exam.html#

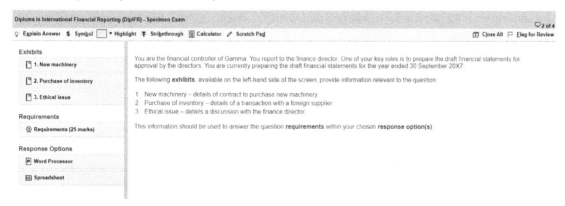

Once you have started the CBE and are in a question, you should note the various elements of the workspace:

- **Introductory information** (on the right side of the screen) – this usually contains background information about the company and a list of the exhibits that are provided.

- **Exhibits** – to open an exhibit, click on the button on the left side of the screen. When you click on an exhibit button, a new window is opened containing the exhibit information. The exhibits contain the question scenario, broken down into smaller sections and are necessary for answering the question. Each requirement will only relate to one exhibit, so to avoid too much clutter on your screen, you should only have one exhibit open at a time.

- **Requirement(s)** – the question requirements are opened via the clickable button on the left side of the screen. When you click the requirement button, a new window is opened containing the requirements.

- **Response option(s)** – the response options are where you present your answer. For Question 1, you will usually be provided with a spreadsheet only. For the remaining questions, you will usually be provided with both a word processor and a spreadsheet. The response options are opened by clicking on the button on the left side of the screen.

Once you have opened the requirements, the relevant exhibit and the response option, the screen will start to get very cluttered. To help you manage all this information, you can re-arrange how each of these windows looks on screen. The windows can all be moved around on the screen and can be re-sized (by clicking on the bottom right of an exhibit): you need to attempt some questions in the CBE specimen to get used to how the windows move and how you can arrange them. As each requirement will only relate to one exhibit, you should only have one exhibit open at a time.

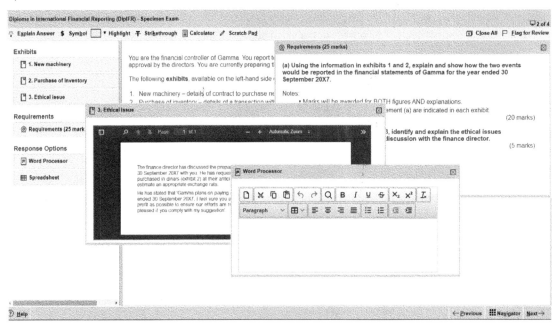

Syllabus learning outcome E2. Work on relevant response options, using available functions and technology, as required by the workspace

CBE tools can be used to support the exam success skills of answer planning (exam success skill 3) and efficient numerical analysis (exam success skill 4).

Response options

Questions may present you with both a word processor response option and a spreadsheet response option, or they may just include a spreadsheet (eg in question 1) or just a word processor, if the answer required is mainly discursive. Where you have both options available, remember you can answer using both response options for a single requirement. For example, if the requirement asked for calculations and then an explanation of these calculations, we recommend you perform the calculations in the spreadsheet and type your explanation in the word processor. To make it clear for the marker, you should clearly label your calculations and then reference them in your explanation in the word processor.

Within the workspace and response options, there are several functions that will help you plan and type up your answer, such as highlighting and formatting text, undo and redo, and copy and paste.

There are many functions and formulae that can be used in the spreadsheet, so you are advised to access the CBE specimen as soon as possible to make sure you are able to use them.

You can copy and paste text and numbers from an exhibit into the word processor and spreadsheet however you may need to reformat if copying from a table so be careful.

Other workspace functions

There is a **scratch pad** function available if you want to make rough notes. The contents of the scratch pad will be saved on screen for you for the duration of your exam, however, they will not be marked. Therefore, we recommend you do all your planning and note taking within the response option itself. That way your planning will be visible to you as you type up your answer and will be visible to the examiner once your exam is submitted. If you run out of time to complete your answer, you may score a small number of marks for the contents of your plan.

The workspace also contains a **calculator** function (you can use your own calculator, but it must not have the ability to enter and store data).

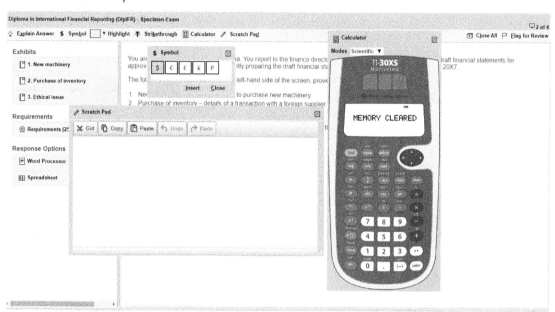

Syllabus learning outcome E3. Navigate windows and computer screens to create and amend responses to exam requirements, using the appropriate tools

This supports the exam success skills of managing information (exam success skill 1), correct interpretation of requirements (skill 2), answer planning (exam success skill 3), and time management (exam success skill 6).

Requirements

By now, you should be starting to feel more comfortable toggling between the various elements of the CBE – the exhibits, the requirement(s) and the response option(s). We recommend that you copy the requirements and paste them into the word processor response option. You can then use the requirements as the basis of your answer plan and you can close the requirements window, which will make the workspace less cluttered. Another benefit to copying the requirements like this is that the requirements will be visible as you type up your answer, helping you to stay focussed on what you have actually been asked to do.

Navigation tools

What about switching between questions? This can be done by accessing the **navigator** function on the bottom right-hand corner of the workspace:

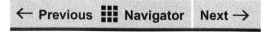

If you feel you need to move on but haven't finished what you wanted to say (perhaps you're stuck, or you are concerned about time) the navigator gives you the option to **flag** the question for review at a later stage to make sure that you haven't forgotten about it. There is also a **help** function which provides an overview of the instructions for both the workspace and the exam itself.

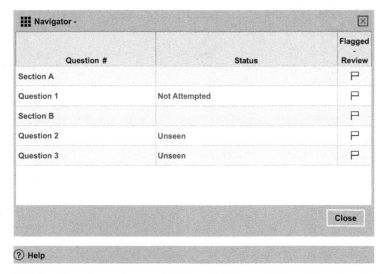

Syllabus learning outcome E4. Present data and information effectively, using the appropriate tools

This supports the exam success skill of **effective writing and presentation** (exam success skill 5).

The formatting functionality in the word processor response option will help you to produce a more professional-looking answer. However, keep it simple. Tables, headings, bold text and underlining may all be useful where appropriate but no marks are available for different font sizes or styles for headings.

Summary

Make use of the questions available in the CBE specimen and in the three past exams available in the CBE practice software. This will help to familiarise you with the various elements of the CBE and how you can make use of them when answering questions.

Although there are syllabus outcomes on employability and technology skills, demonstration of these skills **won't specifically attract marks** in the same way that you are rewarded for technical skills. However, familiarity with the technology that you are given in the CBE will help **you perform effectively in the exam**.

Suggested approach to exam questions

We recommend the following approach to answering an exam question in a CBE:

Step 1	Work out what time you should finish the question. All questions are 25 marks, so you should spend approximately 49 minutes on each. Allocate this time between each requirement in the question.
Step 2	Copy the question requirements into your chosen response option. Then read the requirements and analyse them. Underline each sub-requirement separately and identify the verb(s) used in the requirement. Ask yourself what each sub-requirement means.
Step 3	Read and analyse the scenario. Use active reading as discussed in Exam success skill 1. You may want to note relevant IFRS Accounting Standards, or issues you have identified, in your chosen response option under the relevant requirement, as you read each exhibit. Each requirement will relate to one exhibit only, so to avoid too much clutter on your screen, we recommend you only have open the exhibit that is relevant to the requirement you are addressing.

Step 4	Prepare an answer plan. We recommend you do this in your chosen response option, under the relevant requirement. Use key words from the requirement as headings. In Question 1 (the consolidation question), you do not need to make a plan, but you should make notes on the group structure and draw up a proforma for the consolidated statement you are required to prepare.
Step 5	Complete your answer. We recommend that you present discursive answers in the word processor response option. If you need to prepare a longer calculation or working, we recommend that you use the spreadsheet response option and then cross reference from the word processor to the spreadsheet, so that the marker can see what you have done.

Question practice

Question practice is a core part of learning new topic areas. When you practice questions, you should focus on improving your Exam success skills – personal to your needs – by obtaining feedback or through a process of self-assessment. Practising as many exam-style questions as possible will be the key to passing this exam. You should use word and excel to type up your answers as this will help you get used to typing, rather than writing, your answers, which is good preparation for your CBE. You should attempt questions under timed conditions and ensure you produce full answers to the discussion parts as well as doing the calculations. Also ensure that you attempt all mock exams under exam conditions.

INTRODUCTION

Questions

1 Omega 15 (December 2011) (amended)   49 mins

You are the financial controller of Omega. Omega has subsidiaries located in a number of different countries. All subsidiaries currently prepare financial statements using applicable local accounting standards. Local regulations allow financial statements to be prepared either using local accounting standards or IFRS Accounting Standards. The directors are giving serious consideration to using IFRS Accounting Standards from the year ending 30 September 20X2 onwards. They are also keen to begin producing sustainability disclosures and would like to understand more about the IFRS Sustainability Disclosure Standards, particularly in respect of climate-related matters. One of the directors is not familiar with IFRS Accounting Standards and IFRS Sustainability Disclosure Standards and has identified a number of issues about which he is uncertain. Relevant information is provided in the exhibit.

Exhibit – Director's queries

Query 1

Before I can agree with using IFRS Accounting Standards I need to understand how the standard setting process works. Someone told me there are four different bodies involved! Please give me a brief description of each one of these, highlighting their role in the standard setting process.

Query 2

I am aware of the IASB's *Conceptual Framework for Financial Reporting* (Conceptual Framework) but I'm not clear on what the role of the *Conceptual Framework* is in developing IFRS Accounting Standards and whether there are benefits to having a *Conceptual Framework*.

Query 3

I have heard that there is a new standard setting body called the International Sustainability Standards Board (ISSB). So I can get a better understanding of this new area, can you tell me what the role and purpose of the ISSB is?

I'm particularly interested in any standards that would require us to disclose information on climate-related matters. Can you please explain what might be required under the IFRS Sustainability Disclosure Standards?

Query 4

I know that we recently entered into a lease agreement for a new delivery vehicle. The lease is for two years and I'm surprised to be told that under IFRS Accounting Standards this means we will now have to include both an asset and a liability in our statement of financial position relating to this lease. As far as I am concerned we just rent this vehicle – how can it be our asset and why do we need to show a liability for rent we will pay in the future? I know that we have full autonomy to use this specific vehicle as we wish for the two year period.

Requirements

(a)   Prepare a response to queries 1 to 3 raised by the director.

The mark allocation for each query is as follows:

Query 1–5 marks

Query 2–7 marks

Query 3–6 marks

(18 marks)

(b)   For Query 4, apply the definitions of an asset and a liability given in the *Conceptual Framework* along with the principles of IFRS 16 *Leases*, to discuss whether it is correct under IFRS Accounting Standards to recognise an asset and a liability for the lease of the delivery vehicle.   **(7 marks)**

(Total = 25 marks)

2 Mocca

49 mins

Mocca, a company with a year end 31 March 20X2, applies IFRS 15 *Revenue from Contracts with Customers* to report revenue transactions in the financial statements. Relevant information is provided in the exhibits.

Exhibit 1 – Sale of plant with call option

On 1 March 20X1, Mocca sold some plant for $500,000. The sale contract included a call option that gave Mocca the right to repurchase the plant for $550,000 on or before 30 April 20X2.

Exhibit 2 – Long term contract

On 1 October 20X0 Mocca entered into a contract in which performance obligations are deemed to be satisfied over time. The contract was expected to take 27 months and be completed on 31 December 20X2. The customer gains control over the asset as it is constructed. The percentage of performance obligation satisfied is calculated on the input basis using the contract costs incurred to date as a proportion of total contract costs.

The total contract price and estimated total contract costs are:

	$'000
Total contract revenue	12,500
Estimated total cost of contract	5,500

The correctly reported profit or loss results for the contract for the year ended 31 March 20X1 were:

	$'000
Revenue recognised	3,500
Contract expenses recognised	(2,660)
Profit recognised	840

Details of the progress of the contract at 31 March 20X2 are:

	$'000
Contract costs incurred to date	4,800
Amount invoiced to date	8,125
Total cash received to date	7,725

There was no trade receivable or contract asset or liability recognised at 31 March 20X2.

Exhibit 3 – Sale of goods and services

On 1 April 20X1, Mocca sold a machine to a customer. Mocca invoiced the customer for $500,000 on 1 April 20X1 and the customer paid $500,000 to Mocca on 15 May 20X1. The terms of sale stated that Mocca would service and maintain the machine for a four-year period from 1 April 20X1. Mocca normally charges an annual fee of $37,500 for a service and maintenance arrangement of this nature. The normal selling price of the machine without a service and maintenance arrangement was $450,000.

Requirements

(a)   IFRS 15 deals with accounting requirements for contracts in respect of which performance obligations are satisfied over time.

Describe the issues of revenue and profit recognition in contracts where performance obligations are satisfied over time.   **(5 marks)**

(b)   Explain and show how the above transactions would be treated in the financial statements of Mocca for the year ended 31 March 20X2.

The marks are allocated as follows:

Exhibit 1 – Sale of plant with call option	**(5 marks)**
Exhibit 2 – Long term contract	**(6 marks)**
Exhibit 3 – Sale of goods and services	**(9 marks)**

Note. You should assume that all transactions described here are material.

(Total = 25 marks)

3 Kolya (December 2015) (amended)   49 mins

Kolya is preparing its financial statements for the year ended 30 September 20X5. The exhibits provide information relevant to the question.

Exhibit 1 – Machine contract

On 1 September 20X5, Kolya sold a machine to a customer, Page. Kolya also agreed to service the machine for a two-year period from 1 September 20X5 for no additional charge. The total amount payable by Page for this arrangement was agreed to be:

- $800,000, if Page paid by 31 December 20X5
- $810,000, if Page paid by 31 January 20X6
- $820,000, if Page paid by 28 February 20X6

The directors of Kolya consider that it is highly probable that Page will pay for the products in January 20X6. The stand-alone selling price of the machine was $700,000 and Kolya would normally expect to receive $140,000 in consideration for providing two years' servicing of the machine. The alternative amounts receivable are to be treated as variable consideration.

Exhibit 2 – Right of return

On 20 September 20X5, Kolya sold 100 identical items to a customer for $2,000 each. The items cost Kolya $1,600 each to manufacture. The terms of sale are that the customer has the right to return the goods for a full refund within three months. After the three-month period has expired the customer can no longer return the goods and payment becomes immediately due. Kolya has entered into transactions of this type with this customer previously and can reliably estimate that 4% of the products are likely to be returned within the three-month period.

Exhibit 3 – Sale with a volume discount incentive

On 1 January 20X4 Kolya began an arrangement to sell goods to a third party – Birch. The price of the goods was set at $100 per unit for all sales in the two-year period ending 31 December 20X5. However, if sales of the product to Birch exceed 60,000 units in the two-year period ending 31 December 20X5, then the selling price of all units is retrospectively set at $90 per item.

Sales of the goods to Birch in the nine-month period ending on 30 September 20X4 totalled 20,000 units and this volume of sales per month was not expected to change before 31 December 20X5.

However, in the year ended 30 September 20X5, total sales of the goods to Birch were 35,000 and based on current orders from Birch, the estimate was revised. The directors of Kolya estimated that the total sales of the goods to Birch in the two-year period ending 31 December 20X5 would be more than 60,000 units.

Exhibit 4 – Non-refundable payment

On 30 November 20X4, Kolya entered into a one-year contract to sell goods to a large global chain of retail stores. The customer committed to buy at least $30 million of products over the one year contract. The contract required Kolya to make a non-refundable payment of $3 million to the customer at the inception of the contract. The $3 million payment is to compensate the customer for the changes required to its shelving to accommodate Kolya's products. Kolya duly paid this $3 million to the customer on 30 November 20X4.

Requirements

(a) Explain, with relevant calculations, how Kolya should account for the contract with Page (Exhibit 1) in its financial statements for the year ended 30 September 20X5.   **(9 marks)**

(b) Explain, with relevant calculations, how Kolya should account for the sale with a right of return (Exhibit 2) in its financial statements for the year ended 30 September 20X5.   **(5 marks)**

(c) Explain, with relevant calculations, how much revenue can be recognised by Kolya in relation to the sale with the volume discount incentive (Exhibit 3) in both the year ended 30 September 20X4 and the year ended 30 September 20X5.   **(6 marks)**

(d)   Using the information in Exhibit 4, explain how Kolya should account for the $3 million payment to its
        customer.   **(5 marks)**

                                                                                    (Total = 25 marks)

4 Delta (December 2019) (amended)   **49 mins**

Delta is preparing its financial statements for the year ended to 30 September 20X7. The exhibits provide
information relevant to the question.

Exhibit 1 – Sale of product with right of return

On 1 April 20X7 Delta sold a product to a customer for $121,000. This amount is payable on 30 June 20X9. The
manufacturing cost of the product for Delta was $80,000. The customer had a right to return the product for a full
refund at any time up to and including 30 June 20X7. At 1 April 20X7, Delta had no reliable evidence regarding the
likelihood of the return of the product by the customer. The product was not returned by the customer before
30 June 20X7 and so the right of return for the customer expired. On both 1 April 20X7 and 30 June 20X7, the cash
selling price of the product was $100,000. A relevant annual rate to use in any discounting calculations is 10%.

Exhibit 2 – Machine contract

On 1 January 20X7 Delta signed a contract to construct a machine for one of its customers and to subsequently
provide servicing facilities relating to the machine. Delta commenced construction on 1 February 20X7 and the
construction took two months to complete. Delta incurred the following costs of construction:

*   Materials $1 million.

*   Other direct costs $2 million.

*   Allocated fixed production overheads $1 million. This allocation was made using Delta's normal overhead
        allocation model.

On 1 April 20X7 the machine was delivered to the customer. The customer paid the full contract price of
$7.5 million on 31 May 20X7. The servicing and warranty facilities are for a three-year period from 1 April 20X7.
This is not considered to be an onerous contract at 30 September 20X7. In the six-month period from 1 April 20X7
to 30 September 20X7 Delta incurred costs of $200,000 relating to the servicing and this rate of expenditure is
estimated to continue over the remainder of the three-year period. Delta would normally expect to earn a profit
margin of 20% on the provision of servicing facilities of this nature.

The normal stand-alone selling price of the machine is $7 million. Both the machine and the servicing facilities are
capable of being sold independently of each other.

Requirements

(a)   IFRS 15 *Revenue from Contracts with Customers* contains principles which underpin the timing of the
        recognition of revenue from contracts with customers and the measurement of that revenue.

        Explain the principles underpinning the TIMING of revenue recognition and the MEASUREMENT of that
        revenue which are outlined in IFRS 15. You should provide examples of revenue transactions to support
        your explanations of these key principles.   **(12 marks)**

(b)   Explain and show how the transactions in Exhibits 1 and 2 would be reported in the financial statements of
        Delta for the year ended 30 September 20X7.

        The marks are allocated as follows:

        Exhibit 1 – Sale of product with right of return   **(7 marks)**
        Exhibit 2 –Machine contract   **(6 marks)**

                                                                                    (Total = 25 marks)

5 Delta (December 2021)   49 mins

Delta prepares financial statements to 30 September each year, and operates in a number of different business sectors.

The following **exhibits**, available on the left-hand side of the screen, provide information relevant to the question:

(1)   Sale of a machine – details of the sale of a machine with a repair and maintenance service.

(2)   Sale and leaseback – details of the sale and leaseback of a factory.

This information should be used to answer the question **requirement** within your chosen **response option(s)**.

Exhibit 1 – Sale of a machine

On 1 April 20X5, Delta sold a machine to a customer. The machine was manufactured by Delta in March 20X5 and then included in Delta's inventories at its cost price of $250,000. The machine was delivered to the customer on 1 April 20X5. As well as providing the machine, Delta also agreed to provide the customer with a maintenance and repair service of the machine for three years from the date of sale. Delta regularly provides maintenance and repair services on a 'stand-alone' basis to other customers. The total price payable by the customer for both the machine and the maintenance and repair service was $500,000. The customer paid this amount on 31 May 20X5. The normal stand-alone selling price of the machine at 1 April 20X5 was $420,000. The normal stand-alone selling price for a three-year repair and maintenance contract for such a machine at 1 April 20X5 was $180,000.

On 1 September 20X5, the machine developed a major fault and Delta carried out repairs on the machine during September 20X5 costing a total of $30,000. Following these repairs, the directors of Delta reviewed the condition of the machine and estimated that:

Requirements

(1)   They would need to carry out further repairs to the machine in the future.

(2)   The total additional cost of repairs to the machine between 1 October 20X5 and the end of the three-year maintenance and service period would be $155,000.

(3)   These repairs would occur evenly over the remaining term of the contract.

You can ignore the time value of money when preparing your answer to exhibit 1.   **(14 marks)**

Exhibit 2 – Sale and leaseback

On 1 October 20X4, Delta sold a factory to company X for $30 million, its fair value at that date. The factory was included in the property, plant and equipment of Delta at a carrying amount of $20 million. On 1 October 20X4, Delta entered into an agreement with X to lease the factory for a ten-year period, being its useful life to Delta. There was no provision in the lease to extend the lease beyond this non-cancellable period. The estimated economic life of the factory on 1 October 20X4 was 30 years.

Under the terms of the lease, Delta was required to make ten annual lease payments of $2 million, the first payment being due on 30 September 20X5. The rate of interest implicit in the lease was 8% per annum and the present value of the lease payments was $13.42 million. The payment due on 30 September 20X5 was made on the due date.   **(11 marks)**

Requirement

Using the information in exhibits 1 and 2, explain and compute the amounts which would be recognised by Delta in its financial statements for the year ended 30 September 20X5 and state where in these financial statements they should be presented. Marks will be awarded for BOTH figures AND explanations.

Note. The mark allocations are indicated against each exhibit.

(Total = 25 marks)

6 Omikron

49 mins

Omikron, a public limited company with a year end of 30 June 20X8, applies IAS 36 *Impairment of Assets*. The information contained in the following exhibits is relevant to the impairment review carried out by Omikron during the year.

Exhibit 1 – Cash generating unit

Omikron acquired a taxi business on 1 January 20X8 for $230,000. The carrying amounts of the assets of the business at that date based on fair value less costs of disposal were as follows:

	$'000
Vehicles	120
Intangible assets (taxi licence)	30
Trade receivables	10
Cash	50
Trade payables	(20)
	190

On 1 February 20X8, the taxi company had three of its vehicles stolen. The fair value less costs of disposal of these vehicles was $30,000 and because of non-disclosure of certain risks to the insurance company, the vehicles were uninsured. As a result of this event, Omikron wishes to recognise an impairment loss of $45,000 (inclusive of the loss of the stolen vehicles) due to the decline in the value in use of the cash generating unit, that is the taxi business. On 1 March 20X8 a rival taxi company commenced business in the same area. It is anticipated that the business revenue of Omikron will be reduced by 25% leading to a decline in the present value in use of the business which is calculated at $150,000. The fair value less costs of disposal of the taxi licence has fallen to $25,000 as a result of the rival taxi operator. The fair values less costs of disposal of the other assets have remained the same as at 1 January 20X8 throughout the period.

Exhibit 2 – Individual asset

Omikron has a single substantial asset, the SyMIX which it uses to manufacture computer chips. The carrying amount of the SyMIX after four years is $5 million (cost of $7 million, accumulated depreciation on a straight line basis of $2 million). There is no expected residual value. Due to a breakthrough in technology in the manufacture of computer chips, Omikron now expects the machine to produce 30% less than expected over the rest of its estimated useful life of ten years. Net future cash flows for the next five years, based on management's best estimate after taking the 30% cut into account, are ($'000):

Year	1	2	3	4	5
Future cash flows	600	660	710	755	790

The expected growth rates for the following years are:

Year	6	7	8	9	10
Future cash flows	2%	(1)%	(7)%	(16)%	(30)%

If the machine was sold now it would realise $3.2 million, net of selling costs. The discount rate to be applied to the future cash flows is 10%. Relevant discount factors are as follows:

Year	PV factor at 10%
1	0.90909
2	0.82645
3	0.75131
4	0.68301
5	0.62092
6	0.56447
7	0.51316
8	0.46651
9	0.42410
10	0.38554

Requirements

IAS 36 *Impairment of Assets* requires that where there has been an impairment in the value of an asset, the carrying amount should be written down to the recoverable amount. The phrase 'recoverable amount' is defined as 'the higher of an asset's fair value less costs of disposal and its value in use'.

(a) (i)   Describe the circumstances which indicate that an impairment loss relating to an asset may have occurred.   **(6 marks)**

 (ii) Explain how IAS 36 deals with the recognition and measurement of the impairment of assets.   **(7 marks)**

(b) Explain how the transactions described in Exhibit 1 and Exhibit 2 would be accounted for in the financial statements of Omikron in its financial statements. In respect of Exhibit 1, candidates should show the treatment of the impairment loss at 1 February 20X8 and 1 March 20X8.

The marks allocated are as follows:

Exhibit 1 – Cash generating units   **(7 marks)**
Exhibit 2 – Individual assets   **(5 marks)**

(Total = 25 marks)

7 Dougal   49 mins

Part (a) and (b) adapted from December 2015. Part (c) adapted from June 2010.

Dougal is an entity which is engaged in the construction industry and prepares financial statements to 30 September each year. The financial statements for the year ended 30 September 20X5 are shortly to be authorised for issue. The exhibits provide information relevant to the question.

Exhibit 1 – Property

On 1 October 20X0, Dougal purchased a large property for $20 million and immediately began to lease the property to Edha under an operating lease. Annual rentals were $2 million. On 30 September 20X4, the fair value of the property was $26 million. Under the terms of the lease, Edha was able to cancel the lease by giving six months' notice in writing to Dougal. Edha gave this notice on 30 September 20X4 and vacated the property on 31 March 20X5. On 31 March 20X5, the fair value of the property was $29 million. On 1 April 20X5, Dougal immediately began to convert the property into ten separate flats of equal size which Dougal intended to sell in the ordinary course of its business. Dougal spent a total of $6 million on this conversion project between 31 March 20X5 and 30 September 20X5. The project was incomplete at 30 September 20X5 and the directors of Dougal estimate that they need to spend a further $4 million to complete the project, after which each flat could be sold for $5 million. Dougal uses the fair value model to measure property whenever permitted by IFRS Accounting Standards.

Exhibit 2 – Machine

On 1 August 20X5, Dougal purchased a machine from a supplier located in a country whose local currency is the groat. The agreed purchase price was 600,000 groats, payable on 31 October 20X5. The asset was modified to suit Dougal's purposes at a cost of $30,000 during August 20X5 and brought into use on 1 September 20X5. The directors of Dougal estimated that the useful life of the machine from date of first use was five years.

Relevant exchange rates were as follows:

• 1 August 20X5 – 2.5 groats to $1
• 1 September 20X5 – 2.4 groats to $1
• 30 September 20X5 – 2.0 groats to $1
• 31 October 20X5 – 2.1 groats to $1

Exhibit 3 – Sale of properties

On 30 June 20X5 the directors of Dougal decided to dispose of two properties in different locations. Both properties were actively marketed by the directors from 1 July 20X5 and sales are expected before the end of December 20X5.

Summary details of the two properties are as follows:

Property	Carrying amount at 30 September 20X4	Depreciable amount at 30 September 20X4	Estimated remaining useful life at 30 September 20X4	Estimated fair value less costs to sell at 30 June 20X5
	$'000	$'000	$'000	$'000
A	25,000	15,000	30 years	28,000
B	22,000	16,000	40 years	18,000

Property A was available for sale without modifications from 1 July 20X5 onwards. On 30 September 20X5 the directors of Dougal were reasonably confident that a sale could be secured for $28 million. However, after the year-end property prices in the area in which property A is located started to decline. This was due to an unexpected adverse local economic event in October 20X5. Following this event the directors of Dougal estimated that property A would now be sold for $22 million less selling costs and they are very confident that this lower price can be achieved.

Property B needed repair work carried out on it before a sale could be completed. This repair work was carried out in the two-week period beginning 10 October 20X5. The costs of this repair work are reflected in the estimated fair value less costs to sell figure for property B of $18 million (see above). This estimate remains valid.

Required

Explain and show how the events described in Exhibits 1 to 3 would be reported in the financial statements of Dougal for the year ended 30 September 20X5.

The marks are allocated as follows:

Exhibit 1 – Property	**(10 marks)**
Exhibit 2 – Machine	**(7 marks)**
Exhibit 3 – Sale of properties	**(8 marks)**
	(Total = 25 marks)

8 Gamma (December 2020) (amended)   49 mins

Gamma prepares financial statements to 30 September each year.

The following **exhibits** provide information relevant to the question:

Exhibit 1: Purchase of machine

On 1 November 20X4, Gamma placed an order for machinery which was to be used in a new business venture. The initial cost of the machinery was $30 million. The machinery was delivered on 30 November 20X4. The machine required further development and installation at Gamma's premises. This was carried out by the supplier and took from 1 December 20X4 until 30 April 20X5. The total additional cost of this development and installation was $60 million. The supplier allowed Gamma two months credit from the date of completion of the installation. On 30 June 20X5, Gamma paid $90 million to the supplier.

Following the installation of the machinery, the employees attended a training course to ensure they could operate the machinery. The training was completed on 15 May 20X5 at a total cost of $1 million. Under legal regulations in the country in which Gamma is situated, a safety certificate is necessary for the machinery to be legally used. On 31 May 20X5, the machinery underwent a government inspection and a safety certificate was issued. The cost of the inspection and the safety certificate, paid on 30 June 20X5, was $600,000. Due to economic uncertainties, the machinery was not brought into use until 31 July 20X5.

The new business venture in which the machinery is being used is one which qualifies for preferential loans. These loans are of 12 months duration and carry a fixed annual interest rate of 4%. They are available only on 1 November each year. Therefore on 1 November 20X4, Gamma borrowed $90 million and repaid this amount, including accrued interest, on 31 October 20X5.

The estimated useful life of the machinery is ten years. However, the machinery's engine will require replacement after five years. The current replacement cost of the engine is $24 million. Gamma estimates that the replacement cost of the engine in five years' time will be $30 million. **(15 marks)**

Exhibit 2: Sale of land

Immediately prior to the 30 September 20X5 year end, Gamma sold land located adjacent to its head office to a third party at a price of $16 million with an option to purchase the land back on 1 November 20X5 for $16 million plus a premium of 3%. On 30 September 20X5 the market value of the land was $25 million and the carrying amount was $12 million. The cash received from this transaction eliminated Gamma's bank overdraft at 30 September 20X5. The managing director of Gamma has instructed the finance director to account for the transaction as a sale, and to include a profit on disposal in the statement of profit or loss for the year ended 30 September 20X5. The directors of Gamma are paid a bonus if a profit target for the reporting period is achieved. The finance director is currently experiencing financial difficulties in her personal affairs.

Requirement

(a)   Using the information in Exhibit 1, explain and show how the purchase of the machinery would be reported in the financial statements of Gamma for the year ended 30 September 20X5. **(15 marks)**

(b)   Using the information in Exhibit 2:

(i)   Explain how the sale of land should have been reported in in the financial statements of Gamma for the year ended 30 September 20X5. **(5 marks)**

(ii)   Identify and explain the ethical issues confronting the finance director. **(5 marks)**

Note. Marks will be awarded for BOTH figures AND explanations. **(Total = 25 marks)**

9 Gamma (December 2021) 49 mins

You are the financial controller of Gamma. You report to the finance director. One of your key roles is to prepare the draft consolidated financial statements for approval by the board. Gamma prepares consolidated financial statements to 30 September each year. Gamma has a number of subsidiaries who operate in a number of different business sectors.

The following **exhibits** provide information relevant to the question:

(1)   Disposal of subsidiary – details of a disposal during the year ended 30 September 20X5.

(2)   Construction of power plant – details of the power generating plant constructed during the year ended 30 September 20X5, and your discussion with the finance director of Gamma.

This information should be used to answer the question **requirements** within your chosen **response option(s)**.

Exhibit 1 – Disposal of subsidiary

On 31 May 20X5, Gamma disposed of its 75% holding in subsidiary A for $75 million. Gamma acquired these shares many years ago for a cash consideration of $40 million. Subsidiary A operates in a market sector which is different from that of the rest of the Gamma group. Its disposal was the result of a strategic decision by the directors of Gamma that the group should withdraw from that particular sector.

When Gamma purchased the shares in subsidiary A, the net assets of subsidiary A had a fair value of $48 million. None of the assets and liabilities of subsidiary A which were measured in the initial fair value exercise undertaken at the date of subsidiary A's acquisition were included in the financial statements of subsidiary A at 30 September 20X4.

When Gamma acquired its controlling interest in subsidiary A, the directors elected to measure the non-controlling interest in subsidiary A at its fair value of $13 million at the date of acquisition. No impairment of the goodwill on acquisition of subsidiary A has ever been necessary. On 1 October 20X4, the net assets of subsidiary A had a total carrying amount of $62 million. During the year ended 30 September 20X5, subsidiary A made a post-tax profit of $6.6 million. This profit accrued evenly over the year. Subsidiary A had no other comprehensive income. Subsidiary A paid a dividend of $3.6 million on 31 March 20X5. This was the only dividend paid by subsidiary A during the year ended 30 September 20X5.

Gamma incurred an income tax liability of $7 million on the disposal of the shares in subsidiary A.

Exhibit 2 – Construction of power plant

On 1 November 20X4, Gamma commenced the construction of a power plant. The total cost of constructing the power plant was $30 million. Gamma completed the construction of the power plant on 28 February 20X5 and began to use the power plant on 31 March 20X5. The estimated useful life of the power plant is 20 years from the date it is first depreciated.

The construction of the power plant caused a certain amount of environmental damage. The directors of Gamma estimate that, should the damage be rectified at the end of the useful life of the power plant, the cost of this rectification work would be $20 million. There are no legal requirements for such work to be carried out in the jurisdiction in which Gamma operates. However, in the past whenever Gamma has caused environmental damage by its business processes, the company has always rectified the damage, whether or not legally required to do so.

An appropriate discount rate to use in any discounting calculations is 8% per annum. Using this rate at 28 February 20X5, the present value of $1 payable in 20 years' time is approximately 21 cents.

The finance director has discussed the preparation of the financial statements with you. He has requested you not to include any of the implications of the environmental damage in the financial statements for the year ended 30 September 20X5. He has stated that Gamma plans on paying a profit-related bonus to all employees for the year ended 30 September 20X5. He said to you, 'I feel sure you agree with me that we need to report as healthy a profit as possible to ensure our efforts are rewarded with an appropriate bonus.'

Requirements

(a) Using the information in exhibits 1 and 2, explain and show how the following events would be reported in the consolidated financial statements of Gamma for the year ended 30 September 20X5:

   (i)   Disposal of subsidiary   **(12 marks)**
   (ii) Construction of power plant   **(9 marks)**

   Notes:

   •   Marks will be awarded for BOTH figures AND explanations.

   •   In this part of the question you should IGNORE the implications of your discussion with the finance director.

(b) Using the information in exhibit 2, identify and explain the ethical threats you face as a result of your discussion with the finance director. Your explanation should refer to relevant fundamental ethical principles.

                                                                                                         (4 marks)

                                                                                                  (Total = 25 marks)

10 Wiltshire

49 mins

You are the finance director of Wiltshire, a listed company which applies IFRS 16 *Leases.*

Wiltshire is a recycling company which collects waste, sorts it and sells it to third parties. Wiltshire is both a lessee and lessor. The company's new managing director is having difficulty understanding the accounting treatment and disclosure of assets leased by Wiltshire as lessor. She also requires advice as to how three new lessee arrangements entered into in the year ended 31 December 20X1 would be accounted for. The exhibits provide information relevant to the question.

Exhibit 1 – Lease of vehicles

Wiltshire, has outsourced its waste collection in one area to another provider called Waste and Co and pays an annual amount of $1.4 million to Waste and Co for its services. Waste and Co purchased the vehicles for $3.8 million and uses them exclusively for Wiltshire's waste collection. The vehicles are painted with the Wiltshire name and colours. Wiltshire has use of the vehicles exclusively for waste collection and the vehicles are expected to be used by Wiltshire for nearly all of their 10 year economic lives. If a vehicle breaks down or no longer functions, Waste and Co must provide replacement vehicles fitted with the same waste disposal containers and equipment and painted with Wiltshire's name and colours.

Exhibit 2 – Lease of machinery

On 1 January 20X1, Wiltshire leased a machine under a five year lease. The useful life of the asset to Wiltshire was four years and there is no residual value.

The annual lease payments are $6 million payable in arrears each year on 31 December. The present value of the future lease payments at 1 January 20X1 was $24 million using the interest rate implicit in the lease of approximately 8% per annum. At the end of the lease term legal title remains with the lessor. Wiltshire incurred $0.4 million of direct costs of setting up the lease.

Exhibit 3 – Sale and leaseback of head office building

Wiltshire sold its Head office building for $6 million, its fair value, to a finance company on 1 January 20X1 when the carrying amount was $3.6 million. The same building was immediately leased back from the finance company for a period of 20 years, being its useful life to Wiltshire. The lease rentals for the period are $441,000 payable annually in arrears. The interest rate implicit in the lease is 7%. The present value of the lease payments is $5 million. The transaction constitutes a sale in accordance with IFRS 15 *Revenue from Contracts with Customers.*

Requirements

(a) Prepare a memorandum for the managing director explaining the basics of accounting for leased assets used by lessors in the accounts of listed companies (in full compliance with the relevant IFRS Accounting Standards). Your memorandum should be set out in sections as follows:

(i) Outline the factors, which can influence the decision as to whether a particular lease is a finance lease or an operating lease. **(3 marks)**

(ii) Illustrate your answer using the following non-cancellable lease details as an example:

- Fair value of the leased asset: $100,000

- Lease payments: five annual payments in advance of $20,000 each

- Estimated residual value at the end of the lease: $26,750 of which $15,000 is guaranteed by the lessee. The interest rate implicit in the lease is 10%

Explain whether this lease should be considered a finance lease or an operating lease under the provisions of IFRS 16. **(4 marks)**

(b)   Explain how the transactions described in Exhibits 1–3 would be accounted for in the financial statements of Wiltshire Co for the year ended 31 December 20X1 in accordance with IFRS 16.

The marks allocated are as follows:

Exhibit 1 – Lease of vehicle	**(7 marks)**
Exhibit 2 – Lease of machinery	**(4 marks)**
Exhibit 3 – Sale and leaseback	**(7 marks)**

(Total = 25 marks)

11 Delta (June 2015) (amended)   49 mins

Delta is an entity which prepares financial statements to 31 March each year. The following information relevant to these financial statements is provided in the exhibits:

Exhibit 1 – Sale and leaseback

On 1 April 20X4, Delta sold a property for $48 million to raise cash to expand its business. The transaction constituted a sale under IFRS 15 *Revenue from Contracts with Customers*. The carrying amount of the property on 1 April 20X4 was $50 million and its fair value was $55 million. The estimated future useful life of the property on 1 April 20X4 was 40 years. On 1 April 20X4, Delta began to lease this property on a ten-year lease. The annual lease rentals for the first five years of the lease were set at $1 million. For the final five years of the lease, the rentals were set at $1.5 million. Both of these rental amounts were below the market rental for a property of this nature. The present value of the lease payments is $9 million and the implicit interest rate in the lease is 5.9%.

Exhibit 2 – Shares in Epsilon

On 1 April 20X4, Delta purchased 1 million options to acquire shares in Epsilon, a listed entity. Delta paid 25c per option, which allows Delta to purchase shares in Epsilon for a price of $2 per share. The exercise date for the options was 31 December 20X4. On 31 December 20X4, when the market value of a share in Epsilon was $2.60, Delta exercised all its options to acquire shares in Epsilon. In addition to the purchase price, Delta incurred directly attributable acquisition costs of $100,000 on the purchase of the 1 million shares in Epsilon. Delta regarded the shares it purchased in Epsilon as part of its trading portfolio. However, Delta did not dispose of any of the shares in Epsilon between 31 December 20X4 and 31 March 20X5. On 31 March 20X5, the market value of a share in Epsilon was $2.90.

Exhibit 3 – Ethical issue

On 30 November 20X4 Delta decided to sell a property. This property was correctly classified as held for sale in accordance with IFRS 5 *Non-Current Assets Held For Sale and Discontinued Operations*.

The finance assistant has reduced the carrying amount of the property in Delta's draft financial statements to its fair value less costs to sell of $13.2 million. She has charged the corresponding impairment loss of $1.5 million to the statement of profit or loss and other comprehensive income for the year ended 31 March 20X5. The draft financial statements showed a loss of $0.9 million for the year to 31 March 20X5.

Following review of the draft financial statements, the finance director has instructed the finance assistant to reverse the impairment loss and to present the property in non-current assets at its carrying amount prior to the impairment loss. The finance assistant is seeking to achieve a promotion and is therefore keen to impress the finance director. The finance director commented to the finance assistant that he likes to work with people who he can trust to carry out his instructions without complaint.

Requirements

(a)   Explain and show how the events in Exhibits 1 and 2 should be reported in the financial statements of Delta for the year ended 31 March 20X5.

The marks allocated are as follows:

Exhibit 1 – Sale and leaseback   **(11 marks)**
Exhibit 2 – Shares in Epsilon   **(9 marks)**

(b)   Using the information in Exhibit 3 identify and explain the financial reporting and ethical issues confronting the finance assistant.   **(5 marks)**

(Total = 25 marks)

12 Gamma (June 2019) (amended)   49 mins

Gamma prepares its financial statements to 31 March each year. The following exhibits contain information relevant to the question:

Exhibit 1 – Sale and leaseback of property

On 1 April 20X6, Gamma sold a property to entity A for its fair value of $1,500,000. The transaction constituted a sale in accordance with IFRS 15 *Revenue from Contracts with Customers*. The carrying amount of the property in the financial statements of Gamma at 1 April 20X6 was $1,000,000. The estimated economic life of the property on 1 April 20X6 was 20 years. On 1 April 20X6, Gamma entered into an agreement with entity A under which Gamma leased the property back. The lease term was for five years, with annual rentals of $100,000 payable in arrears. The useful life of the property to Gamma was five years. The annual rate of interest implicit in the lease was 10% and the present value of the future lease payments on 1 April 20X6 was $379,100.

Exhibit 2 – Investment property valuation

Gamma has several investment properties which are measured using the fair value model. Gamma determines the fair value of each investment property by using the amount of 'new-build value less obsolescence'. Valuations are conducted by a member of the board of directors. In order to determine the obsolescence, the board member takes account of the age of the property and the nature of its use. According to the board, this method of calculation is complex but gives a very precise result, which is accepted by the industry. There are sales values for similar properties in similar locations available as well as market rent data per square metre for similar industrial buildings.

Exhibit 3 – Share options

On 1 April 20X5 Gamma granted share options to 500 sales staff. The entitlement of each member of staff depended on the achievement of overall sales targets in the three-year period to 31 March 20X8. Details are as follows:

•   Cumulative sales less than $100 million: 100 options each
•   Cumulative sales between $100 million and $150 million: 150 options each
•   Cumulative sales more than $150 million: 200 options each

The options had a fair value of $1.20 per option on 1 April 20X5. This had increased to $1.30 per option by 31 March 20X6 and by 31 March 20X7 the fair value of an option was $1.35 per option.

When the options were granted and at 31 March 20X6 management estimated that cumulative sales in the three-year period would be $130 million. However, following a very good year in the year to 31 March 20X7, that estimate was revised to $160 million.

Required

(a)   Using the information in Exhibit 1 explain and show how the transaction would be reported in the financial statements of Gamma for the year ended 31 March 20X7.   **(12 marks)**

(b)   Using the information in Exhibit 2, discuss whether the valuation technique used by Gamma is acceptable with reference to the principles of IFRS Accounting Standards.   **(10 marks)**

(c)   Using the information in Exhibit 3, compute the charge to Gamma's statement of profit or loss and other comprehensive income for the year ended 31 March 20X7 and the amount included in Gamma's statement of financial position at 31 March 20X7.   **(3 marks)**

(Total = 25 marks)

13 Gamma (December 2019)   49 mins

Gamma prepares its financial statements to 30 September each year. Exhibits 1 and 2 contain information relevant to these financial statements:

Exhibit 1 – Purchase of equity shares in a key supplier

On 1 October 20X6, Gamma purchased 200,000 equity shares in entity A, a key supplier. Entity A's shares are listed on the local stock exchange. This share purchase did not give Gamma control or significant influence over entity A but Gamma intends to retain the shares in entity A as a long-term strategic investment.

Gamma paid $2.40 per share for these shares. This amount represents their fair value at the date of purchase. Additionally, brokers charge a fee of 2% of the amounts paid to buy or sell a share on the stock exchange on which entity A's shares are quoted.

On 31 March 20X7, entity A paid a dividend of 25 cents per share. For the last few years entity A has made just one dividend payment each year, in the month of March.

On 30 September 20X7, information received from the local stock exchange regarding entity A's share price was:

- Broker's bid price (the price the broker will pay to buy a share) – $2.70 per share
- Broker's ask price (the price which the broker requires when selling a share) – $2.90 per share

Exhibit 2 – Jointly manufactured product

On 1 October 20X6, Gamma entered into an agreement with entity B to manufacture and sell a product.

Under the terms of the agreement, pricing decisions, manufacturing specifications and selling decisions must be agreed by both entities. Any relevant obsolescence risk or bad debt risk is jointly borne by both entities.

Entity B completes the first stage and the partially manufactured product is then transferred to Gamma who completes the manufacture and delivers the product to the customer. Gamma invoices the customer and collects payment.

Entity B receives no payment for the goods they have manufactured until they are sold and the customer has paid Gamma.

Revenue from the sale of the completed product is shared equally between Gamma and entity B. Each month Gamma pays entity B its share of any amounts received from customers in the previous month. Under the terms of the agreement, the payments to entity B must be made within two weeks of the end of each month.

Financial data relevant to the agreement for the year ended 30 September 20X7 is as follows:

Relating to the manufacture of the product:

	Entity B $m	Gamma $m
Manufacturing costs	8	7
Inventories at 30 September 20X7	2	3.8 (note (i))

Relating to the sale of the product:

	$m
Revenue	22
Trade receivables at 30 September 20X7 (note (ii))	5
Bad debts written off (note (iii))	0.1

Notes:

(i) $2.1 million of this cost related to costs incurred by entity B and $1.7 million related to costs incurred by Gamma. All inventory is measured using IAS 2 *Inventories*.

(ii)   Amounts received from customers during September 20X7 were $1.5 million.

(iii)   No further bad debts are expected.

Requirements

Explain and show how the two events detailed in Exhibits 1 and 2 would be reported in the financial statements of Gamma for the year ended 30 September 20X7. Where alternative reporting treatments are permitted in Exhibit 1, you should explain and show both alternatives. Marks will be awarded for BOTH figures AND explanations.

The marks are allocated as follows:

Exhibit 1 – Purchase of equity shares in a key supplier	**(13 marks)**
Exhibit 2 – Jointly manufactured product	**(12 marks)**

(Total = 25 marks)

14 Omega (September 2020) 49 mins

Omega is a listed entity and you are the financial controller. The financial statements of Omega for the year ended 31 March 20X5 are currently being prepared. One of Omega's directors has sent you three questions regarding the financial statements.

The director's questions are contained in the exhibits.

Exhibit 1 – Right-of-use asset

When I looked at the note which gave details of our property, plant and equipment, a separate component appeared for the first time this year. This component was described as a right-of-use asset. Upon further investigation, I discovered that this related to a warehouse which we started to lease on 1 October 20X4 to provide us with more capacity. The warehouse is being leased on a five-year lease contract at an annual rental of $500,000, payable in arrears. There is no option to extend the lease at the end of the five-year period. Based on current annual interest rates (10%), these rentals have a total present value of $1,895,000. The useful life of the warehouse to us is five years.

We incurred direct costs of $105,000 when arranging this lease with the owner. The carrying amount of the right-of-use asset which is shown in the financial statements is $1.8 million. I don't understand this at all. In particular, I have three questions about this that I would like you to answer:

- The warehouse would cost at least $10 million to purchase outright and has an economic life of around 25 years. How can it be presented as Omega's asset in these circumstances?

- Where does the figure of $1.8 million come from?

- Apart from the right-of-use asset, how else will this transaction affect our financial statements? I don't need detailed workings here, just explanations.

Exhibit 2 – Segment reporting

I know that, because we're a listed entity, we are required to disclose details of the financial performance and financial position of different business segments in the notes to our financial statements. I thought it would be interesting to compare the segment report in our financial statements with that of a key competitor. When I did this, I found myself very confused. Our segment report was based on the performance and position by geographical area whereas our competitor's report was based on the performance and position by product type.

How can this be correct when both of us are preparing our financial statements in accordance with IFRS Accounting Standards, is there not a definition of a 'segment' that would be applied to all businesses?

Exhibit 3 – Immaterial transactions

You may know that the contract for cleaning our Head Office has been given to a firm which is controlled by my brother. This contract was approved in the normal way and I was not involved in the approval process to avoid any perception of a conflict of interest as my brother and I are known to holiday and socialise together. The contract has normal commercial terms and is very insignificant in the context of Omega as an entity. I'm very surprised, therefore, to see details of this contract disclosed in our financial statements when many other much more financially significant contracts are not disclosed in the same detail. Surely this disclosure is unnecessary when the monetary amounts are so small and there is nothing 'out of the ordinary' about the contract?

Requirement:

Provide answers to the questions raised by one of Omega's directors relating to the financial statements for the year ended 31 March 20X5.

The marks are allocated as follows:

Exhibit 1 – Right-of-use asset	**(11 marks)**
Exhibit 2 – Segment reporting	**(8 marks)**
Exhibit 3 – Immaterial transactions	**(6 marks)**
	(Total = 25 marks)

15 Omega (December 2021)   49 mins

You are the financial controller of Omega, a listed entity with a number of subsidiaries. Your managing director has recently returned from a seminar which discussed a wide range of business issues. Some of these issues related to the preparation of the financial statements. The managing director has prepared a list of questions for you which have arisen as a result of her attendance at the seminar.

The following **exhibits** provide information relevant to the question:

(1)   *Conceptual Framework* – details of a question from the managing director relating to the *Conceptual Framework for Financial Reporting*

(2)   Brand names – details of a question regarding the inclusion of brand names in the statement of financial position

(3)   Segment reports – a query from the managing director regarding the consistency of segment reports when compared with a competitor

This information should be used to answer the question **requirement** within the **response option** provided.

Exhibit 1 – *Conceptual Framework*

One of the presenters at the seminar I attended was explaining the work of the International Accounting Standards Board (the Board). From time to time she referred to the *Conceptual Framework for Financial Reporting*. I thought the Board set individual international financial reporting standards (IFRS Accounting Standards) to deal with specific issues of financial reporting. What is this 'Conceptual Framework' and how does it relate to individual IFRS

Accounting Standards issued by the IASB? I don't want a detailed description of this *Conceptual Framework* but rather a very brief overview of its content and purpose and how it fits into the overall financial reporting process.

(8 marks)

Exhibit 2 – Brand names

One of the topics covered during the seminar was a discussion on whether brand names should be included as assets in the financial statements. I looked at our consolidated financial statements and noticed the disclosure note for intangible assets included a separate heading 'Brands'. The finance director has provided me with an analysis of this figure, and it all relates to brands acquired through the acquisition of subsidiaries. However, the Omega brand name itself was not included at all. Surely this is inconsistent – the Omega brand name is associated with well known and popular products developed by Omega. This brand name is probably as valuable as the brand names associated with the subsidiaries we've acquired in recent years. I thought financial statements had to be consistent in their treatment of items. Please explain this apparent inconsistency to me. Please also explain how brand names which are recognised on acquisition are measured and whether they should be amortised. **(11 marks)**

Exhibit 3 – Segment reports

The seminar referred to the need for companies to provide information about the financial performance and financial position of different segments of their business in a note to their financial statements. They provided an example of the disclosures provided by a listed entity of a similar size to Omega. On returning from the seminar, I compared the segmental disclosures we had been shown with the segmental disclosures which Omega makes. The way Omega identifies and discloses segmental information was totally different from the seminar example. How can this be right – I thought financial statements needed to be prepared on a consistent basis?

I also looked at the financial statements of one of our key competitors. This competitor is an unlisted family run business which has grown very rapidly and is now not much smaller in size than the Omega group. They operate in the same economic sectors as we do. However, their financial statements make no segmental disclosures. Please explain how not applying the segmental reporting requirements is acceptable when this company is preparing the financial statements using IFRS Accounting Standards. **(6 marks)**

Requirements

Provide answers to the questions asked by the managing director in exhibits 1–3. You should justify your answers with reference to relevant IFRS Accounting Standards.

Note. The mark allocations are indicated against each exhibit.

(Total = 25 marks)

16 Delta (December 2022)   49 mins

Delta prepares financial statements to 30 September each year.

The following **exhibits** provide information relevant to the question:

(1)   Purchase of assets – provides details of the purchase of a brand name and inventory during the period.

(2)   Interest free loans – provides details of loans to employees made in the year ended 30 September 20X5.

(3)   Manufacturing process – provides details of a project to improve a manufacturing process.

This information should be used to answer the question **requirements** within your chosen **response option(s)**.

Requirements

(a)   Using the information in exhibits 1 and 2, explain and show how the transactions described should be accounted for and reported in the financial statements of Delta for the year ended 30 September 20X5.

(16 marks)

(b)   Using the information in exhibit 3, explain and show how the transactions described there should be accounted for and reported in the financial statements of Delta for the years ended 30 September 20X4 **and** 20X5.   **(9 marks)**

(Total = 25 marks)

Notes.

- The mark allocations are indicated in each exhibit.
- Marks will be awarded for BOTH figures AND explanations.

Exhibit 1 – Purchase of assets

Hams, a well-known retailer, became insolvent on 1 April 20X5 and began to sell off its assets. On 1 July 20X5, Delta purchased the Hams brand name, together with a quantity of inventory. The purchase agreement provided for payments of $60 million for the brand name and $20 million for the inventory. Between 1 July 20X5 and 30 September 20X5, Delta sold 75% of the inventory for net proceeds of $18 million. The remainder of the inventory related to a product range which was to be discontinued. On 15 October 20X5, Delta sold the remainder of this inventory to a single customer for net proceeds of $4.5 million. Delta intends to continue to sell goods under the Hams brand name for the foreseeable future and as such, considers that the useful life of the brand name is indefinite. Apart from the product range which is to be discontinued, demand for products sold under the Hams brand name continues to be buoyant.   **(9 marks)**

Exhibit 2 – Interest free loans

On 1 October 20X4, Delta made loans totalling $12.1 million to some key employees. The loans are interest-free provided these employees continue to remain employed and provide services to Delta for the two-year period from 1 October 20X4 to 30 September 20X6, when the loans become repayable. All the employees who received these loans are expected to remain employed and provide services in this two-year period. The market rate for a similar loan from Delta would normally be 10% per annum.   **(7 marks)**

Exhibit 3 – Manufacturing process

In the year ending 30 September 20X4, Delta had begun a project which was seeking to identify new and improved ways of manufacturing its key products. Expenditure incurred in that year was as follows:

- On 1 January 20X4: the purchase of machinery costing $15 million to be used exclusively on the project. The directors estimated that at 30 June 20X5, the machinery would be sold for $1.5 million as it would no longer be required.
- From 1 January 20X4 to 30 September 20X4: ongoing project costs totalling $1 million per month.

On 30 September 20X4, the directors of Delta were unsure about the technical feasibility and commercial viability of this project.

Details of the project for the year ended 30 September 20X5 were as follows:

- From 1 October 20X4 to 31 December 20X4, the ongoing costs related to the project continued at a rate of $1 million per month.
- On 31 December 20X4, the technical feasibility and commercial viability of the project was confirmed.
- From 1 January 20X5 until 30 June 20X5, Delta incurred expenditure on the project at a rate of $2 million per month.
- The project was completed on 30 June 20X5 and the new manufacturing process became available to use from that date. The process was actually brought into use from 1 August 20X5.
- On 30 June 20X5, the directors of Delta considered that the project would provide Delta with a significant economic advantage over its rivals for a five-year period.
- On 30 June 20X5, the machinery purchased on 1 January 20X4 was advertised for sale. It was sold for $1.8 million on 31 July 20X5.

(9 marks)

  BPP LEARNING MEDIA

17 Worldwide Fuels

49 mins

Worldwide Fuels, a public limited company, is preparing its financial statements for the year ending 30 November 20X9. The financial controller has asked for your assistance in accounting for the information within the exhibits.

Exhibit 1 – Decommissioning nuclear facilities

Worldwide Fuels is required to decommission its nuclear facilities at the end of their useful lives. Worldwide Fuels has a provision for decommissioning the group's radioactive facilities over their useful life which relates to the complete demolition of the facility within 50 years of it being taken out of service. The provision is based on future prices and is discounted using a current market rate of interest.

The movement in the provision for the year is as follows:

	$m
Balance at 1 December 20X8	675
Adjustment arising from change in price levels (charged to reserves)	33
Charged in the year to profit or loss	125
Adjustment due to change in decommissioning techniques (charged to reserves)	27
Balance at 30 November 20X9	860

In addition, decommissioning costs of $1,231 million (undiscounted) have been incurred in the current year that have not yet been accounted for.

Exhibit 2 – Legal case

On 15 May 20X9, Worldwide Fuels was notified that an employee was taking legal action against Worldwide in respect of injury caused to the employee whilst operating equipment that was not fitted with required safety guards. Worldwide Fuels defended the case but considered, based on the progress of the case up to 30 November 20X9, that there was a 75% probability they would have to pay damages of $20 million to the employee. The case was ultimately settled by Worldwide Fuels paying damages of $18 million to the employee on 12 December 20X9.

Requirements

Provisions are particular kinds of liabilities. It therefore follows that provisions should be recognised when the definition of a liability has been met. The key requirement of a liability is a present obligation and thus this requirement is critical also in the context of the recognition of a provision. IAS 37 *Provisions, Contingent Liabilities and Contingent Assets* deals with this area.

(a)   (i)   Explain why there was a need for detailed guidance on accounting for provisions. **(7 marks)**

      (ii)   Explain the circumstances under which a provision should be recognised in the financial statements according to IAS 37. **(6 marks)**

(b)   Explain how the transactions described in Exhibit 1 and Exhibit 2 would be accounted for in the financial statements of Worldwide for the year ended 30 November 20X9 in accordance with IAS 37.

    The marks allocated are as follows:

    Exhibit 1 – Decommissioning **(7 marks)**
    Exhibit 2 – Legal case **(5 marks)**

(Total = 25 marks)

18 Delta (June 2012) (amended)   49 mins

Delta is preparing its financial statements for the year ended 31 March 20X2. The exhibits contain information relevant to the question.

Exhibit 1 – Mineral extraction

On 1 April 20X1, Delta purchased some land for $10 million. Delta purchased the land in order to extract minerals from it. During the six months from 1 April 20X1 to 30 September 20X1, Delta incurred costs totalling $3.5 million in preparing the land and erecting extraction equipment. This process caused some damage to the land. Delta began extracting the minerals on 1 October 20X1 and the directors estimate that there are sufficient minerals to enable the site to have a useful life of ten years from that date. Further damage to the land is caused as the minerals are extracted.

Delta is legally obliged to rectify the damage caused by the preparation and mineral extraction. The directors estimate that the costs of this rectification on 30 September 20X1 will be as follows:

(1) $3 million to rectify the damage caused by the preparation of the land
(2) $200,000 for each year of the extraction process to rectify damage caused by the extraction process itself

Following this rectification work the land could potentially be sold to a third party for no less than its original cost of $10 million.

An annual discount rate appropriate for this project is 12%. The present value of $1 payable in ten years' time with an annual discount rate of 12% is 32.2 cents. The present value of $1 payable in 9½ years' time with an annual discount rate of 12% is 34.1 cents.

Exhibit 2 – Share options

On 1 April 20X1, Delta granted 20,000 share options to each of 100 senior executives. The options vest on 31 March 20X4, provided the executives remain with Delta throughout the period ending on 31 March 20X4 and providing the share price of Delta is at least $1.60 on that date. Relevant data relating to the share options is as follows:

	Market value of:	
Date	Granted option	Delta share
1 April 20X1	$0.84	$1.20
31 March 20X2	$0.90	$1.28

On 1 April 20X1, estimates suggested that 95 of the executives would remain with Delta throughout the period. This estimate changed to 92 executives on 31 March 20X2.

Exhibit 3 – Legal case

At 31 March 20X2, Delta was engaged in a legal dispute with a customer who alleged that Delta had supplied faulty products that caused the customer actual financial loss. The directors of Delta consider that the customer has a 75% chance of succeeding in this action and that the likely outcome should the customer succeed is that the customer would be awarded damages of $1 million. The directors of Delta further believe that the fault in the products was caused by the supply of defective components by one of Delta's suppliers. Delta has initiated legal action against the supplier and considers there is a 70% chance Delta will receive damages of $800,000 from the supplier. Ignore discounting in this part of the question.

Exhibit 4 – Ethical issues

On 1 April 20X1, Delta entered into a contract for the right to use a property for 10 years in exchange for annual lease payments of $2.5 million per annum. The draft financial statements for the year ended 31 March 20X2 do not include a lease liability or related asset and lease payments made to date have been recorded as an expense in the statement of profit or loss.

A new financial controller joined Delta shortly after the financial year end of 31 March 20X2 and is presently reviewing the draft financial statements to prepare for the upcoming audit and to begin making a loan application to finance expansion of the business. The financial controller has advised that the lease relating to the property should be recognised in the statement of financial position, but the managing director, who did a brief accountancy course ten years ago, strongly disagrees. The managing director wishes to continue to charge the lease payments to profit or loss. The managing director feels that the arrangement does not meet the criteria for recognition in the statement of financial position, and has made it clear that showing the lease in the statement of financial position could jeopardise both the company's upcoming loan application and the financial controller's future prospects at Delta.

Requirements

(a)   Explain and show how the events in Exhibits 1 to 3 would be reported in the financial statements of delta for the year ended 31 March 20X2.

The mark allocation is as follows:

Exhibit 1 – Mineral extraction	**(9 marks)**
Exhibit 2 – Share options	**(5 marks)**
Exhibit 3 – Legal case	**(3 marks)**

(b)   Using the information in Exhibit 4:

(i)	Identify and explain the financial reporting issues	**(3 marks)**
(ii)	Identify and explain the ethical issues arising	**(5 marks)**

(Total = 25 marks)

19 Epsilon (December 2019) (amended)   49 mins

Epsilon, a company with a year end of 30 September 20X7, is listed on a securities exchange. A director of Epsilon has a number of questions relating to the application of IFRS Accounting Standards in its financial statements for the year ended 30 September 20X7. Relevant information is included in Exhibits 1–3.

Exhibit 1 – Inconsistencies

I have recently been appointed to the board of another company which is growing very quickly and will probably seek a securities exchange listing in the next few years. As part of my familiarisation process, I've been reviewing their financial statements which they state comply with IFRS Accounting Standards. I have been comparing them with the financial statements of Epsilon. There appear to be some inconsistencies between the two sets of financial statements:

- The financial statements of the other company contain no disclosure of the earnings per share figure and there is no segmental analysis despite this company having a number of divisions with different types of business. Epsilon gives both of these disclosures.

- Both Epsilon and this other company have received government grants to assist in the purchase of a non-current asset. We have deducted the grant from the cost of the non-current asset. They have recognised the grant received as deferred income.

Please explain the apparent inconsistencies to me.

Exhibit 2 – Pending legal cases

At a recent board meeting, we discussed legal cases which customers A and B are bringing against Epsilon in respect of the supply of products which were allegedly faulty. We supplied the goods in the last three months of the financial year.

We have reliably estimated that if the actions succeed, we are likely to have to pay out $10 million in damages to customer A and $8 million in damages to customer B.

Epsilon's legal advisers have reliably estimated that there is a 60% chance that customer A's claim will be successful and a 25% chance that customer B's claim will be successful.

I know we have insurance in place to cover us against claims like this. It is highly probable that any claims which were successful would be covered under our policy. Therefore I would have expected to see a provision for legal claims based on the likelihood of the claims succeeding. However, I would also have expected to see an equivalent asset in respect of amounts recoverable from the insurance company. The financial statements do contain a provision for $10 million but no equivalent asset. Disclosure of the information relating to both of the claims and the associated insurance is made in the notes to the financial statements. How can it be the correct accounting treatment to include a liability but not the corresponding asset, given the above facts?

Exhibit 3 – Statement of profit or loss and other comprehensive income

I've been reviewing the statement of profit or loss and other comprehensive income and it appears to be in two sections. The first section appears to be entitled 'profit or loss' and the second 'other comprehensive income'. It appears that the tax charge is included in the 'profit or loss' section of the statement as there is no tax charge included in the 'other comprehensive income' section of the statement. I have a number of questions regarding this statement:

- How do we decide where to put a particular item of income or expenditure?

- Where does the tax relating to 'other comprehensive income' get shown?

- Do the above points have an impact on the computation of performance evaluation indicators which will be of interest to shareholders?

Requirements

Provide answers to the questions raised by the director in Exhibits 1–3. You should justify your answers with reference to relevant IFRS Accounting Standards.

The mark allocation is as follows:

Exhibit 1 – Inconsistencies **(7 marks)**
Exhibit 2 – Pending legal cases **(12 marks)**
Exhibit 3 – Statement of profit or loss and other comprehensive income **(6 marks)**

(Total = 25 marks)

20 Omicron 2 (December 2011) (amended)   49 mins

Omicron prepares financial statements to 30 September each year. It applies IAS 19 *Employee Benefits* in accounting for its short and long term employee benefits. The exhibits provide information relevant to the question.

Exhibit 1 – Defined benefits plan

Omicron makes contributions to a defined benefit post-employment benefit plan for its employees. Relevant data is as follows:

(1)   At 1 October 20X0 the plan obligation was $35 million and the fair value of the plan assets was $30 million.

(2)   The actuary advised that the current service cost for the year ended 30 September 20X1 was $4 million. Omicron paid contributions of $3.2 million to the plan on 30 September 20X1. These were the only contributions paid in the year.

(3)   The appropriate annual rate at which to discount the plan liabilities was 6% on 1 October 20X0 and 5.5% on 30 September 20X1.

(4)   The plan paid out benefits totalling $2 million to retired members on 30 September 20X1.

(5)   At 30 September 20X1 the plan obligation was $41.5 million and the fair value of the plan assets was $32.5 million.

Exhibit 2 – Defined contributions plan

Under the terms of the defined contributions plan, Omicron does not guarantee any return on the contributions paid into the fund. The company's legal and constructive obligation is limited to the amount that is contributed to the fund.

The following details relate to this scheme:	$m
Fair value of plan assets at 30 September 20X1	21
Contributions paid by company for year to 30 September 20X1	10
Contributions paid by employees for year to 30 September 20X1	10
Amounts owed to the pension plan at 30 September 20X1	2

Requirements

Explain:

(a)   (i)   The difference between a defined contribution and a defined benefit plan. Your explanation should include an analysis of which party bears the risks attaching to the level of benefits.   **(4 marks)**

        (ii)   The difference, in the financial statements of contributing employers, between the method of accounting for contributions to defined contribution plans and contributions to defined benefit plans.   **(3 marks)**

        (iii)   How actuarial gains and losses are reported.   **(3 marks)**

(b)   Compute the amounts that will appear in the statement of profit loss and other comprehensive income of Omicron for the year ended 30 September 20X1 and the statement of financial position at 30 September 20X1 in respect of its defined benefit and defined contribution pension plans.

      The marks are allocated as follows:

Exhibit 1 – Defined benefits plan	**(12 marks)**
Exhibit 2 – Defined contributions plan	**(3 marks)**

      Note. You should indicate where in each statement the relevant amounts will be presented.

(Total = 25 marks)

21 Delta (June 2022)   **49 mins**

Delta prepares financial statements to 31 March each year.

The following exhibits provide information relevant to the question:

(1)   Post-employment benefits – provides details of benefits for existing and previous employees.

(2)   Sale of goods – provides details of the sale of goods with a right of return.

This information should be used to answer the question requirement within your chosen response option(s).

Exhibit 1 – Post-employment benefits Delta has provided two types of post-employment benefit plans for its employees (members). Both plans are administered by separate legal entities.

Plan A provides the benefits for the majority of the employees of Delta. The contributions paid into Plan A are invested to produce appropriate growth in the value of the plan. The ultimate level of post-employment benefits receivable by members of this plan depends on the level of contributions made and the returns received on the investment of those contributions.

Membership of plan B is restricted to the directors and other senior employees of Delta. The contributions paid into Plan B are invested to make optimal returns. However, post-employment benefits payable to Plan B members are based on the salary of the relevant employee at the date of their retirement and their length of service with Delta.

Relevant details of the two plans for the year ended 31 March 20X5 are as follows:

Plan A

	$'000
Contributions payable by Delta to the plan for the year	45,000
Benefits paid to ex-employees in the year	30,000
Fair value of plan assets at 1 April 20X4	240,000
Fair value of plan assets at 31 March 20X5	275,000
Current service cost – year ended at 31 March 20X5	42,000

Plan B

	$'000
Contributions payable by Delta to the plan for the year	15,000
Benefits paid to ex-employees in the year	9,000
Present value of obligation to pay future benefits as at 1 April 20X4	190,000
Present value of obligation to pay future benefits as at 31 March 20X5	220,000
Fair value of plan assets at 1 April 20X4	140,000
Fair value of plan assets at 31 March 20X5	165,000
Current service cost – year ended at 31 March 20X5	14,000

Details relevant to both plans are:

- Contributions into the plans and also benefits payable by the plans are paid evenly on a monthly basis across the year ended 31 March 20X5.

- Where required, a relevant discount rate to apply to any calculations is 8% per annum.   **(14 marks)**

Exhibit 2 – Sale of goods

On 1 March 20X5, Delta sold and delivered 200 identical items to a customer for $5,000 each. The items cost Delta $3,000 each to manufacture. The terms of sale are that the customer has the right to return the goods within two months and will receive a full refund. After the two month period has expired, the customer can no longer return the items and payment for all items becomes immediately due. Delta has entered into transactions of this type with this customer previously and can reliably estimate that 5% of the products are likely to be returned within the two month period. During March 20X5, the customer returned six of the items. No change was necessary to the original estimate of the total number of goods which would be returned by the customer in the two month period from 1 March 20X5 to 30 April 20X5.   **(11 marks)**

Requirement

Using the information in exhibits 1 and 2, explain and show how the transactions described there should be accounted for and reported in the financial statements of Delta for the year ended 31 March 20X5.

Notes.

- The mark allocations are indicated in each exhibit.
- Marks will be awarded for BOTH figures AND explanations.

                (Total = 25 marks)

22 Kappa (June 2016) (amended)   49 mins

Kappa is preparing its financial statements for the year ended 30 September 20X6. The exhibits contain information relevant to the question.

Exhibit 1 – Interest-free loan

On 1 October 20X5, Kappa made an interest free loan to an employee of $800,000. The loan is due for repayment on 30 September 20X7 and Kappa is confident that the employee will repay the loan. Kappa would normally require an annual rate of return of 10% on business loans.

Exhibit 2 – Loan to entity X

On 1 October 20X5, Kappa made a three-year loan of $10 million to entity X. The rate of interest payable on the loan was 8% per annum, payable in arrears. On 30 September 20X8, Kappa will receive a fixed number of shares in entity X in full settlement of the loan. Entity X paid the interest due of $800,000 on 30 September 20X6 and entity X has no liquidity problems. Following payment of this interest, the fair value of this loan asset at 30 September 20X6 was estimated to be $10.5 million.

Exhibit 3 – Equity investment in entity Y

On 1 October 20X5, Kappa purchased an equity investment in entity Y for $12 million. The investment did not give Kappa control or significant influence over entity Y but the investment is seen as a long-term one. On 30 September 20X6, the fair value of Kappa's investment in entity Y was estimated to be $13 million.

Exhibit 4 – Loan notes

Kappa anticipates capital expenditure in a few years and so invests its excess cash into short- and long-term financial assets so it can fund the expenditure when the need arises. Kappa will hold these assets to collect the contractual cash flows, and, when an opportunity arises, Kappa will sell financial assets to re-invest the cash in financial assets with a higher return.

As part of this policy, Kappa purchased $50,000 par value of loan notes at a 10% discount on their issue on 1 October 20X5. The redemption date of these loan notes is 30 September 20X9. An interest coupon of 3% of par value is paid annually on 30 September. Transaction costs of $450 were incurred on the purchase. The annual internal rate of return on the loan notes is 5.6%. At 30 September 20X6, due to a decrease in market interest rates, the fair value of these loan notes had increased to $51,000.

Requirements

(a)   One of the matters addressed in IFRS 9 *Financial Instruments* is the initial and subsequent measurement of financial assets. IFRS 9 requires that financial assets are initially measured at their fair value at the date of initial recognition. However, subsequent measurement of financial assets depends on their classification for which IFRS 9 identifies three possible alternatives.

Explain the three classifications which IFRS 9 identifies for financial assets and the basis of measurement which is appropriate for each classification. You should also identify any exceptions to the normal classifications which may apply in specific circumstances.   **(8 marks)**

(b)   Explain and show how the transactions contained in Exhibits 1 to 4 would be reported in the financial statements of Kappa for the year ended 30 September 20X6.

The mark allocation is as follows:

Exhibit 1 – Interest-free loan	**(5 marks)**
Exhibit 2 – Loan to entity X	**(4 marks)**
Exhibit 3 – Equity investment in entity Y	**(3 marks)**
Exhibit 4 – Loan notes	**(5 marks)**
	(Total = 25 marks)

23 Seltec   49 mins

Seltec is a public limited company with a year-end date of 30 September 20X7. Seltec processes and sells edible oils. You are the Seltec's financial accountant, reporting to the finance director. She has asked for your assistance in accounting for various financial instrument transactions Seltec has entered into in the year. The exhibits provide information relevant to the question.

Exhibit 1 – Fair value hedge

Seltec uses forward and futures contracts to protect it against fluctuation in the price of edible oils. Where forwards are used the company often takes delivery of the edible oil and sells it shortly afterwards. The contracts are constructed with future delivery in mind but the contracts also allow net settlement in cash as an alternative. The net settlement is based on the change in the price of the oil since the start of the contract. Seltec uses the proceeds of a net settlement to purchase a different type of oil or purchase from a different supplier. Where futures are used these sometimes relate to edible oils of a different type and market than those of Seltec's own inventory of edible oil. The company intends to apply fair value hedge accounting to these contracts in order to protect itself from earnings volatility.

Exhibit 2 – Convertible loan note

On 1 October 20X6 Seltec issued a $6 million convertible loan note. The quoted rate of interest on the loan note was 2% per annum, payable on 30 September in arrears. The loan note was repayable at an amount of $7 million on 30 September 20X9. As an alternative to repayment the lender may choose to receive 1 million shares in Seltec (having a nominal value of $1 each).

The required rate of return for providers of this type of loan finance at 1 October 20X6 was 10% per annum.

Exhibit 3 – Cash flow hedge

On 15 August 20X7, Seltec entered into a commitment to supply a large consignment of components to a foreign customer whose currency is the kroner. The agreed value of the order was 25 million kroner and this amount is expected to be paid by the customer on 30 November 20X4. On 15 August 20X7, Seltec entered into a contract to sell 25 million kroner for $13 million on 30 November 20X7. Currency fluctuations in August and September 20X7 were such that on 30 September 20X7 the fair value of this currency contract was $1.1 million (a financial liability). The draft financial statements of Seltec do not include any amounts in respect of this currency contract since it has a zero cost. Seltec wishes to use cash-flow hedge accounting. The currency contract is a perfectly effective hedge of the commitment to supply the components.

Requirements

Advise Seltec how to account for the transactions in Exhibits 1 to 3 above.

The mark allocation is as follows:

Exhibit 1 – Fair value hedge	**(14 marks)**
Exhibit 2 – Convertible loan note	**(6 marks)**
Exhibit 3 – Cash flow hedge	**(5 marks)**

(Total = 25 marks)

24 Delta (December 2012) (amended)   49 mins

Delta, a company with a year end 30 September 20X2, has four outstanding events that need to be reported in the financial statements. Information is provided in the exhibits:

Exhibit 1 – Loan to supplier

On 1 October 20X1, Delta lent $2 million to a supplier in order to assist them with their expansion plans. It is expected that the supplier will to be able to repay us in full with ease. The loan cost $100,000 to arrange, and it has been assumed that the $100,000 will be charged as a cost in the current year. There is no interest payable on this loan to help the supplier's short-term cash flow but the supplier must repay $2.4 million on 30 September 20X3. This will mean no profit will be recognised this year but there will be a nice bonus next year when repayment is received. The effective annual rate of interest on this loan is 6.9%.

Just before the year end, the supplier communicated that the poor economic climate has caused it significant problems. In order to help, the amount repayable by the supplier on 30 September 20X3 has been reduced to $2.2 million.

Exhibit 2 – Purchase of PPE

On 1 October 20X0, Delta bought a large machine for $20 million. This machine has an estimated useful life of eight years, but will need a substantial overhaul on 30 September 20X4 in order to enable it to be used for the final four years of its expected useful life. This overhaul is likely to cost $4 million, based on prices prevailing at 1 October 20X0. If the overhaul occurs, the machine is expected to have a reasonable resale value at the end of its useful life. On 1 October 20X0, the estimated residual value of the machine was $1 million. On 30 September 20X1, this estimate was revised to $1.1 million and on 30 September 20X2, the estimate was revised to $1.2 million. Depreciation was not been charged on this asset in the year to 30 September 20X1 and therefore it is proposed to charge two years' depreciation in the current year.

Exhibit 3 – Legal claim

During the year ended 30 September 20X2, Delta provided consultancy services to a customer regarding the installation of a new production system. The system has caused the customer considerable problems, so the customer has taken legal action against Delta for the loss of profits that has arisen as a result of the problems with the system. The legal department considers that there is a 25% chance the claim can be successfully defended, but a 75% chance that Delta will be required to pay damages of $1.6 million. The legal department is reasonably confident that Delta is covered by insurance against this type of loss and a claim will be made as soon as the outcome of the case is confirmed. No accounting has taken place because the claim is expected to exactly offset against the damages payable.

Exhibit 4 – Forward currency contract

During July and August 20X2 Delta conducted a large marketing effort in Country X. The currency in Country X is the Euro. Delta made no sales to customers in Country X in the year ended 30 September 20X2 but is very confident of making substantial sales to such customers in the year ended 30 September 20X3. In order to hedge against fluctuations in future cash flows, on 5 September 20X2, Delta entered into a contract to sell €20 million for $28 million on 31 October 20X2. Currency fluctuations in September 20X2 were such that on 30 September 20X2 the fair value of this currency contract was $1.1 million (a financial asset). Delta has not yet accounted for this currency contract since it has a zero cost. Delta wishes to use hedge accounting whenever permitted by IFRS Accounting Standards. Delta expects sales to customers in Country X to be at least €22 million in October 20X2.

Requirements

Explain and show how the four events would be reported in the financial statements of Delta for the year ended 30 September 20X2:

Exhibit 1 – Loan to supplier	**(7 marks)**
Exhibit 2 – Purchase of PPE	**(8 marks)**
Exhibit 3 – Legal claim	**(5 marks)**
Exhibit 4 – Forward currency contract	**(5 marks)**

(Total = 25 marks)

25 Epsilon   49 mins

Epsilon is preparing its financial statements to 31 March 20X8. The following information relating to IFRS 9 *Financial Instruments* is provided in the exhibits:

Exhibit 1 – $30 million loan

On 1 April 20X7, Epsilon loaned $30 million to another entity. Interest of $1.5 million is payable annually in arrears. An additional final payment of $35.3 million is due on 31 March 20Y0. Epsilon incurred direct costs of $250,000 in arranging this loan. The annual rate of interest implicit in this arrangement is approximately 10%. Epsilon has no intention of assigning this loan to a third party at any time.

Exhibit 2 – Investment in Greek

On 1 April 20X7, Epsilon purchased 500,000 shares in a key supplier – Greek. The shares were purchased in order to protect Epsilon's source of supply and Epsilon has no intention of trading in these shares. The shares cost $2 per share and the direct costs of purchasing the shares were $100,000. On 1 January 20X8, Greek paid a dividend of 30 cents per share. On 31 March 20X8, the fair value of a share in Greek was $2.25.

Exhibit 3 – Call options

On 1 January 20X8, Epsilon purchased 100,000 call options to purchase shares in Young – an unconnected third party. Each option allowed Epsilon to purchase shares in Young on 31 December 20X8 for $6 per share. Epsilon paid $1.25 per option on 1 January 20X8. On 31 March 20X8, the fair value of a share in Young was $8 and the fair value of a share option purchased by Epsilon was $1.60. This purchase of call options is not part of a hedging arrangement.

Exhibit 4 – Loan to subsidiary

On 1 April 20X7, Epsilon loaned $1,000,000 to a subsidiary. The loan attracts no interest, but is to be paid back in full in a single payment on 31 March 20X9. The market rate of interest for a two year loan on both of the above dates is 6% per annum. At a discount rate of 6% per annum the present value of $1 receivable in two years' time is $0.89.

Requirements

(a)   Explain how IFRS 9 *Financial Instruments* requires entities to select the appropriate measurement basis for a financial asset. You should include any options available to entities regarding classification in your explanation.   **(7 marks)**

You are NOT required to define a financial asset.

(b)   Explain and show how the transactions described in notes 1–4 should be reported in the individual financial statements of Epsilon for the year ended 31 March 20X8. You should assume that Epsilon only measures financial assets at fair value through profit or loss when *required* to do so by IFRS 9. The marks are allocated as follows:

Exhibit 1 – $30 million loan	**(4 marks)**
Exhibit 2 – Investment in Greek	**(5 marks)**
Exhibit 3 – Call options	**(4 marks)**
Exhibit 4 – Loan to subsidiary	**(5 marks)**

(Total = 25 marks)

26 Kirkham   49 mins

Adapted from December 2013 (part (a) and part (b) Exhibits 1 to 3), and June 2014 (part (b) Exhibits 4 and 5)

Kirkham prepares consolidated financial statements to 30 September each year. During the year ended 30 September 20X3 Kirkham entered into the transactions given in the exhibits:

Exhibit 1 – Equity investment

On 1 October 20X2, Kirkham purchased an equity investment for $200,000.

The investment was designated as fair value through other comprehensive income. On 30 September 20X3, the fair value of the investment was $240,000. In the tax jurisdiction in which Kirkham operates, unrealised gains and losses arising on the revaluation of investments of this nature are not taxable unless the investment is sold. Kirkham has no intention of selling the investment in the foreseeable future.

Exhibit 2 – Intra-group sales

On 1 August 20X3, Kirkham sold products to Omega, a wholly owned subsidiary operating in the same tax jurisdiction as Kirkham, for $80,000. The goods had cost Kirkham $64,000. By 30 September 20X3, Omega had sold 40% of these goods, selling the remaining 60% in October and November 20X3.

Exhibit 3 – Payment from customer

On 31 March 20X3, Kirkham received $200,000 from a customer. This payment was in respect of services to be provided by Kirkham from 1 April 20X3 to 31 January 20X4. Kirkham recognised revenue of $120,000 in respect of this transaction in the year ended 30 September 20X3 and will recognise the remainder in the year ended 30 September 20X4. Under the tax jurisdiction in which Kirkham operates, the $200,000 received on 31 March 20X3 was included in the taxable profits of Kirkham for the year ended 30 September 20X3.

Exhibit 4 – Impairment of goodwill

On 1 October 20X2, the total goodwill arising on consolidation in Kirkham's consolidated statement of financial position was $4 million. On 30 September 20X3, the directors reviewed the goodwill for impairment and concluded that the goodwill was impaired by $600,000. There was no tax deduction available for any group company as a consequence of this impairment charge as at 30 September 20X3.

Exhibit 5 – Development expenditure

During the year ended 30 September 20X3, Kirkham correctly capitalised development costs in accordance with IAS 38 *Intangible Assets*. The total amount capitalised was $1.6 million. The development project began to generate economic benefits for Kirkham from 1 July 20X3. The directors of Kirkham estimated that the project would generate economic benefits for five years from that date. The development expenditure was fully deductible against taxable profits for the year ended 30 September 20X3.

Requirements

(a)   When preparing financial statements it is important to ensure that the tax consequences of all transactions are appropriately recognised. IAS 12 *Income Taxes* prescribes the treatment of both current and deferred tax assets and liabilities.

Current tax is the amount of income tax payable or recoverable in respect of the taxable profit or tax loss for a period. Deferred tax is tax on temporary differences. A temporary difference is the difference between the carrying amount of an asset or liability and its tax base. A taxable temporary difference leads to a potential deferred tax liability and a deductible temporary difference leads to a potential deferred tax asset.

Explain how the tax base of both an asset and a liability is computed and state the general requirements of IAS 12 regarding the recognition of both deferred tax liabilities and deferred tax assets. You do not need to identify any of the exceptions to these general requirements which are set out in IAS 12.   **(5 marks)**

(b)   Explain and show how the tax consequences (current and deferred) of the transactions shown in Exhibits 1 to 5 above would be reported in the statement of financial position of Kirkham at 30 September 20X3 and its statement of profit or loss and other comprehensive income for the year ended 30 September 20X3.

The mark allocation is as follows:

Exhibit 1 – Equity investment	**(5 marks)**
Exhibit 2 – Intra-group sales	**(6 marks)**
Exhibit 3 – Payment from customer	**(4 marks)**
Exhibit 4 – Impairment of goodwill	**(2 marks)**
Exhibit 5 – Development expenditure	**(3 marks)**

You should assume that:

- The rate of income tax in the jurisdiction in which Kirkham operates is 25%

- Both Kirkham and Omega are profitable companies which consistently generate annual taxable profits of at least $1,000,000

In answering this part, you do **not** need to consider the possible offset of deferred tax assets against deferred tax liabilities.

(Total = 25 marks)

27 Edgworth (June 2016) (amended)   49 mins

Edgworth, a company with a year end 31 March 20X6, applies IAS 12 *Income Taxes* to report current and deferred tax transactions in the financial statements. The exhibits provide information relevant to the question.

Exhibit 1 – Tax base of assets

(1)   A machine was purchased during the current accounting period for $250,000. Depreciation of $50,000 was charged in arriving at the accounting profit for the current period. A deduction of $100,000 was given against taxable profits by the local tax authorities against the taxable profits of the current period. The remaining cost will be deductible in future periods, either as depreciation or as a deduction on disposal.

(2)   A current asset of $60,000 relates to interest receivable. The related interest income will be taxed on a cash basis when it is received.

Exhibit 2 – Tax base of liabilities

(1) $120,000 is included in trade payables. This amount relates to purchases which qualified for a tax deduction when the purchase was made.

(2) $40,000 is included in accrued liabilities. A tax deduction relating to this liability will be given when the liability is settled.

Exhibit 3 – Edgworth tax transactions

Edgworth prepares financial statements to 31 March each year. The rate of income tax applicable to Edgworth is 20%. The following information relates to transactions, assets and liabilities of Edgworth during the year ended 31 March 20X6:

(1)   Edgworth has an investment property which it carries under the fair value model. The property originally cost $30 million. The property had an estimated fair value of $35 million on 31 March 20X5 and $38 million on 31 March 20X6. In the tax jurisdiction in which Edgworth operates, gains on the fair value of investment properties are not subject to income tax until the properties are disposed of.

(2)   Edgworth has a 40% shareholding in Lowercroft. Edgworth purchased this shareholding for $45 million. The shareholding gives Edgworth significant influence over Lowercroft but not control and therefore Edgworth accounts for its interest in Lowercroft using the equity method. The equity method carrying value of Edgworth's investment in Lowercroft was $70 million on 31 March 20X5 and $75 million on 31 March 20X6. In the tax jurisdiction in which Edgworth operates, profits recognised under the equity method are taxed if and when they are distributed as a dividend or the relevant investment is disposed of.

(3)   Edgworth measures its head office property using the revaluation model. The property is revalued every year on 31 March. On 31 March 20X5, the carrying value of the property (after revaluation) was $40 million and its tax base was $22 million. During the year ended 31 March 20X6, Edgworth charged depreciation in its statement of profit or loss of $2 million and claimed a tax deduction for tax depreciation of $1.25 million. On 31 March 20X6, the property was revalued to $45 million. In the tax jurisdiction in which Edgworth operates, revaluation of property, plant and equipment does not affect taxable income at the time of revaluation.

Requirements

Deferred tax is the tax on temporary differences. Temporary differences are identified on individual assets and liabilities in the statement of financial position. Temporary differences arise when the carrying amount of an asset or liability differs from its tax base.

(a) (i) Explain, using the examples in Exhibit 1, how IAS 12 *Income Taxes* defines the tax base of assets.

(4 marks)

(ii) Explain, using the examples in Exhibit 2, how IAS 12 defines the tax base of liabilities. **(4 marks)**

(iii) Explain how temporary differences are identified as either taxable or deductible temporary differences. **(2 marks)**

(iv) Explain the general criteria prescribed by IAS 12 for the recognition of deferred tax assets and liabilities. You do **not** need to identify any specific exceptions to these general criteria. **(3 marks)**

(b) Assuming that there are no other temporary differences other than those in Exhibit 3 above, calculate:

- The deferred tax liability of Edgworth at 31 March 20X6

- The charge or credit to both profit or loss and other comprehensive income relating to deferred tax for the year ended 31 March 20X6

You should include brief explanations to support your computations. **(12 marks)**

(Total = 25 marks)

28 Omega (June 2014) (amended) 49 mins

You are the financial controller of Omega, a listed company which prepares consolidated financial statements in accordance with IFRS Accounting Standards. The year end of Omega is 31 March and its functional currency is the $. Your managing director, who is not an accountant, has recently prepared a list of questions for you concerning current issues relevant to Omega. The questions are contained in the exhibits:

Exhibit 1 – Purchases from Sigma

One of my fellow directors has informed me that on 1 January 20X4 his spouse acquired a controlling interest in one of our major suppliers, Sigma. He seemed to think that this would have implications for our financial statements. I cannot understand why. Our purchases from Sigma were $1.5 million for each month of our year ended 31 March 20X4 and I acknowledge this is a significant amount for us. However, I can't see how the share purchase on 1 January 20X4 affects our financial statements – all the purchases from Sigma were made at normal market rates, so what's the issue? Please explain this to me and identify any impact on our financial statements.

Exhibit 2 – Advertising costs

You will be aware that we intend to open a new retail store in a new location in the next few weeks. As you know, we have spent a substantial sum on a series of television adverts to promote this new store. We paid for adverts costing $800,000 before 31 March 20X4. $700,000 of this sum relates to adverts shown before 31 March 20X4 and $100,000 to adverts shown in April 20X4. Since 31 March 20X4, we have paid for further adverts costing $400,000. I was chatting to a colleague over lunch and she told me she thought all these costs should be written off as expenses in the year to 31 March 20X4. I don't want a charge of $1.2 million against my 20X4 profits! Surely these costs can be carried forward as intangible assets? After all, our market research indicates that this new store is likely to be highly successful. Please explain and justify the treatment of these costs of $1.2 million in the financial statements for the year ended 31 March 20X4.

Exhibit 3 – Exchange rate fluctuations

As you know, on 1 January 20X4 we purchased a machine for 2 million kroner. At that date the exchange rate was $1 = 10 kroner. We don't have to pay for this purchase until 30 June 20X4. The kroner strengthened against the $ in the three months following purchase and by 31 March 20X4 the exchange rate was $1 = 8 kroner. I thought these exchange fluctuations wouldn't affect our financial statements because we have an asset and a liability denominated in kroner which was initially the same amount. We're depreciating this machine over four years so the future year-end amounts won't be the same, of course. Something I heard at a seminar, but didn't really grasp, made me think I could be mistaken. Please explain the impact of this transaction on our financial statements for the year ended 31 March 20X4.

Exhibit 4 – Fair value of vehicles

As you know, we are considering selling the agricultural vehicles retail division. We need to measure the fair value of the inventory of agricultural vehicles for the purpose of the sale. Three markets currently exist for the vehicles, all of which we have transacted in regularly.

I was provided with the following data relating to The current volume and prices in the three markets:

Market	Sales price per vehicle ($)	Total volume of vehicles sold in the market	Transaction costs per vehicle ($)
A	40,000	150,000	500
B	38,000	750,000	400
C	34,000	100,000	300

I think we should value the vehicles in market A at $39,500 per vehicle as these are the highest net proceeds per vehicle. Please explain whether this valuation would be acceptable under IFRS Accounting Standards and if not, please explain how we should measure the fair value of the vehicles.

Requirements

Provide answers to the issues raised by the managing director.

Exhibit 1 – Purchases from Sigma	**(7 marks)**
Exhibit 2 – Advertising costs	**(6 marks)**
Exhibit 3 – Exchange rate fluctuations	**(7 marks)**
Exhibit 4 – Fair value of vehicles	**(5 marks)**
	(Total = 25 marks)

29 Denshaw (June 2017) (amended)   49 mins

Denshaw, a company with a year end 30 September 20X8, has three events that need to be reported in the financial statements. Information is provided in the exhibits:

Exhibit 1 – Joint arrangement

On 1 October 20X7, Denshaw entered into a joint arrangement with Yankee to jointly operate a delivery depot. Yankee is located, and has major customers in, the same geographical region as Denshaw. Denshaw and Yankee each made the following payments in respect of the arrangement on 1 October 20X7:

- $25 million each to purchase a joint 25-year leasehold interest in a depot which was close to both Denshaw and Yankee's business premises. This depot was to act as headquarters for the delivery vehicles (see below).

- $7.5 million each to purchase a fleet of delivery vehicles. The vehicles have an expected useful life of five years, with no expected residual value. Denshaw and Yankee agreed to jointly use the delivery vehicles to deliver products to their customers, and to share the operating costs of the depot equally. Any delivery charges to customers were levied by Denshaw and Yankee directly at the discretion of the individual entities. During the year ended 30 September 20X8, the total cash cost of operating the depot was $8 million. This was paid equally by Denshaw and Yankee. In the year ended 30 September 20X8, Denshaw charged its customers a total of $2 million in delivery charges.

Exhibit 2 – Purchase of inventory from a foreign supplier

On 1 August 20X8 Denshaw purchased some inventory from a supplier whose functional currency was the dinar. The total purchase price was 3.6 million dinars. The terms of the purchase were that Denshaw would pay for the goods in two instalments. The first instalment payment of 1,260,000 dinars was due on 15 September 20X8 and the second payment of 2,340,000 dinars on 30 October 20X8. Both payments were made on the due dates. Denshaw did not undertake any activities to hedge its currency exposure arising under this transaction. Denshaw sold 60% of this inventory prior to 30 September 20X8 for a total sales price of $480,000. All sales proceeds were receivable in $. After 30 September 20X8 Denshaw sold the remaining inventory for sales proceeds that were in excess of their cost.

Relevant exchange rates are as follows:

- 1 August 20X8 – 6.0 dinars to $1
- 15 September 20X8 – 6.3 dinars to $1
- 30 September 20X8 – 6.4 dinars to $1

Exhibit 3 – Share options

On 1 October 20X7 the board of Denshaw granted key employees share options that are subject to vesting conditions. Details of the award are as follows:

(1) Fifty employees can potentially receive 5,000 options each on 30 September 20X9. The options that vest (see below) will allow the employees to purchase shares in Denshaw at any time in the year to 30 September 20Y0 for $15 per share. The par (or nominal) value of the shares is $1 per share.

(2) The options only vest if the employees remain in employment with Denshaw until 30 September 20X9 and if the share price of Denshaw is at least $20 by that date.

(3) On 1 October 20X7 the board of Denshaw estimated that 5 of the 50 employees would leave in the following two years. Three of the employees left in the year ended 30 September 20X8 and at that date the board considered that a further three would leave in the year to 30 September 20X9.

(4) On 1 October 20X7 the share price of Denshaw was $15. The price had risen to $18 by 30 September 20X8 and the directors are reasonably confident that the price will exceed $20 by 30 September 20X9.

(5) On 1 October 20X7 the directors estimated that the fair value of one of the granted options was $4.50. This estimate had risen to $5 by 30 September 20X8.

Requirements

Explain and show with appropriate calculations how the three events would be reported in the financial statements of Denshaw for the year ended 30 September 20X8:

Exhibit 1 – Joint arrangement	**(7 marks)**
Exhibit 2 – Purchase of inventory from a foreign supplier	**(11 marks)**
Exhibit 3 – Share options	**(7 marks)**

(Total = 25 marks)

30 Gamma (September 2020 (amended))

49 mins

Exhibit 2 adapted from SBR Specimen exam 2

Gamma prepares consolidated financial statements to 31 March each year. Information relevant to the question is provided in the exhibits.

Exhibit 1 – Purchase of machine

On 1 January 20X4, Gamma entered into a firm commitment to purchase a machine from a supplier whose functional currency is the kroner. This firm commitment was not an onerous contract. The cost of the machine was 14.4 million kroner and the agreed delivery date was 30 June 20X4. Gamma was due to pay 14.4 million kroner to the supplier on 31 July 20X4.

On 1 January 20X4, Gamma entered into a forward exchange contract with a bank to purchase 14.4 million kroner for $1.44 million on 31 July 20X4. The forward exchange contract was entered into so as to provide a hedge against the currency risk associated with the firm commitment to purchase the machine.

On 30 June 20X4, Gamma took delivery of the machine and immediately brought the machine into use. Gamma estimated that the machine would have a useful life of five years from 30 June 20X4, with no residual value.

On 31 July 20X4, Gamma paid 14.4 million kroner to the supplier of the machine and received payment of $360,000 from the bank in settlement of the forward exchange contract (see below).

Gamma designated the forward exchange contract as a hedge of the cash flows expected to arise on the purchase of the machine. This contract was a perfectly effective hedge of those cash flows. Gamma wishes to use hedge accounting to reflect the above transactions in its financial statements.

Relevant exchange rates and fair values of the forward exchange contract are as follows:

Date	Exchange rate (kroners to $1)	Fair value of forward contract (favourable to Gamma) $'000
1 January 20X4	10	Nil
31 March 20X4	9.6	60
30 June 20X4	9	160
31 July 20X4	8	360

Exhibit 2 – Provisions

The directors of Gamma receive a cash bonus each year if reported profits for the period exceed a pre-determined target. Gamma has performed in excess of targets in the year ended 31 March 20X5 but financial forecasts for 20X6 are pessimistic.

A new accountant has recently started work at Gamma. She noticed that the provisions balance as at 31 March 20X5 is significantly higher than in the prior year. She made enquiries of the finance director, who explained that the increase was due to substantial changes in food safety and hygiene laws which become effective during 20X6. As a result, Gamma must retrain a large proportion of its workforce. This retraining has yet to occur, so a provision has been recognised for the estimated cost of $2 million. The finance director then told the accountant that such enquiries were a waste of time and would not be looked at favourably when deciding on her future pay rises and bonuses.

Requirements

(a)   Using the information in exhibit 1, explain and show how the purchase of the machine would be reported in the consolidated financial statements of Gamma for the year ended 31 March 20X5.   **(17 marks)**

(b)   Using the information in exhibit 2:

   (i)   Explain and show how this event would be reported in the consolidated financial statements of Gamma for the year ended 31 March 20X5.   **(4 marks)**

   (ii)   Identify and explain the ethical issues confronting the accountant.   **(4 marks)**

(Total = 25 marks)

31 Omega (June 2015) (amended)   49 mins

You are the financial controller of Omega, a listed company which prepares consolidated financial statements in accordance with IFRS Accounting Standards.

Your managing director has raised a number of queries relating to the application of various IFRS Accounting Standards. The information is provided in the exhibits:

Exhibit 1 – Agriculture

The managing director has recently become aware that there is a IFRS Accounting Standard, IAS 41 *Agriculture*, which applies to farming entities. She is not clear why a special standard is needed for farming entities and has questioned whether IAS 41 means that other IFRS Accounting Standards do not apply to farming entities. She has asked you to please explain the main recognition and measurement requirements of IAS 41 Details about disclosures are not required. Your discussion should refer to any areas where the provisions of IAS 41 differ from general IFRS Accounting Standards. She is particularly interested in whether farming entities treat grants from the government in a different way than other entities do.

Exhibit 2 – Smaller entities

The managing director was recently talking to another company in the industry which is a relatively small listed entity. The director of that entity stated that it did not need to comply with the detailed requirements of IFRS Accounting Standards because of the relatively small size of the entity. The managing director would like you to explain whether it is true that there are different accounting rules for smaller entities if so, whether these can be applied to a small listed entity? Details of any different rules are not required.

Exhibit 3 – *Conceptual Framework*

The managing director is aware that the IASB's *Conceptual Framework for Financial Reporting* (Conceptual Framework) has recently been revised. She understands that it recognises a wide range of 'users' but feels this is incorrect as they all have differing needs and the end result is bigger and bigger but less comprehensible sets of accounts. She believes the only users that financial accountants should be interested in are the company's shareholders but would like to understand more about what the *Conceptual Framework* sees as the purpose of financial statements.

Requirements

Provide answers to the questions raised by the managing director.

Exhibit 1 – Agriculture	**(12 marks)**
Exhibit 2 – Smaller entities	**(8 marks)**
Exhibit 3 – *Conceptual Framework*	**(5 marks)**

(Total = 25 marks)

32 Okawa (December 2015) (amended)   49 mins

You are the financial controller of Okawa, a listed company which prepares consolidated financial statements in accordance with IFRS Accounting Standards. Your managing director, who is not an accountant, has recently attended a seminar and has raised two questions for you concerning issues discussed at the seminar. The issues are detailed in the exhibits:

Exhibit 1 – Exploration costs

One of the delegates at the seminar was a director of an entity which is involved in the exploration for, and evaluation of, mineral resources. This delegate told me that under IFRS rules it is possible for individual entities to develop their own policies for when to recognise the costs of exploration for and evaluation of mineral resources as assets. This seems very strange to me. Surely IFRS Accounting Standards require consistent treatment for all tangible and intangible assets so that financial statements are comparable. Please explain the position to me and outline the relevant requirements of IFRS Accounting Standards regarding accounting for exploration and evaluation expenditures.

Exhibit 2 – Buildings for sale

Another delegate was discussing the fact that the entity of which she is a director is relocating its head office staff to a more suitable site and intends to sell its existing head office building. Apparently the existing building was advertised for sale on 1 July 20X5 and the entity anticipates selling it by 31 December 20X5. The year end of the entity is 30 September 20X5. The delegate stated that in certain circumstances buildings which are intended to be sold are treated differently from other buildings in the financial statements. Please outline under what circumstances buildings which are being sold are treated differently and also what that different treatment is.

Required

(a)   The managing director has acknowledged that she needs to better understand the definition of a non-current asset before you respond to the specific questions raised. She understands a non-current asset to be: 'a physical asset of substantial cost, owned by the company, which will last longer than one year'.

Provide an explanation to the managing director of the weaknesses in her understanding of a non-current asset when compared to the definition of assets in the *Conceptual Framework*.   **(5 marks)**

Note. You do not need to refer to either of the notes above to answer this part of the question.

(b)   Provide answers to the questions raised by the managing director in Exhibits 1 and 2.

Exhibit 1 – Exploration costs   **(10 marks)**
Exhibit 2 – Buildings for sale   **(10 marks)**

(Total = 25 marks)

33 Delta (September 2020)   49 mins

Delta prepares financial statements to 31 March each year. Delta applies IAS 12 *Income Taxes* and IAS 41 *Agriculture* in the preparation of its financial statements.

IAS 12 requires that entities recognise deferred tax liabilities on taxable temporary differences and, in certain circumstances, deferred tax assets on deductible temporary differences. Temporary differences are determined by comparing the carrying amount of an asset or liability with its tax base.

IAS 41 sets out the principles of recognition and measurement for biological assets and harvested produce.

Information relevant to the question is provided in the exhibits.

Exhibit 1 – Temporary differences

On 1 October 20X4, Delta purchased an item of plant for $4 million. The estimated useful life of the plant was five years, with no residual value. Under tax legislation in the country in which Delta is located, purchases of plant attract a tax deduction of 50% of the cost in the accounting period in which the plant is purchased and 25% of the cost in each of the following two accounting periods.

On 1 July 20X4, Delta borrowed $20 million from a bank. The loan attracts interest at a rate of 8% per annum on the $20 million borrowed. The interest is payable annually in arrears. The loan is repayable on 30 June 20X9. Under tax legislation in the country in which Delta is located, a tax deduction for the interest on loans is available in the accounting periods in which the interest is actually paid.

On 1 April 20X4, Delta purchased some land for $15 million. Delta uses the revaluation model to measure land in its financial statements. On 31 March 20X5, Delta estimated that the value of the land was $18 million and this amount was recognised in Delta's financial statements. Under tax legislation in the country in which Delta is located, gains on the value of land are not taxable unless or until the land is sold. Delta has no intention of disposing of this land in the foreseeable future.

The rate of corporate income tax in the country in which Delta is located is 20% per annum.

The directors of Delta anticipate that Delta will make taxable profits for the foreseeable future. Delta had no temporary differences at 31 March 20X4.

Exhibit 2 – Agricultural activity

Delta is a farming entity specialising in milk production. Cows are milked on a daily basis. Milk is kept in cold storage immediately after milking and sold to retail distributors on a weekly basis.

On 1 April 20X4, Delta had a herd of 500 cows which were all three years old.

During the year, some of the cows became sick and on 30 September 20X4 20 cows died. On 1 October 20X4, Delta purchased 20 replacement cows at the market for $210 each. These 20 cows were all one year old when they were purchased.

On 31 March 20X5, Delta had 1,000 litres of milk in cold storage which had not been sold to retail distributors. The market price of milk at 31 March 20X5 was $2 per litre. When selling the milk to distributors, Delta incurs selling costs of 10 cents per litre. These amounts did not change during March 20X5 and are not expected to change during April 20X5.

Information relating to fair value and costs to sell is given below:

Date	Fair value of a dairy cow which is:				Costs to sell a cow at market
	1 year old	1½ years old	3 years old	4 years old	
	$	$	$	$	$
1 April 20X4	200	220	270	250	10
1 October 20X4	210	230	280	260	10
31 March 20X5	215	235	290	265	11

Requirement:

Using the information in exhibits 1 and 2, explain, with appropriate computations, how Delta should report these transactions in the financial statements for the year ended 31 March 20X5.

Note. Marks will be awarded for explanations as well as for computations.

The marks are allocated as follows:

Exhibit 1 – Temporary differences **(12 marks)**
Exhibit 2 – Agricultural activity **(13 marks)**

(Total = 25 marks)

34 Delta (June 2021)

49 mins

Delta prepares financial statements to 31 March each year. Delta has a number of subsidiaries which operate in a number of different business sectors.

The following **exhibits** provide information relevant to the question:

Exhibit 1 – Cattle and sheep

Omega has a herd of 300 cattle which are all six months old on 31 March 20X5 and a herd of 200 sheep which are all one year old at 31 March 20X5. The herd of cattle will be sold when the cattle are two years old. The herd of sheep is expected to be sold within the next 12 months.

There are two markets available to Omega in which they could sell the cattle and the sheep, Market 1 and Market 2. Market 1 is the principal market in which cattle could be sold but Omega sells its sheep in both Market 1 and Market 2 in roughly equal proportions. Therefore, neither Market 1 nor Market 2 can be identified as the principal market in which Omega could sell sheep.

Relevant market prices and relevant costs of sale at 31 March 20X5 are as follows:

	Market 1		Market 2	
	Cattle	Sheep	Cattle	Sheep
	$	$	$	$
Gross selling price per animal	80	61	85	63
Transport costs per animal	4	3	5	4
Selling costs per animal	2	2	3	4

(10 marks)

Exhibit 2 – Purchase of shares

Kappa has a portfolio of equity shares which is regarded as a trading portfolio. On 1 January 20X5 Kappa purchased 20,000 shares in a listed entity and added these shares to the trading portfolio. Kappa purchased the shares for $5.25 per share and paid a commission to the broker of 20 cents per share. Due to favourable market conditions Kappa retained these shares and they were still part of the trading portfolio at 31 March 20X5. These shares are listed on a single stock exchange. Relevant market prices (per share) are as follows:

Date	Bid price	Offer price
	$	$
1 January 20X5	5.00	5.25
31 March 20X5	5.80	6.10

(8 marks)

Exhibit 3 – Acquisition of subsidiary

On 1 October 20X4 Delta acquired a new subsidiary, Zeta. The net assets of Zeta included a factory with a carrying amount of $6 million. $3.2 million of this amount was attributable to the buildings element. The useful life of the buildings element at 1 October 20X4 is 40 years. Delta intends to continue to use the factory for the same purpose as it was being used by Zeta prior to its acquisition. However, the factory could be used for administrative purposes with virtually no conversion costs.

Relevant fair value measurements for the factory at 1 October 20X4 are as follows:

	Land element	Buildings element	Total	Future life of buildings element
	$ million	$ million	$ million	
Use as a factory	3.4	3.8	7.2	40 years
Use for administrative purposes	3.5	4.0	7.5	50 years

Delta uses the cost model to measure its property, plant and equipment in its consolidated financial statements.

(7 marks)

Requirement

Using the information in exhibits 1–3, explain and compute the amounts that would be recognised by Delta in its consolidated financial statements for the year ended 31 March 20X5 and state where in these financial statements they should be presented. Marks will be awarded for BOTH calculations AND explanations.

Note. The mark allocations are indicated in each exhibit.

(Total = 25 marks)

35 Omega (December 2022)   49 mins

You are the financial controller of Omega. The consolidated financial statements of Omega for the year ended 30 September 20X5 were authorised for issue on 31 October 20X5. These statements were further discussed at a directors' meeting held on 15 November 20X5. One of the directors, who is not an accountant, has approached you with some queries relating to these financial statements.

The following **exhibits** provide information relevant to the question:

(1)   Assets of subsidiary – details the assets of a subsidiary of Omega operating in the farming sector.

(2)   Post year end – details of events occurring after the year end and discussed at a board meeting on 15 November 20X5.

(3)   Inventory – details of inventory bought from a foreign supplier.

This information should be used to answer the question **requirement** within the **response option** provided.

Requirement

Provide answers to the queries raised by one of Omega's directors detailed in exhibits 1, 2, and 3, relating to the consolidated financial statements for the year ended 30 September 20X5.

Note. The mark allocations are indicated in each exhibit.

(Total = 25 marks)

Exhibit 1 – Assets of subsidiary

As you know, we acquired a new subsidiary during the year ended 30 September 20X4. This subsidiary operates several different farms, which contain both cattle and sheep. We dealt with all the initial consolidation procedures last year and I understand how all of that works. However, I am not sure how we have measured the assets of this subsidiary at 30 September 20X5. I thought that assets were generally measured based on what they cost. I understand how that would work for this subsidiary in the case of the purchase of farm machinery, or the purchase of cattle or sheep from the market. I am not clear, though, how you would measure the cattle and sheep subsequently born on the farm as there is no cost of purchase. The same would apply to inventory items like meat or milk. Please explain how we measured the assets of this subsidiary in its statement of financial position. When do profits and losses relating to farming assets get recognised, given that there is often no real 'cost' of acquisition?

(12 marks)

Exhibit 2 – Post year end

At our board meeting, the finance director provided us with a summary of three events which had occurred in the period immediately after 30 September 20X5. These were:

(1)   The settlement of a legal case which a former employee had brought against one of our subsidiaries. The case was in respect of alleged unfair dismissal on 31 December 20X4. At 30 September 20X5, our legal team estimated that the case was likely to result in our paying $500,000 to this employee. On 20 October 20X5, the case was settled, and the subsidiary was required to pay $560,000, including court costs.

(2) A fire at one of the factories of another subsidiary on 11 October 20X5. This fire caused damage which is likely to cost $2 million to rectify. The subsidiary does have the necessary resources to finance this work. There was no insurance in place to cover this cost.

(3) The launch of a new product on 10 November 20X5 by a competitor. This product is likely to provide significant competition to one of the key products of another subsidiary. As the subsidiary may need to reduce its selling prices, estimates suggest the net realisable value of the inventories of this subsidiary at 30 September 20X5 could be $250,000 lower than its cost.

I'm a little confused about how these events should have been reflected in the financial statements for the year ended 30 September 20X5. I know that the group financial statements were authorised for issue on 31 October 20X5. Please explain the appropriate treatment of each item in our financial statements.

(8 marks)

Exhibit 3 – Inventory

On 1 August 20X5, Omega bought some inventory from a supplier based in a country whose currency is the groat. The invoiced amount was 840,000 groats. Omega paid for the goods on 31 August 20X5. Omega sold these goods to customers based in that country during October 20X5 for 1 million groats, and it looks like we made a healthy profit on the sale of those goods after the year end. I am unsure how this transaction would have been recognised in the financial statements for the year ended 30 September 20X5, given that the financial records of all of our group companies are prepared in $ and the exchange rate has changed throughout the period of this transaction (see the table below). Please explain the appropriate financial reporting treatment to me.

Table of exchange rates

Date	Exchange rate (groats to $1)
1 August 20X5	6
31 August 20X5	7
30 September 20X5	8

(5 marks)

36 Delta (June 2019) (amended)   49 mins

Delta prepares financial statements to 31 March each year. The information in the exhibits is relevant for the year ended 31 March 20X7.

Exhibit 1 – Granting of options to sales staff

On 1 April 20X5, Delta granted share options to 100 sales staff. The options are due to vest on 31 March 20X8.

The granting of the options was subject to two conditions:

• The staff member remains employed by Delta on 31 March 20X8.

• The sales revenue of Delta grows by a cumulative amount of at least 40% in the three-year period ending on 31 March 20X8 (see the table below).

Cumulative growth in revenue in the three-year period	Number of options each employee is entitled to (subject to satisfying other vesting conditions)
Between 40% and 50%	200
Over 50%	250

On 1 April 20X5, the fair value of a share option was $4.20. This had increased to $4.50 by 31 March 20X6 and to $4.80 by 31 March 20X7.

During the two years ended 31 March 20X7, expectations of revenue growth and employee retention in the three-year period ending on 31 March 20X8 changed as follows:

	Growth in revenue		Employees leaving	
	In the year	Expected cumulative growth in the three-year period	In the year	Expected FUTURE departures in the three-year vesting period
Year ended 31 March				
20X6	12%	42%	10	20
20X7	18%	54%	5	9

You can assume that this transaction was correctly accounted for by Delta in its financial statements for the year ended 31 March 20X6.

Exhibit 2 – Granting of share appreciation rights to senior executives

On 1 October 20X5, Delta granted 500 share appreciation rights to 20 senior executives. The rights are redeemable in cash on 30 September 20X9 provided the executives remain employed by Delta until at least 30 September 20X9.

On 1 October 20X5, Delta estimated that two of the 20 executives would leave in the period from 1 October 20X5 to 30 September 20X9 and this estimate remained unchanged at 31 March 20X6.

During the year ended 31 March 20X7, one executive left Delta and on that date Delta estimated that the other 19 executives would remain in employment until 30 September 20X9 and so be entitled to the share appreciation rights.

On 1 October 20X5, the fair value of a share appreciation right was estimated to be $6. The fair value of a right had increased to $6.20 by 31 March 20X6 and to $6.40 by 31 March 20X7.

You can assume that this transaction was correctly accounted for by Delta in its financial statements for the year ended 31 March 20X6.

Exhibit 3 – Granting of share options to a director

On 1 April 20X6, Delta granted one of its directors the right to choose either 2,400 shares in Delta or a cash payment equal to the value of 2,000 shares on the settlement date, 31 March 20X8. The director must remain in employment for two years following the grant date.

Delta's market share price was $6.10 per share on 1 April 20X6 and $6.90 on 31 March 20X7. Theta has estimated that the grant date fair value of the share alternative is $5.50 per share.

Requirements

(a) It has become increasingly common for entities to use share-based payment methods and the most common example is to grant employees share options as part of a remuneration package. These options often vest at the end of a specified period, and are subject to vesting conditions. IFRS 2 *Share-based Payment* has been issued to provide financial reporting guidance for entities which engage in this type of transaction.

  (i) Explain how share options granted to employees with a future vesting date and subject to vesting conditions should be recognised and measured in the financial statements of the employing entity. Your explanation need only include the treatment of non-market based vesting conditions. **(6 marks)**

  (ii) Explain what would be the changes to your answer if instead the entity granted share appreciation rights which are payable in cash to the employees at the end of the vesting period. **(3 marks)**

(b) Briefly explain and show how the transactions described in Exhibits 1, 2 and 3 would be reported in the financial statements of Delta for the year ended 31 March 20X7.

The mark allocation is as follows:

Exhibit 1 – Granting of options to sales staff **(6 marks)**
Exhibit 2 – Granting of share appreciation rights to senior executives **(5 marks)**
Exhibit 3 – Granting of share options to a director **(5 marks)**

(Total = 25 marks)

37 Dart
49 mins

Part (a) and (c) adapted from June 2015, part (b) adapted from June 2010

Dart and its wholly owned subsidiary, Kappa, both prepare individual financial statements to 31 March each year. The exhibits provide information relevant to the question.

Exhibit 1 – Dart's share options

On 1 April 20X4, Dart granted share options to 100 senior executives. The options vest on 31 March 20X7. The number of options granted per executive depend on the cumulative revenue for the three years ended 31 March 20X7. Each executive will receive options as follows:

Cumulative revenue for the three years ended 31 March 20X7	Number of options per executive
Less than $180m	Nil
At least $180m but less than or equal to $270m	200
More than $270m	300

Dart's revenue for the year ended 31 March 20X5 was $50 million. The directors of Dart have produced reliable budgets showing that the revenues of Dart for the next two years are likely to be:

- Year ended 31 March 20X6 – $65 million
- Year ended 31 March 20X7 – $75 million

On 1 April 20X4, the fair value of these share options was $3 per option. This figure had increased to $3.60 per option by 31 March 20X5 and was expected to be $5 per option by 31 March 20X7. All of the 100 executives who were granted the options on 1 April 20X4 were expected to remain as employees throughout the three-year period from 1 April 20X4 to 31 March 20X7.

Exhibit 2 – Kappa's share-based payments

Kappa had the following share-based payment arrangements in force during the year ended 31 March 20X5:

(1) On 1 April 20X3, Kappa granted options to 500 employees to subscribe for 400 shares each in Kappa on 31 March 20X7, providing the employees still worked for Kappa at that time. On 1 April 20X3, the fair value of each option was $1.50.

In the year ended 31 March 20X4, ten of these employees left Kappa and at 31 March 20X4, Kappa expected that 20 more would leave in the three-year period from 1 April 20X4 to 31 March 20X7. Kappa's results for the year ended 31 March 20X4 were below expectations and at 31 March 20X4 the fair value of each option had fallen to 25 cents. Therefore, on 1 April 20X4 Kappa amended the exercise price of the original options. This amendment caused the fair value of these options to rise from 25 cents to $1.45.

During the year ended 31 March 20X5, five of the employees left and at 31 March 20X5, Kappa expected that ten more would leave in the two-year period from 1 April 20X5 to 31 March 20X7. The results of Kappa for the year ended 31 March 20X5 were much improved and at 31 March 20X5, the fair value of a re-priced option was $1.60.

(2)   On 1 April 20X3, Kappa granted share appreciation rights to 50 senior employees. The number of rights to which each employee becomes entitled depends on the cumulative profit of Kappa for the three years ended 31 March 20X6:

- 1,000 rights per employee are awarded if the cumulative profit for the three-year period is below $500,000.

- 1,500 rights per employee are awarded if the cumulative profit for the three-year period is between $500,000 and $1 million.

- 2,000 rights per employee are awarded if the cumulative profit for the three-year period exceeds $1 million.

On 1 April 20X3, Kappa expected that the cumulative profits for the three-year period would be $800,000. After the disappointing financial results for the year ended 31 March 20X4, this estimate was revised at that time to $450,000. However, given the improvement in results for the year ended 31 March 20X5, the estimate was revised again at 31 March 20X5 to $1,100,000.

On 1 April 20X3, the fair value of one share appreciation right was $1.10. This estimate was revised to $0.90 at 31 March 20X4 and to $1.20 at 31 March 20X5. All the senior employees are expected to remain employed by Kappa for the relevant three-year period. The rights are exercisable on 30 June 20X6.

Requirements

(a)   IFRS 2 *Share-based Payment* defines a share-based payment transaction as one in which an entity receives goods or services from a third party (including an employee) in a share-based payment arrangement. A share-based payment arrangement is an agreement between an entity and a third party which entitles the third party to receive either:

- Equity instruments of the entity (equity-settled share-based payments); or

- Cash or other assets based on the price of equity instruments of the entity (cash-settled share-based payments).

Share-based payment arrangements are often subject to vesting conditions which must be satisfied over a vesting period.

For both cash-settled **and** equity-settled share-based payment arrangements, explain:

(i)   The basis on which the arrangements should be measured

(ii)   The criteria which are used to allocate the total value of the arrangement to individual accounting periods

(iii)   The accounting entries (debit and credit) required during the vesting period   **(6 marks)**

(b)   Using the information in Exhibit 1, explain and show how the share options should be reported in the individual financial statements of Dart for the year ended 31 March 20X5. Ignore deferred tax.   **(5 marks)**

(c)   Using the information in Exhibit 2:

(i)   Explain how Kappa's share options would be reported in the individual financial statements of Kappa for the year ended 31 March 20X5.   **(9 marks)**

(ii)   Explain how Kappa's share appreciation rights would be reported in the individual financial statements of Kappa for the year ended 31 March 20X5.   **(5 marks)**

Ignore deferred tax.   **(Total = 25 marks)**

38 Roma (June 2016) (amended)

49 mins

Roma has a year end 31 March 20X6. It has four outstanding events that need to be reported in its financial statements. Information is provided in the exhibits:

Exhibit 1 – Employee share options

On 1 April 20X4, Roma granted 2,000 employees 1,000 share options each. The options are due to vest on 31 March 20X7 provided the relevant employees remain in employment over the three-year period ending on 31 March 20X7.

On 1 April 20X4, the directors of Roma estimated that 1,800 employees would qualify for the options on 31 March 20X7. This estimate was amended to 1,850 employees on 31 March 20X5, and further amended to 1,840 employees on 31 March 20X6.

On 1 April 20X4, the fair value of an option was $1.20. The fair value increased to $1.30 by 31 March 20X5 but, due to challenging trading conditions, the fair value declined after 31 March 20X5. On 30 September 20X5, when the fair value of an option was 90 cents, the directors repriced the options and this caused the fair value to increase to $1.05. Trading conditions improved in the second half of the year and by 31 March 20X6 the fair value of an option was $1.25. Any additional costs that have occurred as a result of the repricing of the options on 30 September 20X5 should be spread over the remaining vesting period from 30 September 20X5 to 31 March 20X7.

Exhibit 2 – Legal case

On 1 August 20X5, Roma supplied some products it had manufactured to customer C. The products were faulty and on 1 October 20X5 C commenced legal action against Roma claiming damages in respect of losses due to the supply of the faulty products. Upon investigating the matter, Roma discovered that the products were faulty due to defective raw materials supplied to Roma by supplier S. Therefore on 1 December 20X5, Roma commenced legal action against S claiming damages in respect of the supply of defective materials. Since that date Roma has consistently estimated that it is probable that both of the legal actions, the action of C against Roma and the action of Roma against S, will succeed.

On 1 October 20X5, Roma estimated that the damages Roma would have to pay to C would be $5 million. This estimate was updated to $5.2 million as at 31 March 20X6 and $5.25 million as at 15 May 20X6. This case was eventually settled on 1 June 20X6, when Roma was required to pay damages of $5.3 million to C.

On 1 December 20X5, Roma estimated that they would receive damages of $3.5 million from S. This estimate was updated to $3.6 million as at 31 March 20X6 and $3.7 million as at 15 May 20X6. This case was eventually settled on 1 June 20X6, when S was required to pay damages of $3.75 million to Roma.

Exhibit 3 – Related party transactions

On 1 June 20X5, the spouse of one of the directors of Roma purchased a controlling interest in entity X, a long-standing customer of Roma. Sales of products from Roma to entity X in the two-month period from 1 April 20X5 to 31 May 20X5 totalled $800,000. Following the share purchase by the spouse of one of the directors of Roma on 1 June 20X5, Roma began to supply the products at a discount of 20% to their normal selling price and allow entity X three months' credit (previously entity X was only allowed one month's credit, Roma's normal credit policy). Sales of products from Roma to entity X in the ten-month period from 1 June 20X5 to 31 March 20X6 totalled $6 million. On 31 March 20X6, the trade receivables of Roma included $1.8 million in respect of amounts owing by entity X.

Exhibit 4 – Acquired brand

On 1 April 20X5 Roma acquired a new subsidiary, Omicron. The directors of Roma carried out a fair value exercise as required by IFRS 3 *Business Combinations* and concluded that the brand name of Omicron had a fair value of $10 million and would be likely to generate economic benefits for a ten-year period from 1 April 20X5. They further concluded that the expertise of the employees of Omicron contributed $5 million to the overall value of Omicron. The estimated average remaining service lives of the Omicron employees was eight years from 1 April 20X5.

Requirements

Explain and show how the three events would be reported in the financial statements of Roma for the year ended 31 March 20X6:

Exhibit 1 – Employee share options **(10 marks)**
Exhibit 2 – Legal case **(6 marks)**
Exhibit 3 – Related party transaction **(5 marks)**
Exhibit 4 – Acquired brand **(4 marks)**

(Total = 25 marks)

39 Gamma (June 2022)

49 mins

Gamma prepares financial statements to 31 March each year. You are a trainee accountant employed by Gamma and report to the finance director (FD) of Gamma. One of your key responsibilities is to prepare the first draft of Gamma's published financial statements. You have recently received an email from the FD regarding the financial statements for the year ended 31 March 20X5 but are unsure how to respond. You would like to ask the advice and assistance of a friend who is a fully ACCA qualified accountant with more technical knowledge, but they are not employed by Gamma.

The following exhibits provide information relevant to the question:

(1)   Email – an email from the finance director.
(2)   Attachment 1 to the email – provides details relating to shares granted to ten of Gamma's executives.
(3   Attachment 2 to the email – details the revaluation of property.

This information should be used to answer the question requirements within your chosen response option(s).

Exhibit 1 – Email

To: Trainee accountant
From: Finance director
Subject: Potential bonuses dependent on performance
Date: 5 April 20X5

It is very important that the upcoming set of financial results of Gamma show a favourable financial performance and position. If the results are good, then potentially there are big bonuses available for all staff, including you! There are a couple of complex transactions which have occurred in the year ended 31 March 20X5 which you may be unsure how to deal with in your preparation of the draft financial statements. They are set out in the two attachments to this email. I have also included the way in which I would like you to deal with them in your draft. I have tried to identify treatments which will show Gamma in as favourable a position as possible.

Exhibit 2 – Attachment 1 to the email

On 1 April 20X4, we granted ten of our senior executives 12,000 shares each in Gamma. These shares will vest on 31 March 20X7 provided the executives remain employed by Gamma until then. One of these executives is likely to retire in the next couple of years but the other nine are almost certain to stay employed until at least 31 March 20X7. The shares will be issued on 31 March 20X7. As an alternative to receiving the 12,000 shares, each executive could, on 31 March 20X7, receive a cash payment equal to the value of 10,000 shares on that date.

The market price of Gamma shares on 1 April 20X4 was $10 per share and this has increased to $12 by 31 March 20X5. My finance specialists tell me that the fair value of the share alternative was $9 on 1 April 20X4, increasing to $9.50 by 31 March 20X5.

Do not worry about all this detail as although we have given them the choice, the executives are almost certain to take up the shares rather than the cash, so all we need to do is to recognise the share issue when it happens on 31 March 20X7. Therefore, you do not have to include this in the financial statements until then.   **(10 marks)**

Exhibit 3 – Attachment 2 to the email

I want to measure Gamma's property at its market value from the start of the year (1 April 20X4). Gamma has not used the revaluation model before. The property was previously recognised in the financial statements on 1 April 20X4 at its carrying amount of $20 million. $10 million of this amount relates to the land element of the property and $10 million to the buildings element. A report from a qualified surveyor has indicated that its market value on 1 April 20X4 was $30 million. The report said that $12 million of this value was attributed to the land element and $18 million to the buildings element. The profit on revaluation will improve our reported pre-tax profit and provide a nice improvement to financial performance this year. It is likely the company will use this property for 20 more years from 1 April 20X4 but do not worry about accounting for depreciation – future increases in value of the property will be more than enough to cancel depreciation out.

If we sold the property, we would have to pay tax at 25% on any profit made. The tax department has informed me that the tax base of the property on 1 April 20X4 was nil because the property qualified for very favourable tax treatment when purchased. You need not worry about any of this though; we have no immediate intention of disposing of this property, so we can leave tax considerations related to the revaluation until later.   **(10 marks)**

Requirements

(a)   Using the information in exhibits 2 and 3, explain and show how the transactions described should be accounted for in the financial statements of Gamma for the year ended 31 March 20X5. Your answer to (a) should NOT include discussion of any ethical issues.   **(20 marks)**

Notes.

*   The mark allocations are indicated in each exhibit.
*   Marks will be awarded for BOTH figures AND explanations.

(b)   Using the information in exhibit 1, explain THREE ethical issues confronting you as a result of the email from the finance director and the associated attachments and whether you should ask for assistance from your fully ACCA qualified friend who is not employed by Gamma.   **(5 marks)**

(Total = 25 marks)

40 Belloso   49 mins

Belloso is finalising its consolidated financial statements for the year ended 31 December 20X1. It has three outstanding issues to address. Information relevant to the question is provided in the exhibits.

Exhibit 1 – Contract with Alesso

Belloso has a contractual agreement with Alesso, whereby Alesso holds items of Belloso's inventory in its stores for a trial period of 6 months from 1 September 20X1. The items cost $30,000 and have a retail value of $42,000.

Belloso retains the right to set the selling price of the inventory. When Alesso sells the inventory to a customer, legal title passes from Belloso to the customer. At the end of each month, Alesso is required to remit to Belloso any revenue relating to the inventory that it has sold.

Alesso has paid a refundable deposit of $10,000 to hold the inventory in its stores. The deposit is deducted by Alesso, on a proportionate basis, from the revenue remitted to Belloso each month. At the end of the trial period Alesso is required to return any unsold inventory to Belloso in return for any remaining deposit. In return for selling the products, Alesso receives a commission of 10% of any sales made, payable at the end of the 6 month trial.

As at 31 December 20X1, Alesso had sold goods with a retail value of $28,000 which cost $20,000. Alesso correctly deducted $6,667 from the amount paid in respect of these goods to reflect a proportion of the deposit paid. In the year ended 31 December 20X1, Belloso has removed all of the inventory from its records and has recorded the deposit and payments received as revenue in the statement of profit or loss.

Exhibit 2 – Convertible bonds

On 1 January 20X1 Belloso issued 50,000 5% $20 convertible bonds at par. The bonds can be redeemed at par on 31 December 20X4 or converted into ordinary shares at the rate of 5 ordinary shares for each $20 bond.

Belloso has credited the proceeds of the issue to non-current liabilities. The interest is payable annually in arrears and $250,000 has been accrued in finance costs. The interest rate on similar bonds without conversion rights is 7% per annum.

Discount factors which may be relevant are as follows:	Discount rate	
	5%	7%
	$	$
Present value of $1 receivable in 3 years	0.864	0.816
Cumulative present value of $1 receivable at the end of years 1–3	2.723	2.624

Exhibit 3 – Investment in Nefyn

On 1 April 20X1 Belloso acquired 25% of the $1 ordinary shares in Nefyn for a total of $340,000. Belloso subsequently appointed two out of a total of five directors onto Nefyn's board. Nefyn earned a profit for the year to 31 December 20X1 of $430,000 and paid a dividend totalling $35,000 to ordinary shareholders on 31 May 20X1. Belloso has recorded the acquisition cost of $340,000 within investments and the dividend received within investment income. There is no evidence of impairment of the investment at the year end. You can assume that the profits accrued evenly over the year.

Exhibit 4 – Decommissioning of plant

On 1 January 20X1 Belloso purchased a waste processing plant for $1.3 million. The plant has an estimated useful life of 5 years after which time Belloso is required to decommission and restore the land on which the plant is located. The cost of decommissioning and restoration is estimated at $150,000 and a relevant discount rate is 8%. Belloso will depreciate the plant on a straight-line basis. The estimated residual value of the plant at the end of the five year period is nil. Belloso has not made any accounting entries in relation to the decommissioning of the plant. When using a discount rate of 8%, the present value of $1 payable in five years is 68.1 cents.

Requirements

Explain and show how the four events should be reported in the consolidated financial statements of Belloso for the year ended 31 December 20X1:

Exhibit 1 – Contract with Alesso	**(7 marks)**
Exhibit 2 – Convertible bonds	**(6 marks)**
Exhibit 3 – Investment in Nefyn	**(6 marks)**
Exhibit 4 – Decommissioning of plant	**(6 marks)**
	(Total = 25 marks)

41 Delta (December 2013) (amended)   49 mins

Delta is preparing its financial statements to 30 September 20X3. The outstanding issues in the exhibits have not yet been accounted for.

Exhibit 1 – Investment in loan notes

On 1 April 20X3, Delta subscribed for 40 million $1 loan notes in Epsilon. The loan notes were issued at 90 cents and under the terms of issue were redeemable at $1.20 on 31 March 20X8. Interest is payable on 31 March in arrears at 4% of par value. This represents an effective annual rate of return for Delta of 9.9%. Delta's intention is to hold the loan notes until redemption.

 BPP LEARNING MEDIA   49

Exhibit 2 – Disposal of a component

On 1 June 20X3, Delta decided to dispose of the trade and assets of a business it had acquired several years previously. This disposal does not involve Delta withdrawing from a particular market sector. The carrying amounts on 1 June 20X3 of the assets to be disposed of were as follows:

	$m
Goodwill	10
Property, plant and equipment	20
Patents and trademarks	8
Inventories	15
Trade receivables	10
	63

Delta offered the business for sale at a price of $46.5 million, which was considered to be reasonably achievable. Delta estimated that the direct costs of selling the business would be $500,000. These estimates have not changed since 1 June 20X3 and Delta estimates that the business will be sold by 31 March 20X4 at the latest.

None of the assets of the business had suffered obvious impairment at 1 June 20X3. At that date the inventories and trade receivables of the business were already stated at no more than their recoverable amounts.

Exhibit 3 – Lease arrangements

During the year Delta entered into two lease arrangements:

(1)   A nine-month lease of an item of plant commencing on 1 August 20X3. A payment of $180,000 was made on 1 August 20X3. The economic life of the plant is five years.

(2)   A four year lease of 500 tablet computers for its staff. The market price of each tablet is approximately $800, with a useful life of four years. Lease payments of $240 per year per tablet are payable in advance, commencing on 1 April 20X3. The present value of the lease payments is $800 per tablet computer, equivalent to a finance rate of 13.7% per annum.

Delta's accounting policy is to apply any optional exemptions permitted by IFRS 16 *Leases*.

Exhibit 4 – Termination payments

During the year, Delta decided to restructure its workforce in order to reduce the number of employees. As a result, on 31 July 20X3, Delta made an offer to 100 employees to terminate their employment on 31 December 20X3 in exchange for a one off payment of $15,000 each, payable on 31 December 20X3. On 31 August 20X3, 45 employees formally accepted the offer and 55 declined it. The number of employees who accepted the offer was not as high as Delta expected, and therefore on 15 September 20X3 Delta announced that it would mandate that 30 employee contracts would be terminated on 31 December 20X3, but it had yet to identify the employees affected or the details of any termination benefit payable. On 3 October 20X3, Delta communicated to the 30 identified employees that their employment would end on 31 January 20X4 and that they would each receive a payment of $15,000 on that date. All employees would continue to be paid at their usual rates up until their employment ended.

Requirements

Explain and show how the four events would be reported in the financial statements of Delta for the year ended 30 September 20X3:

Exhibit 1 – Investment in loan notes	**(6 marks)**
Exhibit 2 – Disposal of component	**(7 marks)**
Exhibit 3 – Lease arrangements	**(6 marks)**
Exhibit 4 – Termination payments	**(6 marks)**

(Total = 25 marks)

42 Delta (December 2020)   49 mins

Delta prepares financial statements to 30 September each year.

The following **exhibits** provide information relevant to the question.

Exhibit 1: Share-based payment

On 1 October 20X3, Delta granted 3,000 share options to 50 senior executives. The options are due to vest on 30 September 20X6. In order to be entitled to exercise the options, the executives had to remain in employment until at least 30 September 20X6.

On 1 October 20X3, Delta estimated that 10 executives would leave prior to 30 September 20X6. This estimate was confirmed when the financial statements for the year ended 30 September 20X4 were prepared. However, during the year ended 30 September 20X5, the estimate of the total number of executives expected to leave before 30 September 20X6 was revised to 12.

On 1 October 20X3, the fair value of a share option was $2.50. At 30 September 20X4 and 20X5, the fair value of the option was $2.00 and $2.80 respectively.

On 1 April 20X5, because of disappointing financial results, Delta modified the terms of the arrangement with the senior executives by decreasing the exercise price. The results of this modification were to increase the fair value of a share option from $2.10 to $2.70.

Exhibit 2: Sale of two properties

On 1 September 20X5, Delta decided to sell two properties which were surplus to requirements. Both properties were measured under the cost model.

Property 1

Property 1 was available and advertised for immediate sale in its current condition. This property had a carrying amount of $50 million on 1 September 20X5. The property was being actively marketed at a realistic selling price of $60 million. The advertising agents have advised that a sale should be achievable within three months of 1 September 20X5. The agents will charge a commission of 5% of the selling price.

Property 2

Property 2 required essential repair work to be undertaken on it prior to it being in a condition to be offered for sale. This work is planned for October 20X5 and is expected to cost $10 million. This property had a carrying amount of $40 million at 30 September 20X5. The selling agents have advised that once the work has been carried out, the property could realistically be sold for $45 million. The agents' commission will also be 5% of the selling price.

Neither property 1 nor property 2 will be able to generate any income for Delta after 1 September 20X5, other than through sale.   **(10 marks)**

Exhibit 3: Sale of two business units

On 1 June 20X5 Delta sold two business units. The first unit was a business segment in its own right. Delta made a decision to withdraw from this particular business segment and concentrate on its 'core' business. This segment generated post-tax profits of $5 million from 1 October 20X4 to 31 May 20X5. On 1 June 20X5, the net assets of the segment were $50 million. The sale proceeds were $54 million.

The second sale was one of Delta's distribution centres as a result of a decision to rationalise the way in which Delta distributed its products. The net assets of the distribution centre were $10 million and it was sold for $12 million.

The income tax rate applicable to Delta is 20%.   **(5 marks)**

Requirements

(a) Using the information in Exhibit 1, explain and compute the amounts that would be recognised by Delta in its financial statements for the year ended 30 September 20X5 and state where in the financial statements they should be presented. **(10 marks)**

(b) Using the information in Exhibits 2 and 3, explain how each event would be measured and recognised in Delta's financial statements for the year ended 30 September 20X5. **(15 marks)**

Notes:

1   Marks will be awarded for BOTH figures AND explanations.
2   The mark allocations for part (b) are indicated in Exhibits 2 and 3.

(Total = 25 marks)

43 Omega (December 2020) (amended)   49 mins

You are the financial controller of Omega, a listed entity involved in the exploration for and evaluation of mineral resources. One of Omega's directors has raised some queries following his review of the consolidated financial statements for the year ended 30 September 20X5.

The following **exhibits** provide information relevant to the question:

Exhibit 1: Exploration and evaluation assets

When I looked at our financial statements, I saw a note which gave a breakdown of our exploration and evaluation assets. I compared it with that of a competitor and I have the following three questions.

First, both notes showed the breakdown of the exploration and evaluation assets figure into various categories but they are not presenting the same categories despite both companies operating in similar ways. How can this be right when both companies use IFRS Accounting Standards to prepare their financial statements?

Second, why does neither company include the costs of developing mineral resources as part of the exploration and evaluation assets figure? As a key part of both of our businesses, should these costs not be recognised as part of this figure?

Finally, the financial statements state that we measure our exploration and evaluation assets using the cost model while the competitor's state they use the revaluation model. Is this an acceptable inconsistency when both companies are preparing financial statements in accordance with IFRS Accounting Standards? **(7 marks)**

Exhibit 2: Events after 30 September 20X5

When I read two notes to our financial statements, they seemed to contradict each other. One of the notes referred to a legal case from December 20X4 in which we were being sued for damages by a customer. We originally thought Omega would have to pay damages of $5 million but the case was finally settled for $5.5 million on 20 October 20X5. The financial statements at 30 September 20X5 presented a liability for $5.5 million, despite this only being confirmed after the year end.

A second note referred to the major fire in one of our factories on 15 October 20X5. The damage caused to the factory is estimated at $5.75 million. However, the note says that no adjustments have been made to the amounts recognised in the financial statements for the year ended 30 September 20X5 in respect of the damage caused by the fire. This will have a significant, but temporary impact on the cash flow of the business, however, it will not cause our own going concern status to be in doubt.

The two events are not being treated consistently despite the financial amounts being similar. Please can you explain these apparent inconsistencies?

I am aware that a major customer, owing us a significant amount, became insolvent on 20 November 20X5. We are unlikely to recover much, if any, of this debt. Why don't the financial statements contain at least a note explaining to our shareholders what has happened?

I am aware that the financial statements were authorised for issue on 15 November 20X5. **(10 marks)**

Exhibit 3: Sustainability disclosures

I am aware that our stakeholders have requested that we provide sustainability disclosures as part of our annual report, and given that the business is involved in exploration for and evaluation of mineral resources, this is likely to be significant. I have read the IFRS Sustainability Disclosure Standards and I am aware that disclosures should include sustainability-related risks and opportunities and climate-related risks and opportunities, but I would like to understand this in more detail. Please could you explain these terms in more detail, including how they might apply to Omega. **(8 marks)**

Requirement

Provide answers to the queries raised in Exhibits 1–3 relating to the consolidated financial statements for the year ended 30 September 20X5. These financial statements were authorised for issue on 15 November 20X5.

Note. The mark allocations are indicated in each exhibit.

(Total = 25 marks)

44 Townsend

49 mins

Townsend is a publicly listed company reporting to a year end of 31 March. Information relevant to the question is provided in the following exhibits.

Exhibit 1 – Information for years ended 31 March 20X4 and 20X5

The issued share capital of Townsend at 31 March 20X3 was $10 million. Its shares are denominated at 25 cents each. Townsend's earnings attributable to its ordinary shareholders for the year ended 31 March 20X3 were also $10 million, giving an earnings per share of 25 cents.

Year ended 31 March 20X4

On 1 July 20X3 Townsend issued eight million ordinary shares at full market value. On 1 January 20X4 a bonus issue of one new ordinary share for every four ordinary shares held was made. Earnings attributable to ordinary shareholders for the year ended 31 March 20X4 were $13,800,000.

Year ended 31 March 20X5

On 1 October 20X4 Townsend made a rights issue of shares of two new ordinary shares at a price of $1.00 each for every five ordinary shares held. The offer was fully subscribed. The market price of Townsend's ordinary shares immediately prior to the offer was $2.40 each. Earnings attributable to ordinary shareholders for the year ended 31 March 20X5 were $19,500,000.

Exhibit 2 – Information for year ended 31 March 20X6

On 1 April 20X5 Townsend issued $20 million 10% convertible loan stock at par. The terms of conversion (on 1 April 20X8) are that for every $100 of loan stock, 25 ordinary shares will be issued at the option of loan stockholders. Alternatively the loan stock will be redeemed at par for cash. Also on 1 April 20X5 the directors of Townsend were awarded share options on 12 million ordinary shares exercisable from 1 April 20X8 at $1.50 per share. The average market value of Townsend's ordinary shares for the year ended 31 March 20X6 was $2.50 each. The income tax rate is 20%. Earnings attributable to ordinary shareholders for the year ended 31 March 20X6 were $25,200,000. The share options have been correctly recorded in the financial statements.

Requirements

(a) IAS 33 *Earnings per Share* sets out requirements for the calculation and presentation of earnings per share in financial statements of listed entities. The requirements include the disclosure of basic earnings per share and, where an entity has potential ordinary shares in issue, the additional disclosure of diluted earnings per share in certain circumstances.

    (i) Explain the meaning of the term 'potential ordinary shares' and provide one example of potential ordinary shares OTHER THAN convertible loans. **(2 marks)**

    (ii) Explain how the diluted earnings per share is calculated and when it needs to be disclosed. **(3 marks)**

    (iii) Discuss the view that the basic EPS should be based upon not only existing issued shares but also on other shares which are in substance 'share equivalents' and have a dilutive effect on the basic EPS. **(6 marks)**

(b) Using the information in Exhibit 1, calculate Townsend's basic earnings per share for the years ended 31 March 20X4 and 20X5 including comparative figures. **(9 marks)**

(c) Using the information in Exhibit 2, calculate Townsend's basic and diluted earnings per share for the year ended 31 March 20X6 (comparative figures are not required). **(5 marks)**

(Total = 25 marks)

45 Gamma (June 2021)   49 mins

Gamma prepares financial statements to 31 March each year.

The following **exhibits** provide information relevant to the question:

Exhibit 1 – Lease of machine

On 1 October 20X4 Gamma began to lease a machine. The lease gave Gamma the sole right to direct the use of the machine and receive all the economic benefits arising from its use. The lease was for a five-year term, with annual rentals of $200,000 being payable in advance. The first rental was paid on 1 October 20X4 and the final rental is due for payment on 1 October 20X8. The total estimated useful life of the machine on 1 October 20X4 was ten years. There are no terms in the lease agreement that allow the lease to be extended beyond the five-year term. The annual rate of interest implicit in the lease is 8%. On 1 October 20X4 when the first rental was paid Gamma debited $200,000 to profit or loss. Gamma has made no other entries regarding this lease in its draft financial statements for the year ended 31 March 20X5.

8% discount factors which may be relevant are as follows:

Cumulative present value of $1 payable in:

	$
1 year	0.926
2 years	1.783
3 years	2.577
4 years	3.312
5 years	3.993

(9 marks)

Exhibit 2 – Purchase of property

On 1 April 20X4 Gamma purchased an overseas property on credit for 4.4 million crowns. Of the initial carrying amount, 60% of the value of the property was attributed to the buildings element. On 1 April 20X4 Gamma estimated that the useful life of the buildings element was 40 years. On 30 June 20X4 Gamma paid 4.4 million crowns to the seller.

Gamma uses the revaluation model to measure property. On 31 March 20X5 Gamma estimated that the fair value of the property was 4.8 million crowns. The only entries made by Gamma in its draft financial statements regarding the purchase of the property were to record the cash paid on 30 June 20X4 as an operating expense in the statement of profit or loss.

Relevant exchange rates are:

Date	Exchange Rate
1 April 20X4	2 crowns to $1
30 June 20X4	1.76 crowns to $1
31 March 20X5	1.60 crowns to $1

(8 marks)

Exhibit 3 – Additional information

1 The draft financial statements of Gamma for the year ended 31 March 20X5 show a profit after tax of $10 million. This amount is before taking account of the implications of the information in exhibits 1 and 2.

2 On 1 April 20X4 Gamma had 70 million ordinary shares and 50 million preference shares in issue. The preference shares are irredeemable, and any preference dividends are discretionary.

3 On 1 October 20X4 Gamma made a 1 for 4 rights issue. The new shares were issued at a price of $1 per share. On 1 October 20X4 the shares of Gamma had a listed price of $1.50 immediately before the rights issue. The rights issue was fully taken up.

4 On 31 December 20X4 Gamma paid a dividend of $3 million to its ordinary shareholders and $2 million to its preference shareholders. These were the only dividends paid by Gamma in the year ended 31 March 20X5.

Requirements

(a) Using the information in exhibits 1 and 2, explain and show how the lease of machine and purchase of property would be reported in the financial statements of Gamma for the year ended 31 March 20X5. Marks will be awarded for BOTH calculations AND explanations.

   Note. The mark allocations are indicated in each exhibit. **(17 marks)**

(b) Using the information in exhibit 3 and the adjustments for the lease and purchase of property in part (a), compute the earnings per share of Gamma for the year ended 31 March 20X5. Comparative figures and explanations of your calculations are not required. **(8 marks)**

(Total = 25 marks)

46 Gamma (December 2022)   49 mins

Gamma, a listed entity, prepares financial statements to 30 September each year. You are a trainee accountant employed by Gamma and report to the finance director (FD) of Gamma. You also own a small number of equity shares in Gamma. One of your key responsibilities is to prepare the first draft of Gamma's published financial statements. You have recently received an email from the FD regarding the financial statements for the year ended 30 September 20X5.

The following **exhibits** provide information relevant to the question:

(1)   Email – an email from the FD.

(2)   Attachment 1 to the email – provides details relating to a sale of goods with a two-year repair service.

(3)   Attachment 2 to the email – details the valuation of a property which is being rented out on short-term leases.

This information should be used to answer the question **requirements** within your chosen **response option(s)**.

Requirements

(a)   Using the information in exhibits 2 and 3, explain and show how the transactions described there should be accounted for in the financial statements of Gamma for the year ended 30 September 20X5.

   Notes.

   - The mark allocations are indicated in each exhibit.
   - Marks will be awarded for BOTH figures AND explanations.
   - Ignore taxation.
   - Your answer to part (a) should NOT discuss any ethical issues.

   (17 marks)

(b)   Using the information in exhibit 1, and your answer to part (a) of this question, compute the earnings per share of Gamma for the year ended 30 September 20X5.

   Note. Explanations are NOT required for part (b).

   (3 marks)

(c)   Using the information in exhibit 1, explain the ethical issues which confront you as a result of the email sent to you from the finance director.

   (5 marks)

   (Total = 25 marks)

(1)   Email – an email from the FD.

(2)   Attachment 1 to the email – provides details relating to a sale of goods with a two-year repair service.

(3)   Attachment 2 to the email – details the valuation of a property which is being rented out on short-term leases.

Exhibit 1 – Email

To: Trainee accountant
From: Finance director
Subject: Earnings per share (EPS) calculation
Date: 30 September 20X5

As you will know, we have issued 1.5 million new equity shares at full market value on 1 February 20X5, taking our total number of shares in issue to 6 million shares. It is very important that the upcoming set of financial results of Gamma show a favourable financial performance to impress the new shareholders. There are a couple of relatively complex events which have occurred in the year ended 30 September 20X5 which you may be unsure how to deal with in your preparation of the draft financial statements. These events are described in the two attachments to this email. I have also included the way in which I would like you to deal with them in the financial statements. Assuming you follow my instructions, then the profit for the year (after tax) of Gamma for the year will be $1.8 million. Given that the number of shares in issue at the start of the year was 4.5 million, that would give EPS of 40 cents, which is highly satisfactory. Given you also own shares in Gamma, this should be to your advantage.

You should be aware that your annual performance appraisal, which I am responsible for, is due shortly.

Exhibit 2 – Attachment 1 to the email

On 31 March 20X5, we sold a large machine to a major customer. The normal selling price of the machine is $800,000 but we sold it to the customer for $840,000. This is because the sale includes an agreement to provide an after-sales repair service for the machine for a two-year period from 31 March 20X5. We would normally expect to charge a fee of $80,000 per annum to provide this service for a machine of this nature but we offered this customer a good deal because they provide us with so much business. I can reliably estimate that the machine will only cost us about $50,000 each year to repair on average. So far, the only repair cost we have incurred is expenditure of $20,000. I want you to recognise $840,000 in revenue for the current period. I would like you to show the $20,000 as an asset for now. Until we know the total actual repair costs for the two-year period, I do not want subjective amounts affecting our profit. Overall, my suggestions seem reasonable as the customer paid us $840,000 on 30 June 20X5.

(12 marks)

Exhibit 3 – Attachment 2 to the email

As you know, we have a large investment property which we rent out to tenants on short leases.

We have chosen to apply the cost model to our investment property. The current carrying amount of the property is $1.2 million. We have recently negotiated a lease with new tenants who will begin to rent the property from 1 October 20X5. Due to a surplus of properties available for rental, we have had to reduce the amount we are charging the new tenants. This has affected the resale value of the property, which is currently estimated at $900,000 after selling costs. On the basis that we continue to rent the property out to tenants, then the present value of all future rental payments would be around $1 million. We may be embarking on a restructuring in the near future, although nothing has been firmly decided yet. If we do restructure, then the property could be put to an alternative use and the present value of the future net cash inflows generated by the property could be reliably estimated as at least $1.3 million. Therefore, I am satisfied that the current carrying amount of the property is fully justified.

(5 marks)

47 Ontario

49 mins

Exhibits 1 and 2 adapted from June 2016, Exhibit 3 adapted from June 2013

You are the financial controller of Ontario, a listed entity which prepares consolidated financial statements in accordance with IFRS Accounting Standards. The managing director, who is not an accountant, has recently attended a business seminar at which financial reporting issues were discussed. Following the seminar, she reviewed the financial statements of Ontario for the year ended 31 March 20X6. Based on this review she has prepared a series of queries relating to those statements, contained in the exhibits:

Exhibit 1 – Impairment of financial assets

'One of the issues discussed at the seminar was 'impairment of financial assets'. On reviewing our financial statements I have noticed that we have two types of financial assets – Type A (those measured at amortised cost) and Type B (those measured at 'fair value through profit or loss'). It appears we carry out impairment reviews of Type A assets but not Type B assets. Please explain to me why this is the case and also please explain exactly how an impairment review of Type A assets is carried out.'

Exhibit 2 – Accounting policies

'During a break-out session I heard someone talking about accounting policies and accounting estimates. He said that when there's a change of these items sometimes the change is made retrospectively and sometimes it's made prospectively. Please explain the difference between an accounting policy and an accounting estimate and give me an example of each. Please also explain the difference between retrospective and prospective adjustments and how this applies to accounting policies and accounting estimates.'

Exhibit 3 – Segment reporting

'One of the topics discussed at the seminar was segment reporting. I believe I heard someone say that segment reporting varies from company to company depending on its internal structure. Please explain how we should identify the segments we use to provide our segment reporting information. I do not need to know the detailed content of a segment report.'

Requirements

Provide answers to the questions raised by the managing director.

The mark allocation is:

Exhibit 1 – Impairment of financial assets	**(8 marks)**
Exhibit 2 – Accounting policies	**(7 marks)**
Exhibit 3 – Segment reporting	**(10 marks)**

(Total = 25 marks)

48 Omega (December 2014) (amended)　　49 mins

Your managing director has raised a number of queries relating to the application of various IFRS Accounting Standards. The managing director's queries are contained in the exhibits.

Exhibit 1 – Operating segments

'I was very confused by the note that presented financial information relating to our operating segments. This note bears very little resemblance to the equivalent note included in the financial statements of our major competitor Rival. Please explain how the two notes can be so different when both companies operate in the same industry.'

Exhibit 2 – Share based payments

'The notes to our financial statements refer to equity settled share-based payments relating to the granting of share options. When I joined Omega, I was granted share options but I can only exercise those options if I achieve certain performance targets in my first three years as managing director. I know that other directors are also granted similar option arrangements. I don't see why they affect the financial statements when the options are granted though, because no cash is involved unless the options are exercised. Please explain to me exactly what is meant by an 'equity settled share-based payment'. Please also explain how, and when, equity settled share-based payments affect the financial statements of entities that grant them to their employees. I would like to know how such 'payments' are measured, over what period the 'payments' are recognised, and exactly what accounting entries are involved.'

Exhibit 3 – Non-current assets held for sale

'I was confused when I looked at the statement of financial position and saw that the assets and liabilities were divided up into three sections and not two. The current and non-current sections I understand but I don't understand the 'non-current assets held for sale' and 'liabilities directly associated with non-current assets held for sale' sections. Please explain the meaning and accounting treatment of a non-current asset held for sale. Please also explain how there can be liabilities directly associated with non-current assets held for sale.'

Exhibit 4 – Cash generating units

'I noted that we carried out an impairment exercise based on our 'cash-generating units'. I thought impairment reviews had to be carried out on individual assets and I'm not quite sure what a cash generating unit actually is. Please explain what a cash generating unit is and why the impairment may have been based on it rather than individual assets.'

Requirements

Provide answers to the following questions raised by your managing director.

Exhibit 1 – Operating segments	**(8 marks)**
Exhibit 2 – Share based payments	**(8 marks)**

Exhibit 3 – Non-current assets held for sale   **(4 marks)**
Exhibit 4 – Cash generating units   **(5 marks)**
         (Total = 25 marks)

49 Omega (June 2022)   **49 mins**

You are the financial controller of Omega, a listed entity. One of Omega's directors has raised some queries regarding the preparation of the consolidated financial statements of Omega for the year ended 31 March 20X5.

The following exhibits provide information relevant to the question:

(1)   Acquisition of subsidiary – three queries relating to the acquisition of a controlling interest in NewSub on 30 September 20X4.

(2)   Financial statements – two queries specifically on the consolidated statement of profit or loss and other comprehensive income.

This information should be used to answer the question requirement within the response option provided.

Exhibit 1 – Acquisition of subsidiary

Currently unlisted and has two separate business segments which will complement the activities of our existing group very well. I have been examining the most recent published financial statements of NewSub which are prepared using full IFRS Accounting Standards. There are a few things that I do not understand about these financial statements and I would appreciate your help.

Query 1

The most recent published financial statements of NewSub are for the year ended 31 December 20X4. Given that the Omega group year end is 31 March, this seems to pose a problem when preparing the consolidated financial statements. How do we incorporate the NewSub results given that they are prepared to a different year-end date? Could we require NewSub to change its year end, given we now control the company?

Query 2

A key reason for my reviewing NewSub's published financial statements was to find out how revenues and profits are split between its two business segments. I have found the segmental reports which we include in our consolidated financial statements very useful when considering the performance of the business segments of our existing group. However, when I examined the financial statements of NewSub, I found none of the segment disclosures that I see when I review the consolidated financial statements of Omega. How can NewSub's financial statements be in accordance with full IFRS Accounting Standards without this information? Does NewSub's lack of segmental reporting mean we can ignore segmental reporting for NewSub in our consolidated financial statements for the year ended 31 March 20X5?

Query 3

I have noticed that NewSub has some investment properties. A note to NewSub's financial statements states that these properties are measured using the cost model. I believe that the Omega group policy is to measure investment properties using the fair value model. This is in line with full IFRS Accounting Standards, so the NewSub policy must be wrong. On that basis, how should we deal with the investment properties of NewSub in the consolidated financial statements of Omega? Now that we control NewSub, should we require NewSub to change its accounting policy in its own individual financial statements?   **(17 marks)**

Exhibit 2 – Financial statements

I thought it would be useful for me to review the consolidated financial statements of Omega for the year ended 31 March 20X4 to help me to assess those prepared for the year ended 31 March 20X5. I also looked at the financial statements of one of our key competitors, Rival. I have the following questions concerning the statements of profit or loss and other comprehensive income of Omega and Rival.

Query 1

I can see similarities between the statements for Omega and Rival. Both show revenue, finance costs, profit before tax, and income tax expense on the face of the statement. However, many of the other line items in the statements seem to be totally different. In particular, the classification of operating expenses into various categories in the Omega statement is completely different from the classification in the Rival statement. How can this be when both statements are allegedly prepared in accordance with full IFRS Accounting Standards?

Query 2

I am not clear how you decide which items are shown in the 'profit or loss' section and which are shown in the 'other comprehensive income' section. Are entities allowed a free choice in this matter and would it change how performance might be assessed? **(8 marks)**

Requirement

Provide answers to the queries raised by one of Omega's directors detailed in exhibits 1 and 2, relating to the consolidated financial statements for the year ended 31 March 20X5.

Note. The mark allocations are indicated in each exhibit.

(Total = 25 marks)

50 Whitebirk 49 mins

Whitebirk has met the definition of a small or medium-sized entity (SME) in its jurisdiction and wishes to comply with the IFRS for SMEs Accounting Standard. Whitebirk currently prepares its financial statements under full IFRS Accounting Standards and has a reporting date of 30 November 20X2. Information relevant to the question is provided in the exhibits.

Exhibit 1 – Acquisition of Close

Whitebirk purchased 90% of Close, a SME, on 1 December 20X1. The purchase consideration was $5.7 million and the value of Close's identifiable assets was $6 million. The value of the non-controlling interest at 1 December 20X1 was measured at $0.7 million. Whitebirk has used the full goodwill method to account for business combinations and the life of goodwill cannot be estimated with any accuracy. Whitebirk wishes to know how to account for goodwill under the IFRS for SMEs Accounting Standard.

Exhibit 2 – R&D expenditure

Whitebirk has incurred $1 million of research expenditure to develop a new product in the year to 30 November 20X2. Additionally, it incurred $500,000 of development expenditure to bring another product to a stage where it is ready to be marketed and sold.

Exhibit 3 – Investment properties

Whitebirk purchased some properties for $1.7 million on 1 December 20X1 and designated them as investment properties under the cost model. No depreciation was charged as a real estate agent valued the properties at $1.9 million at the year end.

Exhibit 4 – Intangible assets

Whitebirk has an intangible asset valued at $1 million on 1 December 20X1. The asset has an indefinite useful life, and in previous years had been reviewed for impairment. As at 30 November 20X2, there are no indications that the asset is impaired.

Requirements

(a) The principal aim when developing accounting standards for small to medium-sized enterprises (SMEs) is to provide a framework that generates relevant, reliable, and useful information which should provide a high quality and understandable set of accounting standards suitable for SMEs. There is no universally agreed definition of an SME and it is difficult for a single definition to capture all the dimensions of a small or medium-sized business. The main argument for separate SME accounting standards is the undue cost burden of reporting, which is proportionately heavier for smaller firms.

  (i) Comment on the different approaches which could have been taken by the International Accounting Standards Board (IASB) in developing the IFRS for SMEs Accounting Standard, explaining the approach finally taken by the IASB. **(6 marks)**

  (ii) Discuss the main differences and modifications to IFRS Accounting Standards which the IASB made to reduce the burden of reporting for SMEs, giving specific examples where possible and include in your discussion how the Board has dealt with the problem of defining an SME. **(8 marks)**

(b) Discuss how the transactions described in Exhibits 1 to 4 should be dealt with in the financial statements of Whitebirk at 30 November 20X2, with reference to the IFRS for SMEs Accounting Standard.

The mark allocation is as follows:

Exhibit 1 – Acquisition of Close **(4 marks)**
Exhibit 2 – R&D expenditure **(3 marks)**
Exhibit 3 – Investment property **(2 marks)**
Exhibit 4 – Intangible assets **(2 marks)**

(Total = 25 marks)

51 Epsilon (June 2021) 49 mins

You are the financial controller of Epsilon, a listed entity with a number of subsidiaries. The consolidated financial statements of Epsilon for the year ended 31 March 20X5 are currently being prepared. One of the directors of Epsilon has raised some queries which have arisen as a result of her review of the draft consolidated financial statements.

The following **exhibits** provide information relevant to the question:

Exhibit 1 – New subsidiary

I know during the year ended 31 March 20X5 we acquired Newby. Newby is a small company which operates in the construction industry. I also know that the shares in Newby were previously owned equally by three family members, and that Newby's borrowing was a bank loan. I had a look at Newby's audited individual financial statements for the current year. The audit report identified no issues with how the financial statements had been prepared but I don't understand how this can be correct. Newby is located in the same country as we are and is subject to the same regulatory regime. The financial statements of Newby do not appear to be wholly compliant with full International Financial Reporting Standards (IFRS Accounting Standards). For example, the notes to Newby's financial statements state that all borrowing costs are expensed as they are incurred despite some of these borrowings relating to the construction of a new factory. Furthermore, the notes to Newby's financial statements don't appear to contain all the disclosures required by full IFRS Accounting Standards.

Please can you answer the following questions (I don't need to know the mechanics of the consolidation process – I know that already):

(1) Please explain why Newby has been allowed to prepare individual financial statements which don't appear to wholly comply with full IFRS Accounting Standards.

(2) Please explain if Newby will need to use full IFRS Accounting Standards in its own financial statements now that it's part of our group. **(8 marks)**

Exhibit 2 – Investment

You will know that during the year we made a strategic long-term investment in Sandy, an entity which is a vital part of our supply chain. I believe we purchased 40% of the shares, which carry one vote each, and that this gave us the right to appoint four of the ten directors. The other six directors are independent of each other – they don't always agree when voting. I was expecting to see Sandy included as a subsidiary in our consolidated financial statements but instead the investment has been shown as a single figure in our consolidated statement of financial position. The carrying amount of the investment is presented as $40 million but, given the share price, I have calculated the fair value as $42 million. I thought that equity investments that weren't consolidated needed to be measured at fair value. Please explain:

(1)   Why we aren't including Sandy as a subsidiary in our consolidated financial statements.

(2)   What method will have been used to arrive at the carrying amount of $40 million rather than measuring the investment at fair value.   **(9 marks)**

Exhibit 3 – Measurement change

The draft financial statements indicate that in the current period we began measuring our inventory of raw materials using the weighted average cost formula. In previous periods we measured all our inventories using the first in first out formula. I have a number of questions here:

(1)   Are we allowed to change the measurement method in this way?

(2)   If we do change the measurement method for our inventory of raw materials shouldn't we change it for all of our inventories?

(3)   How do we ensure that the financial statements for this year are comparable with those of last year given that a different measurement method has been used for raw materials inventory?   **(8 marks)**

Requirement

Provide answers to the queries raised by one of Epsilon's directors relating to the consolidated financial statements for the year ended 31 March 20X5. The queries you need to address appear in exhibits 1–3.

Note. The mark allocations are indicated in each exhibit.

(Total = 25 marks)

52 Alpha (December 2019)   **49 mins**

Alpha, a parent with a subsidiary Beta, is preparing the consolidated statement of financial position at 30 September 20X7. The draft statements of financial position for both entities as at 30 September 20X7 are given below:

	Alpha $'000	Beta $'000
Assets		
Non-current assets:		
Property, plant and equipment (note 1)	966,500	546,000
Development project (note 1)	0	20,000
Investment in Beta (note 1)	450,000	0
	1,416,500	566,000
Current assets:		
Inventories (note 2)	165,000	92,000
Trade receivables	99,000	76,000
Cash and cash equivalents	18,000	16,000
	282,000	184,000
Total assets	1,698,500	750,000

	Alpha $'000	Beta $'000
Equity and liabilities		
Equity		
Share capital ($1 shares)	360,000	160,000
Retained earnings	570,000	360,000
Other components of equity	102,000	0
Total equity	1,032,000	520,000
Non-current liabilities:		
Long-term borrowings (note 3)	300,000	85,000
Pension liability (note 4)	187,500	0
Deferred tax (note 1 and 2)	69,000	54,000
Total non-current liabilities	556,500	139,000
Current liabilities:		
Trade and other payables	70,000	59,000
Short-term borrowings	40,000	32,000
Total current liabilities	110,000	91,000
Total equity and liabilities	1,698,500	750,000

Note 1 – Alpha's investment in Beta

On 1 April 20X7, Alpha acquired 120 million shares in Beta. Alpha made a payment of $450 million in exchange for these shares. The individual interim financial statements of Beta showed a balance of $340 million on its retained earnings on 1 April 20X7.

The directors of Alpha carried out a fair value exercise to measure the identifiable assets and liabilities of Beta at 1 April 20X7. The following matters emerged:

- Plant and equipment having a carrying amount of $440 million had an estimated fair value of $480 million. The estimated remaining useful life of this plant and equipment at 1 April 20X7 was four years.

- An in-process development project of Beta's had a carrying amount of $8 million and a fair value of $18 million. During the six-month period from 1 April 20X7 to 30 September 20X7, Beta incurred further development costs of $12 million relating to this project. These costs were correctly capitalised in accordance with the requirements of IAS 38 *Intangible Assets*. No amortisation of the capitalised costs of this project was required prior to 30 September 20X7.

- The fair value adjustments have not been reflected in the individual financial statements of Beta. In the consolidated financial statements, the fair value adjustments will be regarded as temporary differences for the purposes of computing deferred tax. The rate of deferred tax to apply to temporary differences is 20%.

On 1 April 20X7, the directors of Alpha measured the non-controlling interest in Beta at its fair value on that date. On 1 April 20X7, the fair value of an equity share in Beta was $3.80.

Note 2 – Intra-group trading

Since 1 April 20X7, Alpha has supplied a product to Beta. Alpha applies a mark-up of 25% to its cost of supplying this product. Sales of the product by Alpha to Beta in the period from 1 April 20X7 to 30 September 20X7 totalled $30 million. One-third of the products which Alpha has supplied to Beta since 1 April 20X7 were still unsold by Beta at 30 September 20X7. Any adjustment which is necessary in the consolidated financial statements as a result of these sales will be regarded as a temporary difference for the purposes of computing deferred tax. The rate of deferred tax to apply to temporary differences is 20%. No amounts were owing to Alpha by Beta in respect of these sales at 30 September 20X7.

Note 3 – Long-term borrowings

Prior to 1 October 20X6, Alpha had no long-term borrowings. On 1 October 20X6, Alpha borrowed $300 million to finance its future expansion plans. The term of the borrowings is five years and the annual rate of interest payable on the borrowings is 6%, payable in arrears. Alpha charged the interest paid on 30 September 20X7 as a finance cost in its financial statements for the year ended 30 September 20X7.

The borrowings are repayable in cash at the end of the five-year term or convertible into equity shares on that date at the option of the lender. If the borrowings had not contained a conversion option, the lender would have required an annual return of 8%, rather than 6%. Discount factors which may be relevant are as follows:

Discount factor	Present value of $1 payable at the end of year 5	Cumulative present value payable at the end of years 1–5 inclusive
6%	74.7 cents	$4.21
8%	68.1 cents	$3.99

Note 4 – Pension liability

Alpha has established a defined benefit pension plan for its eligible employees. The statement of financial position of Alpha at 30 September 20X7 currently includes the estimated net liability at 30 September 20X6. The following matters relate to the plan for the year ended 30 September 20X7:

- The estimated current service cost was advised by the actuary to be $60 million.

- On 30 September 20X7, Alpha paid contributions of $70 million into the plan and charged this amount as an operating expense.

- The annual market yield on high quality corporate bonds on 1 October 20X6 was 8%.

- The estimated net liability at 30 September 20X7 was advised by the actuary to be $205 million. No benefits have been paid to date.

Required

Using the draft statements of financial position of Alpha and its subsidiary Beta at 30 September 20X7, and the further information provided in notes 1–4, prepare the consolidated statement of financial position of Alpha at 30 September 20X7. Unless specifically told otherwise, you can ignore the deferred tax implications of any adjustments you make.

Note: You should show all workings to the nearest $'000.

(Total = 25 marks)

53 Alpha (December 2020)   49 mins

Alpha, a parent with one subsidiary, Beta, is preparing the consolidated statement of financial position as at 30 September 20X5.

The following **exhibits** provide information relevant to the question:

Exhibit 1: Financial statement extracts

	Alpha $'000	Beta $'000
Assets		
Non-current assets		
Property, plant and equipment (Exhibit 2)	250,000	170,000
Investments in equity instruments (Exhibits 2 and 4)	180,000	nil
	430,000	170,000

	Alpha $'000	Beta $'000
Current assets		
Inventories (Exhibit 3)	80,000	60,000
Trade receivables	90,000	55,000
Cash and cash equivalents	30,000	25,000
	200,000	140,000
Total assets	630,000	310,000
Equity and liabilities		
Share capital ($1 shares)	160,000	80,000
Retained earnings	150,000	85,000
Other components of equity	60,000	45,000
Total equity	370,000	210,000
Non-current liabilities		
Long-term borrowings	90,000	15,000
Deferred tax	20,000	15,000
Pension liability (Exhibit 5)	50,000	Nil
Total non-current liabilities	160,000	30,000
Current liabilities		
Trade and other payables	70,000	50,000
Current tax payable	30,000	20,000
Total current liabilities	100,000	70,000
Total liabilities	260,000	100,000
Total equity and liabilities	630,000	310,000

Exhibit 2: Alpha's investment in Beta

On 1 October 20X4, Alpha acquired 60 million shares in Beta and gained control of Beta. Alpha made a cash payment of $175 million to the former shareholders of Beta on 1 October 20X4. Alpha incurred acquisition costs of $5 million and has presented the total costs of $180 million as investments in equity instruments.

A condition of the purchase agreement was that Alpha would make a further cash payment to the former shareholders of Beta on 30 September 20X7. The amount of this further cash payment depends on the performance of Beta in the three-year period from 1 October 20X4 to 30 September 20X7. On 1 October 20X4, the fair value of this conditional payment was $60 million. Because the performance of Beta in the year ended 30 September 20X5 was below expectations, the fair value of the conditional payment had reduced to $50 million by 30 September 20X5. Alpha has not made any entries in its own financial statements in respect of this conditional payment.

On 1 October 20X4, Beta had retained earnings of $80 million and other components of equity of $45 million.

On 1 October 20X4, the fair values of Beta's identifiable assets and liabilities were the same as their carrying amounts in the individual financial statements of Beta with the exception of property, plant and equipment which had a carrying amount of $150 million and a fair value of $205 million. On 1 October 20X4, the useful life of this property, plant and equipment was five years. The fair value adjustments should be regarded as temporary differences for the purposes of computing deferred tax. The relevant rate of income tax to use for this purpose is 20%.

The directors of Alpha measured the non-controlling interest in Beta at its fair value at the date of acquisition. On 1 October 20X4, the fair value of the non-controlling interest was $65 million.

Exhibit 3: Intra-group trading

Since 1 October 20X4, Beta has been supplying Alpha with a product. Beta earns a margin of 25% on this product. On 30 September 20X5, the inventories of Alpha included $20 million in respect of the product. There were no outstanding intra-group balances at 30 September 20X5.

Exhibit 4: Impairment review

Alpha undertook an impairment review of its investment in Beta at 30 September 20X5. Beta comprises three cash generating units for impairment review purposes. Relevant details are as follows:

Cash generating unit (CGU)	Percentage of net assets and goodwill	Recoverable amount of CGU at 30 September 20X5
	%	$'000
A	40	100,000
B	35	110,000
C	25	80,000

Exhibit 5: Retirement plan

Alpha has established a defined benefit retirement plan for its current and former employees. Beta has not established such a plan. The statement of financial position of Alpha in Exhibit 1 shows the net defined benefit pension liability at 30 September 20X4.

During the year ended 30 September 20X5, Alpha made a payment of $30 million to the plan. When making this payment, Alpha debited retained earnings and credited cash. This is the only accounting entry which has been made in relation to the plan for the year to 30 September 20X5.

The current service cost for the year ended 30 September 20X5 was $25 million. The net interest cost on the pension liability for the year ended 30 September 20X5 was $2.5 million.

On 30 September 20X5, the defined benefit pension liability was $160 million and the fair value of the plan assets was $105 million.

Requirement

Using the information in Exhibits 1–5, prepare the consolidated statement of financial position of Alpha at 30 September 20X5.

Note. Unless specifically referred to in the exhibits you should ignore deferred tax.

(Total = 25 marks)

54 Alpha (June 2021)   49 mins

Alpha, a parent company with one subsidiary, Beta, is preparing the consolidated statement of financial position (SOFP) as at 31 March 20X5.

The following exhibits provide information relevant to the question:

Exhibit 1 – SOFP of Alpha and Beta

Statements of financial position at March 20X5

	Alpha $'000	Beta $'000
Assets		
Non-current assets		
Property, plant and equipment (Exhibit 2)	240,000	140,000
Financial assets (Exhibit 2 and 4)	182,840	nil
	422,840	140,000
Current assets		
Inventories (Exhibit 3)	70,000	50,000
Trade receivables (Exhibit 3)	80,000	45,000
Cash and cash equivalents (Exhibit 3)	19,360	20,000
	169,360	115,000
Total assets	592,200	255,00
Equity and liabilities		
Share capital ($1 shares)	140,000	60,000
Retained earnings	120,000	45,000
Other components of equity	52,200	35,000
Total equity	312,200	140,000
Non-current liabilities		
Long-term borrowings	120,000	30,000
Deferred tax (Exhibits 2 and 3)	60,000	15,000
Total non-current liabilities	180,000	45,000
Current liabilities		
Trade and other payables	70,000	55,000
Current tax payables	30,000	15,000
Total current liabilities	100,000	70,000
Total liabilities	280,000	115,000
Total equity and liabilities	592,200	255,000

Exhibit 2 – Alpha's investment in Beta

On 1 April 20X3 Alpha acquired 48 million shares in Beta by means of a share exchange. This gave Alpha control of Beta. On 1 April 20X3 Alpha issued two shares in exchange for every three Beta shares acquired when the fair value of an Alpha share was $4.20.

Alpha incurred costs of $2.5 million relating to the issue of Alpha shares and $3.5 million relating to due diligence costs. Alpha included the fair value of the shares issued, plus the above issue and due diligence costs of $6 million, as part of financial assets. On 1 April 20X3 Beta had retained earnings of $25 million and other components of equity of $35 million.

On 1 April 20X3 the fair values of Beta's identifiable assets and liabilities were the same as their carrying amounts in the individual financial statements of Beta with the exception of:

(1)   Property, plant and equipment which had a fair value of $20 million in excess of its carrying amount in the financial statements of Beta. On 1 April 20X3 the useful life of this property, plant and equipment was five years.

(2)   An internally developed brand of Beta which had a fair value of $15 million on 1 April 20X3. On 1 April 20X3 the useful life of this internally developed brand was ten years.

(3)   A contingent liability which had a fair value of $10 million on 1 April 20X3. This contingency was resolved during the year ended 31 March 20X4.

The fair value adjustments should be regarded as temporary differences for the purposes of computing deferred tax. The income tax rate is 20%.

The directors of Alpha measured the non-controlling interest in Beta at its fair value at the date of acquisition. On 1 April 20X3 the fair value of the non-controlling interest was $33 million. The goodwill is not impaired at 31 March 20X5

Exhibit 3 – Intra-group trading

Since 1 April 20X3 Alpha has been supplying goods to Beta. Alpha marks up its cost by 33.33% when computing Beta's invoiced price. On 31 March 20X5 the inventories of Beta included $16 million in respect of these goods. Any unrealised profits should be regarded as temporary differences for the purposes of computing deferred tax. The income tax rate is 20%.

On 28 March 20X5 Beta made a payment of $15 million to Alpha relating to amounts owing in respect of the purchase of these goods. Alpha received and recorded this payment on 3 April 20X5. No other intra-group amounts were outstanding at 31 March 20X5

Exhibit 4 – Alpha's financial assets

On 1 April 20X3 Alpha made a loan of $40 million to a key supplier. Alpha incurred costs of $2 million in arranging the loan. The terms of the loan were that interest of $2.5 million is payable annually in arrears on 31 March. On 31 March 20X6 the loan is repayable at a premium. The effective annual rate of interest on this loan (which can be used in all relevant calculations) is approximately 7%. Alpha did not elect to measure this loan asset at fair value through profit or loss. On 1 April 20X3, Alpha estimated that the probability of payment of the interest due on 31 March 20X4 was 100% so that the 12-month expected credit losses relating to this loan were zero.

On 31 March 20X4, Alpha received the interest payment of $2.5 million which was due on that date. On 31 March 20X4, Alpha measured the loan at its amortised cost with no loss allowance deemed necessary as the assessment of expected credit loss was unchanged from initial recognition.

During the year ended 31 March 20X5, the supplier began to face significant financial difficulties and just before 31 March 20X5 Alpha received reliable information that the supplier was insolvent. The supplier was not able to make the further payment of $2.5 million which was due on 31 March 20X5 and Alpha was told that the only further amount which will be received in respect of this loan will be a payment of $30 million on 31 March 20X6. Based on this information, Alpha considered that the loan to the supplier was credit impaired at 31 March 20X5.

The financial assets of Alpha at 31 March 20X5 as shown in exhibit 1 include the carrying amount of the loan to the supplier as correctly measured at 31 March 20X4. No entries have yet been made regarding this loan in the current period.

Requirement

Using exhibits 1–4, prepare the consolidated statement of financial position of Alpha at 31 March 20X5. Explanations of consolidation procedures are not required. Unless specifically referred to in the exhibits you should ignore deferred tax.

Note. You should show all workings to the nearest $'000.

(Total = 25 marks)

55 Alpha (June 2022)

49 mins

Alpha, a parent with one subsidiary, Beta, is preparing the consolidated statement of financial position as at 31 March 20X5.

The following exhibits provide information relevant to the question:

(1) Financial statements extract – an extract of the statements of financial position (SOFP) of Alpha and Beta at 31 March 20X5.

(2) Alpha's investment in Beta – details of Alpha's investment in Beta which are relevant to the question.

(3) Intra-group trading – details of intra-group trading.

(4) Power plant – details of Alpha's construction of a power plant during the year ended 31 March 20X5.

(5) Convertible loan – details of a new convertible loan taken out by Alpha on 1 April 20X4.

This information should be used to answer the question requirement within the response option provided.

Exhibit 1 – Financial statements extract

Statements of financial position of Alpha and Beta at 31 March 20X5

	Alpha $'000	Beta $'000
Assets		
Non-current assets		
Property, plant and equipment (Exhibits 2 and 4)	380,000	185,000
Investments in equity instruments (Exhibit 2)	170,000	nil
	550,000	185,000
Current assets		
Inventories (Exhibit 3)	90,000	65,000
Trade receivables	100,000	50,000
Cash and cash equivalents	35,000	20,000
	225,000	135,000
Total assets	775,000	320,000
Equity and liabilities		
Share capital ($1 shares)	200,000	100,000
Retained earnings	160,000	80,000
Other components of equity	70,000	20,000
Total equity	430,000	200,000
Non-current liabilities		
Long-term borrowings (Exhibits 4 and 5)	200,000	20,000
Deferred tax	20,000	10,000
Total non-current liabilities	220,000	30,000
Current liabilities		
Trade and other payables	85,000	60,000
Current tax payables	40,000	30,000
Total current liabilities	125,000	90,000
Total liabilities	345,000	120,000
Total equity and liabilities	775,000	320,000

Exhibit 2 – Alpha's investment in Beta

On 1 April 20X3, Alpha acquired 80 million shares in Beta and gained control of Beta. Alpha made a cash payment of $160 million to the former shareholders of Beta on 1 April 20X3. Alpha incurred acquisition costs of $10 million and has presented the total costs of $170 million as investments in equity instruments.

A condition of the purchase agreement was that Alpha would make a further cash payment of $66.55 million to the former shareholders of Beta on 31 March 20X6. Alpha has not made any entries in its own financial statements in respect of this deferred payment. A suitable discount rate to use, where relevant, is 10% per annum. Using this rate, the present value of $1 payable in three years' time is approximately 75.132 cents.

On 1 April 20X3, Beta had retained earnings of $60 million and other components of equity of $20 million.

On 1 April 20X3, the fair values of Beta's identifiable assets and liabilities were the same as their carrying amounts in the individual financial statements of Beta with the exception of property, plant and equipment which had a carrying amount of $160 million and a fair value of $190 million. On 1 April 20X3, the useful life of this property, plant and equipment was five years. The fair value adjustments should be regarded as temporary differences for the purposes of computing deferred tax. The relevant rate of income tax to use for this purpose is 20%.

The directors of Alpha measured the non-controlling interest in Beta on 1 April 20X3 at its proportionate share of the net assets at that date. There has been no goodwill impairment since the date of acquisition.

Exhibit 3 – Intra-group trading

Since 1 April 20X3, Alpha has been supplying Beta with a product. Alpha applies a mark-up of 20% to its production cost when establishing an invoiced price for sales of the product to Beta. On 31 March 20X5, the inventories of Beta included $24 million in respect of these purchases. There were no intra-group balances outstanding at 31 March 20X5.

Exhibit 4 – Power plant

On 1 August 20X4, Alpha began to construct a power plant. The construction cost was $60 million and the construction was completed on 30 November 20X4. The plant was available for use from that date. Following a formal opening ceremony, the plant was brought into use on 1 January 20X5. Alpha estimated that the useful life of the plant was ten years. On 1 July 20X4, Alpha borrowed $60 million to finance the construction of the power plant. The interest payable on this borrowing was 8% per annum, payable in arrears on 30 June each year. On 31 March 20X5, the property, plant and equipment of Alpha incorrectly included $62.01 million in respect of the power plant, made up as follows:

	$'000
Cost of constructing power plant	60,000
Finance cost of loan taken out to finance construction of the power plant ($60 million × 8% × 9/12)	3,600
	63,600
Depreciation from 1 January 20X5 (63,600 × 1/10 × 3/12)	(1,590)
	62,010

Exhibit 5 – Convertible loan

On 1 April 20X4, Alpha borrowed $80 million. The interest payable on this borrowing is 5% per annum, payable in arrears on 31 March each year. Alpha recorded the first interest payment of $4 million on 31 March 20X5 as a finance cost and included $80 million in respect of this borrowing in its long-term borrowings at 31 March 20X5.

The principal sum of $80 million (together with any accrued interest due) is repayable on 31 March 20X9. The lenders have the option to receive equity shares in Alpha at 31 March 20X9 as an alternative to receiving repayment of the principal amount. If this option were not available, then the lenders would have required annual interest at a rate of 7% per annum.

Present value factors which may be relevant are as follows:

	5%	7%
Present value of $1 payable in five years	78.4 cents	71.3 cents
Cumulative present value of $1 payable at the end of years 1–5	$4.329	$4.10

Required

Using the information in exhibits 1–5, prepare the consolidated statement of financial position of Alpha at 31 March 20X5. Unless specifically referred to in the exhibits you should ignore deferred tax.

Note. Explanations of consolidation procedures are not required.

(Total = 25 marks)

56 Alpha (December 2022)   49 mins

Alpha, a parent company with one subsidiary, Beta, is preparing the consolidated statement of financial position (SOFP) as at 30 September 20X2.

The following **exhibits** provide information relevant to the question:

(1) SOFP of Alpha and Beta – draft statements of financial position for Alpha and Beta as at 30 September 20X2.
(2) Alpha's investment in Beta – provides details of Alpha's investment in Beta.
(3) Intra-group trading – provides details of intra-group trading between Alpha and Beta.
(4) Investment in Drax – provides details of an investment in Drax on 1 October 20X1.
(5) Restoration costs – provides details of costs relating to the extraction of minerals.

This information should be used to answer the question **requirement** within the **response option** provided.

Requirement

Prepare the consolidated statement of financial position of Alpha at 30 September 20X2. You need only consider the deferred tax implications of any adjustments you make where the question specifically refers to deferred tax.

Note. You should show all workings to the nearest $'000 and no explanations of consolidation adjustments are required.

(Total = 25 marks)

Exhibit 1 – SOFP of Alpha and Beta

Statements of financial position as at 30 September 20X2

	Alpha $'000	Beta $'000
Assets		
Non-current assets		
Property, plant and equipment (Exhibit 2)	680,000	430,000
Intangible assets (Exhibit 5)	3,000	
Investments (Exhibits 2 and 4)	398,000	
	1,081,000	430,000
Current assets		
Inventories (Exhibit 3)	30,000	28,000
Trade receivables	16,700	9,800
Cash and cash equivalents	12,000	6,450
	58,700	44,250
Total assets	1,139,700	474,250
Equity and liabilities		
Equity		

	Alpha $'000	Beta $'000
Share capital ($1 shares)	380,000	100,000
Retained earnings	703,000	340,000
Total equity	1,083,000	440,000
Non-current liabilities		
Long-term borrowings	4,200	8,900
Deferred tax	3,750	4,500
Total non-current liabilities	7,950	13,400
Current liabilities		
Trade and other payables	18,960	11,400
Short-term borrowings	29,790	9,450
Total current liabilities	48,750	20,850
Total equity and liabilities	1,139,700	474,250

Exhibit 2 – Alpha's investment in Beta

On 1 October 20X0, Alpha acquired 75 million shares in Beta, paying cash of $380 million for these shares. Beta had a retained earnings balance of $275 million on the date of acquisition. On the date of acquisition, the directors measured the non-controlling interest in Beta at its fair value of $98 million.

The directors of Alpha carried out a fair value exercise to measure the identifiable assets and liabilities of Beta at 1 October 20X0 and identified the following:

- Plant and equipment with a carrying amount of $220 million had a fair value of $240 million. The estimated remaining useful life of this plant and equipment at 1 October 20X0 was five years.

- On 1 October 20X0, the notes to the financial statements of Beta disclosed a contingent liability. On 1 October 20X0, the fair value of this contingent liability was reliably measured at $4 million. The contingency was resolved in the year ended 30 September 20X1.

- A customer list used by Beta had a fair value of $1.6 million. This customer list was not recognised in the individual financial statements of Beta as it was internally generated. The directors of Alpha considered that the useful life of this list was four years from 1 October 20X0.

These fair value adjustments have not been reflected in the individual financial statements of Beta. In the consolidated financial statements, the fair value adjustments will be regarded as temporary differences for the purposes of calculating deferred tax. The relevant tax rate for determining deferred tax is 20%.

No impairment of the goodwill on acquisition of Beta was evident when the review was carried out on 30 September 20X1. On 30 September 20X2, the directors of Alpha carried out a further review and concluded that the recoverable amount of the net assets of Beta at that date was $500 million. Beta is regarded as a single cash generating unit for the purpose of measuring goodwill impairment.

Exhibit 2 – Intra-group trading

Alpha sells goods to Beta and applies a mark-up of 20% on the cost of these supplies. Sales of these goods from Alpha to Beta during the year to 30 September 20X2 totalled $15 million. One quarter of these goods were still in Beta's inventory on 30 September 20X2.

Any adjustment which is necessary in the consolidated financial statements as a result of these sales will be regarded as a temporary difference for the purposes of calculating deferred tax.

The relevant tax rate for determining deferred tax is 20%. No amounts were owed by Beta to Alpha in respect of these sales at 30 September 20X2.

Exhibit 4 – Investment in Drax

On 1 October 20X1, Alpha purchased 25% of the equity shares of Drax at a cost of $18 million giving it significant influence over Drax. On the date of purchase, Drax had net assets with a carrying amount of $70 million. On 1 October 20X1, there was no significant difference between the fair values of the net assets of Drax and their carrying amounts. Drax's net assets on 30 September 20X2 were $79 million.

Alpha's investment in Drax has not suffered any impairment since acquisition.

Exhibit 5 – Restoration costs

On 1 October 20X1, Alpha purchased a licence to extract minerals from a new site for a five-year period. The costs of the extraction licence were recognised in intangible assets and amortised appropriately. Local legislation requires the site owner to restore any environmental damage at the end of the five-year licence. The cost of restoration includes landscaping and other groundworks which are expected to cost $4 million and will take place at the end of the five-year period. Alpha will capitalise these costs as part of the extraction licence.

No entries have been recorded in the draft financial statements of Alpha for these restoration costs.

An appropriate discount rate for determining the present value of future payments is 10%. At this rate, the present value of $1 payable in five years is 62.1 cents.

57 Alpha (December 2012) (amended to 25 marks)   49 mins

Alpha, Beta and Gamma are members of the same group and have a reporting date of 30 September 20X2. The exhibits provide information relevant to the question.

Exhibit 1 – Statements of profit or loss and other comprehensive income

STATEMENTS OF PROFIT OR LOSS AND OTHER COMPREHENSIVE INCOME

	Alpha	Beta	Gamma
	$'000	$'000	$'000
Revenue	240,000	150,000	120,000
Cost of sales	(190,000)	(110,000)	(70,000)
Gross profit	50,000	40,000	50,000
Distribution costs	(7,000)	(6,000)	(8,000)
Administrative expenses	(10,000)	(7,000)	(8,000)
Profit from operations	33,000	27,000	34,000
Investment income	15,300	Nil	Nil
Finance cost	(8,000)	(4,900)	(7,300)
Profit before tax	40,300	22,100	26,700
Income tax expense	(10,100)	(6,000)	(6,700)
Net profit for the period	30,200	16,100	20,000
Other comprehensive income	4,000	Nil	Nil
Total comprehensive income	34,200	16,100	20,000

Exhibit 2 – Purchase of shares in Beta

On 1 October 20X1, Alpha purchased 80% of the equity shares of Beta. As part of the purchase consideration Alpha agreed to make a payment of $30 million to the shareholders of Beta on 30 September 20X3. This payment was contingent on the post-acquisition profits of Beta reaching a specified level in the two-year period ending on 30 September 20X3. The directors of Alpha assessed that the fair value of this contingent consideration was $20 million on 1 October 20X1 and debited $20 million to the cost of investment in Beta. They reassessed the fair value of the contingent consideration at $22 million on 30 September 20X2. The directors of Alpha made no change to the carrying amount of the cost of investment in Beta as a result of this reassessment.

Alpha incurred incremental legal and professional fees of $1.5 million in connection with the acquisition of Beta and debited these costs to the cost of investment in Beta. $500,000 of this amount related to the costs of issuing the Alpha shares.

Exhibit 3 – Fair value exercise

The directors of Alpha carried out a fair value exercise on the net assets of Beta on 1 October 20X1. The fair values of the net assets of Beta were the same as their carrying amounts with the exception of:

- Plant and equipment that had a carrying amount of $80 million and a fair value of $84 million. The estimated remaining useful life of this plant and equipment was two years at 1 October 20X1. Depreciation of plant and equipment is charged to cost of sales.

- An intangible asset that had a fair value of $6 million but was not recognised by Beta because it was internally developed. The useful life of this asset was estimated at 18 months from 1 October 20X1. Amortisation of intangible assets is charged to cost of sales.

Exhibit 4 – Other information regarding Beta

- On 1 October 20X1, Alpha made a loan of $40 million to Beta at a fixed annual interest rate of 5%. Both Alpha and Beta have correctly accounted for the interest on this loan in their individual statements of profit or loss and other comprehensive income.

- On 31 March 20X2, Beta paid a dividend of $10 million to its equity shareholders.

Exhibit 5 – Purchase of shares in Gamma

- On 1 January 20X2, Alpha and another investor both purchased 50% of the equity capital of Gamma for a cash payment of $50 million. These investments enabled the two investors to jointly control Gamma.

- On 31 March 20X2, Gamma paid a dividend of $10 million to its equity shareholders.

- The recoverable amount of the investment in Gamma by Alpha was estimated at $50 million on 30 September 20X2.

Exhibit 6 – Inter-company sales

Alpha supplies products used by Beta and Gamma. Sales of the products to Beta and Gamma during the year ended 30 September 20X2 were as follows (all sales were made at a profit margin of 20%):

- Sales to Beta $25 million
- Sales to Gamma (all since 1 January 20X2) $12 million

At 30 September 20X2, the inventories of Beta and Gamma included the following amounts in respect of goods purchased from Alpha.

	$'000
Beta	5,000
Gamma	4,000

Exhibit 7 – Share based payments

On 1 October 20X1, Alpha granted 1,000 senior employees 2,500 share options each, provided they remained as employees for the two years ending 30 September 20X3. On 1 October 20X1, the fair value of one share option was $5 and this had increased to $5.40 by 30 September 20X2. On 1 October 20X1, the directors estimated that 950 employees would qualify for these options. At 30 September 20X2, this estimate was 960 employees. Ignore the deferred tax implications of this transaction.

Exhibit 8 – Other comprehensive income of Alpha

On 1 September 20X1, Alpha entered into a contract to sell €60 million for $85 million. This contract was to hedge against an expected sales receipt from a customer on 31 January 20X2 that was denominated in €. On 30 September 20X1, the contract was a financial asset with a fair value of $1 million. Alpha designated the contract as a cash-flow hedge of the expected future sales in € and credited $1 million to other comprehensive income in the year ended 30 September 20X1. On 31 January 20X2, the sales in € were made to the customer and the customer paid for the goods on that date. On 31 January 20X2, the fair value of the contract to sell €60 million for $85 million was $5 million. Therefore Alpha credited a further $4 million to other comprehensive income and recorded the sales revenue at €60 million, translated at the spot rate of exchange on that date.

Exhibit 9 – Investment by Alpha in Zeta

On 1 October 20X1, Alpha purchased 100,000 equity shares in Zeta for $10 per share. The investment did not give Alpha control or significant influence over Zeta and was designated by Alpha as fair value through other comprehensive income. Alpha incurred transaction costs of $50,000 which it recorded as part of its finance costs. During the period Alpha received a dividend of $2 per share from Zeta and at 30 September 20X2 the fair value of a Zeta share was $11. Alpha recorded both the dividend and the increase in fair value of its holding as investment income.

Requirement

Using the information given in Exhibits 1 to 9, prepare the consolidated statement of profit or loss and other comprehensive income for Alpha for the year ended 30 September 20X2. You do not need to consider the deferred tax effects of any adjustments you make.

Note. You should show all workings to the nearest $'000.

(Total = 25 marks)

58 Abiola (June 2016) (amended)   49 mins

Abiola's investments include subsidiaries, Busayo and Cuca. The exhibits provide information relevant to the question.

Exhibit 1 – Statements of profit or loss and other comprehensive income

The statements of profit or loss and other comprehensive income and summarised statements of changes in equity of the three entities for the year ended 31 March 20X6 were as follows:

STATEMENTS OF PROFIT OR LOSS AND OTHER COMPREHENSIVE INCOME

	Abiola $'000	Busayo $'000	Cuca $'000
Revenue (Exhibits 4 and 5)	360,000	210,000	190,000
Cost of sales (Exhibits 2–4)	(240,000)	(110,000)	(100,000)
Gross profit	120,000	100,000	90,000
Distribution costs	(20,000)	(16,000)	(15,000)
Administrative expenses	(30,000)	(19,000)	(18,000)
Investment income (Exhibits 6 and 7)	19,800	Nil	Nil
Finance costs (Exhibit 8)	(12,000)	(17,000)	(13,000)
Profit before tax	77,800	48,000	44,000
Income tax expense	(15,000)	(12,000)	(11,000)
Profit for the year	62,800	36,000	33,000
Other comprehensive income:			
Items that will not be reclassified to profit or loss			
Gains/(losses) on financial assets designated at fair value through other comprehensive income (Exhibit 6)	Nil	Nil	Nil
Total comprehensive income	62,800	36,000	33,000

Exhibit 2 – Abiola's investment in Busayo

On 1 April 20W4, Abiola acquired 80% of the equity shares of Busayo and gained control of Busayo. On 1 April 20W4, the fair value of the net assets of Busayo was equivalent to their carrying amounts at the date of acquisition.

Abiola measured the non-controlling interest in Busayo using the proportion of net assets method and correctly recognised goodwill on acquisition of $8 million in the consolidated financial statements of Abiola. No impairment of goodwill on acquisition of Busayo has been necessary up to and including 31 March 20X5.

On 31 March 20X6, the annual impairment review of the goodwill on acquisition of Busayo indicated that the recoverable amount of the total net assets of Busayo (including the goodwill) at that date was $180 million. Busayo is regarded as a single cash generating unit for impairment purposes. Any impairment of goodwill should be charged to cost of sales.

The carrying amount of the net assets of Busayo at 31 March 20X6 were $174,000,000.

Exhibit 3 – Abiola's Investment in Cuca

On 1 October 20X5, Abiola acquired 60% of the equity shares in Cuca and gained control of Cuca. As part of the acquisition price:

- Abiola agreed to pay a total of $24.2 million to the former shareholders of Cuca on 30 September 20X7. Abiola's incremental borrowing rate at 1 October 20X5 was 10% per annum.

- Abiola agreed to pay a further amount to the former shareholders of Cuca on 31 December 20X9 if the cumulative profits of Cuca for the four-year period from 1 October 20X5 to 30 September 20X9 exceed $150 million. On 1 October 20X5, the fair value of this obligation was measured at $40 million. On 31 March 20X6, this fair value was remeasured at $42 million.

On 1 October 20X5, the fair values of the net assets of Cuca were the same as their carrying amounts in the financial statements of Cuca with the exception of:

- Property – whose fair value exceeded the carrying amount by $25 million ($10 million of this excess relates to land). The estimated remaining useful life of the buildings element of the property at 1 October 20X5 was 20 years.

- Plant and equipment – whose fair value exceeded the carrying amount by $8 million. The estimated remaining useful life of the plant and equipment of Cuca at 1 October 20X5 was four years.

All depreciation of property, plant and equipment is charged to cost of sales. You can assume that the profit of Cuca for the year ended 31 March 20X6 accrued evenly over the year.

No impairment of the goodwill on acquisition of Cuca is necessary in the consolidated financial statements of Abiola for the year ended 31 March 20X6.

Exhibit 4 – Intra-group trading

Abiola supplies a component used by both Busayo and Cuca. Abiola earns a profit margin of 10% on these supplies. Details of the sales of the component, and the holdings of inventory of the component by group entities, are as follows:

	Busayo $'000	Cuca $'000
Sales of the component (for Cuca all sales after 1 October 20X5)	15,000	8,000
Inventory of component at 31 March 20X5 (at cost to Busayo/Cuca)	2,000	Nil
Inventory of component at 31 March 20X6 (at cost to Busayo/Cuca)	3,000	2,800

Exhibit 5 – Revenue of Abiola

On 1 October 20X5, Abiola sold a large machine to a customer for a total price of $51.2 million and credited $51.2 million to revenue. As part of the sales agreement, Abiola agreed to provide annual servicing of the machine for four years from 1 October 20X5 for no additional payment. The normal selling price of this without any annual servicing would have been $60 million and Abiola would normally charge the customer an annual fee of $1 million to service the machine. You should ignore the time value of money in respect of this transaction.

Exhibit 6 – Abiola's other investment

Apart from its investments in Busayo and Cuca, Abiola has one other investment – in entity X. Abiola purchased this equity investment on 1 July 20X5 for $40 million and designated the investment as fair value through other comprehensive income. In order to protect against a prolonged decline in the fair value of the investment in entity X, Abiola purchased a put option to sell this investment. The cost of the option was $6 million and the option was regarded as an effective hedge against a prolonged decline in the fair value of the investment in entity X.

On 31 March 20X6, the fair value of the equity investment in entity X was $37 million and the fair value of the put option was $8.7 million. Apart from recognising the investment in entity X and the put option at cost, Abiola has made no other entries in its draft financial statements. Abiola wishes to use hedge accounting whenever permitted by IFRS Accounting Standards.

Exhibit 7 – Dividends and investment income

During the year, Busayo paid dividends of $12,000,000. Cuca paid dividends of $11,000,000 on 1 February 20X6. All of the investment income of Abiola has been correctly recognised in the individual financial statements of Abiola.

Exhibit 8 – Bond issue

On 1 April 20X5, Abiola issued a convertible zero-coupon bond to a single institutional investor. The bond will be redeemed or converted into equity shares on 31 March 20Y0. If the investor chooses to redeem the bond on 31 March 20Y0, the investor will receive $362.32 million. The incremental borrowing rate of Abiola on 1 April 20X5 is 10% per annum. The present value of $1 received in five years at a discount rate of 10% per annum is 62.1 cents.

Requirement

Using the information provided in Exhibits 1 to 8, prepare the consolidated statement of profit or loss and other comprehensive income of Abiola for the year ended at 31 March 20X6. You do not need to consider the deferred tax effects of any adjustments you make.

Note. You should show all workings to the nearest $'000.

(Total = 25 marks)

59 Alpha (September 2020)   49 mins

Alpha, a parent company with one subsidiary, Beta, is preparing the consolidated statement of profit or loss and other comprehensive income for the year ending 31 March 20X5. The exhibits provide information relevant to the question.

Exhibit 1 – Draft financial statements

The draft statements of profit or loss and other comprehensive income for the year ending 31 March 20X5 are as follows:

	Alpha $'000	Beta $'000
Revenue (Exhibit 3)	64,800	39,000
Cost of sales (Exhibits 3 and 5)	(26,000)	(16,000)
Gross profit	38,800	23,000
Distribution costs	(5,000)	(2,000)
Administrative expenses	(9,000)	(3,500)
Investment income (Exhibits 2 and 4)	7,000	0
Finance costs (Exhibit 2)	(4,000)	(2,500)
Profit before tax	27,800	15,000
Income tax expense	(7,000)	(4,000)
Profit for the year	20,800	11,000
Other comprehensive income:		
Items that will not be reclassified to profit or loss:		
Gains on property revaluation (Exhibit 5)	5,000	3,000
Other comprehensive income for the year:	5,000	3,000
Total comprehensive income for the year	25,800	14,000

Exhibit 2 – Alpha's investment in Beta

On 1 April 20X3, Alpha acquired 180 million equity shares in Beta. On that date Beta had 200 million equity shares in issue. Alpha made a cash payment of $60 million to the former shareholders of Beta on 1 April 20X3 and agreed to make a further payment of $26.62 million on 31 March 20X6.

Alpha had correctly accounted for the deferred payment in its financial statements for the year ended 31 March 20X4 but has made no further entries in its financial statements for the year ended 31 March 20X5. An appropriate annual rate to use in any discounting calculations is 10%. At a discount rate of 10% per annum the present value of $1 payable in three years is $0.7513.

On 31 December 20X4, Beta paid a dividend of $5 million. This was the only dividend paid by Beta in the year ended 31 March 20X5 and was appropriately recognised by Alpha.

On 1 April 20X3, Alpha made a long-term loan to Beta of $25 million. The loans are included in the financial statements of Beta at this amount. These long-term loans attract interest at an annual rate of 8%. Both Alpha and Beta have correctly accounted for this interest in their individual financial statements for the year ended 31 March 20X5.

No impairments of the goodwill on acquisition of Beta have been evident up to and including 31 March 20X5.

Exhibit 3 – Intra-group trading

Alpha supplies Beta with a raw material which it uses in its production process. Alpha applies a mark-up of one-third to its cost. Sales of the raw material by Alpha to Beta in the year ended 31 March 20X5 totalled $10 million. On 31 March 20X4 and 20X5, the inventories of Beta included goods costing $2 million and $3 million respectively which had been purchased from Alpha.

Exhibit 4 – Alpha's other investments

Apart from its investments in the equity shares and loans of Beta, Alpha has a portfolio of equity investments which are correctly classified as fair value through profit or loss. The investment income of Alpha for the year ended 31 March 20X5 currently correctly includes dividend income from this portfolio. However, the carrying amount of the portfolio has not yet been adjusted to its fair value at 31 March 20X5. On 31 March 20X5, the carrying amount of the portfolio was $32 million and its fair value $33.5 million.

Exhibit 5 – Revaluation of property, plant and equipment (PPE)

Both Alpha and Beta measure their PPE using the revaluation model. PPE is re-measured at the end of each financial year.

In previous periods Alpha had recorded net revaluation losses of $3.5 million. These losses were correctly accounted for under the requirements of IAS 16 *Property, Plant and Equipment*.

In the financial statements of Alpha for the year ended 31 March 20X5, re-measurement gains of $5 million were entirely recognised in other comprehensive income. These gains related to the same properties which had previously suffered revaluation losses.

Beta has only ever recorded revaluation gains. All depreciation and impairments of PPE are recognised in cost of sales.

Exhibit 6 – Equity settled share based payment scheme

On 1 April 20X3, Alpha granted 500 senior executives 4,000 share options each. The options vest on 31 March 20X7. The options only vest for senior executives who remain employed by Alpha on 31 March 20X7. The following information is relevant:

Date	Fair value of option ($)	Number of executives for whom the option is expected to vest
1 April 20X3	1.20	400
31 March 20X4	1.35	420
31 March 20X5	1.50	450

This transaction was correctly accounted for in the financial statements of Alpha for the year ended 31 March 20X4 and the cost was recognised as an administrative expense. However, no further entries have yet been made in the financial statements for the year ended 31 March 20X5.

Requirement:

Prepare the consolidated statement of profit or loss and other comprehensive income of Alpha for the year ended 31 March 20X5. Where relevant you should round all figures to the nearest $'000.

Note. Ignore deferred tax.

(Total = 25 marks)

60 Alpha (December 2021) 49 mins

Alpha, a parent with one subsidiary, Beta, is preparing the consolidated statement of profit or loss and other comprehensive income for the year ended 30 September 20X5.

The following **exhibits** provide information relevant to the question:

(1)   Financial statement extracts – statements of profit or loss and other comprehensive income of Alpha and Beta for the year ended 30 September 20X5

(2)   Alpha's investment in Beta – details of Alpha's investment in Beta which are relevant to the question

(3)   Intra-group trading – details of intra-group trading

(4)   Alpha's hedging transactions – details of Alpha's hedging of foreign currency transactions

This information should be used to answer the question **requirement** within the **response option** provided.

Exhibit 1 – Financial statement extracts

Statements of profit or loss and other comprehensive income for the year ended 30 September 20X5

	Alpha	Beta
	$'000	$'000
Revenue (Exhibit 3)	290,000	240,000
Cost of sales (Exhibits 2–3)	(130,500)	(132,000)
Gross profit	159,500	108,000
Other income (Exhibits 2–4)	20,000	Nil
Distribution costs	(15,000)	(12,000)
Administrative expenses	(55,000)	(50,000)
Finance costs	(30,000)	(28,000)
Other expenses (Exhibit 4)	(1,000)	Nil
Profit before tax	78,500	18,000
Income tax expense	(15,000)	(4,000)
Profit for the year	63,500	14,000
Other comprehensive income:		
Items that will not be reclassified subsequently to profit or loss:		
Cash flow hedges (Exhibit 4)	18,000	Nil
Total comprehensive income for the year	81,500	14,000

Exhibit 2 – Alpha's investment in Beta

On 1 October 20X4, Alpha made a cash payment of $185 million to purchase 48 million of Beta's 60 million issued equity shares and gain control of Beta. On 1 October 20X4, the net assets of Beta as shown in the individual financial statements of Beta totalled $180 million. The fair values of Beta's identifiable assets and liabilities were the same as their carrying amounts in the individual financial statements of Beta with the exception of:

(1) Property, plant and equipment (PPE) which had a fair value of $18 million in excess of its carrying amount in the financial statements of Beta. On 1 October 20X4, the useful life of this PPE was six years.

(2) An internally developed patent relating to one of Beta's products which had a fair value of $20 million on 1 October 20X4. On 1 October 20X4, the useful life of this internally developed patent was ten years.

(3) Inventory which had a fair value of $1.5 million in excess of its carrying amount in the financial statements of Beta. All this inventory was disposed of in the year ended 30 September 20X5.

The fair value adjustments should be regarded as temporary differences for the purposes of computing deferred tax. The relevant rate of income tax to use for this purpose is 20%. On 1 October 20X4, the directors of Alpha measured the non-controlling interest in Beta based on Alpha's proportionate share of the net assets of Beta at the date of acquisition. On 1 July 20X5, Beta paid a dividend of $10 million. Alpha included its share of this dividend in 'other income' in its own individual financial statements. On 30 September 20X5, the directors of Alpha tested the goodwill on acquisition of Beta for impairment as required by IAS 36 – Impairment of Assets. The directors decided that Beta represented a single cash-generating unit for this purpose and that its recoverable amount at 30 September 20X5 was $225 million.

All depreciation, amortisation and impairment charges are made to cost of sales.

Exhibit 3 – Intra-group trading

Since 1 October 20X4, Alpha has been supplying Beta with a product (product X). Alpha makes a profit of 25% on the invoiced price for these supplies of product X. During the year ended 30 September 20X5, Alpha sold $20 million of product X to Beta and invoiced Beta for this amount. At 30 September 20X5, the inventories of Beta included $3.2 million of product X purchased from Alpha. Since 1 October 20X4, Alpha has been providing Beta with administrative services. Alpha charged Beta a total of $6 million for these services during the year ended 30 September 20X5. Alpha recognised this amount in 'other income' and Beta recognised the amount as an administrative expense.

Exhibit 4 – Alpha's hedging transactions

Alpha uses cash flow hedge accounting for its hedging transactions whenever the relevant criteria set out in IFRS 9 *Financial Instruments* are met. Alpha recognises any hedge ineffectiveness in other income or other expenses as appropriate.

On 1 September 20X5, Alpha entered into two firm commitments to purchase products from overseas suppliers in the year ended 30 September 20X6. The first commitment to purchase products was for delivery on 1 November 20X5 (Contract A) and the second for delivery on 1 December 20X5 (Contract B). Alpha entered into two separate derivative contracts to hedge the currency risk associated with these firm commitments. Both of these contracts meet the required IFRS 9 criteria to enable hedge accounting to be used. The financial statements of Alpha for the year ended 30 September 20X5 include $18 million relating to other cash flow hedges but do not contain any amounts in respect of either the fair values of the firm future commitments or the fair values of the hedging derivatives for Contract A or B. You are given the following details concerning the fair values at 30 September 20X5:

	Commitment for delivery on:	
	1 November 20X5 (Contract A)	1 December 20X5 (Contract B)
	$'000	$'000
Future commitment – increase in fair value at 30 September 20X5	5,500	6,000
Derivative – positive fair value at 30 September 20X5	5,600	5,800

Requirements

Using exhibits 1–4, prepare the consolidated statement of profit or loss and other comprehensive income of Alpha for the year ended 30 September 20X5. Unless specifically referred to in the exhibits you should ignore deferred tax.

Note. Explanations of consolidation procedures are not required.

(Total = 25 marks)

Answers

1 Omega 15 (December 2011) (amended)

Top tips. This was a detailed question on this area of the syllabus, and goes to show that you must be familiar with the whole syllabus if you are going to pass DipIFR.

Query 1 was reasonably straightforward if you knew at least the names of the bodies, as their functions are quite self-explanatory after that – the IFRS Advisory Council, for example, provides advice about IFRS Accounting Standards. Query 2 tested your understanding of the role of the *Conceptual Framework*. Query 3 brought in a new topic area regarding the role and purpose of the ISSB, a very current topic in financial reporting. For Query 4, you were required to discuss how the definitions of two elements of financial statements (assets and liabilities) as defined in the *Conceptual Framework*, are applied to a lease agreement. Note that the requirement specifically asks you to apply the definitions in the *Conceptual Framework*, so make sure you cover this in your answer.

Easy marks. Queries 1 and 3 contained relatively easy knowledge marks. There were marks available in part (b) (Query 4) for the definition of an asset and of a liability.

(a) **Query 1 – Regulatory bodies**

IFRS Foundation

The Foundation is responsible for the standard-setting process as a whole, and seeks to ensure that the standard-setting bodies have appropriate work plans and are financed accordingly.

International Accounting Standards Board

The IASB is the IFRS Foundation's independent standard-setting body, which develops and publishes IFRS Accounting Standards. In doing this it follows a transparent due process, including the publication of consultation documents such as exposure drafts and discussion papers.

IFRS Advisory Council

The IFRS Advisory Council advises the IASB on a range of issues, such as the appropriateness of its work plan and future priorities. It also advises on single projects with an emphasis on practical and implementation issues.

IFRS Interpretations Committee

The IFRS Interpretations Committee reviews accounting issues that have arisen (or could arise) in the context of IFRS Accounting Standards, and provides authoritative guidance on them.

Query 2 – *Conceptual Framework*

The *Conceptual Framework* forms the theoretical conceptual basis for determining which transactions should be recognised in the financial statements, how transactions should be measured (historical cost or current value) and reported – ie how they are presented or communicated to users. The use of a *Conceptual Framework* leads to a 'principles-based' system whereby accounting standards are developed from an agreed conceptual basis with specific objectives.

The *Conceptual Framework* describes the objective of, and the concepts for, general purpose financial reporting. The purpose of the *Conceptual Framework* is to:

- Assist the IASB to develop IFRS Accounting Standards that are based on consistent concepts;

- Assist preparers to develop consistent accounting policies when no Accounting Standards applies to a particular transaction or other event, or when a Accounting Standards allows a choice of accounting policy; and

- Assist all parties to understand and interpret the Accounting Standards.

(Conceptual Framework: para. SP1.1)

The use of a *Conceptual Framework* helps to avoid standards being developed on a haphazard basis in response to issues being identified with a particular accounting treatment which resulted in attempts to standardise accounting practice in that area, without regard to the relative importance of that issue or the consistency with other accounting standards. Without a *Conceptual Framework*, there is a risk that the development of standards may be subject to political interference from interested parties. Where there is a conflict of interest between user groups on which policies to choose, policies deriving from a *Conceptual Framework* will be less open to criticism as there is a conceptual basis on which the decisions are being made.

The *Conceptual Framework* defines existing and potential investors, lenders and other creditors as the primary users of financial statements (Conceptual Framework: para. 1.2). However it does accept that general purpose financial statements cannot provide all the information those primary users need, nor does it address the needs of other users of the financial statements. Given the diversity of user requirements, there may be a need for a variety of accounting standards, each produced for a different purpose (and with different concepts as a basis). It is not clear, however, whether having a *Conceptual Framework* makes the task of preparing and then implementing standards any easier than without a *Conceptual Framework*.

Query 3 – *International Sustainability Standards Board (ISSB)*

The ISSB was formed to address the increased global interest in sustainability and the stakeholder need for information in this area. Prior to the formation of the ISSB, there were many different sources of guidance and regulatory requirements which caused difficulties for preparers and users of reports.

The four key objectives of the ISSB are:
- To develop standards for a global baseline of sustainability disclosures
- To meet the information needs of investors
  - To enable companies to provide comprehensive sustainability information to global capital markets
  - To facilitate interoperability with disclosures that are jurisdiction-specific and/or aimed at broader stakeholder groups

To help achieve these objectives the ISSB has issued two Sustainability Disclosure Standards IFRS S1 *General Requirements for Disclosure of Sustainability-related Financial Information* and IFRS S2 *Climate-related Disclosures*.

The IFRS Sustainability Standards are not mandatory and therefore Omega will not be required to apply the standards, however given the company's interest in disclosing sustainability information, particularly relating to climate-related matters, the ISSB Standards may provide a framework for providing such disclosures.

Looking specifically at IFRS S2, the objective is to require an entity to disclose information about its climate-related risks and opportunities that could be reasonably expected to affect an entity's prospects, that is, it's future cash flows, its access to capital and its cost of capital.

Climate related risks include physical risks, such as the risks associated with adverse weather conditions, or transition risks which are the risks that arise as a result of transitioning to a lower carbon economy.

Information regarding climate-related risks and opportunities are disclosed in four categories:
- **Governance** – so users can understand the governance processes, control and procedures used to monitor, manage and oversee climate-related risks and opportunities
- **Strategy** – so users can understand an entity's strategy for managing climate-related risks and opportunities
- **Risk management** – so users can understand an entity's processes to identify, assess, prioritise and monitor climate-related risks and opportunities
- **Metrics and targets** – so users can understand an entity's performance in relation to its climate-related risks and opportunities, including progress towards any climate-related targets

(b)   IFRS 16 *Leases* requires a lessee to recognise a right-of-use asset and a lease liability for each lease it enters into (with limited exceptions).

For an agreement to be classified as a lease under IFRS 16, it must give the lessee the right to control the use of an identified asset. It appears this is the case for Omega as the director has stated that Omega has full autonomy to use the specific vehicle as it wishes.

The *Conceptual Framework* defines an asset as 'a present economic resource controlled by the entity as a result of past events' and an economic resource is 'a right that has the potential to produce economic benefits' (Conceptual Framework: para. 4.2). Applying this definition to the lease of the vehicle:

- there is a **past event** as Omega has entered into a lease agreement

- Omega can **control** the vehicle as it has full autonomy to use the vehicle as it wishes

- through Omega's right to control the use of the vehicle, it has the **potential to produce economic benefits**, eg by delivering products to customers so that sales can be made, and therefore is a **present economic resource**.

A liability is defined as 'a present obligation of the entity to transfer an economic resource as a result of past events' (Conceptual Framework: para. 4.2).

The lease liability meets this definition: the lessee has a responsibility (**present obligation**) as a result of entering into the lease agreement (**past event**) to pay the lease rentals (**transfer of economic benefits**, ie cash) as they become due.

Therefore it is correct to recognise an asset and a liability for this lease under IFRS Accounting Standards.

2 Mocca

Marking guide

	Marks
Revenue recognition	2
Satisfied over time	2
Time value of money	1
Satisfy performance obligations	1
Control not transferred	2
If option lapses	2
Control as contract progresses	1
Revenue	2
Costs	1
Profit	½
Trade receivable	½
Contract asset	1
Separate performance obligations	1
Standalone prices	1
Calculations	7
Total	25

Marks

(a) Revenue recognition is an important issue in financial reporting. Revenue is often the largest figure in the statement of profit or loss. IFRS 15 *Revenue from Contracts with Customers* requires that revenue can be recognised when an entity has performed its performance obligations, that is when control over the goods and services promised in a contact pass to a customer. **When control passes**, the **performance obligation has been satisfied** and revenue is said to have been realised.

1 + 1

The major issues are ascertaining exactly when each performance obligation is fulfilled, and managing the conflict between the concepts of prudence and accruals.

As a contract where performance obligations are satisfied over time can span several accounting periods, if no revenue were recognised until the end of the contract, this would certainly be prudent but would **not be in accordance with the accruals concept**. The financial statements would show all of the profit in the final period, when in fact some of it had been earned in prior periods. This is remedied by **recognising attributable profit** as the performance obligations are satisfied, as long as ultimate profitability is expected. Any foreseeable loss is recognised immediately.

1 + 1

The **time value of money** could also be an issue in a contract where performance obligations are satisfied over time, for example if there is a long delay between when an entity satisfies a performance obligation and when the customer is due to pay the promised consideration.

1

<u>5</u>

(b) **Exhibit 1 – Sale of plant with call option**
IFRS 15 states that revenue can be recognised when an entity satisfies its performance obligations by transferring **control** of a promised good or service to a customer. In this case, the customer does not obtain control of the plant, because the call option means that that the customer's ability to use and obtain benefit from the plant is limited to the period 1 March 20X1 to 30 April 20X2.

1

As **control has not been transferred**, Mocca cannot recognise revenue and must account for the transaction as a **financing arrangement**, because the exercise price is above the original selling price. Mocca must continue to recognise the plant as an asset and recognise the cash received as a financial liability. The difference of $50,000 is recognised as a finance cost.

1 + 1

If, on 30 April 20X2, the **option lapses** unexercised, the customer will then obtain control of the plant. In this case, Mocca **must will derecognise the plant and recognise revenue of $550,000** (the $500,000 already received plus the $50,000 charged to interest).

1 + 1

<u>5</u>

Exhibit 2 – Long term contract
IFRS 15 requires revenue to be recognised as control over the asset is transferred to the customer. In this case, the control is passed to the customer over time as the contract progresses. Revenue is recognised based on contract costs incurred to date as a proportion of total costs.

1

	$'000
Costs incurred to date	4,800
Total costs	5,500
% completion	87.3%

  BPP LEARNING MEDIA

<u>Revenue</u>   1

Total revenue that can be recognised as $12,500 × 87.3% = $10,913

Some revenue has already been recognised in the prior year and therefore we must
calculate the additional revenue that can be recognised in the current year   1
($10,913 – $3,500) = $7,413
<u>Costs</u>

Contract costs incurred and recognised in the current year are total contract costs
incurred – costs recognised in the prior year ($4,800 – $2,660) = $2,140

<u>Profit</u>   1

Profit recognised in the year in respect of this contract is $7,413 – $2,140 = $5,273
<u>Trade receivable</u>   ½

A trade receivable is recognised in respect of amounts invoiced but not yet received:
$8,125 – $7,725 = $400

<u>Contract asset</u>   ½

A contact asset is recognised for revenue recognised to date but not yet invoiced

	$'000
Total revenue recognised	10,913
Amount invoiced to date	8,125
Contract asset	2,788

1

6

Exhibit 3 – Sale of goods and services

IFRS 15 regards a transaction such as this as being made up of two separately
identifiable performance obligations – the supply of the machine and the supply of the
servicing agreement.   ½

The total revenue of $500,000 would need to be allocated between the two separate
performance obligations in proportion to their stand-alone selling prices.   ½

The selling price of the machine is $450,000 and the normal selling price of the supply
of services is $150,000 (4 × $37,500). The total stand-alone selling prices therefore
total $600,000.   1

Revenue of **$375,000** ($500,000 × 450,000/600,000) is allocated to the supply of the
machine. The balance of revenue of **$125,000** is allocated to the supply of services.   1 + ½

On 1 April 20X1, Delta would recognise revenue from the supply of the machine of
$375,000 because control has passed to the customer.   ½

On the same date Delta would recognise a receivable of $500,000.   ½

The balance of $125,000 is initially recognised as deferred income.   ½

On 15 May 20X1, the receivable of $500,000 is de-recognised when the payment was
received from the customer.   ½

In the year ended 31 March 20X2, service revenue of $31,250 ($125,000 × ¼) can be
recognised.   1

The closing balance of deferred income on 31 March 20X2 will be $93,750
($125,000 – $31,250).   ½

$31,250 of this balance will be shown as a current liability as this refers to service revenue to be recognised in the year ended 31 March 20X2.   1

The balance of deferred income of $62,500 ($125,000 – $31,250 – $31,250) is shown as a non-current liability.   1

9
———
25

3 Kolya (December 2015) (amended)

> **Top tips.** This question covered IFRS 15 *Revenue from Contracts with Customers*. Part (a) required you to account for a transaction where goods and servicing were bundled together, part (b) was a transaction where a customer has a right of return. Part (c) was a contract in which the customer received a volume discount incentive. Part (d) was about a compensation payment paid by the supplier to the customer, something which you may not have seen before.
>
> **Examining team's comments.** In part (a) most candidates displayed an awareness that there were two performance obligations, one satisfied at a point in time and one satisfied over a period of time. On the whole candidates found the issue of measuring the total revenue and allocating this to the individual components more challenging and a variety of different mistakes were made here. It would be beneficial for future candidates to study the model answer to this part carefully.
>
> Answers to part (b) varied considerably. Candidates who had not studied IFRS 15 tended to either conclude that no revenue should be recognised until the return period expired or to conclude that revenue should be recognised in full, with a 'provision' for future refunds. Neither of these approaches fully accords with the IFRS 15 'expected value approach'.
>
> For part (c), marks were often lost by candidates due to: 1. a failure to fully use the monthly sales made in the nine-month period to 30 September 20X4 to predict the likely level of sales in the two-year period from 1 January 20X4 to 31 December 20X5; and 2. recording twelve months' sales at $100 per unit in the year ended 30 September 20X4 (rather than nine months from 1 January 20X4). The majority of candidates correctly concluded that ultimately all the goods would be sold to Birch at a price of $90 per unit.

[References: IFRS 15: paras. 9–10, 22, 25, 27, 29, 31–32]

Marking scheme

Marks

(a)   **Exhibit 1 – Machine contract**

Kolya has **two** performance obligations – to provide the machine and provide the servicing.   1

The total transaction price consists of a fixed element of $800,000 and a variable element of $10,000 or $20,000.   1

The variable element should be included in the transaction price based on the probability of its occurrence. Therefore a variable element of $10,000 should be included and the total transaction price will be $810,000.   1

The transaction price should be allocated to the performance obligations based on their stand-alone fair values. In this case, these are $700,000:$140,000 or 5:1.   1

Therefore $675,000 ($810,000 × 5/6) should be allocated to the obligation to supply the machine and $135,000 ($810,000 × 1/6) to the obligation to provide two years' servicing of the machine.   ½ + ½

The obligation to supply the machine is satisfied fully in the year ended 30 September 20X5 and so revenue of $675,000 in respect of this supply should be recognised.   1

Marks

Only 1/24 of the obligation to provide the servicing is satisfied in the year ended 30
September 20X5 and so revenue of $5,625 ($135,000 × 1/24) in respect of this supply
should be recognised.

1

On 30 September 20X5, Kolya will recognise a receivable of $810,000 based on the
expected transaction price. This will be reported as a current asset.

½
½ + ½
+ ½

On 30 September 20X5, Kolya will recognise deferred income of $129,375 ($810,000 –
$675,000 – $5,625). $67,500 ($129,375 × 12/23) of this amount will be shown as a current
liability. The balance of $61,875 ($129,375 – $67,500) will be non-current.

9

(b) **Exhibit 2 – Right of return**

When the customer has a right to return products, the transaction price contains a
variable element.

1

Since this can be reliably measured, it is taken account of in measuring the revenue and
the total revenue will be $192,000 (96 × $2,000).

1

$200,000 (100 × $2,000) will be recognised as a trade receivable.

1

$8,000 ($200,000 – $192,000) will be recognised as a refund liability. This will be shown
as a current liability.

1

The total cost of the goods sold is $160,000) (100 × $1,600). Of this amount, only
$153,600 (96 × $1,600) will be shown as a cost of sale. The other $6,400 ($160,000 –
$153,600) will be shown as a right of return asset under current assets.

1
5

(c) **Sale with a volume discount incentive**

The consideration payable by Birch is variable as it depends on the volume of sales in the
two-year period. However, at 30 September 20X4, Kolya can reliably estimate the outcome
and conclude that the volume discount threshold is not expected to be exceeded (sales for 9
months: 20,000 × 24/9 = 53,333). The revenue included for the 9 month period ended 30
September 20X4 will be booked at $100 per unit and will be $2 million (20,000 × $100).

1
1
1

During the year ended 30 September 20X5, actual sales volumes and estimates change such
that the cumulative revenue should now be booked at $90 per unit. It is now expected that
the volume discount threshold will be exceeded. This means that the cumulative revenue
relating to these goods at 30 September 20X5 will be $4,950,000 ((20,000 + 35,000) × $90).

1

1

The revenue which will actually be booked by Kolya for the year ended 30 September 20X5
will be $2,950,000 ($4,950,000 – $2m recognised in 20X4).

1
6

(d) **Non-refundable payment**

The $3 million compensation payment to the customer is **not** in exchange for a distinct good or
service that transfers to Kolya as Kolya does not obtain control of any rights to the customer's
shelves.

1

Consequently, IFRS 15 requires the $3 million payment to be treated as a **reduction of the
transaction price** rather than a purchase from a supplier.

1

The $3 million payment should not be recorded as a reduction in the transaction price until Kolya
recognises revenue from the sale of the goods.

1

Mark

Therefore, on 30 November 20X4, Kolya should initially recognise the $3 million paid as a **contract asset** within current assets (since it is a one year contract) with the following accounting entry:

1

DEBIT   Contract asset $3m
CREDIT   Cash $3m

When Kolya sells the goods to the customer, the amount of revenue recognised should be after deducting 10% ($3m/$30m) of the invoice price.

1

5

25

4 Delta (December 2019) (amended)

Marking scheme

Marks

(a) The timing of the recognition of revenue under IFRS 15 *Revenue from Contracts with Customers* depends on the type of performance obligation the entity has under the contract with the customer. A performance obligation is a distinct promise to transfer goods or services to the customer (sense of the point only required).

1

IFRS 15 requires that revenue should be recognised when (or as) a particular performance obligation is satisfied.

1

In many cases (eg the sale of goods in the ordinary course of business), performance obligations are satisfied at a point in time. In such cases, the revenue is recognised at the point control of the goods is transferred to the customer.

2

In some cases (eg a contract to construct an asset for use by a customer), performance obligations are satisfied over a period of time. In such cases, the proportion of the total revenue recognised is the proportion of the performance obligation which has been satisfied by the reporting date.

2

The measurement of revenue is based on the transaction price. The transaction price is the amount of consideration to which an entity expects to be entitled in exchange for transferring the promised goods and services to the customer.

1

In many cases, where the consideration for the transaction is fixed and payable immediately after the revenue has been recognised (eg most sales of goods), the transaction price is the invoiced amount less any sales taxes collected on behalf of third parties.

1

Where the due date for payment of the invoiced price is 'significantly different' (certainly more than 12 months) from the date of recognition of the revenue, then the time value of money should be taken into account when measuring the transaction price. This means that the revenue recognised on the sale of goods with deferred payment terms would be split into a 'sale of goods' component and a financing component.

2

Where the total consideration due from the customer contains variable elements (eg the possibility that the customer obtains a discount for bulk purchases depending on the total purchases in a period), then the transaction price should be based on the best estimate of the total amount receivable from the customer as a result of the contract.

2

12

(b) **Exhibit 1 – Sale of product with right of return**

Under the principles of IFRS 15, revenue cannot be recognised on 1 April 20X7 because at that date the consideration is variable and the amount of the variable consideration cannot be reliably estimated.   1

However, on 1 April 20X7 $80,000 would be removed from inventory and included as a 'right to recover asset' (any reasonable description of this would be permitted).   1

Revenue of $100,000 (the present value of $121,000 receivable in two years) is recognised on 30 June 20X7 when the uncertainty regarding potential returns is resolved.   1

On the same day, the 'right to recover asset' will be de-recognised and transferred to cost of sales.   1

Delta will also recognise finance income of $2,500 ($100,000 × 10% × 3/12) in the year ended 30 September 20X7.   2

At 30 September 20X7, Delta will recognise a trade receivable of $102,500 ($100,000 + $2,500).   <u>1</u>

<u>7</u>

Exhibit 2 – Machine contract
                                                                                    1

IFRS 15 states that where a contract contains more than one distinct performance obligation, a company allocates the transaction price to all separate performance obligations in proportion to the stand-alone selling price of the good or service underlying each performance obligation.

Total revenue of $7.5 million is divided into sales and service elements. Total costs of servicing are $1.2 million ($200,000 × 2 × 3). Adding a normal gross margin of 20% gives a stand-alone selling price of $1.5 million ($1.2m ÷ 0.8).   2

Revenue from the sale of the machine of $6.176 million (7/8.5 × 7.5m) is recognised on 1 April 20X7, when the machine is delivered to the customer.   1

Service revenue is recognised on a straight line basis over the three year period, resulting in deferred revenue in the first two years. $221,000 (1.5/8.5 × $7.5m × 6/36) is recognised in the year ended 20X7, with deferred revenue of $1.103 million (1.5/8.5 × 7.5 × 30/36). This is split into current liabilities of $0.441 million ($1.103m × 12/30) and non-current liabilities of $0.662 million ($1.103m × 18/30).   <u>2</u>

<u>6</u>

<u>25</u>

5 Delta (December 2021)

> **Top tips.** This question required you to explain and show the accounting treatment of two separate issues in the financial statements of Delta:
>
> (1) The sale of a machine with an ongoing commitment by the seller to repair and maintain the machine for a three-year period following the sale.
>
> (2) The sale and leaseback of a factory.
>
> There was lots to explain in both of these issues, however, the examiner commented that many answers provided were not in sufficient depth to earn the marks available. For example, issue 1 was worth 14 marks, 4 of which were for workings, so as a rough guide, to gain the remaining 10 marks, you needed to have made around 10 well-explained points. As always though, you need to apply good exam technique and manage your time appropriately. You should spend no more than $14 \times 1.95 = 27$ minutes addressing Exhibit 1 1 and 21 minutes on Exhibit 2.
>
> **Examining team comments.**
>
> The following aspects relevant to **Exhibit 1** were less well dealt with:
>
> - The calculation of the revenue recognised in the current period relating to the 'repair and maintenance aspect' of the transaction. Since the sale took place on 1 April 20X5 – six months before 30 September 20X5 (the year-end) – only 6/36 of the total revenue amount should have been recognised. Many candidates stated that 12/36 of the total revenue amount should have been recognised.
>
> - The treatment of the unrecognised revenue as deferred income in the statement of financial position at 30 September 20X5. 12/30 of this amount should have been a current liability and 18/30 a non-current liability.
>
> - Identification and subsequent treatment of the repair and maintenance contract as an onerous contract at 30 September 20X5.
>
> Errors in Exhibit 2 that were apparent reasonably often included:
>
> - Recognising a right-of-use asset as the present value of the lease payments. This is not appropriate for a sale and leaseback.
>
> - Stating that the profit on sale of the factory was the difference between the sales proceeds and the carrying amount, without allowing for the necessary recognition of the right-of-use asset and the lease liability.
>
> - Incorrect allocation of the closing lease liability into its current and non-current portions. Many candidates stated that the current liability was the total rental payment in the following period. This does not allow for the fact that, since the rental payments are made at the end of the reporting period, the rental payment made in the following period is partly applied to the settlement of the finance cost for the following period.
>
> - Inappropriate references to the sale and leaseback arrangement creating a finance lease or operating lease. Such distinctions are no longer relevant for lessees following the publication of IFRS 16 *Leases*.

Marking scheme

Marks

Sale of machine

Under the principles of IFRS 15 *Revenue from Contracts with Customers* the sale of the machine comprises two performance obligations – the delivery of the machine and the provision of a three-year repair and maintenance service.

1

In the case of the delivery of the machine, the performance obligation is satisfied **fully on 1 April 20X5**, when the customer took control of the machine. Therefore **all the revenue attributable to the delivery of the machine** is recognised on that date.

½ + ½

The machine will be removed from the inventory of Delta on 1 April 20X5 and its cost ($250,000) recognised in cost of sales. ½

In the case of the repair and maintenance service, the performance obligation is satisfied **over time** – in the **three-year period from 1 April 20X5 to 31 March 20X8**. IFRS 15 would require that this revenue is recognised over that three-year period. ½ + ½

It is clear from the total invoiced amount and the stand-alone selling prices of the two components of the transaction that the machine is being sold at a discount. ½

Where a bundle of goods and/or services are sold at a discount, IFRS 15 requires that, unless the discount is obviously attributable to one or more of the components of the bundle, the discount should be allocated to the components in proportion to their stand-alone selling prices. 1

Therefore the revenue from the delivery of the machine will be $350,000 (W1) and the revenue from the maintenance and repair service will be $150,000 (W1). 1 (W1) + ½ (W1)

The revenue from the delivery of the machine of $350,000 (W1) will be recognised **in full** in the year ended 30 September 20X5. ½

The revenue which will be recognised in respect of the maintenance service will be $25,000 (W2). The unrecognised revenue will be shown as a contract liability (as deferred income). $50,000 (W2) of this liability will be a current liability and the balance of $75,000 (W2) will be a non-current liability. 2½ (W2) + 1 (explanation)

The $30,000 cost of repairing the machine in the six months ended 30 September 20X5 will be shown as an operating cost in the year ended 30 September 20X5 (probably under cost of sales). ½

Since the future expected repair costs to the machine are $155,000 and the future revenue to be recognised under the repair and maintenance service is $125,000, then under the principles of IAS 37 *Provisions, Contingent Liabilities and Contingent Assets* the contract has become an **onerous** contract. ½ + ½

Under the principles of IAS 37, Delta needs to make a **provision** at 30 September 20X5 for the **net cost** of fulfilling the service. The net cost of fulfilling the service is **$30,000** ($155,000 – $125,000). ½ + ½

Since the net costs of the onerous contract are expected to accrue evenly over its remaining duration, the amount of the provision which will be shown as a current liability will be **$12,000** ($30,000 × 12/30). The balance of **$18,000** ($30,000 – $12,000) will be non-current. 1

Marks available 14

Workings

1   *Allocation of revenue between machine and maintenance and repair service*

	$	Allocation of transaction price ($500,000)	
Stand-alone fair value of machine	420,000	420/600 × $500,000 = $350,000	1
Stand-alone fair value of maintenance and repair service	180,000	180/600 × $500,000 = $150,000	½
Total	600,000		1½

2   *Recognition of revenue on repair and maintenance service*

Total revenue (W1)		$150,000	½
Amount recognised in the year ended 30 September 20X5	(6/36 × $150,000)	$25,000	½
Deferred income	($150,000 – $25,000)	$125,000	½
Current liability	($150,000 × 12/36)	$50,000	½
Non-current liability	(balance)	$75,000	½
			2½

Sale and leaseback

Because the factory is being leased back for only 10 of its 30 years of remaining economic life, the transaction would be regarded as a sale under the principles of IFRS 15.

1

Under the principles of IFRS 16 *Leases* the factory would be de-recognised by Delta and a 'right of use asset' recognised in its place.

(principle) 1

The initial carrying amount of the right of use asset will be a proportion of the previous carrying amount of the factory. This proportion will be the ratio of the present value of the future lease payments compared with the fair value of the factory at the date of sale.

(principle) 1

The initial carrying amount of the right of use asset for Delta will therefore be $8.95 million ($20 million × $13.42 million/$30 million).

1

Delta will also recognise a lease liability of $13.42 million.

1

The net result of derecognising the factory and recognising the right of use asset and the lease liability is that Delta will recognise a profit on sale of $5.53 million** ($30 million + $8·95 million – $20 million – $1342 million).

1½

The right of use asset will be depreciated over the the shorter of the lease term and the useful life, which here are both 10 years.10-year lease term, so for the year ended 30 September 20X5 Delta will charge depreciation of $895,000 ($8.95 million × 1/10).

½ + ½

The closing carrying amount of the right of use asset will be $8,055,000 ($8.95 million – $895,000). This will be shown as a non-current asset in Delta's statement of financial position.

½ + ½

Delta will recognise a finance cost of $1,073,600 (W3). The closing lease liability will be $12,493,600 (W3). $1,000,512 (W3) of this liability will be a current liability and the balance of $11,493,088 (W3) will be non-current (W3).

2½

11

25

Tutorial note.

An alternative method of arriving at the profit on sale to be recognised is to calculate the **amount of any gain or loss** on the sale which relates to the **rights transferred** to the buyer.

Step 1: Calculate the total gain = fair value – carrying amount = $30 million – $20 million = **$10 million**

Step 2: Calculate the gain which relates to the **rights retained** = gain × present value of lease payments/fair value = $10 million × $13.42 million/$30 million = $4.47 million

Step 3: The gain relating to **rights transferred** is the balancing figure: Gain – gain on rights retained = $10 million – $4.47 million = $5.53 million

So the relevant journal entry would be:

	DR	CR
	$ million	$ million
Cash	30	
Right-of-use asset	8.95	
PPE		20
Lease liability		13.42
Gain on sale (to P/L)		5.53

3   *Computation and split of closing lease liability*

Year ended 30 September	Opening liability (PV) $	Finance cost (8%) $	Rental payment $	Closing liability $	
20X5	13,420,000	8% × 13,420,000 = 1,073,600	(2,000,000)	12,493,600	1
20X6	12,493,600	8% × 12,493,600 = 999,488	(2,000,000)	11,493,088	1

The current liability at 30 September 20X5 is $1,000,512 ($12,493,600 – $11,493,088).   ½

2½

6 Omikron

[References: IAS 36: paras. 6–12]

Marking guide

	Marks
External indicators	3
Internal indicators	3
Impairment definition	1
Recoverable amount definition	2
Impairment loss	2
Cash generating unit	2
Calculations Feb 20X8	3
Calculations Mar 20X8	3
Conclusion	1
DCF calculation	3
Impairment loss calc	1½
Carrying amount	½
Total	**25**

(a)   (i)   Indicators will include the following.

External factors

- A significant decrease in the market value of an asset in excess of normal passage of time.

- Significant **adverse changes** in the **markets** or **business** in which the asset is used.

- Adverse changes to the **technological**, **economic** or **legal environmental** of the business.

- Increase in **market interest rates** likely to adversely affect the **discount ratio** used to calculate **value in use**.

- Where interest rates increase, adversely affecting recoverable amounts.

- The carrying amount of an entity's asset exceeding its market capitalisation.

Internal factors

- Adverse changes to the method of use of the asset.

- Indications suggest the **economic performance** of the asset will be **worse** than expected.

- Physical damage or obsolescence has occurred.

- For new assets, **cost increases** adversely affect profitability.

- Where **actual cash flows are less than estimated** cash flows if an asset is valued in terms of 'value in use'.

- Where the **management** intend to **reorganise** the **entity**.

(ii) **Recognition and measurement of impairment**

IAS 36 states that if an **asset's carrying amount** is **higher than** its **recoverable amount**, an **impairment loss** has occurred. The **recoverable amount** is **defined** as the **higher** of the **asset's fair value less costs of disposal** and its **value in use**. If the recoverable amount is less than the carrying amount, then the resulting impairment loss should be charged as an expense in the statement of profit or loss. When an **impairment loss occurs** for a **revalued asset**, the **impairment loss** should be charged to the **revaluation surplus**, any **excess** is then charged to the **statement of profit or loss**.

Where it is not possible to measure impairment for individual assets, the loss should be measured for a cash generating unit. **Impairment losses** for **cash generating units** should be **allocated initially** to **goodwill**, **then** to all **other assets** on a **pro rata basis**. Impairment losses should only be reversed if there has been a change in the estimates used to determine the asset's recoverable amount since the last impairment loss was recognised.

After impairment losses have been recognised, the depreciation (amortisation) charges should be revised.

(b) **Exhibit 1 – Cash generating unit**

At 1 February 20X8

	1.1.X8	Impairment loss	1.2.X8
	$'000	$'000	$'000
Goodwill (230 – 190)	40	(15)	25
Intangible assets	30		30
Vehicles	120	(30)	90
Sundry net assets	40		40
	230	(45)	185

An impairment loss is recognised for the stolen vehicles. The balance of $15,000 is allocated to goodwill in the cash generating unit.

At 1 March 20X8

	1.2.X8	Impairment loss	1.3.X8
	$'000	$'000	$'000
Goodwill	25	(25)	–
Intangible assets	30	(5)	25
Vehicles	90		90
Sundry net assets	40		40
	185	(30)	155

A further impairment loss of $30,000 is recognised. The recoverable amount falls to the higher of net selling price (190 – 5 – 30) or value in use (150). There is no indication that other tangible assets are impaired. The loss is applied initially to the intangible assets and then to goodwill.

Exhibit 2 – Individual asset

It is necessary to find the value in use in order to determine what the impairment loss is.

Year	Long-term growth rate	Future cash flows $'000	PV factor at 10%	Discounted future cash flows $'000
1		600	0.90909	545
2		660	0.82645	545
3		710	0.75131	533
4		755	0.68301	516
5		790	0.62092	491
6	+2%	806	0.56447	455
7	–1%	798	0.51316	409
8	–7%	742	0.46651	346
9	–16%	623	0.42410	264
10	–30%	436	0.38554	168
Total				4,272

The impairment loss is calculated by comparing the carrying amount ($5m) with the higher of value in use ($4.272m) and fair value less costs of disposal ($3.2m).

The impairment loss is therefore $5m – $4.272m = $728,000 which is an expense in the statement of profit or loss.

The new carrying amount of the SyMIX is $4,272 million.

7 Dougal

Top tips. This is typical question requiring you to explain three different issues. Exhibit 1 required you to recognise and account for an investment property. You also had to consider the accounting treatment of the property when it changed use. Note that IFRS 16 *Leases* retains the distinction between finance and operating leases for lessors, though not for lessees. Exhibit 2 required you to account for a purchase of a machine from a foreign supplier and to contrast the treatment of the machine itself (non-monetary item) with the liability (monetary).

In Exhibit 3, there were easy marks essentially for applying the basic provisions of IFRS *5 Non-current Assets Held for Sale and Discontinued Assets.* This is a fundamental standard that you should be very familiar with.

Examining team's comments. On the whole, candidates found Exhibit 1 of this question challenging. Many candidates did not appreciate that the property being leased out was an investment property, so that fair value changes would be recognised in profit or loss rather than other comprehensive income. A number of others incorrectly stated that the property would satisfy the 'held-for-sale' criteria in IFRS 5. Others regarded the conversion project as a construction contract when no evidence was provided of the existence of any third-party buyers to support this. Only a minority correctly applied IAS 2 to this situation.

Exhibit 2 of this question was generally well answered. A significant minority of candidates made a careless error of multiplying the foreign currency (groat) figure to convert into $ rather than dividing it. A smaller minority of candidates seemed unaware of the distinction between monetary and non-monetary items in a 'foreign currency context'. Therefore there were some examples of the 're-translation' of PPE, which was not appropriate. A minority of candidates incorrectly stated that the exchange differences on re-translation should be recognised in other comprehensive income rather than profit or loss.

Answers in respect of exhibit 3 were somewhat disappointing. Many candidates failed to recognise that the decline in value of property A was caused by an event after the end of the reporting period and so would be classified as non-adjusting. Many candidates did not appreciate that property B could not be classified as held for sale until the necessary repair work was carried out.

	Marks

Marking scheme

Exhibit 1 – Property

From 1 October 20X0, the property would be regarded as an investment property since it is being held for its investment potential rather than being owner occupied or developed for sale. — ½ + ½

The property would be measured under the fair value model. This means it will be measured at its fair value each year end, with any gains or losses on remeasurement recognised in profit or loss. — ½ + ½

On 31 March 20X5, the property ceases to be an investment property because Dougal begins to develop it for sale as flats. — ½ + ½

The increase in the fair value of the property from 30 September 20X4 to 31 March 20X5 of $3 million ($29m – $26m) would be recognised in P/L for the year ended 30 September 20X5. — ½ + ½

Since the lease of the property is an operating lease, rental income of $1 million ($2m × 6/12) would be recognised in P/L for the year ended 30 September 20X5. — ½ + ½

When the property ceases to be an investment property, it is transferred into inventory at its then fair value of $29 million. This becomes the initial 'cost' of the inventory. — ½ + ½

The additional costs of $6 million for developing the flats which were incurred up to and including 30 September 20X5 would be added to the 'cost' of inventory to give a closing cost of $35 million. — 1

The total selling price of the flats is expected to be $50 million (10 × $5m). Since the further costs to develop the flats total $4 million, their net realisable value is $46 million ($50m – $4m), so the flats will be measured at a cost of $35 million. — ½ + ½ + ½ + ½

The flats will be shown in inventory as a current asset. — $\frac{1}{10}$

Exhibit 2 – Machine

The machine and the associated liability would be recorded in the financial statements using the rate of exchange in force at the transaction date – 2.5 groats to $1. Therefore the initial carrying amount of both items is $240,000 (600,000/2.5). — 1

The liability is a monetary item so it would be retranslated at the year end of 30 September 20X5 using the closing rate of two groats to $1 at $300,000 (600,000/2) and shown as a current liability. — 1 + ½

The exchange difference of $60,000 ($300,000 – $240,000) is recognised in profit or loss – in this case a loss. — 1

The machine is a non-monetary asset measured under the cost model and so is not retranslated as the exchange rate changes. — 1

The modification costs of $30,000 are added to the cost of the machine to give a total cost figure of $270,000. — ½

The machine is depreciated from 1 September 20X5 (the date it is brought into use) and so the depreciation for the year ended 30 September 20X5 is $4,500 ($270,000 × 1/5 × 1/12). — 1

The machine will be shown as a non-current asset at a closing carrying amount of $265,500 ($270,000 – $4,500). — $\frac{1}{7}$

Marks

Exhibit 3 – Sales of properties

From 1 July 20X5 property A would be regarded as held for sale under the principles of IFRS 5 *Non-current Assets Held for Sale and Discontinued Operations*. The property is available for immediate sale in its present condition and is being actively marketed at a reasonable price. On the other hand property B would not, since it cannot be sold until necessary repairs are carried out.

1

Property A would be depreciated up to the date of classification as held for sale but not thereafter. Therefore, depreciation of $375,000 ($15,000,000 × 1/30 × 9/12) would be necessary in the year to 30 September 20X5.

1

The property would be removed from non-current assets and shown in current assets or in a separate section of the assets side of the statement of financial position.

1

It would be measured at the lower of its carrying amount of the date of classification of $24,625,000 ($25,000,000 – $375,000) and its fair value less costs to sell of $28,000,000 – $24,625,000 in this case.

1

The decline in property prices affecting this property relates to an economic event occurring after the end of the reporting period. Therefore, it would be regarded as a non-adjusting event after the reporting period. The event would be disclosed as a note to the financial statements but the decline in value would not be recognised.

1

Property B would be depreciated for the whole period and would remain in non-current assets. The depreciation required for the year ended 30 September 20X5 would be $400,000 ($16,000,000 × 1/40).

1

The fact that its fair value less costs to sell is estimated at $18 million whilst the carrying amount prior to any write down is $21,600,000 ($22,000,000 – $400,000) is prima-facie evidence of impairment.

1

Given that the property is to be sold – even though it cannot be classified as held for sale at 30 September 20X5 – this is the best indicator of the recoverable amount of the property.

<u>1</u>

<u>8</u>

<u><u>25</u></u>

8 Gamma (December 2020) (amended)

Top tips. In this question you were required to explain two accounting issues – the purchase of a machine (financed by borrowing and which required subsequent development and the replacement of an engine) and the sale of land. You also had to identify and explain the ethical issues confronting the finance director. Ethical issues will always be tested in Question 2 of the exam, for a maximum of 5 marks. Good exam technique in approaching ethical issues is to refer to the fundamental principles of the IESBA's *Code of Ethics* and to identify potential breaches or threats to those fundamental principles.

A common error noted by the examiner's report in relation to part (a) was to select the incorrect date to begin depreciating the machine. The correct date to commence depreciation was 31 May 20X5, the date the machine was available for use following the issue of the inspection and safety certificate.

ANSWERS

Marking scheme

	Marks

Exhibit 1 – Purchase of machine

Under the principles of IAS 16 *Property, Plant and Equipment* (PPE) the machine will be recognised as an asset in PPE from 30 November 20X4, the date of delivery.　　½ (principle)

Under the principles of IAS 16, the **installation costs and the costs of the inspection and the safety certificate** will be included in the initial carrying amount of PPE **because** these costs are necessarily incurred in getting the machine ready for use.　　½ + ½

$30 million will be added to PPE on 30 November 20X4, a further $60 million in the period from 1 December 20X4 to 30 April 20X5, and $600,000 on 15 May 20X5.　　½

Under the principles of IAS 16, employee training costs **cannot** be recognised as part of the carrying amount of PPE. They are specifically excluded by IAS 16. Therefore these costs (of $1 million) will be shown as an **operating expense** in the statement of profit or loss and other comprehensive income for the year ended 30 September 20X5.　　½ + ½

Under the principles of IAS 23 *Borrowing Costs* **borrowing costs** which are **directly** attributable to the acquisition of an asset should be included as part of the carrying amount of that asset.　　½ + ½ (principle)

The costs which are eligible for such treatment are those incurred in the period starting from the date expenditure is incurred on the asset and ending on the date the asset is ready for use.　　½ (principle)

In this case, that means that the relevant period is the six months from 1 December 20X4 until 31 May 20X5 and the relevant borrowing costs to capitalise will be $1.8 million ($90 million × 4% × 6/12).　　½ + 1

This means that the total depreciable amount of the PPE will be $92.4 million ($30m + $60m + $600,000 + $1.8m).　　½

Under the principles of IAS 16, depreciation commences when an asset is ready for use (1 June 20X5) rather than when it is brought into use (31 July 20X5).　　½ (principle)

Under the principles of IAS 16, a single physical asset which has two or more significant components with different useful lives is regarded as two assets for depreciation purposes.　　½ (principle)

In this case, one component is the engine element with an initial carrying amount of **$24 million** – its fair value at the **date of acquisition**. The estimated future replacement cost is not relevant.　　½ + ½

The depreciation of this component for the year ended 30 September 20X5 will be $1.6 million (**$24m** × **1/5** × 4/12).　　½ + ½

The residual component has a carrying amount of $68.4 million ($92.4m – $24m) and its depreciation for the year ended 30 September 20X5 will be $2,280,000 ($68.4m × 1/10 × 4/12).　　½ + ½

100   BPP LEARNING MEDIA

The total depreciation expense in the statement of profit or loss and other comprehensive income for the year ended 30 September 20X5 will be $3,880,000 ($1.6 million + $2,280,000). This will be presented as an **operating** expense.

½ + ½

The balance in PPE on 30 September 20X5 will be **$88,520,000** ($92.4m – $3,880,000). This will be presented under **non-current assets**.

½ + ½

The finance cost on the loan for the current year will be **$3.3 million** ($90m × 4% × 11/12). The amount not capitalised of **$1.5 million** ($3.3m – $1.8m) will be shown as a finance cost in the statement of **profit or loss and other comprehensive income**.

½ + ½ + ½

The closing loan balance will be $93.3 million ($90m + $3.3m). This will be presented as a **current** liability.

½ + ½

15

Exhibit 2 – Sale of land

(i) **Accounting treatment**

The sale of land is a repurchase agreement under IFRS 15 *Revenue from Contracts with Customers* as Gamma has an option to buy the land back from the third party and, therefore, control has not transferred as the purchaser's ability to use and gain benefit from the land is limited.

1

Gamma must treat the transaction as a financing arrangement and record both an asset (the land) and a financial liability (the cash amount received which is repayable to the third party).

1

Gamma should not have derecognised the land from the financial statements because the risks and rewards of ownership have not been transferred. The substance of the transaction is a loan of $16 million, and the 3% 'premium' on repurchase is effectively an interest payment. As the transaction is immediately prior to the reporting date, no interest is recognised in the year to 30 September 20X5.

1

Recording the transaction as a sale is an attempt to manipulate the financial statements in order to show an improved profit figure and more favourable cash position.

1

The sale must be reversed and the land reinstated at its carrying amount before the transaction. The repurchase, ie the repayment of the loan, takes place one month after the year end, and so this is a current liability:

Debit	Property, plant and equipment	$12m
Debit	Retained earnings (to reverse profit on disposal (16–12))	$4m
Credit	Current liabilities	$16m

1

5

Marks

(ii) **Ethical issues**

Professional accountants are required to comply with the fundamental principles of IESBA's *Code of Ethics*. This includes objectivity, which means not allowing bias, conflict of interest or undue influence of others to override professional or business judgements. The finance director is suffering from financial difficulties herself which creates pressure to meet profit targets in order to achieve her bonus. This is a self-interest threat to the objectivity of the finance director as it could result in her choosing to record the transaction incorrectly in order to achieve her bonus.

2

Professional accountants must act with integrity, which requires honesty. The integrity of the finance director appears to be threatened in this situation if she applies the accounting treatment as instructed by the managing director. The effect of the sale just before the year end was to improve profits and to eliminate the bank overdraft, making the cash position look better. However, this is not an honest reflection of the actual position and performance of Gamma.

1

Professional accountants must also comply with the principle of professional behaviour, which requires compliance with relevant laws and regulations. In this case the suggested accounting treatment does not conform to IFRS Accounting Standards. It is not clear whether the finance director is aware of this or not. If she is not aware that the treatment is incorrect, and she records the transaction as instructed, then she will have breached the principle of professional competence. If she is aware, it may be that the finance director is facing an intimidation threat as she may be under undue pressure from the managing director to record the transaction as instructed, even though she knows the accounting treatment to be incorrect.

2

5
25

9 Gamma (December 2021)

Top tips. This question required you to explain and show the accounting treatment for two issues:

(1) The disposal of a subsidiary that operated in a market sector that is different from that of the rest of the Gamma group.

(2) The construction of a power generating plant during the year that caused environmental damage.

The question also covered the ethical issues arising in the scenario.

The question specifically asked for an *explanation* of the issues (as well as calculations). The examiner noted that many candidates did not provide explanations. A significant proportion of the marks are available for the narrative, so to score well in the question, you must provide some explanations in your answer. There were some relatively easy marks to be gained for some of these explanations – eg for requirement (a)(ii), stating that depreciation and finance costs are charged in the statement of profit or loss and that property, plant and equipment is presented as a non-current asset in the statement of financial position.

It may have surprised you to see group accounting covered in a question other than Question 1, however, group accounting can be covered anywhere in the exam and so you should be prepared for this in future exams.

BPP LEARNING MEDIA

This was the first time that ethics has been examined in DipIFR and the examiner reported that the answers produced by candidates were disappointing with some candidates not providing any answer to this part of the question. Ethics will be examined in Question 2 of every DipIFR exam, so it is worth revising the BPP Study Text content on this area and practising the ethics questions in this Kit. Your answer should refer to the principles of the Code of Ethics and should be applied to the scenario presented.

Examining team comments.

The examining team report stated that for requirement (a)(i), 'Very few candidates realised that, given the facts signposted in the question ('withdraw from the sector'), the disposal of the subsidiary would constitute a discontinued operation in the consolidated financial statements of Gamma. This meant that most candidates did not score any of the marks that were available for identifying this issue and its implications for the scenario.'

In relation to requirement (a)(ii): 'many candidates failed to appreciate that asset would be depreciated from the date it became available for use (28 February 20X5) rather than the date it was actually brought into use (31 March 20X5). This often caused candidates to compute an incorrect amount for the unwinding of the discount on the provision that was necessary as a result of the environmental damage.'

Marking scheme

			Marks

(a) (i) **Disposal of subsidiary**

Under the principles of IFRS 5 *Non-current Assets Held for Sale and Discontinued Operations* Subsidiary A will be regarded as a discontinued operation by the Gamma group. This is because subsidiary A is a component of the group which has been disposed of during the period and which represents a separate major line of the business for the group. Gamma is completely withdrawing from this sector.   1

IFRS 5 requires that the Gamma group discloses **a single amount** in the statement of profit or loss and other comprehensive income comprising the **post-tax profit or loss** of subsidiary A for the period up to the date of disposal and the **post-tax profit or loss on the disposal of subsidiary A.** This single amount is required to be **analysed in further detail** but this analysis **can be shown in the notes** to the financial statements.   3 (6 × ½ mark)

The post-tax profit or loss of subsidiary A for the year to the date of disposal will be **$4.4 million** ($6.6 million × 8/12). Given that subsidiary A was a **75%** subsidiary, $1.1 million ($4.4 million × 25%) of this amount will be attributed to the **non-controlling interests** in subsidiary A.   1 + ½ + ½

The consolidated post-tax profit on disposal will be $16.9 million (W1).   5½ (W1)

The total amount to be shown as a discontinued operation will be $21.3 million ($4.4 million + $16.9 million).   ½
      ___
      12

Working

1 *Profit on disposal of subsidiary A*

	$'000	
Disposal proceeds	75,000	½
Net assets at date of disposal (62,000 + 6,600 × 8/12 − 3,600)	(62,800)	½ + ½ + ½
Unimpaired goodwill at date of disposal (40,000 + 13,000 − 48,000)	(5,000)	½ + ½ + ½
Non-controlling interest at date of disposal (13,000 + 25% (62,800 − 48,000))	16,700	½ + 1
Tax payable by Gamma on the disposal	(7,000)	½
	16,900	5½

Marks

(ii) **Construction of power plant**

Although Gamma has **no** legal obligation to rectify the environmental damage caused by the construction of the power plant, under the principles of IAS 37 *Provisions, Contingent Liabilities and Contingent Assets* Gamma has a **constructive obligation** to rectify the damage. This is **because**, by its past actions, Gamma has created a valid expectation that it will do so at the end of the power plant's life.

½ + ½ + ½

Under the principles of IAS 37, the provision will be measured at the **present value** of the future expected payment. The amount will be **$4.2 million** ($20 million × 0.21 (W1)).

½ + 1 (W1)

As the date for payment of the liability approaches, the discount unwinds. The unwinding of the discount is shown as a finance cost in the consolidated statement of profit or loss for the year ended 30 September 20X5.

(principle) ½

The relevant finance cost in this case will be for seven months – from the date construction of the asset is complete.

(principle) ½

Therefore the finance cost for the year ended 30 September 20X5 will be $196,000 ($4.2 million × 8% × 7/12 (W1)).

1

The closing provision will be $4,396,000 ($4.2 million + $196,000 (W1)). This will be shown as a non-current liability in the consolidated statement of financial position of Gamma as at 30 September 20X5.

½ (W1) + ½

Under the **principles** of IAS 16 *Property, Plant and Equipment* the initial obligation to rectify the environmental damage will be shown as part of the initial construction cost of the power plant. Therefore the total initial cost will be $34.2 million ($30 million + $4.2 million (W2)).

½ + ½ (W2)

Under the principles of IAS 16, the power plant will be depreciated from the date it is ready for use, which in this case is 28 February 20X5. Therefore the depreciation charge for the year ended 30 September 20X5 will be shown as an expense in the consolidated statement of profit or loss of $997,500 ($34.2 million × 1/20 × 7/12 (W2)).

½ + ½ (W2)

The carrying amount of the power plant at 30 September 20X5 in the consolidated statement of financial position will be $33,202,500 (W2) ($34.2 million – $997,500). This will be shown as a **non-current asset**.

½ + ½ (W2)

9

Workings

1   *Provision*

	$	
PV of provision ($20 million × 0.21)	4,200,000	1
Unwinding of discount ($4.2 million × 8% × 7/12)	196,000	1
Closing provision at 30 September 20X5	4,396,000	½
		2½

2   *Carrying amount of power plant*

	$	
Cost of construction	30,000,000	
Environmental damage provision ($20 million × 0.21)	4,200,000	
	34,200,000	½
Depreciation ($34,200,000 × 1/20 × 7/12)	(997,500)	½
Carrying amount at 30 September 20X5	33,202,500	½
		1½

(b)   The situation that the financial controller has been presented with means that the fundamental principles of **objectivity** (not to compromise professional judgements because of conflict of interest or undue influence) and **professional competence and due care** (acting diligently and in accordance with IFRS Accounting Standards – in this case IAS 37) are under threat.

The discussion with the finance director means that the financial controller faces a **self-interest threat**. This is because the financial controller is due to receive a bonus based on the reported profit for the period. Therefore there is a potential inducement to prepare the financial statements in such a way that reported profit is maximised. Inclusion of an environmental provision would lead to a finance cost and additional depreciation, both of which would depress reported profits.

In addition to a self-interest threat, the financial controller would also face an **intimidation threat**. This is because the financial controller reports to the finance director and would therefore be accustomed to following his directives. It would be difficult to avoid doing this even if these directives were apparently in breach of fundamental ethical principles.

4
―
25

Note. Other relevant points re: the ethics of this situation, sensibly made, will receive credit.

10 Wiltshire

Tutorial note. This question has been included in this Exam Practice Kit because it provides good practice of the topic areas covered, however, the requirements in this question are more detailed than would usually be seen in a DipIFR exam.

Marking guide

	Marks
Factors to consider	3
Indicators of finance lease	2
Calculation of PV	1
Conclusion	1
Identifiable	2
Exclusive use	2
Right to direct use	2
Right to operate	1
Carrying amount ROU asset	2
Liability	2
Sale and leaseback discussion	2
Calculations	5
Total	**25**

(a) **Memorandum**

To: Managing director
From: Finance director
Date: XX.XX.20X2
Subject: Accounting for leases

[References: IFRS 16: paras. 61–84]

(i) **Factors determining type of lease for a lessor – finance or operating**

In deciding whether a particular lease should be classified as a finance or operating lease the substance of the transaction should be considered, rather than its strict legal form. The determining factor is who has the **risks and rewards of ownership**. For a finance lease, the risks and rewards of ownership are transferred to the lessee. For an operating lease, the risks and rewards remain with the lessor.

Finance lease

In deciding whether the lease is a finance lease, IFRS 16 gives examples of situations that individually or in combination would normally lead to a lease being classified as a finance lease:

(1) The lease **transfers ownership** of the underlying asset to the lessee by the end of the lease term;

(2) The lessee has the **option to purchase** the underlying asset at a price expected to be **sufficiently lower than fair value** at the exercise date, that it is reasonably certain, at the inception date, that the option will be exercised;

(3) The lease term is for a **major part of the economic life** of the underlying asset even if title is not transferred;

(4) The present value of the lease payments at the inception date amounts to at least **substantially all** of the fair value of the underlying asset; and

(5) The underlying asset is of such **specialised** nature that only the lessee can use it without major modifications.

(ii) IFRS 16 says that a lessor should classify a lease as a finance lease if substantially all of the risks and rewards of ownership have been transferred to the lessee.

One factor identified by IFRS 16 is whether the present value of the lease payments is equal to substantially all of the fair value of the leased asset.

The lease payments that need to be discounted are:

- The five annual instalments of $20,000 each
- The residual value of $15,000 guaranteed by the lessee

The IFRS requires the lease payments to be discounted using the rate implicit in the lease which is 10%.

Time	Cash flow	Discount factors	Present value
0	20,000	1	20,000
1	20,000	$1/1.1$	18,182
2	20,000	$1/(1.1)^2$	16,529
3	20,000	$1/(1.1)^3$	15,026
4	20,000	$1/(1.1)^4$	13,660
5	15,000	$1/(1.1)^5$	9,314
			92,711

The present value of the lease payments ($92,711) does not exceed the $100,000 fair value of the asset, but is more than 90% of it, and can therefore be considered to be substantially all of the fair value. Consequently, the lease should be classified as a finance lease under the provisions of IFRS 16 since substantially all the risks and rewards of ownership appear to have been transferred.

[References: IFRS 16: paras. 9, B9, 23–32, 99–100]

(b) **Exhibit 1 – Lease of vehicles**

The issue here is whether the arrangement with the private sector provider Waste and Co is, or contains, a lease, even if it does not take the legal form of a lease. The **substance of the arrangement should be considered**. Key factors to consider are as follows.

(i)   Is there an **identifiable asset**?

(ii)   Does the customer have the right to **obtain substantially all the economic benefits** from use of the asset throughout the period of use?

(iii)   Who has the **right to direct how and for what purpose the asset is used**?

(iv)   Does the customer **have the right to operate the asset throughout the period of use** without the supplier having the right to change those operating instructions?

The answer in each case is yes.

(i)   The vehicles which cost Waste & Co $3.8 million are an identifiable asset. Although Waste and Co can substitute another vehicle if one of the existing vehicles needs repairing or no longer works, this substitution right is not substantive because of the significant costs involved in fitting out the vehicle for use by Wiltshire.

(ii)   Wiltshire has exclusive use of the vehicles for the period of use. It therefore has a right to obtain substantially all the economic benefits from the use of the assets.

(iii)   Wiltshire controls the vehicles, since it stipulates how they are painted, and ostensibly owns them because they must be painted with Wiltshire's name. It therefore has the right to direct how and for what purpose the asset is used.

(iv)   As indicated in (ii) above, Wiltshire has the right to operate the asset throughout the period of use, although it has outsourced the driving to Waste and Co.

The arrangement is **a lease**. A **right-of-use asset** should be recorded, and a **lease liability** set up, equal to the present value of the lease payments.

Exhibit 2 – Lease of machinery

Wiltshire controls the use of the machinery and expects to gain economic benefits from its use, this meets the definition of an asset. Wiltshire has an obligation to pay the lease payments in the future, this meets the definition of a liability.

On 1 January 20X1 recognise:

A right-of-use asset of $24.4 million. This is comprised of the $24 million present value of lease payments **not** paid at the 1 January 20X1 commencement date plus the 'initial direct costs' incurred in setting up the lease of $0.4 million.

A lease liability of $24 million. This is the present value of lease payments **not** paid at the commencement date.

On 31 December 20X1 recognise In the statement of profit or loss:

A finance cost of $1.9 million ($24m × 8%).

A depreciation charge of $6.1 million ($24.4/4 years).

The asset is depreciated from the commencement date (1 January 20X1) to the earlier of the end of the asset's useful life (four years) and the end of the lease term (five years).

On 31 December 20X1 recognise In the statement of financial position:

The right of use asset at carrying amount of $18.3 million.

The lease liability in non-current liabilities at $15.5 million and in current liabilities at £4.4 million. (see Working)

Working:

Lease liability

	$m
b/d at 1 January 20X1	24.0
Interest (24 × 8%)	1.9
Instalment in arrears	(6.0)
c/d at 31 December 20X1	19.9
Interest (19.9 × 8%)	1.6
Instalment in arrears	(6.0)
c/d at 31 December 20X2	15.5

The lease liability at 31 December 20X1 is split between current and non-current:

	$m
Non-current liability (owed at 31 December 20X1)	15.5
Current liability (bal. fig.) = instalment (0.441) less finance cost (0.344)	4.4
Total liability at 31 December 20X1	19.9

Exhibit 3 – Sale and leaseback

IFRS 16 requires an initial assessment to be made regarding whether or not the transfer constitutes a sale. This is done by determining when the performance obligation is satisfied in accordance with IFRS 15 *Revenue from Contracts with Customers*. In this case, we are told in the question that the IFRS 15 criteria have been met. IFRS 16 therefore requires that, at the start of the lease, Wiltshire should measure the right-of-use asset arising from the leaseback of the building at the proportion of the previous carrying amount of the building that relates to the right-of-use retained. This is calculated as carrying amount × present value of lease payments/fair value. The present value of lease payments was given in the question as $5 million, which is the lease liability.

On 1 January 20X1 derecognise the building at $3.6 million and recognise:

A right-of-use asset ($3.6m × $5m/$6m = $3m) and a gain of $0.4 million.

Wiltshire only recognises the amount of gain that relates to the rights transferred to the finance company.

The gain on sale of the building is $2,400,000 ($6,000,000 – $3,600,000), of which:

$(2,400,000 × 5,000,000/6,000,000) = $2,000,000 relates to the rights retained.

The balance, $(2,400,000 – 2,000,000) = $400,000, relates to the rights transferred to the buyer.

At 1 January 20X1, Wiltshire should account for the transaction as follows:

	Debit $	Credit $
Cash	6,000,000	
Right-of-use asset	3,000,000	
Building		3,600,000
Financial liability		5,000,000
Gain on rights transferred		400,000
	9,000,000	9,000,000

At 31 December 20X1 Recognise in the statement of profit or loss:

A finance charge of $0.35 million (see working) and a depreciation charge of $0.15 million. The right-of-use asset should be depreciated over the shorter of the useful life of the asset and the lease term. Here these are both 20 years: $3 million ÷ 20 years = $0.15 million.

At 31 December 20X1 Recognise in the statement of financial position:

The right-of -use asset at carrying amount $2.85 million ($3m – 0.15m)

The lease liability in non-current liabilities at $4.812 million and in current liabilities at £0.097 million (see Working).

Working:

Lease liability

	$m
b/d at 1 January 20X1	5.0
Interest (5 × 7%)	0.350
Instalment in arrears	(0.441)
c/d at 31 December 20X1	4.909
Interest (4.909 × 7%)	0.344
Instalment in arrears	(0.441)
c/d at 31 December 20X2	4.812

The lease liability at 31 December 20X1 is split between current and non-current:

	$m
Non-current liability (total owed at 31 December 20X2)	4.812
Current liability (bal. fig.) = instalment (0.441) less finance cost (0.344)	0.097
Total liability at 31 December 20X1	4.909

11 Delta (June 2015) (amended)

Top tips. Exhibit 1 covered sale and leaseback transactions. Because the fair value of the proceeds from the sale were less than the fair value of the asset sold, the shortfall of consideration received from the lessor is treated as a prepayment of lease payments by the lessee. Exhibit 2 financial instruments may have been initially daunting, but this question was actually relatively straightforward. Exhibit 3 covered ethical issues. Ensure you discuss the fundamental ethical principles which are threatened in this scenario.

Examining team's comments. On the whole, candidates found Exhibit 1 of this question challenging. A number of candidates did not identify that the share option was a derivative which needed to be measured at fair value through profit or loss. The majority of candidates realised that the shares that were purchased by the exercising of the option needed to be measured at fair value. However many candidates stated that the measurement basis should have been fair value through other comprehensive income, despite the question making it clear that these shares were part of a trading portfolio. This should have led candidates to conclude that the shares should be measured at fair value through profit or loss. As a result many candidates incorrectly stated that the transaction costs should be included in the initial carrying value of the equity investment, rather than being immediately taken to profit or loss.

	Marks

(a) **Exhibit 1 – Sale and leaseback**

As a sale has occurred, the carrying amount of the hotel asset of $50 million must be derecognised. 1

Per IFRS 16, a right-of-use asset should then be recognised at the **proportion of the previous carrying amount** that relates to the right of use **retained**. This amounts to $8.2 million ($50m carrying amount × $9m present value of lease payments/$55m fair value). 1

As the fair value of $55 million is in excess of the proceeds of $48 million, IFRS 16 requires the excess of $7 million ($55m – $48m) to be treated as a prepayment of the lease rentals. Therefore, the $7 million prepayment must be added to the right-of-use asset, bringing the right-of-use asset to $15.2 million ($8.2m + $7m). 1

A lease liability must also be recorded at the present value of lease payment of $9 million. 1

A gain on sale is recognised in relation to the rights transferred to the buyer-lessor. The total gain would be $5 million ($55m fair value – $50m carrying amount). The portion recognised as a gain relating to the rights transferred is $4.2 million ($5m gain × ($55m – $9m)/$55m portion of fair value transferred). 1 + 1

On 1 April 20X4, the double entry to record the sale is: 1

DEBIT	Cash	$48m
DEBIT	Right-of-use asset	$15.2m
CREDIT	Property asset	$50m
CREDIT	Lease liability	$9m
CREDIT	Gain on sale (P/L)	$4.2m

The lease liability is increased for interest and reduced for the lease liability, giving a carrying amount of the lease liability at 31 March 20X5 of $8.53 million (W1). The interest of $0.53 million is charged to profit or loss as a finance cost. 1

The proportion of the carrying amount of the property relating to the right of use retained of $15.2 million (including the $7m lease prepayment) remains as a right-of-use asset in the statement of financial position and is depreciated over the lease term: 1

DEBIT	P/L ($15.2m/10 years)	$1.52m
CREDIT	Right-of-use asset	$1.52m

This results in a net credit to profit or loss for the year ended 31 April 20X5 of $2.15 million ($4.2m – $0.53m – $1.52m). 1

Working:

Lease liability for the year ending 31 March 20X5

	$m
b/d at 1 April 20X4	9.00
Interest (9 × 5.9%)	0.53
Lease payment	(1.00)
c/d at 31 March 20X5	8.53

1

—
11

Marks

Exhibit 2 – Shares in Epsilon

Under the provisions of IFRS 9 *Financial Instruments* the option to acquire shares in Epsilon would be regarded as a derivative financial instrument.   ½

This is because the value of the option depends on the value of an underlying variable (Epsilon's share price), it requires a relatively small initial investment and it is settled at a future date.   ½

A derivative financial instrument is initially measured at its fair value.   ½

In this case fair value will be the price paid – which is $250,000 at 1 April 20X4.   ½

Derivative financial instruments are remeasured to fair value at the reporting date and gains or losses on remeasurement recognised in the statement of profit or loss.   ½

However, in this case the derivative is derecognised on 31 December 20X4, when the option is exercised.   ½

On 31 December 20X4, the investment in Epsilon's shares would be regarded as a financial asset.   ½

Under IFRS 9, financial assets are initially measured at fair value, so the initial carrying amount of the shares in the accounts of Delta will be $2.6 million (1m × $2.60).   ½

The difference between the carrying amount of the new asset – $2.6m and the price paid plus the derecognised derivative – $2.25 million ($2m + $250,000) will be taken to profit or loss for the year ended 31 March 20X5 as investment income. In this case $350,000 will be included as investment income.   ½ + ½

Because the investment in Epsilon is an equity investment, it will continue to be remeasured to fair value at each year end.   1

Because the investment is part of a trading portfolio, the investment is measured at fair value through profit or loss.   ½

Therefore the acquisition costs of $100,000 must be recognised as an expense in the statement of profit or loss for the year ended 31 March 20X5.   ½

The investment is included in the statement of financial position at 31 March 20X5 as a current asset at its fair value of $2.9 million.   ½ + ½

The increase in fair value of $300,000 ($2.9m – $2.6m) is taken to the statement of profit or loss.   ½ + ½
____
9

(b) **Exhibit 3 – Ethical issue**

The finance assistant is at risk of breaching the fundamental ethical principle of objectivity. This is due to the clear self-interest threat that arises as the finance assistant is keen to impress the finance director in order to gain a promotion and may therefore comply with the finance director's request even though it would be contrary to IFRS 5.   1

IFRS 5 requires that assets held for sale are carried at the lower of their carrying amount and fair value less costs to sell. The finance director's instruction to re-classify the property as a non-current asset at its previous carrying amount ignores the requirements of IFRS 5 and is therefore wrong. If the finance assistant complies with the finance director's request, she will be breaching the fundamental principle of professional behaviour by not complying with relevant IFRS Accounting Standards.   1 + 1

	Marks

The finance director's comment that he 'likes to work with people he can trust to carry out his instructions without complaint' further threatens the finance assistant's objectivity. The finance assistant may be deterred from acting objectively because she feels intimidated or pressurised by the finance director to comply with his request. — 1

The finance assistant's integrity is under threat because she is being asked to agree to an accounting treatment which she knows is incorrect. If she agrees, then she is being dishonest. — 1
5

12 Gamma (June 2019)

Marking scheme

	Marks

(a) **Exhibit 1 – Sale and leaseback**

Because the sale of the building by Gamma satisfies the requirements in IFRS 15 Revenue from Contracts with Customers Gamma will de-recognise the building on 1 April 20X6. — 1

Gamma will recognise a 'right of use asset' on 1 April 20X6. — 1

The right of use asset will be measured as a percentage of the previous carrying amount of $1 million which relates to the right of use retained by Gamma. This percentage is 25.27% ($379,100/$1.5 million).

This means that the carrying amount of the right of use asset will be $252,700 ($1 million × 25.27%). — 2

The gain on sale of property to be recognised in Gamma's statement of profit or loss is restricted to the rights transferred to entity A. The total gain is $500,000 ($1.5m – $1m). The percentage of this gain to be recognised is 74.73% (100% – 25.27%). This means that the gain which will be recognised will be $373,650 ($500,000 × 74.73%). — 2

The right of use asset will be depreciated over the shorter of the useful life to Gamma and the lease term, which here are both five years. Therefore depreciation of $50,540 ($252,700 × 1/5) will be charged in the statement of profit or loss. — 2

The statement of financial position at 31 March 20X7 will show a right of use asset of $202,160 ($252,700 – $50,540) under non-current assets. — 1

Gamma will show a finance cost of $37,910 ($379,100 × 10%) in the statement of profit or loss for the year ended 31 March 20X7. — 1

The closing lease liability will be $317,010 ($379,100 + $37,910 – $100,000). — 1

The amount of the overall liability which is current will be $68,299 ($100,000 – ($317,010 × 10%)).

The balance of the liability of $248,711 ($317,010 – $68,299) will be non-current. — 1
12

Tutorial note: *The amount of the gain on sale which is recognised by Gamma could alternatively be computed as follows:*

$$\text{The total gain} \times \frac{(\text{The fair value of the asset} - \text{the lease liability})}{\text{The fair value of the asset}}$$

Marks

In this case this would give:

$500,000 × (($1,500,000 − $379,100)/$1,500,000) = $373,633 (difference to above $373,650 due solely to rounding))

Candidates who adopt an approach of this nature will receive full credit.

(b) **Exhibit 2 – Investment property**

IAS 40 *Investment Property* allows two methods for valuing investment property: the

fair value model and the cost model. If the fair value model is adopted, then the investment property must be valued in accordance with IFRS 13 *Fair Value Measurement.* 1

Fair value is the price that would be received to sell an asset or paid to transfer a liability in an orderly transaction between market participants at the measurement date. 1

Fair value is a market-based measurement rather than specific to the entity, so a company is not allowed to choose its own way of measuring fair value. 1

Valuation techniques must be those which are appropriate and for which sufficient data is available. Entities should maximise the use of relevant observable inputs and minimise the use of unobservable inputs. 1

IFRS 13 establishes a hierarchy for the inputs that valuation techniques use to measure fair value: 1

Level 1 – Quoted prices (unadjusted) in active markets for identical assets or liabilities

Level 2 – Inputs other than quoted prices included within Level 1 that are observable for the asset or liability, either directly or indirectly

Level 3 – Unobservable inputs for the asset or liability

Although the directors claim that 'new-build value less obsolescence' is accepted by the industry, it may not be in accordance with IFRS 13. 1

As investment property is often unique and not traded on a regular basis, fair value measurements are likely to be categorised as Level 2 or Level 3 valuations. 1

IFRS 13 mentions three valuation techniques: the market approach, the income approach and the cost approach. A market or income approach would usually be more appropriate for an investment property than a cost approach. The 'new-build value less obsolescence' (cost approach) does not take account of the Level 2 inputs such as sales value (market approach) and market rent (income approach). Nor does it take account of reliable estimates of future discounted cash flows, or values of similar properties. 2

In conclusion, Gamma must apply IFRS 13 to the valuation of its investment property, taking account of Level 2 inputs. 1

10

(c) **Exhibit 3 – Share options**

The cumulative amount recognised at 31 March 20X7 is 500 × 200 × $1.20 × 2/3 = $80,000. This is shown in the statement of financial position as part of equity. 1

The cumulative amount recognised at 31 March 20X6 is 500 × 150 × $1.20 × 1/3 = $30,000. 1

Therefore the amount recognised in the SPLOCI for the year is $50,000 ($80,000 − $30,000). 1

3

25

13 Gamma (December 2019)

	Marks

Exhibit 1 – Purchase of equity shares in a key supplier

Under the principles of IFRS 9 *Financial Instruments* equity investments must be measured at fair value because the contractual terms associated with the investment do not entitle the holder to specific payment of interest and principal (sense of the point only needed).   1

The fair value of the investment in entity A at the date of purchase is $480,000 (200,000 × $2.40).   ½

The amount actually paid for the shares (incorporating broker's fee) in entity A on 1 October 20X6 was $489,600 (480,000 × 1.02).   ½

The difference between the price paid for the shares and their fair value is $9,600 ($489,600 – $480,000). This difference is regarded as a transaction cost by IFRS 13 *Fair Value Measurement*.   1

IFRS 9 would normally require equity investments to be measured at fair value through profit or loss.   1

Where financial assets are measured at fair value through profit or loss, transaction costs are recognised in profit or loss as incurred. Therefore in this case, $9,600 would be taken to profit or loss on 1 October 20X6.   1

Under the principles of IFRS 13, the fair value of an asset is the amount which could be received to sell the asset in an orderly transaction. Where the asset is traded in an active market (as is the case for the investment in entity A), then fair value should be determined with reference to prices quoted in that market.   1

Therefore the fair value of the investment in entity A at the year end is $540,000 (200,000 × $2.70).   1

The year-end fair value of $540,000 is unaffected by the broker's fees which would be incurred if the shares were to be sold – these fees are not a component of fair value measurement.   ½

The change in fair value of $60,000 ($540,000 – $480,000) between 1 October 20X6 and 30 September 20X7 would be taken to profit or loss at the end of the reporting period.   1

The dividend received of $50,000 (200,000 × 25 cents) would be recognised as other income in profit or loss at 31 March 20X7.   1

Because the shares in entity A are not held for trading, Gamma has the option to make an irrevocable election on 1 October 20X6 to measure the shares at fair value through other comprehensive income.   1

Were this election to be made, then the transaction cost would be included in the initial carrying amount of the financial asset, making this $489,600.   1

The difference between the closing fair value of the investment and its initial carrying amount is $50,400 ($540,000 – $489,600). This is recognised in other comprehensive income.   1

The dividend income of $50,000 is still recognised in profit or loss regardless of how the financial asset is measured.   ½
   ——
   13
   ——

Marks

Exhibit 2 – Joint manufacture of a product with entity B

Under the principles of IFRS 11 *Joint Arrangements* the agreement with entity B is a joint arrangement. This is because key decisions, eg pricing and selling decisions, manufacturing specifications, require the consent of both parties and so joint control is present.   2

IFRS 11 would regard the type of arrangement with entity B as a joint operation. This is because the two parties have rights to specific assets and liabilities relating to the arrangement and no specific entity has been established.   2

Because of the type of joint arrangement, each entity will recognise specific assets and liabilities relating to the arrangement (exact wording not necessary – just sense of the point).   1

This means that Gamma will recognise revenues of $11 million ($22m × 50%).   1

Gamma will recognise bad debt expense of $50,000 ($100,000 × 50%).   1

Gamma's trade receivables at 30 September 20X7 will be $2.5 million ($5m × 50%).   1

Gamma will show a payable to entity B of $750,000 ($1.5m × 50%) 30 September 20X7.   1

Gamma's inventories at 30 September 20X7 will be $1.7 million ($3.8m – $2.1m).   1½

Gamma's cost of sales will be $5.3 million ($7m – $1.7m).   1½

                                                                                                12

                                                                                                25

14 Omega (September 2020)

Top tips. This question asked you to answer three questions from a director of a listed company. The topics covered were leasing (IFRS 16), segment reporting (IFRS 8) and related party transactions (IAS 24). As with all questions in the DipIFR exam, there were 25 marks available, which translates to roughly 49 minutes. You should split this time between the three questions according to the marks available for each: so approximately 21 minutes for question 1 (11 marks × 1.95 minutes per mark), 16 minutes for question 2 and 11 minutes for question 3. Make sure you move on from each question at the end of the time allocated so that you can make a good attempt at each. A good approach to tackling each question is to state the relevant principle(s) from the IFRS Accounting Standard and then explain how this applies to the issue you are dealing with.

Examining team's comments.

The examiner's report identified some common errors and themes, which included the following:

- For question 1, 'Despite the fact that the question stated no numerical workings were required a number of candidates computed the finance cost on the lease liability and attempted to split the closing liability into its current and non-current components. All that was required in this case was an explanation of these features.'

- For question 2, 'Some candidates spent too much time in question 2 focussing on the definition of an operating segment. There were 3 marks available for this but in some cases candidates did not move on to discuss the implications for the segmental disclosures that are required and the reason they could differ from entity to entity.'

- 'Answers to question 3 were generally good and there are no common errors to report.' (Examiner's report – September 2020)

Marks

Exhibit 1 – Right-of-use asset

IFRS 16 *Leases* requires a lessee to recognise a right-of-use asset in all circumstances other than for very short leases (of one year or less) or for low value assets. A warehouse lease for five years is neither of these, so recognition of a non-current asset will be required in our financial statements.

2

The initial carrying amount of the right-of-use asset comprises the present value of the lease payments plus any direct costs we incurred in arranging the lease.

1 (principle)

In this case, therefore, the initial carrying amount at 1 October 20X4 will be $2 million ($1,895,000 + $105,000).

1

The right-of-use asset is included as a separate component of property, plant and equipment and depreciated over the shorter of the lease term and its useful life.

1 (principle)

The depreciation of the asset for the year ended 31 March 20X5 will be $200,000 ($2m $\times$ 1/5 $\times$ 6/12).

1

Therefore the carrying amount of the right-of-use asset at 31 March 20X5 will be $1,800,000 ($2m – $200,000).

1

When the right-of-use asset is recognised, a lease liability is also recognised. It is initially measured at the present value of the lease payments – $1,895,000 in this case.

1 (principle)

The liability will be increased by a finance cost. This cost is based on the carrying amount of the liability and the rate of interest implicit in the lease.

1 (principle)

The finance cost will be charged as an expense in the statement of profit or loss.

½ (principle)

When the lease rentals are paid, they will be treated as a repayment of the lease liability.

½ (principle)

Since a lease rental is due for payment six months after the year end, $500,000 of the lease liability will be treated as a current liability. The balance will be non-current.

1 (principle)
_____
11

Exhibit 2 – Segment reporting

IFRS 8 *Operating Segments* requires entities to which it applies to provide a segment report based on its operating segments.

1 (principle)

An operating segment is a **business component** for which **discrete financial information is available** and whose operating results are regularly reviewed by the **chief operating decision maker** (exact words not needed).

3

The chief operating decision maker is the person (or persons) who assesses performance and allocates resources (exact words not needed).

1

Omega assesses performance and allocates resources on a geographical basis whereas our competitor more than likely does this on a 'product type' basis (mark for coming to a logical conclusion).

1

Notwithstanding the above, IFRS 8 normally requires **all** entities to give details of revenues by geographical area and by product type and non-current assets by geographical area.

1 (principle)

However, the above is not required if the information could only be made available at a prohibitive cost. This may explain the discrepancy between the segment reports.

1
___
8

  BPP
LEARNING
MEDIA

Marks

Exhibit 3 – Immaterial transactions

Under the principles of IAS 24 *Related Party Disclosures* your brother's firm is a related party of Omega.

1 (principle)

This is because the firm is controlled by the close family member (your brother) of a member of the key management personnel of Omega (yourself).

2

IAS 24 requires that the existence of all related party relationships be disclosed together with details of any transactions and outstanding balances (exact words not needed).

2

IAS 24 regards related party relationships as material by their nature so the fact that the transaction is financially insignificant and ordinary to Omega is not relevant in terms of requiring the disclosure.

1 (principle)
<u>6</u>
<u>25</u>

15 Omega (December 2021)

Top tips. This question was a standard Question 4 in that it presented several queries from a director which you were required to answer. You must make sure you answer the queries presented, and not regurgitate all your knowledge on the topic raised. While there are marks available for stating relevant parts of the relevant IFRS Accounting Standard, no credit will be given for providing narrative which is not relevant to the director's query, even if that narrative is technically correct.

Query 1 in this question concerned the *Conceptual Framework*. This was very straightforward knowledge if you had revised this area. Although it is not examined often, the *Conceptual Framework* is the fundamental basis of IFRS Accounting Standards. As such it is worth your time to understand its role and purpose, and to understand the key principles it establishes, such as the definitions of the elements of the financial statements (assets, liabilities, equity, income and expenditure) and the qualitative characteristics of useful information.

Examining team comments.

The examining team report commented that, as in previous sittings, many candidates presented very short answers to this question, indicating poor time management. It is important that you work out how many minutes you should be spending on each question, and on each part of each question and then stick to that when preparing your answers. For this question, you should split this time as approximately 15 minutes on Exhibit 1, 21 minutes on Exhibit 2 and 11 minutes on Exhibit 3.

Marking guide

Marks

Conceptual Framework

The *Conceptual Framework* (Framework) is a document which sets out the **objectives** and **concepts** for general purpose financial reporting. The *Framework* provides the foundations for the International Financial Reporting Standards (IFRS Accounting Standards) but it is not a standard itself.

1 + ½

These concepts are set out in a number of **distinct chapters** in the document. These chapters address issues **such as** the overall objective of general purpose financial reporting which is to provide financial information which is useful to existing and potential investors, lenders and other creditors.

A further chapter details the qualitative characteristics of useful financial information. **(Other examples of chapter titles up to 1 mark would be acceptable – the question makes clear that only a general overview is needed.)** ½ + 1

A key purpose of the Framework is to **assist the International Accounting Standards Board (the Board) in developing** and revising individual IFRS Accounting Standards which are based on consistent concepts. Therefore the **concepts underpinning any specific Accounting Standard should generally be consistent** with those outlined in the *Framework*. ½ + ½

The *Framework* does not override the provisions of any specific IFRS Accounting Standards. In the rare circumstances that the Board decided to issue a new or revised standard which is in conflict with the *Framework*, the Board would highlight the fact and explain the reasons for the departure in the Basis for Conclusions to the standard. (up to) 2

A further purpose of the Framework is to help preparers to develop consistent accounting policies for areas which are not covered by a IFRS Accounting Standard (eg cryptocurrency) or where there is choice of accounting policy, and to assist all parties to understand and interpret IFRS Accounting Standards. 1 + 1

8

Brand names

A brand name is an intangible asset and so the recognition and measurement requirements are to be found in IAS 38 *Intangible Assets*. ½

IAS 38 states that the recognition of brand names (and other intangible assets) in the statement of financial position depends on **how they arose**. Brand names which are **purchased** can be recognised as assets. ½ + ½

Where a brand name is purchased in an individual transaction, then the brand name can be recognised at its original purchase cost. 1

When a parent company acquires a subsidiary company, the purchase consideration needs to be allocated to the individual assets and liabilities which are to be included in the consolidated statement of financial position. Any amount of the consideration which cannot be allocated is presented as goodwill on acquisition. (overall principle, however worded) 1

Marks

A brand name acquired as part of the acquisition of a subsidiary can be recognised as an asset in the consolidated financial statements if it is **identifiable**. This **means** that the asset is either capable of being sold separately or arises from contractual or other legal rights, regardless of whether or not these rights are transferable. This is **even if** it is not recognised in the individual financial statements of the subsidiary. (sense of the point) ½ + 1 + ½

Where a brand name associated with the acquisition of a subsidiary is regarded as identifiable, then it is initially recognised at its **fair value at the date of acquisition**. ½

The brand name associated with Omega itself (the parent company) is an internally developed intangible asset from the perspective of Omega. (principle) ½

Unless internally developed intangibles relate to the cost of developing a specific product or process, they cannot be recognised as assets because their 'cost' cannot be established reliably. This explains why brand names associated with acquired subsidiaries can be recognised in the consolidated financial statements but the Omega brand name cannot. (sense of the point) 1 + (conclusion) ½

Brand names which are recognised should be included as intangible assets and written off (amortised) over their estimated useful lives. 1

Where the useful lives of brand names are assessed as being **indefinite**, then **no** amortisation charge is necessary but the brand name needs to be reviewed for possible impairment at the end of **every** financial reporting period, **irrespective** of whether or not indicators of impairment are present.

½ + ½ + ½ + ½

11

Segment reports

The issue of segmental disclosures is addressed in IFRS 8 *Operating Segments*. IFRS 8 requires that segmental disclosures are made with reference to key operating segments of the business. (overall sense of the point)

1

IFRS 8 says that an operating segment is one which **earns revenues** and incurs expenses, whose results are regularly reviewed by the **chief operating decision maker** and for which **discrete financial information** is available.

½ + ½ + ½

The term 'chief operating decision maker' is a role, not a manager with a specific title. The function is to assess performance and allocate resources. This role is often undertaken by the chief executive officer but there could be circumstances where the role is undertaken by a group of directors.

The segments which are reported are identified because:

(1)   They exceed quantitative thresholds set out in IFRS 8; and

(2)   It will allow users of the financial statements to evaluate the nature of the business activities and the economic environment in which it operates (nature of the products, the production processes, type of customer, distribution methods, regulatory environment).

2

Given that different entities could organise themselves in different ways, the operating segments which are identified and reported could theoretically differ between apparently similar entities.

(conclusion) ½

IFRS 8 only applies to listed entities, so a large unlisted family business would not be required to given segmental disclosures.

1

6

25

16 Delta (December 2022)

Top tips. This question required candidates to explain and show the financial reporting treatment of three issues, namely the purchase of a brand and inventory of an insolvent trader, the provision of interest free loans to employees and a project seeking ways of improving the company's manufacturing process.

The examiners often state that explanations are insufficient, so it is important that you keep practising your explanations, focusing on relevant parts of standards and ensuring that you answer in sufficient detail to gain marks. There did seem to be evidence of candidates doing this more effectively in this question than in previous sittings.

It is also important that you read the scenario carefully and really think about what the relevant standards could be – in this question some candidates did misinterpret the scenario and use the wrong accounting rules to explain the treatment.

Examining team comments.

The examining team report reiterated the importance of providing full explanations, which had seen an improvement in answers to this question. It was noted however that some candidates just provided journals, which on their own will score few marks.

(a)   **Exhibit 1 – Purchase of assets**

IAS 38 *Intangible Assets* states that intangible assets can only be recognised if it is probable that economic benefits attributable to the asset will flow to the entity and the cost of the asset can be measured reliably (principle). **1 mark**

In the case of the purchase of the brand name, both of these conditions are satisfied (conclusion). **0.5 mark**

IAS 38 states that intangible assets should be amortised **over their useful lives** where the useful life is considered to be **finite** (principle). **0.5 mark**

Where the useful life of an intangible asset is considered to be indefinite, then the asset should not be amortised and the useful life would be reviewed annually. **0.5 mark** Additionally, the brand should be reviewed annually for impairment, regardless of whether indicators of impairment are present (principle). **0.5 mark**

Based on the information provided, it would appear that **no impairment 0.5 mark** is necessary and the asset can be shown at a carrying amount of **$60 million**. $60 million would be shown as a **non-current asset**. **0.5 mark**

$18 million would be recognised in **revenue** for the inventories sold during the year ended 30 September 20X5. **1 mark**

In the same period, **$15 million** ($20 million × 75%) would be recognised in **cost of sales**. Both the $18 million and the $15 million would be included in the statement of **profit or loss** for the year ended 30 September 20X5. **1 mark**

Under the principles of **IAS 10** *Events After the Reporting Date* the post year-end date sale of goods held in inventory at the year end is an **adjusting event. 1 mark**

The goods held in inventory have a cost of **$5 million** ($20 million – $15 million) but were sold for $4.5 million. $4.5 million is therefore their **net realisable value. 1 mark**

Under the principles of IAS 2, inventories are measured at the **lower of cost and net realisable value**. Therefore inventories of **$4.5 million** would be recognised as a **current asset. 0.5 mark**

The required write down of **$0.5 million** ($5 million – $4.5 million) would be recognised in the statement of **profit or loss** for the year ended 30 September 20X5. **0.5 mark**

Exhibit 2 – Interest free loans to employees

Under the principles of IFRS 9 *Financial Instruments* the loans are a **financial asset** of Delta. IFRS 9 states that financial assets should initially be recognised at fair value in the financial statements **(principle).** **0.5 mark**

In this case, the initially recognised amount will be $10 million [$12.10/(1.10)2]. **0.5 mark**

The difference of $2.1 million between the amount lent and the financial asset will be regarded as an employee benefit under IAS 19 *Employee Benefits*, and recognised as an expense over the two-year period from 1 October 20X4 to 30 September 20X6 (principle). **1 mark**

Therefore, in the year ended 30 September 20X5, an employment expense of **$1.05 million** (2.10/2) would be recognised in the statement of **profit or loss. 1 mark**

The residual difference of **$1.05 million** ($2.1 million – $1.05 million) would be recognised as a deferred employee compensation **prepayment 1 mark** in the statement of financial position at 30 September 20X5. The prepayment will be shown as a **current asset. 0.5 mark**

Since the cash flows expected from the loan asset are known in terms of their timing and amount and Delta expects to retain the asset and collect the cash flows as they fall due, the loan asset can be measured at amortised cost from 1 October 20X4 (principle – up to). **1 mark**

BPP
LEARNING
MEDIA

This means that Delta will recognise finance income **0.5 mark** of **$1 million** ($10 million × 10%) in its statement of **profit or loss** for the year ended 30 September 20X5. **0.5 mark**

The loan asset at 30 September 20X5 will be **$11 million** ($10 million + $1 million). This will be shown as a **current asset** in the statement of financial position of Delta. **0.5 mark**

Tutorial note. Candidates who recognise the employment cost on an 'amortised cost' basis, ie $1 million ($10 million × 10%) in the year ended 30 September 20X5 and $1.1 million ($11 million × 10%) in the year ended 30 September 20X6 will receive full credit.

(b)   **Exhibit 3 – Manufacturing process**

IAS 38 does not allow any expenditure on a research and development project to be recognised as an asset until the technical feasibility and commercial viability of the project has been established (principle). **1 mark**

After the technical feasibility and commercial viability of the project has been established, expenditure which has previously been shown as an expense in profit or loss cannot be restated as an intangible asset (principle). **1 mark**

This means that, for the year ended 30 September 20X4, the on-going project costs of **$9 million** (9 × $1 million) will have been expensed in the statement of **profit or loss** and the further **$3 million** from 1 October to 31 December 20X4 will be expensed in the profit or loss for the year ending 30 September 20X5. **1 mark**

Under the principles of IAS 16 *Property, Plant and Equipment* (PPE) the machinery purchased on 1 January 20X4 will be regarded as PPE and depreciated over its useful life of 18 months (from 1 January 20X4 to 30 June 20X5). **0.5 mark**

The depreciable amount will be its cost less its estimated residual value **(principle)**. In this case, the depreciable amount is **$13.5 million** ($15 million – $1.5 million). Therefore the monthly depreciation will be **$750,000** ($13.5 million/18). **0.5 mark**

The depreciation of **$6.75 million** (9 × $750,000) for the nine months from 1 January 20X4 to 30 September 20X4 and $2.25 million (3 × $750,000) for the three months from 1 October to 20X4 to 31 December 20X4 will be shown as an **expense** in the statements of profit or loss for 20X4 and 20X5 respectively. **1 mark**

From 1 January 20X5, ongoing expenditure on the project will be able to be recognised as an intangible asset by Delta. This applies to both the on-going project costs and the depreciation of the machinery exclusively used on the project (principle). **1 mark**

Therefore at 30 June 20X5 (the date the project is concluded), the intangible asset will be $16.5 million (6 × $2 million + 6 × $750,000).

IAS 38 requires that intangible assets with finite useful lives be amortised over those lives (principle already rewarded). Amortisation starts from the date the asset is **available for use**, rather than the date it is actually brought into use. In this case, that date is **30 June 20X5. 1 mark**

Therefore amortisation for the year ended 30 September 20X5 will be **$825,000** ($16.5 million × 1/5 × 3/12). **0.5 mark**

The closing carrying amount of the intangible asset will be **$15,675,000** ($16.5 million – $825,000). This will be shown as a **non-current asset** in the statement of financial position of Delta at 30 September 20X5. **0.5 mark**

On 30 June 20X5, the carrying amount of the machinery will be **$1.5 million**. **No further deprecation will be charged** because the machinery is being advertised for sale from that date. **0.5 mark**

A profit on sale of the machinery of **$300,000** ($1.8 million – $1.5 million) will be shown in the statement of **profit or loss** of Delta for the year ended 30 September 20X5. **0.5 mark**

17 Worldwide Fuels

Marking guide

	Marks
Link to CF	3
Creative accounting	3
Obligation	1
User expectations	1
IAS 37 criteria	2
Constructive obligation	2
Future operating losses	2
Decommissioning estimate	2
Link to IAS 16	1
Discounting	4
Legal case	4
Total	**25**

[References: Conceptual Framework: para. 4.26; IAS 16: para. 16; IAS 37: paras. 10, 14, 63–65]

(a)   (i)   Need for guidance on accounting for provisions

Liabilities are 'present obligations of the entity to transfer an economic resource as a result of past events' Provisions are liabilities of uncertain timing or amount, for which the future outflow is probable.

If outcomes are uncertain, then it follows that identifying provisions is very subjective, and so guidance is needed to ensure that financial statements are comparable through time and between entities.

In particular the IASB wishes to **prevent companies providing for future operating losses**, or for any future outflow for which there was either no current obligation, or from which there were likely to be future benefits.

Provisions can be difficult to identify and quantify, reclassification or amendment is common with the passage of time and clarification of events.

Provisions may enable "creative accounting" moving expenses and income between different accounting periods. Once a provision has been set up, it becomes possible to charge expenses directly to it and so bypass the statement of profit or loss. Companies may have engaged in **creative accounting devices** by setting up **large provisions** and subsequently releasing them back to the statement of profit or loss; provisions then became '**income smoothing**' devices.

There is concern over the ways in which provisions have been recognised. In many cases provisions have been **set up where there is no obligation** and in **other cases** companies have **failed to set up provisions where obligations do exist**. So there is scope for income and profit smoothing and **inconsistent reporting between companies**.

The standard should ensure that provisions are recognised and measured on a consistent basis and that sufficient disclosure occurs of the details of the provision to understand its nature, timing and amount.

(ii) **Criteria for recognising provisions**

Under IAS 37, provisions must be recognised in the following circumstances.

(1) There is a **legal** or **constructive obligation** to transfer benefits as a result of past events.

(2) It is probable an outflow of economic resources will be required to settle the obligation.

(3) A reasonable estimate of the amount required to settle the obligation can be made.

(4) If a company can avoid expenditure by its future action, no provision should be recognised.

Constructive obligations emerge when an entity is committed to certain expenditures because of a pattern of behaviour which the public at large would expect to continue. Any alternative course of action which would conceal the constructive obligation could be very onerous. (An example would be a practice of giving customer refunds to preserve goodwill, where there is no legal obligation to do so.)

A constructive obligation for restructuring only exists when the criteria in IAS 37 are satisfied.

If an entity has an onerous contract, the present obligation should be recognised and measured.

No provisions for future operating losses should be recognised.

IAS 37 therefore takes a **statement of financial position perspective** of provisions. It ensures that all **liabilities** are recognised when they are incurred, rather than recognising expenses in the statement of profit or loss only when their payment is certain, or they are actually paid

(b) **Exhibit 1 – Decommissioning**

IAS 37 requires a provision to be the **best estimate** of the expenditure required to **settle** the **obligation** at the **end of the reporting period**. The provision should be capitalised as an **asset** if the expenditure provides access to **future economic benefits**; **otherwise** it should be immediately charged to the **statement of profit or loss**.

IAS 16 *Property, Plant and Equipment* caters for debits set up when assets are created as a result of provisions. Such assets are **written off over** the **life** of the facility and **normal impairment rules** will apply. The additional decommissioning costs of $1,231 million (undiscounted) not yet provided for will be included as a provision (at the discounted amount) in the statement of financial position and a corresponding asset created.

IAS 37 suggests the discount rate should be a pre-tax rate reflecting current market assessments of the time value of money and risks. The **discount rate** should **not reflect risks** which have been **included by adjusting future cash flows**.

The company has also charged the present value of the change in decommissioning techniques of $27 million to reserves in the year. Such a change in the estimated amount of the provision should be capitalised as an asset and depreciated rather than being charged to reserves.

The company also makes reserve adjustments for changes in price levels. This adjustment comprises two elements chargeable to the statement of profit or loss, not reserves:

(i) **Adjustments** to the provision caused by changes in **discount rates**

(ii) An **interest element** representing the **'unwinding' of the discount**, which should be classified as part of interest expenses in the statement of profit or loss

Exhibit 2 – Legal case

The potential payment of damages to the employee is an **obligation arising out of a past event** which can be reliably estimated. Therefore, following IAS 37 *Provisions, Contingent Liabilities and Contingent Assets* a provision is required.

The provision should be for the **best estimate** of the expenditure required to settle the obligation at 30 November 20X9.

Under the principles of IAS 10 *Events After the Reporting Period* evidence of the settlement amount is an adjusting event.

Therefore at 30 November 20X9 a provision of **$18 million** should be recognised as a **current liability** and as an expense in the statement of profit or loss.

18 Delta (June 2012) (amended)

> **Top tips.** This question presented you with four issues, covering different syllabus topics, and so is a good practice question. Remember to show your workings clearly and to give explanations.
>
> In Exhibit 1 the provision for restoration at the end of its useful life should be capitalised, but note that the provision damage already caused by the end of the reporting period should be charged to profit or loss. In Exhibit 2 the cost is measured using the fair value of the options at the grant date.
>
> Exhibit 4 included ethical issues. Ensure you cover discuss the fundamental ethical principles in your answer.

Marking guide

			Marks
(a)		Minerals explanation	3
		Minerals calculations	6
		SBPs explanation	3
		SBPs calculations	2
		IAS 37 explanation	3
(b)	(i)	Accounting issues	3
	(ii)	Ethical issues	5
		Total	**25**

Marking scheme

	Marks

(a)   **Exhibit 1**

Under the principles of IAS 16 *Property, Plant and Equipment* costs of $13.5 million ($10m + $3.5m) will be debited to property, plant and equipment in respect of the cost of acquiring the extraction facility.   ½

The costs of erecting the extraction facility (excluding the land) will be depreciated over a ten-year period, giving a charge in the current period of $175,000 ($3.5m × 1/10 × 6/12).   1

From 1 October 20X1, an obligation exists to rectify the damage caused by the erection of the extraction facility and this obligation should be provided for.   ½

The amount provided is the present value of the expected future payment, which is $966,000 ($3m × 0.322).   1

The amount provided is debited to property, plant and equipment and credited to provisions in non-current liabilities at 1 October 20X1.   ½

The debit to property, plant and equipment creates additional depreciation of $48,300 in the current year ($966,000 × 1/10 × 6/12).   1

At 31 March 20X2 the carrying amount of property, plant and equipment is $14,242,700 ($13.5m − $175,000 + $966,000 − $48,300).   ½

As the date of settlement of the liability draws closer the discount unwinds.   ½

The unwinding of the discount in the current year is $57,960 ($966,000 × 12% × 6/12). This increases the provision in the statement of financial position and finance costs in the statement of profit and loss.   1

The extraction process itself creates an additional liability based on the damage caused **by the end of the reporting period.**   ½

	Marks
The additional amount provided is $34,100 ($200,000 × 6/12 × 0.341).	1
This additional provision causes an extra charge to the statement of profit or loss and other comprehensive income.	½
The carrying amount of the provision at the year end is $1,058,060 ($966,000 + $57,960 + $34,100).	½
	9

Exhibit 2

Under the principles of IFRS 2 *Share-based Payment* this arrangement will be regarded as an equity settled share based payment.   ½

The fair value of the equity settled share based payment will be credited to equity and debited to expenses (or occasionally included in the carrying amount of another asset) over the vesting period.   1

Where the transaction is with employees, fair value is measured as the market value of the equity instrument at the grant date.   ½

The vesting condition relating to the number of executives who remain with Delta is a non-market condition so it is taken into account when estimating the number of options that will vest.   ½

The vesting condition relating to the share price is a market condition so it is taken into account when measuring the fair value of an option at grant date.   ½

Therefore the total estimated fair value of the share based payment is $1,545,600 (92 × 20,000 × $0.84).   1

1/3 of this amount ($515,200) is recognised in the year ended 31 March 20X2.   ½

$515,200 is credited to equity and debited to expenses (or occasionally included in the carrying amount of another asset).   ½

5

Exhibit 3

Under the principles of IAS 37 *Provisions, Contingent Liabilities and Contingent Assets* a provision should be made for the probable damages payable to the customer.   ½

The amount provided should be the amount Delta is most likely to pay to settle the obligation at the end of the reporting period. Ignoring discounting, this is $1 million.   ½

This amount should be credited to liabilities and debited to profit or loss.   ½

Under the principles of IAS 37 the potential amount receivable from the supplier is a contingent asset because its receipt is probable but not virtually certain.   ½

Contingent assets should not be recognised but should be disclosed where there is a probable future receipt of economic benefits – this is the case for the $800,000 potentially receivable from the supplier.   1

3

				Marks

(b)   (i)   **Accounting issue**

The arrangement meets the IFRS 16 criteria for a lease in that there is an identifiable asset and the contract conveys the right to control the use of that asset for a period of time in exchange for consideration.   1

Delta must recognise a right-of-use asset representing its right to use the property and a lease liability representing its obligation to make lease payments. At the commencement date, Delta should recognise the right-of-use asset at the present value of future lease payments, plus initial direct costs plus any lease payments paid on or before commencement of the lease.   1

Delta must initially recognise the liability at the present value of the future lease payments including any payments expected at the end of the lease discounted using the rate implicit in the lease. $\frac{1}{3}$

(ii)   **Ethical issue**

As the financial controller's future position at Delta has been threatened if the managing director's proposed accounting treatment is not adopted, there has been an intimidation threat to the fundamental ethical principles of objectivity and integrity.   1 + 1

Furthermore, as the managing director has flagged the risk that Delta may not secure its future loan finance if the lease is recognised in the statement of financial position, there is an advocacy threat because the financial controller may feel compelled to follow an incorrect accounting treatment to maximise the company's chance of obtaining the loan. The pressure will be greater because the financial controller is new.   1 + 1

When preparing the financial statements, the financial controller should adhere to the fundamental principle of professional behaviour which requires preparing accounts that comply with accounting regulation, eg IFRS Accounting Standards. If the financial controller were to accept the managing director's proposed treatment, this would contravene IFRS 16 and so would be a breach of the fundamental principle of professional behaviour. $\frac{1}{5}$

$\overline{\underline{25}}$

19 Epsilon (December 2019) (amended)

Marking scheme

    Marks

Exhibit 1 – Inconsistencies

It is possible for two sets of financial statement to comply with IFRS Accounting Standards and yet be inconsistent with each other. Some individual IFRS Accounting Standards allow a choice of accounting treatment and some IFRS Accounting Standards are only compulsory for listed entities like Epsilon.   2

Both IFRS 8 *Operating Segments* and IAS 33 *Earnings per Share* are only compulsory for listed entities. The other company is not currently listed and is not required to give either of these disclosures but can do so on a voluntary basis. If the other company obtains a listing, then they will have to give these disclosures.   2

IAS 20 *Accounting for Government Grants and Disclosure of Government Assistance* requires government grants to be recognised in profit or loss on a systematic basis over the period in which the entity recognises as expenses the related cost. However, IAS 20 allows entities to choose from two alternative models for presenting the government grants. These are the approach, which Epsilon uses, which deducts the grant in arriving at the non-current asset's carrying amount and will result in a reduced depreciation charge through profit or loss. The other company uses the allowed alternative of setting up the grant as deferred income and releasing the grant systematically to profit or loss. The net effect on profit or loss will be the same, whichever approach is used. Consistency of choice is required **within** entities. Therefore the other company could continue to use the deferred income approach to present its government grants even after obtaining a listing.

$$\frac{3}{7}$$

Exhibit 2 – Pending legal cases

Provisions are covered by IAS 37 *Provisions, Contingent Liabilities and Contingent Assets*. IAS 37 states that for a provision to be recognised, an obligating event must have incurred before the year end. In this case, both customer A and B were sold the product before the year end so an obligating event has occurred.

2

IAS 37 further states that a provision is only recognised when there is a probable outflow of economic benefits. IAS 37 interprets 'probable' to be 50% or more. This is only the case with the supply to customer A, so it is correct to only recognise a provision for customer A's claim.

3

IAS 37 also states that any provision should be measured based on the best estimate of the likely outflow of economic benefits. In this case, this amount is $10 million.

2

Any liability arising from the legal case brought by customer B would be regarded as a contingent liability because there is only a possible (rather than a probable) chance of an outflow of economic benefits. In this case, it is dealt with by disclosure, rather than provision.

2

In addition to the recognition of a provision in the case of customer A's claim, it is also necessary to disclose key facts relating to the case in the notes to the financial statements.

1

The possible recovery of funds from the insurance company would be regarded as a contingent asset. This would always be the case for possible assets unless it is virtually certain (rather than highly probable) that there will be an inflow of economic benefits. Where there is a probability of an inflow of funds relating to a contingent asset, then this is dealt with by disclosure under IAS 37.

$$\frac{2}{12}$$

Exhibit 3 – Statement of profit or loss and other comprehensive income

The principles underpinning the overall presentation of financial statements are set out in IAS 1 *Presentation of Financial Statements*. IAS 1 requires that all income and expenses are presented in a statement of profit or loss and other comprehensive income.

1

IAS 1 does not allow entities to choose whether to present income and expenses in the profit or loss or the other comprehensive income section of the statement. IAS 1 states that, unless required or permitted by a specific IFRS Accounting Standard, all items of income and expense should be presented in the profit or loss section of the statement.

2

IAS 1 states that the tax relating to items of other comprehensive income is either shown as a separate line in the 'other comprehensive income' section of the statement or netted off against each component of other comprehensive income and disclosed in the notes to the financial statements.

2

The key implication of an item being presented in other comprehensive income rather than profit or loss is that the item would not be taken into account when measuring earnings per share, an important performance indicator for listed entities like Epsilon.

$$\frac{1}{\frac{6}{25}}$$

20 Omicron 2 (December 2011) (amended)

Top tips. IAS 19 has a reputation for being one of the harder parts of the syllabus, but questions one should not be taxing once you have practised the area sufficiently. Part (a)(i) was straightforward, and you should be looking to get all three marks here. Part (a)(ii) was also not difficult, and two out of three marks here was eminently attainable. These are not areas on which you should be struggling. Part (a)(iii) is something that you should really know, and at the very least you could have gained one mark for stating the method that you use here.

Easy marks. Part (a)(i) was especially easy.

Examining team's comments.

Part (a)

Areas showing good knowledge:

- The majority of candidates correctly compared and contrasted the key features of the two types of scheme.

Areas where mistakes were common:

- Some candidates seemed unclear on the differing accounting treatments and often seemed to confuse them. A particularly common error was to state that contributions under a defined benefits scheme were treated as an expense by the employer.

Part (b)

Areas showing good knowledge:

- Most candidates seemed to be aware that the net pension liability appeared in the statement of financial position and that the amounts included in the statement of profit or loss were the actuarially determined amounts.

Areas where mistakes were common:

- Showing the closing liability in liabilities and the asset under assets instead of netting them off.
- Calculating the service charge and the interest earned on the closing balances instead of the opening ones.
- Not explaining clearly where in the statement of financial position and statement of profit or loss the various amounts should be included. For example, not specifying that the net liability was a non-current one and whether or not the expenses were operating or financial expenses.

[References: IAS 19: paras. 8, 51–52, 63–86]

Marking guide

	Marks
DC definition	2
DB definition	2
Accounting DB	1
Accounting DB	2
Actuarial	3

DB SFP	6
DB SPL	6
DC calculations	3
Total	**25**

(a) (i) A defined contribution plan is one where the value of the retirement benefits paid out (ie pensions) depends on the value of the plan, which is itself dependent on the value of contributions made. The party who makes contributions and receives benefits bears the risk here, since if the value of the plan falls then so do the benefits paid out.

In a defined benefit plan, by contrast, the value of retirement benefits paid out is defined in advance, and is not affected by the value of the plan. The risk here is with the plan operator because if the plan does not have sufficient funds to pay out the defined benefits then these must be made up.

(ii) Payments into defined contribution plans are expenses in the year of employment, and are accounted for in the same way as eg salaries.

Defined benefit plans require an entity to set up a separate plan , and to record the plan's assets, liabilities, income and expenses. It is common to have a net liability, meaning that the obligations to pay pensions in the future is bigger than the value of the assets owned by the fund.

Employees' contributions are paid into the plan, and increase the plan's assets. It is up to the entity to ensure that the plan has sufficient assets to be able to pay its future benefits.

(iii) Actuarial gains and losses are known as remeasurements (in IAS 19 and must be recognised immediately within other comprehensive income (OCI)). Amounts presented in OCI are not recycled to profit or loss in subsequent periods. This represents a change from the previous treatment, which allowed a choice of methods for recognition of remeasurements. The requirement to recognise remeasurements immediately in OCI results in volatility in OCI as actuarial gains and losses can vary significantly from period to period.

(b) **Note 1**

STATEMENT OF FINANCIAL POSITION – NON-CURRENT LIABILITIES	$'000
Benefit obligation	(41,500)
Plan asset	32,500
	(9,000)
CURRENT LIABILITIES	
Other payables (Note 2)	(2,000)
STATEMENT OF PROFIT OR LOSS AND OTHER COMPREHENSIVE INCOME	
Operating expenses	
Staff costs (Note 2)	(10,000)
Current service cost	(4,000)
Finance costs	
Interest cost (6% × $35m)	(2,100)
Expected return on assets (5% × $30m)	1,800
Other comprehensive income	
Actuarial losses	(2,900)

Notes to the financial statements

1   *Reconciliation of movement in defined benefit obligation*

Statement of financial position – non-current liabilities	$'000
Opening net liability	5,000
Expenditure (4,000 + 2,100)	6,100
Income (1,800 + 3,200)	(5,000)
Actuarial losses	2,900
Closing net liability	9,000

2   *PV of benefit obligation*

	$'000
At start of period	35,000
Current service cost	4,000
Interest cost	2,100
Benefits paid out	(2,000)
Actuarial loss (β)	2,400
	41,500

3   *Fair value of plan assets*

	$'000
At start of period	30,000
Expected return on assets	1,800
Contributions received	3,200
Benefits paid out	(2,000)
Actuarial loss (β)	(500)
	32,500

Exhibit 2 – Defined contribution plan

No assets or liabilities will be recognised for the defined contribution plan, other than current liabilities to reflect the amount due to be paid to the pension plan at year end. The contributions paid by the company of $10 million will be charged to profit or loss. The contributions paid by the employees will not be a cost to the company but will be adjusted in calculating employee's net salary. The net asset of the defined contribution pension plan are not shown in the company's statements of financial position.

21 Delta (June 2022)

Top tips. This question required candidates to explain and show the accounting treatment of two issues in the consolidated financial statements of Delta, namely:

1.   Retirement benefit plans

2.   Sale of goods with a right of return

It is important that candidates can differentiate between the two main types of pension plan (defined contribution and defined benefit) as the accounting treatments of the two types are very different.

Easy marks. These are available for identifying which plan is defined contribution and which is defined benefit, and then explaining the accounting for the defined contribution plan which is usually very straightforward. In part 2 there were also straightforward marks available for applying knowledge of sale or return transactions to the scenario.

Examining team's comments. Answers to the first part of the question were very disappointing. The majority of candidates seemed unable to distinguish between a defined contribution plan and a defined benefit plan. Answers to the second part of the question were much better.

Exhibit 1 – Post-employment benefit plans

The relevant standard to apply here is IAS 19 *Employee Benefits*. Since the benefits payable to plan A members are dependent on the value of the investment fund, plan A is a defined contribution plan. **1 mark**

This means that the liability of Delta is limited to the payment of contributions into the plan. Delta has no responsibility for the adequacy of the plan or payments to the former employees. **1 mark**

Therefore the contributions payable by Delta for the period of **$45 million** will be shown as an **employment expense in the statement of profit or loss. 1 mark** The current service cost is irrelevant to the financial reporting of amounts relating to a defined contribution plan. **1 mark**

The benefits paid to the former employees are paid by the plan and so are not relevant to Delta. Neither is the fair value of the plan assets. **1 mark**

Since the benefits payable to plan B members are based on final salary and length of service of the relevant employee, plan B is a defined benefit plan. **0.5 mark**

This means that the difference between the present value of the obligation (the liability of the plan to pay future benefits) and the fair value of the plan assets is reflected in the statement of financial position of Delta as a net liability or a net asset (*principle*). **0.5 mark**

Therefore the statement of financial position of Delta will record a net liability of **$55 million** ($220 million – $165 million) at 31 March 20X5. This will be shown as **a non-current liability**. **0.5 mark**

Since there is no guarantee that the contributions payable to the plan will be sufficient to fund the benefits, it is the current service cost which is shown as an operating expense in the statement of profit or loss (*principle*). In this case, the relevant expense is **$14 million**. **1mark**

Since, for plan B, Delta has a constructive obligation to fund any deficits, it is appropriate to recognise a net interest cost in the statement of profit or loss. This is the net of the interest cost on the liability and the interest income on the assets (*principle – just sense of the point rather than the exact words*). **0.5 mark**

In this case, the net interest cost would be $3·4 million ($14·84 million (W1) – 11·44 million (W1)).

The benefits paid to the former employees are paid by the plan and so are not relevant to Delta.

The liability of the plan to pay future benefits is an estimate which is usually computed with reference to actuarial advice. This means that there will almost always be a difference between the net closing liability/asset after accounting for the other movements recognised in the financial statements and the actuarial valuations at the year end of the plan assets and liability (*principle – just sense of the point rather than the exact words*).

This difference is referred to in IAS 19 as an **actuarial gain or loss** and is recognised in **other comprehensive income**. **1 mark**

In this case, the actuarial loss is $2.6 million (W2).

Workings

1   *Net interest cost – plan B (2 marks in total – ½ each calculation maximum 2)*

	Asset $'000	Liability $'000
Opening balance	140,000	(190,000)
6/12 of the contributions of $15,000 to plan in the period (increasing the asset)	7,500	
6/12 of the benefits of $9,000 paid to employees in the period (reducing both the asset and the liability)	(4,500)	4,500
Average carrying amount of asset and liability in the period	143,000	(185,500)
Interest at 8%	11,440	(14,840)

2   *Actuarial gain or loss – plan B (3 marks in total – ½ each calculation maximum 3)*

NB numbers below in $'000

	$'000
Opening net liability (190,000 – 140,000)	(50,000)
Current service cost	(14,000)
Net interest cost (W1 (14,840) less 11,440) – NB: OF rule applies here	(3,400)
Contributions payable by Delta into plan	15,000
Actuarial (loss)/gain – **balancing figure**	(2,600)
Closing net liability (220,000 – 165,000)	(55,000)

Exhibit 2 – Sale of goods with right of return

The relevant standard to apply here is IFRS 15 *Revenue from Contracts with Customers*.

In order to determine the amount and timing of the revenue to be recognised, Delta needs to identify the contract with the customer and to identify the performance obligations for Delta contained in the contract. In this case, the contract, and the performance obligation, is to supply the items to the customer (sense of the point). **1 mark**

Delta then needs to determine the transaction price. Where the contract gives the customer a right of return, then the transaction price contains a variable element (*principle*). **0.5 mark**

Since the variable element can be reliably measured, then it is taken into account in measuring the transaction price (*principle*). **0.5 mark** This means that the transaction price is $950,000 (200 × $5,000 × 95%). **0.5 mark**

The transaction price needs to be allocated to the separate performance obligations in the contract. Where there is only one performance obligation, this is a straightforward matter (*sense of the point*). **0.5 mark**

Delta then needs to recognise the revenue as the performance obligation is satisfied. Since the performance obligation is to supply the items to the customer, then the revenue is recognised in full on 1 March 20X5 when the items are delivered (*sense of the point*). The revenue recognised on this date is $950,000. **1 mark**

On 1 March 20X5, $1 million (200 × $5,000) will be recognised as a trade receivable. **0.5 mark**

$50,000 ($1 million – $950,000) will be recognised as a refund liability. **0.5 mark** This will be a current liability. **0.5 mark**

The **total** cost of the goods sold is $600,000 (200 × $3,000). This amount will be removed from inventory on 1 March 20X5. **1 mark**

Only $570,000 (200 × $3,000 × 95%) of the above amount will be recognised in cost of sales **0.5 mark**. The other $30,000 ($600,000 – $570,000) will be shown as a right of return asset under current assets **0.5 mark**.

The return of the six items during March 20X5 does not affect the initial recognition of revenue or cost of sales since the original estimate of the total returns is still considered valid (*principle*). **1 mark**

The sales value of the goods returned of $30,000 (6 × $5,000) will be credited to trade receivables and debited to the refund liability (*principle*). **1 mark**

This means that the closing balance of trade receivables will be $970,000 ($1 million – $30,000) and the closing refund liability will be $20,000 ($50,000 – $30,000). **0.5 mark**

The inventory value of the goods returned of $18,000 (6 × $3,000) will be debited to inventory and credited to the right of return asset (*principle*). **0.5 mark**

The closing balance of the right of return asset will be $12,000 ($30,000 – $18,000). **0.5 mark**

22 Kappa (June 2016) (amended)

Top tips. This question was on financial instruments, specifically financial assets. Part (a) required explanation from IFRS 9 of how financial assets are classified and measured. Part (b) required application of the IFRS 9 rules to four transactions. Bear in mind that you need to discuss the treatment and not just show the accounting entries. And while you may not have come across the specific treatment of interest-free loans before, you can apply the principles of IFRS 9 (what is fair value in this case?) and the *Conceptual Framework*.

Easy marks. These are available in part (a) for the discussion of the requirements of IFRS 9 in relation to financial assets.

Examining team's comments. Answers to part (a) were mixed. Most candidates were able to identify that there were three different measurement bases for financial assets dependent on the nature of the cash flows and the business model. However, only a minority of candidates were able to correctly describe when each measurement basis would be appropriate. A minority of candidates mistakenly thought they were being asked to describe the requirements of IFRS 13 *Fair Value Measurement*. This was not asked for and did not attract marks. Other candidates wasted time by referring to the measurement of financial liabilities and equity instruments – the question was clearly focused on financial assets. Most candidates realised that the loan to the employee (part b Exhibit 1) was a financial asset that should be measured at amortised cost. However only about half the candidates realised that the initial carrying amount of the asset (on which the subsequent amortised cost measurement was based) would be the fair value of the loan at its inception (involving discounting).

Answers to part (b) Exhibit 2 were generally rather disappointing. Few candidates appreciated that the three-year loan to company X failed the 'contractual cash flow test', meaning that the loan asset would be classified as fair value through profit or loss. A minority of candidates attempted to compute a 'split presentation' of the financial instrument along the lines of a convertible loan treated as part liability and part equity. All in all, answers to this part were unsatisfactory.

Answers to part (b) Exhibit 3 were generally satisfactory. Almost all candidates appreciated that equity investments had to be measured at fair value. However only some candidates mentioned the need to make an election should Kappa wish to measure the asset at fair value through other comprehensive income.

[References: IFRS 9: paras. 4.1.2–4.1.5, 5.1.1, Appendix A]

Marking scheme

	Marks
(a) The classification and measurement of financial assets is largely based on:	
The business model for managing the asset – specifically whether or not the objective is to hold the financial asset in order to collect the contractual cash flows.	1
Whether or not the contractual cash flows are solely payments of principal and interest on the principal amount outstanding.	1
Where the business model for managing the asset is to hold the financial asset in order to collect the contractual cash flows and the contractual cash flows are solely payments of principal and interest on the principal amount outstanding, then the financial asset is normally measured at amortised cost.	1
Where the business model for managing the asset is to both hold the financial asset in order to collect the contractual cash flows and to sell the financial asset and the contractual cash flows are solely payments of principal and interest on the principal amount outstanding, then the financial asset is normally measured at fair value through other comprehensive income. Interest income on such assets is recognised in the same way as if the asset were measured at amortised cost.	1 + 1

In other circumstances, financial assets are normally measured at fair value through profit or loss. 1

Notwithstanding the above, where equity investments are not held for trading, an entity may make an irrevocable election to measure such investments at fair value through other comprehensive income. 1

Finally an entity may, at initial recognition, irrevocably designate a financial asset as measured at fair value through profit or loss if to do so eliminates or significantly reduces an accounting mismatch. $\frac{1}{8}$

(b) (i) The loan is a financial asset which would initially be recognised at its fair value on 1 October 20X5. ½

Given the fact that Kappa normally requires a return of 10% per annum on business loans of this type, the loan asset should be initially recognised at $661,157 ($800,000/(1.10)^2). 1

An amount of $138,843 ($800,000 – $661,157) would be charged to profit or loss at 1 October 20X5. 1

Because of the business model and the contractual cash flows, this loan asset will subsequently be measured at amortised cost. 1

Therefore **$66,116** ($661,157 × 10%) will be recognised as finance income in the year ended 30 September 20X6. The closing loan asset **$727,273** will be ($661,157 + $66,116). This will be shown as a **current asset** since repayment is due on 30 September 20X7. <div align="right">½ + ½
+ ½
$\overline{5}$

(ii) Since the loan is at normal commercial rates, the loan would initially be recognised at $10 million – the amount advanced. ½

The interest received and receivable of $800,000 would be credited to profit or loss as finance income. 1

In this case, the contractual cash flows are not solely payments of principal and interest on the principal amount outstanding. Therefore the asset would be measured at fair value through profit or loss. 1

A fair value gain of $500,000 ($10.5m – $10m would be recognised in profit or loss. 1

The loan asset of $10.5 million would be shown as a non-current asset. <div align="right">½
$\overline{4}$

(iii) The equity investment would be initially recognised at its cost of purchase – $12 million. 1

The contractual cash flows relating to an equity investment are not solely payments of principal and interest on the principal amount outstanding. Therefore the asset would normally be measured at fair value through profit or loss. This would result in a gain on remeasurement to fair value of $1 million ($13m – $12m) being recognised in profit or loss. 1

Since the equity investment is being held for the long term, rather than as part of a trading portfolio, it is possible to make an irrevocable election on 1 October 20X5 to classify the asset as fair value through other comprehensive income. In such circumstances, the remeasurement gain of $1 million would be recognised in other comprehensive income rather than profit or loss. <div align="right">$\frac{1}{3}$

(iv) These loan notes are an investment in debt instruments where the business model is to collect the contractual cash flows (which are solely payments of principal and interest) and to sell financial assets. This is because Kappa will make decisions on an ongoing basis about whether collecting contractual cash flows or selling financial assets will maximise the return on the portfolio until the need arises for the invested cash. 1

Therefore, they should be measured initially at fair value plus transaction costs: $45,450 ([$50,000 × 90%] + $450). 1

Subsequently, the loan notes should be held at fair value through other comprehensive income under IFRS 9. However, the interest revenue must still be shown in profit or loss. 1

	$
Fair value on 1 October 20X5 ((50,000 × 90%) + 450))	45,450
Effective interest income (45,450 × 5.6%)	2,545
Coupon received (50,000 × 3%)	(1,500)
	46,495
Revaluation gain (to other comprehensive income) [bal. figure]	4,505
Fair value at 30 September 20X6	51,000

1

Consequently, $2,545 of finance income will be recognised in profit or loss for the year, $4,505 revaluation gain recognised in other comprehensive income and there will be a $51,000 loan note asset in the statement of financial position.

$$\frac{\underline{1}}{\frac{5}{25}}$$

23 Seltec

Marking guide

	Marks
Derivatives characteristics	3
Hedge accounting	4
Fair value hedge	5
Convertible initial	3
Convertible subsequent	3
Effective OCI	2
Ineffective PL	1
Liability	2
Release to PL	2
Total	**25**

[References: IFRS 9: paras. 6.5.1–6.5.14; IAS 32: para. 12]

Exhibit 1 – Fair value hedge

IAS 32 *Financial Instruments: Presentation* and IFRS 9 *Financial Instruments* define a **derivative** as a financial instrument or other contract that has all three of the following characteristics.

(1)   Its value changes in response to the change in a specified interest rate, financial instrument price, commodity price, foreign exchange rate, index of prices or rates, credit rating or credit index, or other variable (sometimes called the 'underlying').

(2)   It requires no initial net investment or an initial net investment that is smaller than would be required for other types of contracts that would be expected to have a similar response to changes in market factors.

(3)   It is settled at a future date.

A contract is **not considered to be a derivative where its purpose is to take physical delivery** in the normal course of business, unless the entity has a practice of settling the contracts on a net basis.

In the case of Seltec, while the company often takes physical delivery of the edible oil, it does so only to sell shortly afterwards, and usually settles on a net basis. Thus the **contracts will be considered to be derivative** contracts rather than contracts for purchase of inventory. Derivatives are accounted for at fair value through profit or loss, unless hedge accounting applies.

Hedge accounting

The rules on hedge accounting are set out in IFRS 9 *Financial Instruments*. Before a hedging relationship qualifies for hedge accounting, **all** of the following **conditions** must be met.

(1)   The hedging relationship consists only of eligible hedging instruments and eligible hedged items.

(2)   There must be formal documentation (including identification of the hedged item, the hedging instrument, the nature of the risk that is to be hedged and how the entity will assess the hedging instrument's effectiveness in offsetting the exposure to changes in the hedged item's fair value or cash flows attributable to the hedged risk).

(3)   The hedging relationship meets all of the following hedge effectiveness criteria:

    (i)   There is an **economic relationship** between the hedged item and the hedging instrument, ie the hedging instrument and the hedged item have values that generally move in the opposite direction because of the same risk, which is the hedged risk;

    (ii)   The **effect of credit risk does not dominate the value** changes that result from that economic relationship, ie the gain or loss from credit risk does not frustrate the effect of changes in the underlyings on the value of the hedging instrument or the hedged item, even if those changes were significant; and

    (iii)   The **hedge ratio of the hedging relationship** (quantity of hedging instrument vs quantity of hedged item) is the same as that resulting from the quantity of the hedged item that the entity **actually hedges** and the quantity of the hedging instrument that the entity **actually uses** to hedge that quantity of hedged item.

A **fair value hedge** is a hedge of the exposure to changes in the fair value of a recognised asset or liability, or an identified portion of such an asset or liability, that is attributable to a particular risk and could affect profit or loss. The **gain or loss** resulting from **re-measuring** the hedging instrument at fair value is **recognised in profit or loss**. The gain or loss on the hedged item attributable to the **hedged risk** should **adjust the carrying amount** of the hedged item and be **recognised in profit or loss**.

Exhibit 2 – Convertible loan Exhibit

Convertible loan Exhibits contain elements of debt and equity. Under IAS 32, the convertible loan Exhibit is required to be classified separately into its debt and equity components on initial recognition.

The initial carrying amount of the debt components, the financial liability, is the present value of the future cash outflows that would occur if the loan is repaid, discounted at 10%. This is 5,557 ($120/(1.10) + 120/(1.10^2)$) 3 + $7,120/(1.10)^3$) and the equity element is 443 ($6,000 - 5,557$).

The financial liability is not held for trading and so is subsequently measured using the amortised cost method. The finance cost each year will be calculated using the effective interest rate on the debt. The finance cost for the year ended 30 September 20X7 is calculated as $5,557 \times 10\%$. The equity element is not subsequently remeasured.

The closing liability balance is calculated as $5,557 \times 1.1 - 2\% \times 6,000 = 5,993$.

Exhibit 3 – Cash flow hedge

The currency contract has not been accounted for correctly. Applying IFRS 9 for a cash flow hedge, the gain or loss on the effective portion of the hedging instrument, which in this case is the currency contract, is recorded in other comprehensive income as an amount that can be recycled to profit or loss.

Any gain or loss on the ineffective portion is recorded in profit or loss.

The fair value of the contract at 30 September 20X7 should be recorded as a liability in the statement of financial position and a corresponding amount shown in OCI for the year.

When the transaction to sell the kroner occurs on 30 November 20X7, the amounts included in OCI will be released to profit or loss.

24 Delta (December 2012) (amended)

Top tips. Remember to show your workings clearly and to give explanations.

In Exhibit 1 the loan, a financial asset, is measured at amortised cost using the effective interest method, in accordance with IFRS 9. In Exhibit 2 the depreciation on the complex asset is calculated on the two identifiable components, the overhaul and the remainder. You should recognise in Exhibit 3 that the provision and potential legal claim need to be accounted for and disclosed separately. There were some easy marks in Exhibit 4 for recognising that the fair value of the contract should be recognised.

Easy marks. Exhibit 3, as long as you note that there is a provision and a separate contingent asset, you should be able to answer this question well.

Examining team's comments.

Exhibit 1

Areas showing good knowledge:

- Most candidates were aware that, whilst the financial asset had a zero coupon rate, the repayment premium meant that there was a finance cost associated with it due to the redemption premium.

- Most candidates were able to compute the finance cost using the effective rate of interest.

Areas where mistakes were common:

- Many candidates were not able to correctly deal with the issue costs of the loan asset. Some incorrectly stated that the costs should be recognised as an immediate expense, whilst others deducted the amount from the initial carrying value, rather than adding it on.

- Few candidates appreciated that the asset had suffered impairment in the current financial period. Where candidates did realise that this had occurred, some incorrectly stated that the loss would be recognised over the remaining term by reducing the effective rate of interest.

Exhibit 2

Areas showing good knowledge:

- Most candidates were aware that depreciation of this complex asset needed to be carried out in two parts.

- Basic depreciation calculations were generally of a satisfactory standard where candidates appreciated the 'complex asset' issue discussed above.

- A number of candidates failed to appreciate that failure to depreciate an asset in a previous period is an accounting error that needs to be adjusted for retrospectively.

Exhibit 3

Areas showing good knowledge:

- Most candidates appreciated that the potential legal claim needed to be provided for as a liability.
- Most candidates realised that the potential re-imbursement was a contingent asset.

Areas where mistakes were common:

- A significant minority of candidates used expected values to compute the provision rather than the most likely outcome.

- A significant minority of candidates stated that the insurance claim should be recognised as an asset.

- A smaller minority of candidates stated that the legal claim should not be provided for, but disclosed.

[References: IFRS 9: paras. 4.1, 5.1–5.2, 5.5; IAS 8: paras. 41–42; IAS 37: paras. 10, 14, 31]

Marking guide

	Marks
Loan explanation	3
Loan calculations	4
IAS 8	1
Complex asset one	2
Asset two	4½
Depreciation total	½
Liability	3
Contingent	2
Hedge accounting	5
Total	**25**

Marking scheme

	Marks

Exhibit 1

The loan to the supplier would be regarded as a financial asset. The relevant accounting standard, IFRS 9, provides that financial assets are normally measured at fair value. — ½

Where the financial asset is held within a business model where the only expected future cash inflows are the receipts of principal and interest and the investor intends to collect these contractual cash flows rather than dispose of the asset to a third party, then IFRS 9 allows the asset to be measured at amortised cost using the effective interest method. — ½

Assuming this method is adopted, then the costs of issuing the loan are included in its initial carrying amount rather than being taken to profit or loss as an immediate expense. This makes the initial carrying value $2.1 million. — 1

Under the effective interest method, part of the finance income is recognised in the current period rather than all in the following period when repayment is due. — ½

The income recognised in the current period is $144,900 ($2.1m × 6.9%). — 1

In the absence of information regarding the financial difficulties of the supplier, the financial asset at 30 September 20X2 would have been $2,244,900 ($2.1m + $144,900). ½

The information regarding financial difficulty of the supplier is objective evidence that the financial asset has suffered impairment at 30 September 20X2. This is then treated as a Stage 3 impairment loss. ½

Impairment is recognised as the present value of expected credit shortfalls over their remaining life **(lifetime expected credit loss)**. Delta is required to reduce the gross carrying amount of the financial asset in the period in which it no longer has a reasonable expectation of recovery. ½

The asset is re-measured at the present value of the revised estimated future cash inflows, using the original effective interest rate. Under the revised estimates the closing carrying amount of the asset would be $2,057,998 ($2.2m/1.069). 1

The reduction in carrying amount of $186,902 ($2,244,900 – $2,057,998) would be charged to profit or loss in the current period as an impairment of a financial asset. ½

Therefore the net charge to profit or loss in respect of the current period would be $42,002 ($186,902 – $144,900). ½

_____

7

Exhibit 2

Omitting to charge depreciation in the prior year where material would be regarded as an error under the principles outlined in IAS 8 _Accounting Policies, Accounting Estimates and Errors_. ½

Where an error has retrospective effect, it is adjusted as a movement on retained earnings in the statement of changes in equity rather than through profit or loss. ½

Because this is a complex asset, the depreciation charge is made on two identifiable components according to their fair values at the date of acquisition. ½

The first 'asset' is the overhaul element which would have a depreciable amount of $4 million. ½

The overhaul is not provided for as it is an intention not an obligation that this will arise and hence the life of the first 'asset' is four years. ½

The depreciation charged on this 'asset' would be $1 million each year. ½

The second 'asset' is the remainder, to which the estimated residual value is allocated entirely. ½

The residual value is an accounting estimate which should be revised at the end of each accounting period. ½

Therefore the depreciable amount for the year ended 30 September 20X1 is $14.9 million ($20m – $4m – $1.1m) 1

This means that the depreciation on this 'asset' for the year ended 30 September 20X1 is $1,862,500 ($14.9m × 1/8). ½

The depreciable amount of this 'asset' for the year ended 30 September 20X2 is $12,937,500 ($16m – $1,862,500 – $1,200,000). 1

Therefore the depreciation charge on this 'asset' for the year ended 30 September 20X2 is $1,848,214 ($12,937,500 × 1/7). 1

The total depreciation charged to profit or loss for the year ended 30 September 20X2 is therefore $2,848,214 ($1m + $1,848,214) and the carrying amount of the asset is $14,289,286 ($2m + $12,289,286) ½

_____

8

Exhibit 3

It is necessary to consider the two parts of this issue separately. ½

ANSWERS

The claim made by our customer needs to be recognised as a liability in the financial statements for the year ended 30 September 20X2.   ½

IAS 37 *Provisions, Contingent Liabilities and Contingent Assets* states that a provision should be made when, at the reporting date:

- An entity has a present obligation arising out of a past event
- There is a probable outflow of economic benefits   ½
- A reliable estimate can be made of the outflow

All three of those conditions are satisfied here, and so a provision is appropriate.

The provision should be measured as the amount the entity would rationally pay to settle the obligation at the reporting date.   ½

Where there is a range of possible outcomes, the individual most likely outcome is often the most appropriate measure to use.   ½

In this case a provision of $1.6 million seems appropriate, with a corresponding charge to profit or loss.   ½

The insurance claim against our supplier is a contingent asset.   ½

IAS 37 states that contingent assets should not be recognised until their realisation is virtually certain, but should be disclosed where their realisation is probable. This appears to be the situation we are in here.   ½

Therefore the contingent asset would be disclosed in the 20X2 financial statements. Any credit to profit or loss arises when the claim is settled.   1
                                                                                                  ―
                                                                                                  5

Exhibit 4
Delta wishes to apply hedge accounting wherever possible. The contract to sell €20 million is a hedging instrument under a cash flow hedge arrangement.   ½

Under IFRS 9, the fair value of the hedging instrument should be recognised in other comprehensive income (OCI) to the extent that it is effective. Any ineffective portion would be recognised in profit or loss.   2

In this case, the hedging instrument is for €20 million and the anticipated sales are €22 million, therefore the full fair value can be recognised in OCI.   ½

The fair value of the hedging instrument should be recognised as a financial asset at 30 September 20X2 and the corresponding amount accumulated in a hedged cash flow reserve.   1

The amount accumulated in the reserve will subsequently be released to profit or loss when the transaction takes place.   1
                                                                                                  ―
                                                                                                  5
                                                                                                  ―
                                                                                                  25

25 Epsilon

	Marks

(a)   Under IFRS 9 *Financial Instruments*, the basis for classifying and measuring financial assets is the business model for managing the financial asset and the contractual cash flow characteristics of the financial asset.   **1**

Where the business model for managing the financial asset is to hold the financial asset to collect the contractual cash flows and where the contractual terms of the financial asset give rise on specified dates to cash flows which are solely payments of principal and interest on the principal amount outstanding, then the financial asset is measured at amortised cost.   **1**

Where the business model for managing the financial asset is to both hold the financial asset to collect the contractual cash flows and to sell the financial asset and where the contractual terms of the financial asset give rise on specified dates to cash flows which are solely payments of principal and interest on the principal amount outstanding, then the financial asset is measured at fair value through other comprehensive income.   **1½**

If a financial asset is not measured at amortised cost or fair value through other comprehensive income, then it is measured at fair value through profit or loss (the default category).   **½**

An entity can make an optional irrevocable election on initial recognition that particular investments in equity instruments which would otherwise be measured at fair value through profit or loss be measured at fair value through other comprehensive income. This election is only possible if the equity investment is not 'held for trading'.   **1½**

Notwithstanding the above, an entity may, at initial recognition, irrevocably designate a financial asset as measured at fair value through profit or loss if to do so would eliminate or reduce a measurement or recognition inconsistency which would otherwise arise from measuring assets or liabilities or recognising gains or losses on them on different bases (an 'accounting mismatch').   **1½**

    7

(b)   **Exhibit 1 – $30 million loan**

Since the business model is to collect the contractual cash flows and the cash flows consist solely of the repayment of principal and interest, this asset is measured at amortised cost.   **1**

The initial carrying amount of the financial asset will be $30.25 million ($30m fair value + $250,000 transaction costs).   **1**

The finance income recorded under investment income category in the statement of profit or loss for the year ended 31 March 20X8 will be $3.025 million ($30.25m × 10%).   **1**

The carrying amount of the financial asset in the statement of financial position at 31 March 20X8 will be $31.775 million ($30.25m + $3.025m – $1.5m).   **1**

    4

Exhibit 2 – Investment in Greek

Since this is an equity investment which Epsilon has no intention of selling, Epsilon can measure the investment at fair value through other comprehensive income (provided irrevocable election on initial recognition has been made).   **1**

Marks

Since the financial asset is measured at fair value through other comprehensive income, the transaction cost (agent's commission) is included in the initial fair value of shares (500,000 × $2 + $100,000).

2

The carrying amount of the financial asset in the statement of financial position at 31 March 20X8 will be $1.125 million based on fair value of shares at the year end (500,000 × $2.25).

1

The difference (fair value gain) of $25,000 ($1.125m – $1.1m) will be recognised in other comprehensive income.

1

Dividend income of $150,000 (500,000 × 30 cents) will be recognised as other income in the statement of profit or loss.

$\frac{1}{5}$

Exhibit 3 – Call options

The call option cannot be measured at amortised cost or fair value through other comprehensive income, so it must be measured at fair value through profit or loss.

1

The initial carrying value of the call option will be $125,000 (100,000 × $1.25).

1

At the year end, the call option will be re-measured to its fair value of $160,000 (100,000 × $1.60).

1

The fair value gain of $35,000 ($160,000 – $125,000) will be recognised in the statement of profit or loss.

$\frac{1}{4}$

Exhibit 4 – Loan to subsidiary

As the business model is to collect the contractual cash flows and the cash flows consist solely of the repayment of principal, this asset is measured at amortised cost.

1

The initial carrying amount of the financial asset is its fair value, which is calculated using the market rate of 6% for a two year loan with the same issue/repayment dates, calculated as ($1m × 0.890) = $890,000.

1

The difference between the fair value and principal of the loan of $110,000 ($1m – 890,000) is the extra cost to Epsilon of not charging a market rate of interest and is recorded as finance income.

1

The finance income recorded for the year ended 31 March 20X8 will be $53,400 ($890,000 × 6%).

1

The carrying amount of the financial asset in the statement of financial position at 31 March 20X8 will be $943,400 ($890,000 + $53,400).

$\frac{1}{5}$

$\frac{}{25}$

26 Kirkham

[References: IAS 12: paras. 5, 15]

(a)   The tax base of an asset is the amount which will be **deductible** for tax purposes against any **taxable economic benefits** which will flow to the entity when the asset is recovered. If these benefits are **not taxable, the tax base equals the carrying amount**.

The tax base of a liability is its **carrying amount**, less any amount which will be **deductible for tax purposes** in respect of that liability in future periods. If the 'liability' is revenue received in advance, the tax base is its **carrying amount, less any revenue which will not be taxable in future periods**.

The general requirements of IAS 12 are that deferred tax liabilities should be recognised on all taxable temporary differences.

IAS 12 states that a deferred tax asset **should** be recognised for deductible temporary differences if it is **probable** that taxable profit will arise in future **against which the deductible temporary difference can be utilised**.

(b)   **Exhibit 1 – Equity investment**

Since the unrealised gain on revaluation of the equity investment is not taxable until sold, there are no current tax consequences.

Since the unrealised gain on revaluation of the equity investment is not taxable until sold, the tax base of the investment is $200,000.

The revaluation creates a **taxable** temporary difference of **$40,000** ($240,000 – $200,000).

This creates a deferred tax liability of **$10,000** ($40,000 × 25%). The liability would be non-current. The fact that there is no intention to dispose of the investment **does not affect the accounting treatment**.

Because the unrealised gain is reported in other comprehensive income, the related deferred tax expense is also reported in **other comprehensive income**.

Exhibit 2 – Intra-group sales

When Kirkham sold the products to Omega, Kirkham would have generated a taxable profit of **$16,000** ($80,000 – $64,000). This would have created a current tax liability for Kirkham and the group of **$4,000** ($16,000 × 25%). This liability would be shown as a **current** liability and charged as an expense in arriving at **profit or loss for the period**.

In the consolidated financial statements the carrying amount of the unsold inventory would be **$38,400** ($64,000 × 60%), with a tax base of **$48,000** ($80,000 × 60%).

In the consolidated financial statements there would be a **deductible** temporary difference of **$9,600** ($38,400 – $48,000) and a potential deferred tax asset of **$2,400** ($9,600 × 25%). This **would** be recognised as a deferred tax asset, because Omega is expected to generate **sufficient taxable profits** against which to utilise the deductible temporary difference.

The deferred tax asset would be recognised as a current asset. The resulting credit would **reduce consolidated deferred tax expense** in arriving at profit or loss.

Exhibit 3 – Payment from customer

The receipt of revenue in advance on 31 March 20X3 would create a **current** tax liability of **$50,000** ($200,000 × 25%) as at 30 September 20X3.

The carrying amount of the revenue received in advance at 30 September 20X3 is **$80,000** ($200,000 – $120,000). Its tax base is nil ($80,000 – $80,000).

The deductible temporary difference of $80,000 would create a deferred tax **asset** of **$20,000** ($80,000 × 25%). The asset can be recognised because Kirkham has **sufficient taxable profits** against which to utilise the deductible temporary difference. It would be recognised as a **current** asset since the remaining revenue is recognised in the next accounting period.

Exhibit 4 – Impairment of goodwill

As there is no tax deduction available in respect of the impairment loss, there is no effect on current tax.

No deferred tax liability arises in respect of goodwill on consolidation when it is created. This is a specific exception referred to in IAS 12.

As a consequence of this, **no adjustment is made for deferred tax** purposes when goodwill is impaired. Therefore there are no deferred tax implications for the consolidated statement of financial position.

Exhibit 5 – Development costs

The development costs were fully tax deductible in the year to 30 September 20X3 – so creating a current tax saving of $375,000 ($1.5m × 25%).

The development costs have a carrying amount of $1.52 million ($1.6m – ($1.6m × 1/5 × 3/12)).

The tax base of the development costs is nil since the **relevant tax deduction has already been claimed**.

The deferred tax liability will be **$380,000** ($1.52m × 25%). All deferred tax liabilities are shown as **non-current**.

27 Edgworth (June 2016) (amended)

Top tips. Deferred tax is examined frequently in DipIFR. If you struggled with this question, you should make sure you revise deferred tax in order to be fully prepared for your exam. Part (a) had some easy marks available for defining the tax base of an asset and liability as per IAS 12. You were then required to use those definitions to compute the tax bases of some assets and liabilities. Part (b) required the computation of the deferred tax liability and the charge/credit to profit or loss and to other comprehensive income.

Easy marks. A few easy marks were available for the definitions in part (a).

Examining team's comments. Despite this topic being frequently tested, candidates found it challenging.

In part (a) not all candidates correctly reproduced the definition. The tax base on the current assets was correctly stated as zero by many candidates though without any relevant explanations. Both questions (a)(i) and (a)(ii), 4 marks each, were challenging for candidates without in-depth knowledge of the core issues of deferred taxes. It is important to read the requirements of the question carefully to avoid producing non-relevant definitions of the temporary differences, taxable and tax deductible, and deferred tax assets/liabilities.

In part (b) all three cases dealt with deferred tax liabilities. Nevertheless, the vast majority of candidates who attempted this question focussed on explaining why there was a deferred tax liability as opposed to a deferred tax asset, and omitted to mention whether a charge or credit is made related to deferred tax. Again it is important to read and understand the requirements before starting an answer. Many candidates made the mistake of calculating deferred tax without using the balance sheet method. Many candidates calculated revaluation surplus and multiplied it by the tax rate. This does not comply with IAS 12 requirements even if correct figures were produced.

[References: IAS 12: paras. 5, 15, 24–37]

Marking guide

	Marks
Tax base assets	4
Tax base liabilities	4
Temporary differences	2
Recognition criteria	3
DT liability calculation	5
Amount to P/L	5½
Amount to OCI	1½
Total	**25**

Marking scheme

			Marks
(a)	(i)	The tax base of an asset is the amount which will be deductible for tax purposes against any taxable economic benefits which will flow to the entity when it recovers the carrying amount of the asset. If those economic benefits will not be taxable, the tax base of the asset is equal to its carrying amount.	2
		In Exhibit 1, an asset is purchased for $250,000 and has already received a tax deduction of $100,000, then the future tax deduction which is available will be $150,000 ($250,000 − $100,000). The tax base of the asset is $150,000.	1
		The interest receivable will generate a taxable economic benefit of $60,000 when it is received in the following period. There is no related tax deduction against this taxable benefit so the tax base of this asset is nil.	1
			4

Marks

(ii) The tax base of a liability is its carrying amount, less any amount which will be deductible for tax purposes in respect of that liability in future periods. In the case of revenue which is received in advance, the tax base of the resulting liability is its carrying amount, less any amount of the revenue which will not be taxable in future periods.

2

In Exhibit 2, the trade payable relates to a purchase which has already been fully deducted for tax purposes. There will be no further deduction when the payable is settled. Therefore in this case the tax base of the liability is $120,000.

1

The accrual of $40,000 relates to an expense which will qualify for a tax deduction only when the liability is settled, the tax base is nil ($40,000 – $40,000).

$\frac{1}{4}$

(iii) A **taxable temporary difference** arises when the carrying amount of an asset exceeds its tax base or the carrying amount of a liability is less than its tax base.

1

A **deductible temporary difference** arises in the reverse circumstances (when the carrying amount of an asset is less than its tax base or the carrying amount of a liability is greater than its tax base).

$\frac{1}{2}$

(iv) IAS 12 requires that (with specific exceptions) deferred tax liabilities are recognised on all taxable temporary differences.

1

IAS 12 allows deferred tax assets to be recognised on deductible temporary differences **when future taxable profits are expected to be available** against which to offset the future tax deductions the deductible temporary differences are expected to generate.

$\frac{2}{3}$

(b) **Deferred tax liability at 31 March 20X6**

Component	Explanation/working	Amount $'000	
Investment property	Carrying amount is $38m. Tax base is $30m. Taxable temporary difference is $8m.	1,600	1½
Investment in Lowercroft	Carrying amount is $75m. Tax base is $45m. Taxable temporary difference is $30m.	6,000	1½
Head office property	Carrying amount is $45m. Tax base is $20.75m ($22m – $1.25m).	4,850	2
		12,450	

Deferred tax charge/(credit) to profit or loss for the year ended 31 March 20X6

Component	Explanation/working	Amount $'000	
Investment property	Opening deferred tax liability is $1m (20% × ($35m – $30m)). Fair value changes are recognised in profit or loss. Tax charge is the difference between the closing and opening liability.	600	1½
Investment in Lowercroft	Opening deferred tax liability is $5m (20% × ($70m – $45m)). Share of profits under the equity method is recognised in profit or loss. Tax charge is the difference between the closing and opening liability.	1,000	1½
Head office property	See working below	(150)	2½
		1,450	

Deferred tax charge/(credit) to other comprehensive income for the year ended 31 March 20X6

Component	Explanation/working	Amount $'000	
Head office property	See working below	1,400	1½
		12	
		25	

Working for deferred tax on property revaluation

The deferred tax liability at 31 March 20X5 is $3.6 million (20% ($40m – $22m)).

At 31 March 20X6, **prior** to revaluation, the carrying amount of the property is $38 million and its tax base is $20.75 million ($22m – $1.25m). The deferred tax liability at this point is $3,450,000 (20% × ($38m – $20.75m)).

The reduction in this liability is $150,000 ($3.6m – $3,450,000). This would be credited to income tax expense in arriving at profit or loss.

Following revaluation the carrying amount becomes $45 million and the tax base stays the same. So the new deferred tax liability is $4,850,000 (20% × ($45m – $20.75m)).

The increase in the deferred tax liability of $1,400,000 ($4,850,000 – $3,450,000) is debited to other comprehensive income.

28 Omega (June 2014) (amended)

Top tips. This question asks you to explain four accounting issues to a non-accountant. It is mainly discursive, but there are some marks available for calculations. Exhibit 1 is about related party relationships and disclosures; it should be fairly clear that this is a related party relationship and should be disclosed, even though all the purchases are apparently at normal rates. Remember to explain **why** Sigma is now a related party of Omega and **what** must be disclosed. Notice that the question is **not** asking for a general discussion about related party transactions and why they must be disclosed.

Exhibit 2 requires you to explain why advertising expenditure cannot be recognised as an intangible asset. Remember that the accruals concept applies here.

Exhibit 3 concerns exchange differences and provided you had revised this area it should have been straightforward.

Exhibit 4 tests the application of the requirements of IFRS 13 *Fair Value Measurement* and required you to recognise that the principal market (if one exists) should be used to determine fair value.

Easy marks. There were easy marks available for the simple calculations in Exhibits 2 and 3.

Examining team's comments. On the whole the answers to this three-part analysis question were satisfactory. In Exhibit 1 a number of candidates incorrectly concluded that Sigma was a subsidiary of Omega and should therefore be consolidated, completely missing the related party issue. On the whole Exhibit 2 was well answered, with the vast majority of candidates appreciating that IAS 38 *Intangible Assets* effectively prohibits the capitalisation of advertising expenditure as an intangible asset. However, not all candidates appreciated that payments made for television advertisements not yet shown should be treated as pre-payments. Many good answers were also provided to Exhibit 3. However, not all candidates appreciated that the purchased machine, being a non-monetary asset that is measured under the cost model, would continue to be reported using the rate of exchange in force at the date of acquisition.

[References: IAS 21: paras. 21–23; IAS 24: paras. 9, 13–24; IAS 38: paras. 8, 18, 29]

Marks

Exhibit 1 – Purchases from Sigma

From 1 January 20X4, Sigma would be regarded as a related party of Omega under IAS 24 *Related Party Disclosures*.

1

This is because Sigma is **controlled** by the **close family member** of one of Omega's **key management personnel**.

½ + ½ + ½

This means that, **from 1 January 20X4**, the purchases from Sigma would be regarded as **related party transactions**.

1

Transactions with related parties need to be **disclosed in the notes** to the financial statements, together with the **nature of the relationship**. It is **irrelevant** whether or not these transactions are at normal market rates.

½ + ½ + ½

The disclosures would state that a company controlled by the spouse of a director supplied goods to the value of $4.5 million (3 × $1.5m) in the current accounting period. It would not be necessary to name the company.

1 + 1
───
7

Exhibit 2 – Advertising costs

Under IAS 38 *Intangible Assets* intangible assets can only be recognised if they are **identifiable** and have a cost which can be reliably measured.

½ + ½ + ½

These criteria are very difficult to satisfy for **internally developed** intangible assets.

½

For these reasons, IAS 38 specifically prohibits recognising advertising expenditure as an intangible asset.

1

The issue of how successful the store is likely to be does not affect this prohibition.

½

Therefore your colleague is correct in principle that such costs should be recognised as expenses.

½

However, the costs would be recognised on an accruals basis.

½

Therefore, of the advertisements paid for before 31 March 20X4, **$700,000** would be recognised as an expense and $100,000 as a pre-payment in the year ended 31 March 20X4.

1

The $400,000 cost of advertisements paid for since 31 March 20X4 would be charged as expenses in the year ended 31 March 20X5.

½
───
6

Exhibit 3 – Exchange rate fluctuations

Under the principles of IAS 21 *The Effects of Changes in Foreign Exchange Rates* the asset and liability would **initially** be recognised at the rate of exchange in force at the **transaction date** – 1 January 20X4. Therefore the amount initially recognised would be **$200,000** (2m kroner × 1/10).

½ + ½ + ½

The liability is a **monetary item** so it is retranslated using the rate of exchange in force at **31 March 20X4**. This makes the closing liability **$250,000** (2m kroner × 1/8).

½ + ½ + ½

The loss on re-translation of $50,000 ($250,000 – $200,000) is recognised in the **statement of profit or loss**.

½ + ½

  BPP LEARNING MEDIA

	Marks

The machine is a **non-monetary** asset carried at **historical cost**. Therefore it continues to be translated using the rate of **10** kroner to $1.   ½ + ½ + ½

Depreciation of **$12,500** ($200,000 × ¼ × 3/12) would be charged to **profit or loss** for the year ended 31 March 20X4.   ½ + ½

The closing balance in property, plant and equipment would be $187,500 ($200,000 – $12,500). This would be shown as a non-current asset in the statement of financial position.   ½

7

Exhibit 4 – Fair value of vehicles

The principles of IFRS 13 *Fair Value Measurement* should be applied when determining fair value. IFRS 13 says that fair value is an exit price in the principal market, which is the market with the highest volume and level of activity. If there is no principal market, the most advantageous market should be used.   ½ + ½ + ½

In Omega's case, market B is clearly the principal market, as this is the market in which the majority of transactions (75%) for the agricultural vehicles occur.   ½ + ½

IFRS 13 makes it clear that the price used to measure fair value must not be adjusted for transaction costs, but should consider transportation costs. Omega has deducted transaction costs in determining the value of $39,500 per vehicle in market A. It should not deduct the transaction costs in arriving at the fair value in the principal market.   ½ + ½

As such, the fair value of the 150 vehicles would be $5,700,000 ($38,000 × 150).   1

The actual sales of the vehicles in either market A or market C could result in a gain or loss to Omega when compared with the fair value of $38,000.   ½

5

25

29 Denshaw (June 2017) (amended)

Marking scheme

	Marks

Exhibit 1 – Joint arrangement

The joint arrangement with Yankee is a joint operation because Denshaw and Yankee have equal rights to the assets and joint obligations for the liabilities relating to the arrangement.   2

In a joint operation, the operators include their share of any jointly held assets. Therefore the property, plant and equipment of Denshaw at 30 September 20X8 will include: 2

– Leasehold property of $25m × 24/25 = $24m
– Plant and equipment of $7.5m × 4/5 = $6m

Marks

In a joint operation, the operators include their share of jointly incurred costs. Therefore the statement of profit or loss of Denshaw for the year ended 30 September 20X8 will include the following costs:

   2

–   Amortisation of lease premium $1 million.
–   Depreciation of plant and equipment $1.5 million.
–   Cash cost of operating the depot $4 million.

Denshaw will also include its own discretionary delivery charges of $2 million as a reduction in its operating costs.

   $\underline{1}$

   $\underline{7}$

Exhibit 2 – Purchase of inventory from a foreign supplier

Under the principles of IAS 21 *The Effects of Changes in Foreign Exchange Rates*, the purchase of inventory on 1 August 20X8 would be recorded using the spot rate of exchange on that date. Therefore Denshaw would recognise a purchase and an associated payable of $600,000 (3.6 million dinars/6).

   2

Denshaw would recognise revenue of $480,000 in the statement of profit or loss because goods to the value of $480,000 were sold prior to 30 September 20X8. At the same time Denshaw would recognise $360,000 ($600,000 × 60%) in cost of sales because the revenue of $480,000 is recognised.

   2

The closing inventory of goods purchased from the foreign supplier would be $240,000 ($600,000 – $360,000) and would be recognised as a current asset. This would not be re-translated since inventory is a non-monetary asset.

   2

The payment of 1,260,000 dinars on 15 September 20X8 would be recorded using the spot rate of exchange on that date therefore the payment would be recorded at $200,000 (1,260,000 dinars/$6.3).

   1

The closing payable of 2,340,000 dinars (3,600,000 dinars – 1,260,000 dinars) is a monetary item therefore would be translated at the rate of exchange in force at the year-end (6.4 dinars to $1). Therefore the closing payable (recorded in current liabilities) would be $365,625 (2,340,000 dinars/$6.4).

   1

The difference between the initially recognised payable ($600,000) and the subsequently recognised payment ($200,000) is $400,000. Since the closing payable is $365,625 (see above), Denshaw has made an exchange gain of $34,375 ($400,000 – $365,625). This gain is recognised in the statement of profit or loss, either under other income category or as a reduction in cost of sales.

   $\underline{3}$

   $\underline{11}$

Exhibit 3 – Share options

The total number of share options that can be awarded is 250,000 (50 × 5,000). At 30 September 20X8 it was estimated that only 44 employees (50 – 3 – 3) would actually receive options and therefore 220,000 options (44 × 5,000) will be awarded.

   2

The transaction is measured using the fair value of the options at the grant date: $4.50. Therefore the total cost of awarding the options is $990,000 (220,000 × $4.50).

   1

The vesting period is two years. Therefore the cost to be recognised in the financial statements for the year ended 30 September 20X8 is $495,000 ($990,000 × ½).

   1

Marks

The statement of profit or loss for the year ended 30 September 20X8 includes an expense of $495,000. This is an employment cost and is included in cost of sales, distribution costs or administrative expenses as appropriate.

1

The statement of financial position at 30 September 20X8 includes a corresponding amount of $495,000 relating to the options. This is presented as a separate component within equity.

1

The accounting entry is:

DEBIT Expense	$495,000	
CREDIT Equity	$495,000	1

7

25

30 Gamma (September 2020 (amended))

Top tips. This question required you to explain and show the accounting treatment for two issues:

(1)   a firm commitment to purchase a machine from a foreign supplier and the arrangement to hedge the associated foreign currency risk

(2)   a provision for training costs.

The question also covered the ethical issues arising in relation to the provision.

Part (a) was challenging and might have seemed daunting given the high number of marks available (17 marks). The key here is to make sure you identify and respond to the issues raised – eg how to account for a firm commitment; how to account for the forward exchange contract on inception, at the reporting date and when settled; and when to recognise the asset and at what amount. You will maximise your chance of gaining marks by making sure you cover all of the issues. It is important to apply exam technique and only spend the allocated amount of time (1.95 marks per minute × 17 marks = 33 minutes) on this part of the question as part (b) was much easier.

Part (b)(i) was straightforward if you knew the rules in IAS 37 to recognise a provision. Part (b)(ii) required you to identify and explain the ethical issues confronting the accountant. Make sure your answer refers to the fundamental ethical principles in the Code of Ethics and any threats to those principles.

Examining team comments.

Answers to part (a) were generally unsatisfactory. A large number of candidates stated incorrectly that the machine would be recognised on 1 January 20X4, the date on which the firm commitment was entered into, rather than 30 June 20X4, the date the machine was delivered and brought into use. Hardly any candidates provided an explanation of why the firm commitment was not recognised on 1 January 20X4. Similarly, hardly any candidates made the initial explanation of the treatment of the hedging derivative that would normally be required under IFRS 9 *Financial Instruments* were hedge accounting not used. A reasonable number of candidates were able to state that the gains arising on the hedging derivative between 1 January 20X4 and 30 June 20X4 were initially recognised in other comprehensive income rather than profit or loss. However very few went on to state that on recognition of the machine on 30 June 20X4 these gains would be deducted from the initial carrying amount of the machine. Only a minority of candidates specifically identified that the gains arising on re-measurement of the derivative in July 20X4 (from the date of recognition of the liability to the date of its settlement) would be initially recognised in other comprehensive income but then reclassified to profit or loss when the liability was settled.

Marks

(a) **Exhibit 1 – Purchase of machine**

The firm commitment to purchase the machine is a non-onerous executory contract until the date of delivery. Therefore, under the principles of IAS 37 *Provisions, Contingent Liabilities and Contingent Assets* no obligation would be recognised in the financial statements of Gamma until the machine was delivered. ½ (principle)

Under the principles of IFRS 9 *Financial Instruments* the forward exchange contract is a derivative financial instrument and so would be classified as fair value through profit or loss. ½

This would normally mean that gains or losses on re-measurement to fair value would be recognised in profit or loss ½ (principle)

However, where the derivative contract is designated as a cash flow hedge of a future firm commitment, IFRS 9 allows the effective portion of the change in fair value to be recognised in other comprehensive income. They will be presented as gains which may subsequently be reclassified to profit or loss. 1½ (principle)

Because the hedge is 100% effective, then in this case the whole of the change in the fair value of the derivative will be recognised in other comprehensive income. ½ (principle)

This means that a gain of $60,000 would be recognised in other comprehensive income of Gamma for the year ended 31 March 20X4 and a further gain of $100,000 ($160,000 – $60,000) recognised in other comprehensive income of Gamma for the year ended 31 March 20X5 (up to 30 June 20X4). 1

Under the principles of IAS 21 *The Effects of Change in Foreign Exchange Rates* on 30 June 20X4 when the asset is delivered, the transaction will be translated using the spot rate at that date. ½ (principle)

This means that $1.6 million (14.4m/9) will be debited to property, plant and equipment and credited to trade payables. 1

Under the principles of IFRS 9, given that hedge accounting is used, the cumulative gains on re-measurement of the derivative which have been recognised to 30 June 20X4 as other comprehensive income will be included in the carrying amount of the property, plant and equipment. 1 (principle)

The cumulative gains will have been accumulated in a cash flow hedge reserve and the inclusion of these gains in property, plant and equipment will be achieved by a direct transfer out of this reserve. This transfer will not affect other comprehensive income. 1 (principle)

This means that $160,000 ($60,000 + $100,000) will be debited to the cash flow hedge reserve and credited to property, plant and equipment. ½

The carrying amount of the property, plant and equipment following this transfer will be $1.44 million ($1.6 million – $160,000). ½

Marks

The property, plant and equipment is a non-monetary asset so its carrying amount will not be affected by future exchange rate fluctuations.

½ (principle)

The property, plant and equipment will be depreciated over its useful life of five years from 30 June 20X4. Therefore depreciation of $216,000 ($1.44m × 1/5 × 9/12) will be charged to profit or loss as an operating expense for the year ended 31 March 20X5.

½ + ½ + ½

The closing balance of property, plant and equipment on 31 March 20X5 will be $1,224,000 ($1.44m – $216,000).

½

For the period from 30 June 20X4 to 31 July 20X4, the further change in fair value of the derivative of $200,000 ($360,000 – $160,000) will be recognised as a gain in other comprehensive income.

½ + ½

The derivative is a financial asset and this asset will be de-recognised on 31 July 20X4 when $360,000 is received from the bank.

½

The liability to pay for the property, plant and equipment will be discharged on 31 July 20X4 by a payment of $1.8 million ($14.4m/8).

1

The loss on exchange of $200,000 ($1.8m – $1.6m) will be recognised in profit or loss as an operating expense.

1

At the same time, the gain on re-measurement of the derivative between 30 June 20X4 and 31 July 20X4 of $200,000 which had previously been recognised in other comprehensive income will be reclassified to profit or loss as a reclassification adjustment.

½

This means that the overall amount recognised in other comprehensive income for the year ended 31 March 20X5 will be a gain of $100,000 ($100,000 gain + $200,000 gain – $200,000 re-classification).

1½
___
17

(b) (i) **Provision**

IAS 37 *Provisions, Contingent Liabilities and Contingent Assets* states that a provision should only be recognised if:

- There is a present obligation from a past event;
- An outflow of economic resources is probable; and
- The obligation can be measured reliably.

2

No provision should be recognised because Gamma does not have an obligation to incur the training costs. The expenditure could be avoided by changing the nature of Gamma's operations and so it has no present obligation for the future expenditure.

1

The provision should be derecognised in the year ended 31 March 20X5. This will reduce liabilities by $2 million and increase profits by the same amount.

1
___
4

Marks

(ii) **Ethical implications**

The finance director is in danger of breaching the fundamental ethical principle of **objectivity** as his ability to be objective is threatened by self-interest. The directors of Gamma receive a bonus based on the profits of Gamma. The finance director has a **personal interest** in ensuring that the profits exceed the pre-determined amount. Although this year the profits have exceeded that amount, it is possible that next year they will not given that the forecasts are pessimistic. The finance director may be attempting to recognise the future training expense in the current year to increase the chance of meeting the bonus target in 20X6.

2

The finance director has incorrectly made a provision when no provision is required. This calls into question the **professional competence** of the finance director as he should be aware that IAS 37 does not permit a provision to be made in such circumstances.

1

The comment made by the finance director (a superior) that such enquiries are a waste of time and would not be looked on favourably when deciding future pay is an **intimidation threat** meant to deter the accountant from acting **objectively**. The finance director is exercising undue influence. The accountant is correct to challenge the finance director and has an ethical responsibility to do so.

$\underline{1}$
$\underline{4}$
$\underline{25}$

31 Omega (June 2015) (amended)

Top tips. This question asks you to explain three accounting issues to a non-accountant and is entirely discursive. The first of these was IAS 41, one of the more peripheral areas of the syllabus. Its inclusion illustrates that you must be careful not to leave out anything in your revision. The second issue was the IFRS for SMEs Accounting Standard (SMEs Accounting Standard). In both cases, only the main provisions were required. The third issue tested your knowledge of the revised *Conceptual Framework*. You should also note your audience, and try to avoid making your answer too technical.

Easy marks. Even a basic knowledge of the SMEs Accounting Standard could have scored a good mark in Exhibit 2. Discussion of the users of financial statements and the purpose of financial statements should have been easy enough in Exhibit 3.

Examining team's comments. This question was not answered well by the majority of candidates attempting it and indeed a reasonable number of candidates did not attempt it at all. As has already been noted in this report, this may be indicative of the fact that these subjects have been regarded as 'fringe' topics and not studied diligently by many candidates. It is very important for candidates to ensure that they have studied the whole of the syllabus.

Exhibit 1 required candidates to explain the applicability of general IFRS Accounting Standards to farming entities and also to outline the main recognition and measurement issues outlined in IAS 41. Candidates were specifically asked about the way government grants relating to agricultural activity need to be accounted for. A number of candidates incorrectly stated that other IFRS Accounting Standards do not apply to farming entities. The majority of candidates incorrectly stated that government grants for agricultural activity are accounted for in the same way as other government grants. Most candidates did have some awareness of the concept of a biological asset, and the difficulty of applying the cost concept to the measurement of such an asset. However the general level of knowledge displayed in this part was rather disappointing.

Exhibit 2 asked candidates to outline the main components of the SMEs Accounting Standard, and explain whether the SMEs Accounting Standard could be used by a small listed entity. Most candidates stated that the small entity in question could use the SMEs Accounting Standard, despite the fact that the SMEs Accounting Standard cannot be used by listed entities, whatever their size. A reasonable minority of candidates incorrectly stated that there was no such thing as the IFRS Accounting Standards Accounting Standard and that all entities have to use full IFRS. A few candidates misinterpreted this part and reflected on the accounting requirements of IFRS 1 *First Time Adoption of IFRS*. As in Exhibit 1, the level of knowledge displayed in Exhibit 2 was rather disappointing.

[References: IAS 20: para. 12; IAS 41: paras. 4–5, 10, 12–13, 34–38, Conceptual Framework: paras. 1.2–1.4]

Marking guide

	Marks
Agriculture	4
Grants	4
Temporary differences	2
Recognition criteria	2
Use of SMEs Accounting Standard	3½
SMEs Accounting Standard vs full IFRS	3½
Advantage of SMEs Accounting Standard	1
Conceptual Framework – users	3
Information needs	2
Total	**25**

Marking scheme

	Marks

Exhibit 1 – Agriculture

Farming entities need a special standard because many of their assets, liabilities, income and expenses are unlike those of other industries, for instance, in no other industry does one asset give birth to another. It is not true that the existence of IAS 41 *Agriculture* means other IFRS Accounting Standards do not apply to farming companies. The general presentation requirements of IAS 1 *Presentation of Financial Statements*, together with the specific recognition and measurement requirements of other IFRS Accounting Standards, apply to farming companies just as much as others.	1
IAS 41 deals with agricultural activity. Two key recognition definitions given in IAS 41 are biological assets and agricultural produce.	½ + ½ + ½
A biological asset is a living animal or plant. Examples of biological assets would be sheep and fruit trees.	1
The criteria for the recognition of biological assets are basically consistent with other IFRS Accounting Standards, and are based around the *Conceptual Framework* definition of an asset, that it is a present economic resource controlled as a result of past events.	1
A key issue dealt with in IAS 41 is that of measurement of biological assets. Given their nature (eg lambs born to sheep which are existing assets), the use of cost as a measurement basis is impracticable.	½ + ½
The IAS 41 requirement for biological assets is to measure them at fair value less costs to sell.	½ + ½

ANSWERS

	Marks

Changes in fair value less costs to sell from one period to another are recognised in profit or loss. — ½

Agricultural produce is the harvested produce of a biological asset. Examples are wool (from sheep) or fruit (from fruit trees). — 1

The issue of measuring 'cost' of such assets is similar to that for biological assets. IAS 41 therefore requires that 'cost' should be fair value less costs to sell at the point of harvesting. This figure is then the deemed 'cost' for the purposes of IAS 2 *Inventories.* — ½ + ½ + ½

Government grants receivable in respect of biological assets are not treated in the way prescribed by IAS 20 *Government grants.* Where such a grant is unconditional, it should be recognised in profit or loss when it becomes receivable. If conditions attach to the grant, it should be recognised in profit or loss only when the conditions have been met. — ½ + ½ + ½

The IAS 20 treatment of grants is to recognise them in profit or loss as the expenditure to which they relate is recognised. This means that recognition of grants relating to property, plant and equipment takes place over the life of the asset rather than when the relevant conditions are satisfied. — 1

$\frac{1}{12}$

Exhibit 2 – Smaller entities

It is true that the International Accounting Standards Board has developed an IFRS for small and medium sized entities (SMEs) which can be used as an alternative to full IFRS Accounting Standards. — ½ + ½

Despite the title of the SMEs Accounting Standard it is not available for all small and medium sized entities. The standard can only be used by entities which are not publicly accountable. Therefore the standard could not be used by the other entity as it is listed. — ½ + ½ + ½

The SMEs Accounting Standard is one single standard which, if adopted, is used instead of all IFRS Accounting Standards. — ½ + ½

The SMEs Accounting Standard omits completely the requirements of IFRS Accounting Standards which are specifically relevant to listed entities, for example, earnings per share and segmental reporting. — ½ + ½

In addition, the subject matter included in the SMEs Accounting Standard has been simplified compared with full IFRS Accounting Standards. For example, research and development costs are always expensed. — ½ + ½ + ½

In general terms, the disclosures required by the SMEs Accounting Standard are considerably less burdensome than for full IFRS Accounting Standards. — 1

A further benefit is that the SMEs Accounting Standard is only updated once every three years, thus reducing the extent of change to financial reporting practice. — 1

$\frac{1}{8}$

Exhibit 3 – *Conceptual Framework*

The IASB's *Conceptual Framework for Financial Reporting* tries to provide a structure for general purpose financial reporting by identifying users and their needs. — 1

The *Conceptual Framework* identifies existing and potential investors, lenders and other creditors as being the main users of the financial statements. The managing director is right, these users do have differing needs but, contrary to the suggestion in the question, they do all need the same useful information from financial statements. — 1 + 1

The *Conceptual Framework* identifies that the objective of general purpose financial statements is to provide useful information to the identified users groups on which they can base decisions relating to providing economic resources to the entity. The *Conceptual Framework* acknowledges that the decisions made depend on the returns the users expect. — 1

To meet the needs of users, the financial statements need to provide users with information about the economic resources of an entity, claims against those resources and changes in those resources and claims in the period and how efficiently and effectively the management of an entity have discharged their stewardship responsibilities relating to those resources.

1

Whether recognising a wide user group and acknowledging their different needs will lead to bigger and more complex sets of accounts is certainly an issue which needs to be addressed. When developing standards the IASB considers what makes financial information relevant. It has been decided that the ability to predict future performance is an essential need of most user groups and therefore the additional cost of preparation can be justified. As long as this test is applied it should ensure no irrelevant information is included.

5
──
25
──

32 Okawa (December 2015) (amended)

Top tips. It was important for this question to know the *Conceptual Framework* definition of an asset. This made it possible to provide a good answer to part (a). Part (b) was a typical discursive question, requiring you to explain two different issues to a non-accountant. Exhibit 1 covered the area of exploration for and evaluation of mineral resources (IFRS 6), which is a peripheral area of the syllabus. Perhaps to balance this out, Exhibit 2 covered the much more mainstream area of assets held for sale (IFRS 5).

Easy marks. Part (b) Exhibit 2 should have been straightforward.

Examining team's comments. Part (b) Exhibit 1 of this question was not well answered. A significant number of candidates seemed totally unaware of the provisions of IFRS 6 *Exploration for and Evaluation of Mineral Resources*. Such candidates made general comments about the recognition of tangible and intangible assets and this could only receive limited credit. Whilst IFRS 6 is not a standard that will appear in every exam it is part of the examinable material for this exam and accordingly candidates should devote part of their study time to this subject.

Part (b) Exhibit 2 was well answered on the whole, with a pleasing level of knowledge being displayed regarding the 'held-for-sale' issues in IFRS 5.

Marking scheme

Marks

(a) The *Conceptual Framework* defines an asset as 'a present economic resource controlled by the entity as a result of past events'. An economic resource is 'a right that has the potential to produce economic benefits'.

1

IAS 1 sets out the defining features of a current asset (intended to be realised during the normal operating cycle or within 12 months of the year end, held for trading or classified as cash or a cash equivalent). All other assets are classified as non-current.

The assistant's definition diverges from this in a number of ways:

(i) A non-current asset **does not have to be physical**. The definition can include intangible assets such as investments or capitalised development costs.

1

Marks

    (ii)   A non-current asset **does not have to be of substantial cost**. An item of   1
immaterial value is unlikely to be capitalised, but this is not part of the definition.

    (iii)   A non-current asset does not have to be legally owned. The accounting principle 1
is based on 'substance over form' and relies on the ability of the entity to **control**
the asset. This means for instance that a lease gives rise to a right-of-use asset in
the financial statements of the lessee in accordance with IFRS 16, even though
legal title of the leased asset remains with the lessor.

    (iv)   It is generally the case that non-current assets will last longer than one year. $\underline{1}$
IAS 16 specifies that property, plant and equipment 'are expected to be used $\underline{5}$
during more than one period'. However, if a non-current asset failed to last longer
than one year, it would **still be classified as a non-current asset during its life**.

(b)   **Exhibit 1 – Exploration costs**

Expenditure on the exploration for, and evaluation of, mineral resources is **excluded**   ½ + ½ + ½
from the scope of standards which might be expected to provide guidance in this area.
Specifically such expenditure is not covered by IAS 16 *Property, Plant and Equipment* or
IAS 38 *Intangible Assets*.

This has meant that, in the absence of any alternative pronouncements, entities would   ½ + ½ + ½
determine their accounting policies for exploration and evaluation expenditures in
accordance with the general requirements of IAS 8 *Accounting Policies, Changes in
Accounting Estimates and Errors*. This could lead to considerable **divergence** of practice
given the diversity of relevant requirements of **other** standard setting bodies.

Given other pressures on its time and resources, the International Accounting Standards   1
Board (IASB) decided in 2002 that it was not able to develop a comprehensive standard
in the immediate future.

However, recognising the importance of accounting for extractive industries generally   1
the IASB issued IFRS 6 *Exploration for and Evaluation of Mineral Resources* to achieve
some level of standardisation of practice in this area.

IFRS 6 requires relevant entities to **determine** a policy specifying which expenditures are   ½ + ½
recognised as exploration and evaluation assets and apply the policy **consistently**.

When recognising exploration and evaluation assets, entities shall consistently classify   1
them as tangible or intangible according to their nature.

Subsequent to initial recognition, entities should consistently apply the cost model or the   1
revaluation model to exploration and evaluation assets.

If the revaluation model is used, it should be applied according to IAS 16 (for tangible   1
assets) or IAS 38 (for intangible assets).

Where circumstances suggest that the carrying amount of an exploration and evaluation
asset may exceed its recoverable amount, such assets should be reviewed for
impairment. Any impairment loss should basically be measured, presented and disclosed $\underline{1}$
in accordance with IAS 36 *Impairment of Assets*. $\underline{10}$

Exhibit 2 – Buildings for sale

The accounting treatment of buildings to be sold is governed by IFRS 5 *Non-current*   ½
Assets Held for Sale and Discontinued Operations.

A building would be classified as held for sale if its carrying amount will be recovered   ½
principally through a sale transaction, rather than through continuing use.

Marks

For this to be the case, the asset must be available for **immediate** sale in its **present** condition. Also management must be **committed** to a plan to sell the asset and an **active programme** to locate a buyer must have been initiated. Further, the asset must be **actively** marketed for sale at a **reasonable** price. In addition, the sale should be expected to be completed within **one year** of the date of classification as held for sale (although there are certain circumstances in which the one-year period can be **extended**). Finally it should be unlikely that significant **changes** to the plan will be made or that the plan will be **withdrawn**.

½ + ½ + ½ + ½ + ½ + ½ + ½+ ½ + ½ + ½

Immediately **prior** to being classified as held for sale, assets should be stated (or re-stated) at their **current** carrying amount under relevant IFRS Accounting Standards. Assets then classified as held for sale should be measured at the **lower** of their **current** carrying amount and their **fair value less costs to sell**. Any write down of the assets due to this process would be regarded as an **impairment** loss and treated in accordance with IAS 36 *Impairment of Assets*.

½ + ½ + ½+ ½ + ½ + ½

Assets classified as held for sale should be presented separately from other assets in the statement of financial position.

$$\frac{1}{\frac{10}{25}}$$

33 Delta (September 2020)

Top tips. In this question, you were required to explain how Delta should report two accounting issues in its financial statements. The question clearly stated the IFRS Accounting Standards you were expected to apply: IAS 12 *Income Taxes* and IAS 41 *Agriculture*. Note that merely reproducing text from the standard that is not relevant to the scenario given will not get you any marks and should be avoided. A good approach to an 'explain' question like this is to state the relevant principles of the standard and then explain how it applies to the scenario given.

Many candidates find deferred tax difficult. In which case, you may prefer to start by explaining the agriculture issue first and the deferred tax issue after that. However, if you do this, make sure you still leave yourself adequate time to make a good attempt at both parts. There are relatively easy marks available in both issues for stating the relevant principles from the standard.

Examining team's comments.

The examiner's report identified some common errors, which included the following:

- Incorrectly stating that there would be no deferred tax recognised on the revaluation of land since Delta had no intention of selling it.

- Confusing deferred tax assets and deferred tax liabilities. A number of candidates stated that the deferred tax impact of the plant purchase was to create an asset rather than a liability. Similarly, some stated that the deferred tax implications of the accrued loan interest created a liability, rather than an asset.

- Not explaining the overall impact of the three deferred tax adjustments on the individual financial statements.

- Incorrectly stating that the overall movement in the fair value less costs to sell is recognised in other comprehensive income, rather than profit or loss.

Exhibit 1 – Temporary differences

The tax base of an asset is the future tax deduction which will be available when the asset generates taxable economic benefits.

½ (principle)

The plant purchased by Delta will have a carrying amount of $3.6 million ($4m – $4m × 1/5 × 6/12).

½

The tax base of the plant will be $2 million ($4m – 50% × $4m).	½
Therefore this transaction will create a **taxable** temporary difference of **$1.6 million** ($3.6m – $2m) and a deferred tax liability of **$320,000** ($1.6m × 20%).	½ + ½ + ½
The tax base of a liability is its carrying amount, less the future tax deduction (if any) which will be available when the liability is settled (exact words not needed).	½
The carrying amount of the liability at 31 March 20X5 is $21.2 million ($20m + $20m × 8% × 9/12).	1
The tax deduction which will be available when the liability is settled will be $1.2 million ($20m × 8% × 9/12).	½
Therefore the tax base of the loan liability will be **$20 million** ($21.2m – $1.2m) and the **deductible** temporary difference will be $1.2 million ($21.2m – $20m).	½ + ½
The deductible temporary difference will create a potential deferred tax asset of $240,000 ($1.2m × 20%).	½
This deferred tax asset can be recognised because Delta is expected to generate taxable income for the foreseeable future.	½ (principle)
The net result of the first two transactions is a charge to income tax expense in the statement of profit or loss of $80,000 ($320,000 – $240,000).	½
Following revaluation of the land, its carrying amount is $18 million and its tax base $15 million, creating a taxable temporary difference of **$3 million** and a deferred tax liability of **$600,000** ($3m × 20%).	½ + ½
Under IAS 12 – *Income Taxes*, this is recognised regardless of the fact that Delta has no intention of disposing of the land for the foreseeable future.	½
Because the revaluation gain is recognised in other comprehensive income as part of items that will not subsequently be reclassified to profit or loss, the related deferred tax is also recognised there as part of the tax relating to other comprehensive income.	1
In the statement of financial position, the deferred tax asset is netted off against the deferred tax liabilities because both relate to the same tax jurisdiction.	½ (principle)
The deferred tax liability which will be shown in the statement of financial position will be **$680,000** ($320,000 – $240,000 + $600,000). IAS 12 requires that deferred tax liabilities should always be shown in **non-current** liabilities.	½ + 1
	12

Exhibit 2 – Agricultural activity

Under the principles of IAS 41 *Agriculture*, the herd of cows will be regarded as a biological asset. Biological assets are measured at their **fair value less costs to sell**.	½ + ½
The carrying amount of the herd at 1 April 20X4 will be $130,000 (500 × ($270 – $10)).	1
When the 20 cows die, $5200 (20 × $260) will be credited to the herd asset and shown as an expense in the statement of profit or loss.	1
When the 20 cows are purchased for $4,200 (20 × $210), the herd asset will be debited with $4,000 (20 × ($210 – $10)).	1
The difference of $200 ($4,200 – $4,000) between the amount paid and the amount recognised as an asset will be shown as an expense in the statement of profit or loss.	1
The intermediate carrying amount of the herd before the year-end revaluation will be $128,800 ($130,000 – $5,200 + $4,000).	1

The carrying amount of the herd at 31 March 20X5 after revaluation will be $126,400 (480 × ($265 − $11) + 20 × ($235 − $11)).   1

The change in the carrying amount of the herd due to the year-end revaluation of $2,400 ($128,800 − $126,400) will be shown as an expense in the statement of profit or loss.   1

Therefore the total charge to profit or loss in respect of the herd for the year ended 31 March 20X5 will be $7,800 ($5,200 + $200 + $2,400).   1

The herd will be shown as a non-current asset in the statement of financial position and disclosed separately.   ½

The milk held by Delta at the year end will be regarded as harvested produce.   ½ (principle)

Under the principles of IAS 41, harvested produce is recognised in inventory at an initial carrying amount of fair value less costs to sell at the point of harvesting.   1 (principle)

In this case, the initially recognised amount will be **$1,900** (1,000 × ($2 − $0.10)). This will be the 'cost' of the inventory which will henceforth be accounted for under **IAS 2 _Inventories_**.   ½ + ½

The inventory of milk will be shown as a **current asset** in the statement of financial position of Delta. The market price of milk is not expected to decline in the near future so there is **no need** for a write-down to net realisable value.   ½ + ½
                                                                                                                                                        13
                                                                                                                                                        25

34 Delta (June 2021)

Top tips. This question required you to explain the accounting treatment of three issues – all three of which require you to apply the provisions of IFRS 13 _Fair Value Measurement_ to determine fair value as well as the provisions of other IFRS Accounting Standards to determine the correct accounting treatment in the financial statements.

For the cattle and sheep, you were provided with market data and should have applied the IFRS 13 principle whereby if more than one market exists, the principal market, if one exists, should be used to determine fair value. If there is no principal market, the most advantageous market should be used. As the cattle and sheep are biological assets under IAS 41 _Agriculture_, they are measured at fair value less costs to sell so the selling costs should be deducted from the computed amount under IFRS 13 to give the amount to recognise in the financial statements.

For the purchase of shares, you should apply the provisions of IFRS 9 _Financial Instruments_ to measure the financial asset at fair value through profit or loss. In determining the fair value, the relevant key principle from IFRS 13 is that the fair value is an _exit_ measure – so you should use the bid price rather than the offer price to calculate the fair value.

For the acquired factory, the key IFRS 13 principle required was that fair value is determined based on the highest and best use of a non-financial asset, despite its current use.

Note that the question asked you to state _where_ in the financial statements each item should be presented. It might have been easy to miss this bit of the requirement if you were focussed on determining the fair value, but it was worth 4 of the available marks and was relatively straightforward. You could use the underline tool or the highlighter tool in the CBE to help you identify all parts of a requirement.

Examining team comments.

On the whole answers to this question were disappointing. This indicated that candidates had not studied IFRS 13 to the depth required.

Common errors included not appreciating that under IFRS 13:

- 'Fair value' means gross selling price less transport costs.
- Where a principal market exists (as for the cattle) 'fair value' is computed with reference to prices prevailing in that market.
- Where no principal market exists (as for the sheep) 'fair value' is computed with reference to the selling prices in the 'most advantageous' market. A fairly common error here was to compute 'fair value' for the sheep based on a 50:50 split between markets 1 and 2 given that the sheep were actually sold equally in the two markets.
- When computing the 'most advantageous' market the decision should be based on fair value less selling costs.
- IFRS 13 fair value is computed with reference to the 'highest and best use' of a non-financial asset, irrespective of the use to which the asset will be put.

Marking scheme

	Marks

Cattle and sheep

Under the principles of IAS 41 *Agriculture* cattle and sheep are biological assets which are measured at fair value less costs to sell in the financial statements.	1
Under the principles of IFRS 13 *Fair Value Measurement* – the fair value of an asset is the price which would be received to sell the asset in an orderly transaction between market participants.	1
Where more than one market exists for the asset, attempts should be made to identify the principal market for the asset. Where the principal market is identified, this market price should be used to establish fair value.	1
In the case of Omega's cattle, these should be measured with reference to market prices in Market 1. The fair value will be the market price in market 1 less the costs of transporting the cattle to market. The selling costs will be a further deduction to arrive at the IAS 41 value.	½ + ½
Therefore the cattle of Omega will be measured at their fair value (300 × ($80 – $4) = $22,800) less costs to sell (300 × $2 = $600). The net measurement will be $22,200 ($22,800 – $600).	1
Because the cattle will be used by Omega for more than 12 months, the cattle will be presented as a non-current biological asset in Delta's consolidated statement of financial position at 31 March 20X5.	½
Where it is not possible to identify a principal market for the sale of an asset, then the entity should use the most advantageous market as a means of identifying fair value.	½
The most advantageous market is the one in which the expected net proceeds (after deducting selling costs) are the higher.	½
In the case of Omega's sheep, the expected net proceeds of sale of sheep in Market 1 are $56 ($61 – $3 – $2) and the expected net proceeds of sale in Market 2 are $55 ($63 – $4 – $4). Therefore Market 1 is the most advantageous market and should be used to measure the fair value of Omega's sheep.	½ + ½ + ½
Therefore the sheep of Omega will be measured at their fair value (200 × ($61 – $3) = $11,600) less costs to sell (200 × $2 = $400). The net measurement will be $11,200 ($11,600 – $400).	1

Because the sheep will be sold by Omega within 12 months, the sheep will be presented as a current biological asset in both Omega and Delta's statement of financial position at 31 March 20X5.

1

10

Purchase of shares

Under the principles of IFRS 9 *Financial Instruments* the trading portfolio would be a financial asset which is measured at fair value through profit or loss because of the business model for managing the financial asset.

½ + ½ + ½

Under the principles of IFRS 13, the fair value would be measured based on the price at which Kappa could sell the shares.

1

Therefore on 1 January 20X5, the shares would be recognised in financial assets at their fair value of $100,000 (20,000 × $5).

1

The difference (of $9,000) between the total price paid for the shares of $109,000 (20,000 × ($5.25 + $0.20)) and their initially recognised fair value of $100,000 would be a transaction cost which would be recognised in the statement of profit or loss for the year ended 31 March 20X5.

1 + 1

On 31 March 20X5, the shares would be re-measured at their fair value of $116,000 (20,000 × $5.80). The re-measurement difference of $16,000 ($116,000 − $100,000) would be recognised in the statement of profit or loss for the year ended 31 March 20X5. The shares would be presented under current assets in the consolidated statement of financial position of Delta at 31 March 20X5.

½ + ½ + 1 + ½

8

Acquisition

Under the principles of IFRS 3 *Business Combinations* the 'cost' of Zeta's factory to Delta will be its fair value at the date of acquisition.

1

Under the principles of IFRS 13, the fair value of a non-financial asset is based on the highest and best use for a potential purchaser, irrespective of the use to which the asset is being put by the user. Therefore the fair value (and the deemed cost to Delta) of the factory at 1 October 20X4 will be $7.5 million.

½ + ½ + 1

The buildings element of the factory will be depreciated over its useful life. Given that Delta will continue to use the building as a factory, rather than for administrative purposes, this will be 40 years.

½ + 1

Therefore the depreciation charge for the year ended 31 March 20X5 will be $50,000 ($4m × 1/40 × 6/12).

1

The closing carrying amount of the factory will be $7,450,000 ($7.5m − $50,000). This will be shown as a non-current asset in Delta's consolidated statement of financial position.

1 + ½

7

25

35 Omega (December 2022)

Top tips. This question required you to explain how certain specific financial reporting issues were dealt with in the financial statements. The explanations needed to be provided to a director who was not an accountant and therefore answers needed to be clearly worded and supported by any relevant calculations.

It is important not to just set out the required journal entries here, as this was not part of the requirement (and your answer should have been directed to a non-accountant who would not understand journal entries anyway).

Make sure you always answer the question as set – the director has some very specific queries so marks would not be available for any irrelevant comments, even if they were technically correct.

Examining team comments.

On the whole answers to this question were very mixed with some students attempting very little (or none) of this question. The performance of those who did attempt the question was again very mixed, with some candidates struggling with some of the technical knowledge.

Time management is particularly important in any examination and a number of candidates need to give this issue further attention.

Exhibit 1 – Assets of subsidiary

IAS 41 *Agriculture* deals with **agricultural activity**. Agricultural activity is the management by an entity of biological transformation and harvest of biological assets for sale or conversion into agricultural produce or into additional biological assets.

A biological asset is a living plant or animal. Cattle or sheep are examples of biological assets. **1 mark**

Agricultural produce is the harvested produce of biological assets. Both milk and meat are examples of agricultural produce. Therefore IAS 41 applies to many of the assets of our farming subsidiary (conclusion). **1 mark**

IAS 41 states that biological assets should normally be measured at fair value less costs to sell in the statement of financial position on initial recognition and at each year end. **1 mark**

Where cattle or sheep are purchased at a market, this means a reliable fair value and related costs can be used to arrive at initial recognised costs and any subsequent increase/decrease at the year end. **1 mark**

In the case of newly born cattle or sheep, the same 'fair value less costs to sell' principle applies. **1 mark**

A gain or loss arising on initial recognition or arising from a change in fair value less costs to sell at the year end are included in profit or loss. **1 mark**

This means that there is immediate recognition of a gain (equal to fair value less costs to sell) in profit or loss as the relevant biological asset is recognised when cattle and sheep are newly born. **0.5 mark**

IAS 41 does allow the 'cost model' to be used for biological assets if fair values cannot be measured reliably but this is unlikely to be true for biological assets like cattle or sheep where market values are available. **1 mark**

IAS 41 states that agricultural produce should be measured at its fair value less costs to sell at the point of harvest (principle). **1 mark**

IAS 41 defines 'harvesting' as the detachment of produce from a biological asset (for example, the milking of a cow) or the cessation of a biological asset's life processes (for example, the slaughter of a cow or a sheep for its meat). **1 mark**

The initial recognition of agricultural produce in the statement of financial position is likely to lead to an equal gain being recognised in the statement of profit or loss. **0.5 mark**

From this point on, agricultural produce would be subject to the recognition and measurement requirements of IAS 2 *Inventories*. Profits or losses on the subsequent sale of agricultural produce would be recognised when such produce was actually sold. **1 mark**

Other assets of our farming subsidiary (for example, farmland, farm machinery or trade receivables) would be measured using the IFRS Accounting Standards relevant to their nature. **1 mark**

Exhibit 2 – Post year end

There is an IFRS Accounting Standard, **IAS 10** *Events after the Reporting Period* which deals with this issue. IAS 10 defines an event after the reporting date as one occurring between the reporting date and the date the financial statements are authorised for issue. **0.5 mark**

IAS 10 further classifies events after the reporting date into adjusting and non-adjusting events (principle).

An adjusting event is one which provides **additional evidence of conditions existing at the reporting date. 0.5 mark** The first event you have queried is **an example of an adjusting event because** it provides confirmation of the amount of a liability which existed at the reporting date (since the unfair dismissal occurred on 31 December 20X4, prior to the year end). **1 mark**

IAS 10 requires that the impact of adjusting events be recognised in the financial statements (principle). **0.5 mark** This means **that we should recognise a liability of $560,000 in the statement of financial position at 30 September 20X5 in respect of this case** and an expense of $560,000 in the statement of profit or loss for the year. **1 mark** We should also make **additional disclosures** if this would assist the users of the financial statements. **0.5 mark**

Non-adjusting events are those events and transactions which provide additional evidence of conditions which arose **after** the reporting date. The fire at the factory is an example of a non-adjusting event. **1 mark**

Non-adjusting events should not be recognised in the financial statements, but should be fully disclosed in the notes to the financial statements if material. **1 mark**

The only exception to the 'non-recognition' rule mentioned above is if the event would be likely to impact on the going concern status of the reporting entity. This exception does not apply here because the subsidiary has the resources to finance the cost of rectifying the fire damage. **1 mark**

The third event you mentioned is **not an 'event after the reporting date' in accordance with IAS 10** as far as our latest financial statements are concerned because it occurred after the financial statements had been authorised for issue. The impact of this event will be shown in the **financial statements for the year ended 30 September 20X6. 1 mark**

Exhibit 3 – Purchase of inventory from a foreign supplier

This purchase is denominated in another currency and so is a foreign currency transaction. The accounting treatment for such transactions is set out in IAS 21 *The Effects of Changes in Foreign Exchange Rates.*

IAS 21 states that foreign currency transactions should initially be recorded at the rate of exchange in force when the transaction occurred **(principle). 1 mark** This means that, in this case, an **inventory and a payable of $140,000** (840,000/6) would be recorded.

The payable is settled on 31 August 20X5. The cash required to settle the payable would have been $120,000 (840,000/7). This means that an exchange gain of **$20,000** (140,000 – 120,000) would be recognised in the **statement of profit or loss. 1 mark**

The closing balance of inventory would have a cost of **$140,000**. This is **because** the inventory measured at cost is a non-monetary item (ie it is not expressed in terms of a monetary amount receivable or payable) and is not retranslated at the year end. **1 mark**

IAS 2 *Inventories* requires that inventories be measured at the lower of cost and net realisable value (NRV) (principle). **1 mark**

The NRV of the inventory is **$125,000** ($1 million/8). The closing exchange rate of 8 is used because NRV is a **monetary** measure. Therefore the closing inventory will be $125,000 and a loss of $15,000 ($140,000 – $125,000) will be recognised in the statement of profit or loss for the year ended 30 September 20X5. **1 mark**

36 Delta (June 2019) (amended)

Marks

(a)

(i) IFRS 2 *Share-based Payment* requires that the total estimated cost of granting share options to employees be recognised over the vesting period. ½

The total estimated cost should be charged as a remuneration expense and credited to equity (IFRS 2 does not specify where in equity the credit should be made). 1

The cumulative charge at the end of each period should be a proportion of the total estimated cost. The proportion should be based on the proportion of the total vesting period which has accrued at the reporting date. 1

The incremental charge is a remuneration expense for any period and should be the difference between the cumulative charge at the end of the period and the cumulative charge at the start of the period. 1

The charge should be based on the fair value of the option at the grant date. This continues to be the case throughout the vesting period – subsequent changes in the fair value of the option are not adjusted for. 1½

Where the vesting conditions are non-market conditions (ie not directly related to any change in the entity's share price), then the cumulative cost at each year end should be estimated based on the expected number of options which will vest at the vesting date. 1

6

(ii) If an entity grants cash-based share appreciation rights to employees rather than share options, then the basic principle of recognising the total estimated cost over the vesting period taking account of relevant vesting conditions is the same. 1

However, since any ultimate payment will be made in cash, the credit entry to account for the remuneration expense is to liabilities rather than equity. 1

Also, since any ultimate payment to the holders of share appreciation rights will normally be based on their fair value either at the vesting date or the payment date, subsequent changes in the fair value of the rights cannot be ignored. Measurement of the remuneration expense will be based on the fair value of the share appreciation rights at each reporting date. 1

3

(b) **Exhibit 1 – Granting of options to sales staff**

The expected total cost of the scheme at 31 March 20X6 was $58,800 (100 – 10 – 20) × 200 × $4.20. 2

Therefore cumulative cost accrued at 31 March 20X6 would have been $19,600 ($58,800 × 1/3). 1

The expected total cost of the scheme at 31 March 20X7 is $79,800 (100 – 10 – 5 – 9) × 250 × $4.20. 2

The cumulative cost accrued at 31 March 20X7 is $53,200 ($79,800 × 2/3). ½

Therefore the amount charged as a remuneration expense to profit or loss for the year ended 31 March 20X7 will be $33,600 ($53,200 – $19,600).

½

6

Exhibit 2 – Granting of share appreciation rights to senior executives

The expected fair value of the total liability at 31 March 20X7 will be $60,800 (500 × 19 × $6.40).

1½

The amount which will be shown as a liability in the statement of financial position at 31 March 20X7 will be the proportion based on the period elapsed since the rights were granted compared with the total vesting period. In this case that proportion is 18/48. Therefore the closing liability will be $22,800 ($60,800 × 18/48). This will be shown as a non-current liability.

1½

The liability which would have been recognised in the statement of financial position at 31 March 20X6 would have been $6,975 (500 × 18 × $6.20 × 6/48).

1

Delta would show a remuneration expense in profit or loss of $15,825 ($22,800 – $6,975) in respect of the share appreciation rights for the year ended 31 March 20X7.

1

5

(c) ### Exhibit 3 – Granting of share options to a director

The right granted to the director represents a share-based payment with a choice of settlement where the counterparty has the choice. In substance, a compound financial instrument has been issued and it needs to be broken down into its equity (equity-settled) and liability (cash-settled) components.

1

The fair value of the equity alternative is $13,200 (2,400 shares × $5.50). The fair value of the cash alternative is $12,200 (2,000 × $6.10). Therefore, the fair value of the equity component of the compound instrument is $1,000 ($13,200 – $12,200).

1

Once the value of the two components have been calculated, the accounting for each follows the normal accounting for an equity-settled or cash-settled share-based payment under IFRS 2, ie the related expense is spread over the vesting period of two years.

1

For the equity component, at 31 March 20X7, Delta should make the following accounting entries:

1

| DEBIT | Profit or loss | $500 |
| CREDIT | Liability ($1,000 × 1/2) | $500 |

The equity component is not remeasured at subsequent year-ends.

For the liability component, at 31 March 20X7, the liability is remeasured using to fair value and Theta should make the following accounting entries:

1

| DEBIT | Profit or loss | $6,900 |
| CREDIT | Liability ($2,000 × $6.90 × 1/2) | $6,900 |

5

25

37 Dart

> **Top tips.** This question asked you to explain and apply the provisions of IFRS 2 on share-based payments. This topic is examined frequently and you are advised to have a good knowledge of it.
>
> **Easy marks.** Parts (a) and (b) had lots of easy marks, and most of the calculations in part (c) were quite straightforward also.
>
> **Examining team's comments.** Part (a) was answered well by most candidates. A minority of candidates lost marks by not addressing the questions specifically enough and writing about share based payments too generally. Some candidates repeated information about IFRS 2 that was given in the question. This clearly attracted no marks.
>
> Part (b) of this question was well answered on the whole, with a number of candidates scoring full marks. Some candidates lost marks by failing to appreciate that, in an equity-settled share-based payment transaction, the credit entry is to equity rather than to liabilities.
>
> Candidates found part (c)(i) challenging on the whole. A reasonable number were able to compute the cost based on the initial share award, by basing the cost on the fair value of the option at the grant date and the expected numbers vesting based on the best estimate at the reporting date. However very few candidates were able to deal with the modification to the award that was necessary because of the fall in Kappa's share price in the year ended 31 March 20X4. It would appear that in general candidates had not studied this aspect of accounting for share based payments.
>
> Answers to part (c)(ii) were on the whole satisfactory. Having said this, only a minority of candidates correctly identified the liability as non-current.

[References: IFRS 2: 7, 10–21, 30–33D]

			Marks
(a)			
	(i)	For equity-settled share-based payment arrangements, the transaction should be measured based on the fair value of the goods or services received, or to be received.	½
		Where the third party is an employee, 'fair value' should be based on the fair value of the equity instruments granted, measured at the grant date.	½ + ½
		For cash-settled share-based payment arrangements, the transaction should be measured based on the fair value of the liability at each reporting date.	½ + ½
	(ii)	The amount recognised should take account of all vesting conditions other than (in the case of equity-settled share-based payment arrangements) market conditions (which are reflected in the measurement of the fair value of the instruments granted).	½ + ½ + ½
	(iii)	For both types of arrangement, the debit entry will normally be to profit or loss unless the relevant expense would qualify for recognition as an asset.	1
		For an equity-settled share-based payment arrangement, the credit entry would be recognised in equity, either as share capital or (more commonly) as an option reserve.	½
		For cash-settled share-based payment arrangements, the credit entry would be recognised as a liability.	½
			6

	Marks

(b)

This equity settled share based payment arrangement should be measured using the fair value of an option on the grant date – $3.00 in this case.　　1

The revenue for the year ended 31 March 20X5, plus the expected revenue for the next two years, indicates that the cumulative revenue for the three years ended 31 March 20X7 is likely to be $190m. Therefore the number of options vesting for each executive is likely to be 200.　　2

This means that the charge to P/L for the year ended 31 March 20X5 should be $20,000 (100 × 200 × $3.00 × 1/3).　　1

The credit entry should be to other components of equity.　　$\frac{1}{5}$

(c)

(i)　　The expected total cost of the arrangement at 31 March 20X4 is 400 × $1.50 × (500 – 10 – 20) = $282,000.　　1

Therefore $70,500 ($282,000 × ¼) would be credited to equity and debited to profit or loss for the year ended 31 March 20X4.　　1

For the year ended 31 March 20X5, the expected total cost of the originally granted options would be 400 × $1.50 × (500 – 10 – 5 – 10) = $285,000.　　1

The cumulative amount taken to profit or loss and recognised in equity at 31 March 20X5 is $142,500.　　1

The additional cost of the repriced options must also be recognised over the three-year period to 31 March 20X7.　　½ + ½

The total additional cost is 400 × ($1.45 – $0.25) × 475 = $228,000.　　1

Therefore the amount recognised in the year ended 31 March 20X5 is $76,000 ($228,000 × 1/3). Therefore the total recognised in equity at 31 March 20X5 is $218,500 ($142,500 + $76,000).　　1

The amount recognised in equity would be shown as 'other components of equity'.　　½

And the charge to profit or loss for the year ended 31 March 20X5 is $148,000 ($142,500 + $76,000 – $70,500).　　1

The amount recognised in profit or loss would be shown as an employment expense.　　$\frac{½}{9}$

(ii)　　For the year ended 31 March 20X4, the expected total cost will be 50 × 1,000 × $0.90 = $45,000.　　1

The amount taken to profit or loss in the prior period, and recognised as a liability, will be $15,000 ($45,000 × 1/3).　　1

At 31 March 20X5, the liability will be 50 × 2,000 × $1.20 × 2/3 = $80,000.　　1

Since the rights are exercisable on 30 June 20X6, the liability will be non-current.　　1

The charge to profit or loss for the year ended 31 March 20X5 will be $65,000 ($80,000 – $15,000). This will be included in employment expenses.　　$\frac{1}{5}$
　　$\frac{}{25}$

38 Roma (June 2016) (amended)

Top tips. This question asked you to explain and show how the four events would be reported in the financial statements of Roma. In Exhibit 1 you had to correctly identify that the share options were equity settled, and then explain how to account for them under IFRS 2. The repricing of the option was tricky, but you could still have gained many of the marks for Exhibit 1 without getting that bit correct. Exhibit 2 was straightforward if you had practiced applying IAS 37. You needed to identify that a provision was required and that a contingent asset should be disclosed. Exhibit 3 required you to spot that related parties were involved. The fact that the spouse of a director was mentioned in the question should have highlighted to you that related parties were potentially an issue – if they didn't, make sure you spot that next time! Exhibit 4 should have been relatively straightforward. You should know that acquired brands can be capitalised and then have to be amortised.

Easy marks. Exhibit 2 had lots of easy marks available for applying your knowledge of provisions and contingent assets. Exhibit 4 had easy marks for discussing basic accounting treatment of acquired intangible assets.

Examining team's comments. Exhibit 1 was generally satisfactorily answered. Candidates found it difficult to deal with the re-pricing. Some candidates used the term 'option reserve' without stating that this is equity and failed to score any marks because 'reserve' may well refer to a liability. Not all candidates wrote that employment expense should be charged to profit or loss under operating costs. Mentioning 'other comprehensive income' is not correct because there are profit or loss and other comprehensive income at the same time. Mentioning provision or reserve cost is not correct either.

Exhibit 2 was a popular part of the question and many candidates correctly classified a claim to S as a contingent asset. But not all of them noted that it was included in the disclosure to the financial statements. Many candidates correctly identified the adjusting event but some incorrectly stated the amount recognised as the best estimate of the amount required to settle the obligation. This should be the estimate made just before the financial statements are authorised for issue. Most candidates mentioned 'provision' without any clarification that this is a liability as opposed to part of equity.

In Exhibit 3 it was necessary for candidates not only to mention related parties but also name them and explain why they should be treated as related parties.

[References: IFRS 2: paras. 7, 10–21, 26–29; IAS 24: paras. 9, 13–24; IAS 37: paras. 10, 14, 31–34; IAS 38: paras. 33–37, 74]

Marking guide

	Marks
SBP explanation and vesting	3
Charge to P/L	1
Charge to equity	2½
Repricing	3½
Provision	3
Contingent asset	3
Revenue	1
Identify related party	2½
Disclosure	1½
Brand name	2
Employees	2
Total	**25**

BPP
LEARNING
MEDIA

Marks

Exhibit 1

IFRS 2 *Share-based Payments* requires that equity-settled share-based payments should be measured based on their **fair value** at the **grant date** multiplied by the **number of options expected to vest** based on estimates at the **reporting date**.
½ + ½ + ½ + ½

The cost should be spread over the **vesting period** – three years in this case.
1

This means that the charge to profit or loss in the year ended 31 March 20X5 will be **$740,000** (1,850 × 1,000 × $1.20 × 1/3).
1

The credit entry will be to **equity**, probably to an **option, or shares to be issued, reserve**.
½ + ½

Based on the **original** arrangements, the **cumulative** balance in equity on 31 March 20X6 will be **$1,472,000** (1,840 × 1,000 × $1.20 × 2/3).
½ + ½ + ½

The impact of the **repricing** on 30 September 20X5 is to charge the **incremental** increase in fair value over the **remaining** vesting period on the same basis as the original charge.
½ + ½ + ½

Therefore the additional credit to equity in respect of the repricing will be $92,000 (1,840 × 1,000 × ($1.05 – $0.90) × 6/18).
½

This means the closing balance in equity will be $1,564,000 ($1,472,000 + $92,000).
½

The charge to profit or loss in the year ended 31 March 20X6 will be **$824,000** ($1,564,000 – $740,000). This will be shown as an **employment expense** under **operating costs**.
1

10

Exhibit 2

The potential liability to pay damages to C needs to be recognised as a provision because the event giving rise to the potential liability (the supply of faulty products) arose **prior** to 31 March 20X6, there is a **probable** transfer of economic benefits and **a reliable** estimate can be made of the amount of the probable transfer.
½ + ½ + ½

The amount recognised should be the best estimate of the amount required to settle the obligation at the reporting date. In this case, this estimate is the one made on **15 May** – just before the financial statements are authorised for issue. Therefore a provision of $5.25 million should be recognised as a **current liability**. There should also be a **charge of $5.25 million to profit or loss**.
½ + ½ +½

The potential amount receivable from S is a contingent asset as it arose from an event prior to the year end but **at the date the financial statements are authorised for issue**, the ultimate outcome is uncertain.
½ + ½ + ½

Contingent assets are **not** recognised as assets in the statement of financial position. Their existence and estimated financial effect is **disclosed** where the future receipt of economic benefits is **probable**. This is the situation here.
½ + ½ + ½

6

Marks

Exhibit 3

Roma would include the **total** revenue of $6.8 million ($6m + $800,000) from entity X receivable in the year ended 31 March 20X6 within its revenue and show $1.8 million within trade receivables at 31 March 20X6.

1

The spouse of a director of Roma would be regarded as **a related party** of Roma because they are **a close family member** of one of the **key management personnel** of Roma.

½ + ½ + ½

From 1 June 20X5, entity X would also be regarded as a related party of Roma because from that date entity X is an entity **controlled by another related party**.

½ + ½

Because entity X is a related party with whom Roma has transactions, then Roma should disclose:

- The nature of the related party relationship.
- The revenue of $6 million from entity X since 1 June 20X5.
- The outstanding balance of $1.8 million at 31 March 20X6. In the current circumstances it may well be necessary for Roma to also disclose the favourable terms under which the transactions are carried out.

1½

5

Exhibit 4

The brand name is capitalised at its **fair value** of $10 million. It is amortised over its **useful life of ten years**, resulting in an expense of $1 million. The carrying amount at the year end is thus $9 million.

1 + 1

In accordance with IAS 38, no asset may be recognised in respect of the employees' expertise, as Roma/Omicron **does not exercise 'control'** over them – they could leave their jobs.

1 + 1

The amount will be recognised as **part of any goodwill** on acquisition of Omicron.

4

25

39 Gamma (June 2022)

Top tips. This question asked you to explain and show the accounting treatment of two separate issues in the financial statements of Gamma – namely the granting of a share based award to senior executives that contained a cash alternative and the revaluation of a building that had previously been measured using the cost model. Candidates were also required to consider an ethical issue in the context of accounting for these items.

The examiners comments show that many candidates did not provide any explanations, and instead only produced calculations. It is important to follow the requirement as set and produce short and clear explanations, applying your knowledge of accounting principles to the scenario. Make sure you practice writing out your answers to improve your performance here as well as making sure your knowledge of key standards is strong enough to make an attempt at every part of the question.

Easy marks. These were available for the basic accounting for an upwards revaluation and then depreciating the asset based on the fair value over the remaining useful life. Candidates always have to consider an ethical issue somewhere in the exam so should have been able to earn marks by applying their knowledge of the Code of Ethics to the scenario.

Examining team's comments. Answers to this question were disappointing. The question clearly asked for explanations as well as calculations but often candidates failed to provide explanations. Answers to issue one – the share based payment – were particularly disappointing. It was evident that the vast majority of candidates were not aware of how to include such awards in the financial statements.

BPP
LEARNING
MEDIA

Attachment 1 to email

The relevant standard is IFRS 2 *Share-based Payment*. Under IFRS 2, the offer of shares to senior executives is a share-based payment transaction which must be recognised in the financial statements. **1 mark**

This particular transaction (a share-based payment transaction with a cash alternative) is treated partly as an equity settled share-based payment transaction and partly a cash settled one. **1 mark**

The fair value of the equity settled element at the grant date is computed by deducting the fair value of the cash alternative at the grant date from the overall fair value of the offer of the shares with the cash alternative. This is because the executives (counterparty) and not the entity have the choice as to whether to take the shares or cash. **1.5 marks**

The fair value of the equity settled part of the transaction is $72,000 [12,000 × $9 (the fair value of the overall share offer) × 9 executives − 10,000 × $10 (the fair value of the cash alternative) × 9]. **1 mark**

The equity settled part of the arrangement is recognised as a remuneration expense over the three-year vesting period based on its fair value at the grant date and the number of shares which are actually expected to vest. **1 mark**

Therefore the amount which is recognised in the year ended 31 March 20X5 is $24,000 ($72,000 × 1/3). **½ mark**

The corresponding credit entry in the statement of financial position is to other components of equity and will not be re-measured. **1 mark**

The remuneration expense associated with the liability component of the arrangement is also recognised over the vesting period and based on the number of shares which are actually expected to be issued on vesting. However, the expense is measured based on the fair value of the liability component at the reporting date. **1 mark**

Therefore the total amount which is recognised in profit or loss as a remuneration expense in the year ended 31 March 20X5 is $384,000 = ((9 × 10,000 × $12 × 1/3) = $360,000 + $24,000 [above]). **1.5 marks**

The corresponding credit entry of $360,000 in the statement of financial position is to non-current liabilities. **½ mark**

Tutorial note. Candidates may present as a journal:

DR	Profit or loss – Remuneration expense	$384,000	
CR	Non-current liability		$360,000
CR	Other components of equity		$24,000

Attachment 2 to email

The relevant standard is IAS 16 *Property, Plant and Equipment* (PPE). Where PPE is revalued and the revaluation shows a surplus, then, unless the surplus is eliminating a previous revaluation deficit on the same asset, the surplus is recognised in other comprehensive income rather than profit or loss. **1 mark**

Since this is a first time revaluation, then a surplus of $10 million ($30 million − $20 million) will be recognised in other comprehensive income. **0.5 marks**

Regardless of future potential increases in value, assets which are revalued still need to be depreciated over their estimated future useful lives . **0.5 marks**

Land generally has an indefinite life, so only the buildings element of the property needs to be depreciated. **0.5 marks**

This means that the depreciation charge on the property for the year ended 31 March 20X5 will be $0.9 million ($18 million × 1/20). $0.9 million will be charged as an expense in the statement of profit or loss. **1 mark**

The carrying amount of the property at 31 March 20X5 will be $29.1 million ($30 million − $0.9 million). This will be presented as part of non-current assets in the statement of financial position. **0.5 marks**

Under the principles of IAS 12 *Income Taxes* a deferred tax liability must be recognised on the revaluation of an asset even if there is no intention to dispose of the asset. **0.5 marks**

ANSWERS

IAS 12 requires that a deferred tax liability be recognised on the difference between the carrying amount of an asset and its tax base. **0.5 marks**

So for this property, the deferred tax liability prior to its revaluation will be $5 million (25% × $20 million (– $0 tax base)). **0.5 marks**

After the revaluation, the deferred tax liability will increase to $7.5 million (25% × $30 million (– $0 tax base)). **0.5 marks**

The increase of $2.5 million following the revaluation will be debited to other comprehensive income. **0.5 marks**

The net credit to other comprehensive income as a result of the revaluation will be $7.5 million ($10 million – $2.5 million). This net credit will be recognised as a revaluation surplus in the statement of financial position as part of 'other components of equity'. **1 mark**

The deferred tax liability on 31 March 20X5 will be $7.275 million ($29.1 million × 25%) 1 mark. This will be presented as a non-current liability in the statement of financial position. **0.5 marks**

The reduction in the deferred tax liability between 1 April 20X4 and 31 March 20X5 will be $0.225 million ($7.5 million – $7.275 million). **1 mark** This will be shown as a credit to the income tax expense in the statement of profit or loss. **0.5 marks**

Tutorial note. Some candidates may mention the option given in IAS 16 for entities which measure PPE using the revaluation model to make a transfer between the revaluation surplus and retained earnings. This transfer is based on the difference between depreciation actually charged on the revalued asset – in this case $0.9 million – and the depreciation which would have been charged had the asset continued to be measured at historical cost. This amount would have been $0.5 million ($10 million × 1/20), so the gross transfer for the year ended 31 March 20X5 would have been $0.4 million ($0.9 million – $0.5 million). Where deferred tax is taken into consideration, the transfer is made net of attributable taxation. The accounting entry in this case would be:

	$m	$m
Credit retained earnings ($0.4 million × (100 – 25)%)		0.30
Debit revaluation surplus	0.30	

Candidates who take this approach will be awarded a maximum of 3 additional marks (but the total for attachment 2 cannot exceed 10 marks).

Email from finance director (FD)

You are in danger of breaching the fundamental ethical principle of objectivity. You have a personal interest in reporting a favourable profit because of the possibility of a profit related bonus. **1 mark**

You also may be breaching the fundamental ethical principle of professional competence. As only part qualified and only part-way through a training programme, you may well not be competent enough to make a decision on the complex transactions outlined by the FD. **1 mark**

You are also breaching the fundamental ethical principle of integrity. It is at least possible that the FD is deliberately seeking to falsify the financial statements. If you are complicit and comply with the instructions of the FD, then there is a danger that this principle will be breached. **2 marks**

It is not appropriate to reveal the detail in the attachments to that email to a friend who is not employed by Gamma. This clearly breaches the fundamental ethical principle of confidentiality. **1 mark**

BPP LEARNING MEDIA

40 Belloso

> **Top tips.** Make sure you consider how you would have answered this question if it was in CBE format. Which response options would you have chosen? Would you have used a combination of both spreadsheet and word processor to submit your answer? For example, you could have typed up the discussion parts in the word processor and performed the calculations in the spreadsheet. If you chose this method of presenting your answer, you must make sure you appropriately label each part of your answer so that the marker can follow what you have done.

Exhibit 1 – Contract with Alesso

This is a consignment arrangement under IFRS 15 *Revenue from Contracts with Customers*. This is demonstrated by the fact that the inventory is controlled by Belloso until it is sold to the customer – Belloso can dictate the selling price and any unsold inventory must be returned to Belloso at the end of the trial period.

At the year end, Belloso retains control over inventory with a cost of $10,000 ($30,000 – $20,000 sold) still held by Alesso. This inventory should therefore be included in Belloso's statement of financial position at 31 December 20X1.

Belloso should only recognise revenue relating to inventory which Alesso has sold on to customers. At the year end, Belloso should recognise a total of $28,000 in revenue, representing the total sales made by Alesso.

Any remaining amount of the $10,000 deposit paid by Alesso is refundable on return of any unsold goods at the end of the trial period. As 31 December 20X1, $6,667 of the deposit has been correctly deducted by Alesso from the revenue remitted to Belloso. Belloso should therefore recognise the remaining $3,333 of the deposit as a current liability at 31 December 20X1.

Under the contract, Alesso is paid a commission of 10% of any sales made, payable at the end of the 6 month trial. Therefore at 31 December 20X1, Belloso should recognise a currently liability payable to Alesso of $2,800 (10% × $28,000).

Exhibit 2 – Convertible bonds

The convertible bonds are compound financial instruments per IAS 32 *Financial instruments: Presentation*. The bonds have the characteristics of both debit and equity. IAS 32 requires that the bonds are separated into an equity component and a debt component and these should be presented separately in the financial statements.

The liability component should be measured first. It is calculated as the present value of the principal and interest payments, discounted at the effective interest rate for an instrument with similar terms but without the conversion option (7%).

	$
Present value of the principal: $1,000,000 payable at the end of three years ($1m × 0.816)	816,000
Present value of the interest: $50,000 payable annually in arrears for three years ($50,000 × 2.624)	131,200
Liability component	947,200
Equity component (Bal fig)	52,800
Proceeds of the bond issue	1,000,000

The liability should be measured at $947,200 and the equity component should be calculated as the residual amount and measured at $52,800. Belloso should therefore reduce the non-current liability recorded to $947,200 and record an equity component of $52,800.

The interest expense for the year to 31 December 20X1 should be calculated at 7% of the liability component.

1 Jan 20X1	Interest (7%)	Payment (5%)	31 Dec 20X1
$	$	$	$
947,200	66,304	(50,000)	963,504

The interest expense of $66,304 should be charged to finance costs and credited to the non-current liability, giving a balance of $963,504 at the year end.

Exhibit 3 – Investment in Nefyn

Belloso has acquired 25% of the ordinary shares of Nefyn and has appointed two of five directors to Nefyn's board. Therefore, under IAS 28 *Investments in Associates*, Belloso is presumed to exercise significant influence over Nefyn. The investment in Nefyn should be classified as an associate and accounted for under the equity method.

In Belloso's consolidated statement of financial position the investment in Nefyn should be measured at cost plus Belloso's 25% share of Nefyn's post-acquisition retained earnings less any impairment.

Belloso's share of Nefyn's earnings, less any impairment charges, should be recognised in consolidated profit or loss.

At 31 December 20X1 the investment in Nefyn should be measured as:

	$
Cost	340,000
Add: Share of post-acquisition earnings ($430,000 × 9/12 × 25%)	80,625
Less: Dividend received (25% × $35,000)	(8,750)
	411,875

In consolidated profit or loss Belloso's share of Nefyn's earnings should be measured at $80,625 and the dividend received should be reversed out of Belloso's investment income.

In the consolidated statement of financial position at 31 December 20X1 the investment in Nefyn should be presented within non-current assets and measured at $411,875.

Exhibit 4 – Decommissioning of plant

The decommissioning and restoration costs are an unavoidable obligation associated with control of the plant. This obligation is reliably measurable and an outflow of resources is highly probable. Therefore a provision for the costs should be made under IAS 37 *Provisions, Contingent Liabilities and Contingent Assets*.

As the costs are not payable until the end of the plant's useful life in five years' time, the provision should be discounted to reflect the time value of money. The discounted cost is $150,000 × 0.681 = $102,150.

At acquisition of the plant this amount should be added to the cost of the plant and credited to provisions. The plant should be measured at $1,300,000 + $102,150 = $1,402,150.

For the year ended 31 December 20X1, Bolloso should recognise:

- $8,172 ($102,150 × 8%) in finance costs to reflect the unwinding of the discount on the provision. This amount should be credited to the provision, resulting in a total provision of $110,322 ($102,150 + $8,172).

- $280,430 ($1,402,150/5) as depreciation of the plant on the straight-line basis. The carrying amount of the plant should therefore be $1,121,720($1,402,150 – $280,430).

41 Delta (December 2013) (amended)

> **Top tips.** This question covered three areas which are fairly central to the syllabus, so if you struggled with any of it then this will give you an indication of where you need to focus your work before the exam. Exhibit 1 on financial instruments was actually not that difficult, even though it was on financial instruments which is a topic which sometimes elicits panic from candidates! It serves as a good illustration of a question where keeping calm pays off, as there were plenty of marks available for simply stating the required treatment of the financial asset on initial recognition.
>
> Exhibit 2 was on a familiar syllabus area. As with Exhibit 1, your approach should be to state the required treatment and then apply it to the question. Be careful, however, not to enter into any long discussions of general accounting principles – keep your answer focused on the question.
>
> Exhibit 3 required the application of the exemptions in IFRS 16. Exhibit 4 was on termination benefits.
>
> **Easy marks.** There are easy marks in Exhibit 1 for computing the cost of the asset, and for stating that it will be split into its current and non-current elements.
>
> **Examining team's comments.** On the whole many candidates failed to score well on this question. Many left out Exhibit 1, which was the least well answered.
>
> *Exhibit 1 – the financial asset*
>
> - Very few discussed the fact that this was valued at amortised cost and even fewer explained why. Some suggested this was a liability not an asset.
>
> - Most identified the initial carrying amount of $36 million but applied the effective rate to $40 million and did not apportion for six months. Most applied the rules for amortised cost valuation but deducted the 4% receivable to arrive at the carrying amount even though this had not been received. This meant that the point about it being a current asset was missed.
>
> *Exhibit 2 – the held for sale business unit*
>
> Of all the parts to this question, this was answered the best. Many understood the impairment issue as well as how to allocate the impairment across the assets in the cash generating unit. The main point missed was the discussion of the held for sale rules and why they applied here.

Marking scheme

	Marks
Exhibit 1	
In line with IFRS 9 *Financial Instruments* financial assets are measured at either amortised cost or fair value, depending on the reason for holding them and the nature of the expected returns from the asset.	1
Here amortised cost is because Delta's objective is to hold the assets to collect the contractual cash flows, and those cash flows consist solely of the repayment of principal and interest by Epsilon.	1
On 1 April 20X3 the asset is recognised at its fair value of $36 million ($40m × 90 cents).	1
The finance income recognised in profit or loss for the six months to 30 September 20X3 is $1.782 million ($36m × 9.9% × 6/12).	1
At 30 September 20X3 the asset's carrying amount is $37.782 million ($36m + $1.782m).	½
This asset will be split into its current and non-current portions.	½
The interest payment due on 31 March 20X4 of $1.6 million ($40m × 4%) will be a current asset.	½
The remaining asset of $36.182 million ($37.782m – $1.6m) will be non-current.	½
	6

Marks

Exhibit 2

The business is held for sale from 1 June 20X3. The held for sale criteria apply because it is being actively marketed at a reasonable price, the assets are ready for sale and the sale is expected to be completed within one year of the date of classification.

1

Under IFRS 5 *Non-current Assets Held for Sale and Discontinued Operations* , on 1 June 20X3 the assets will be classified separately under current assets in the statement of financial position, and depreciation ceases.

1

The assets will be measured at the lower of their current carrying amounts at the date of classification, and their fair value less costs to sell. In this case, they will be re-measured to $46 million ($46.5m – $0.5m).

1

The impairment loss of $17 million ($63m – $46m) will first be allocated to goodwill, taking its carrying amount to nil.

1

None of the remaining impairment loss will be allocated to inventories or trade receivables, because their recoverable amounts are at least equal to their existing carrying amounts.

1

The remaining impairment loss of $7 million ($17m – $10m) will be allocated to the property, plant and equipment and the patents on a pro-rata basis.

1

The closing carrying amounts of the property, plant and equipment and the patents will be $15 million and $6 million respectively.

$\underline{1}$

$\underline{7}$

Exhibit 3

IFRS 16 includes optional recognition exceptions for short term leases and for leases of low value assets. Delta has chosen to apply these recognition exemptions.

1

Short-term leases are leases with a lease term of 12 months or less.

½

The nine-month lease of plant qualifies as a short term lease. The lease payment should be charged to profit or loss on a straight-line basis over the lease term.

1

A charge of $40,000 ($180,000 × 2/9) should be recognised in profit or loss for the year to 30 September 20X3. The remaining lease payment of $140,000 should be recognised as a prepayment in the statement of financial position.

1

The four-year lease of 500 tablets is considered to be a lease of low value assets. Even though the lease of the tablet computers is material to Delta, the exemption can still be applied because the underlying assets, ie the tablets, are individually of low value.

1

The lease payments should be charged to profit or loss on a straight-line basis over the lease term.

½

A charge of $60,000 ($240 × 500 × 6/12) should be recorded in profit or loss, and a prepayment of $60,000 should be recorded in the statement of financial position for the year ended 30 September 20X3.

$\underline{1}$

$\underline{6}$

Exhibit 4

½

The payments of $15,000 which Delta will pay to each of its employees on termination of their employment contracts are termination benefits and should be accounted for under IAS 19 *Employee Benefits*.

IAS 19 states that termination benefits are employee benefits provided in exchange for termination of employment as a result of either an entity's decision to terminate an employee's employment before normal retirement age, or an employee's decision to accept an offer of benefits in exchange for termination of employment. Delta has both of these scenarios in this instance.

1

Marks

For the 45 employees who have accepted Delta's offer of $15,000 payment for termination of employment on 31 December 20X3, Delta should recognise an expense and corresponding liability of $675,000 ($15,000 × 45) on 31 August 20X3, which is the date that the employees accepted Delta's offer. As the amount is due to be settled within 12 months of the reporting date, no discounting is required. As the termination benefits will be paid on 31 December 20X3, the liability will be presented as a current liability at the reporting date of 30 September 20X3.

1 + ½

For the 30 employees who will be forced to end their employment on 31 January 20X4, Delta should not recognise any expense or related liability until Delta can no longer withdraw the offer of termination benefits. IAS 19 considers that to be the date that a plan of termination (which should include details of the number of affected employees, expected termination date and termination benefits payable) is communicated to the affected employees, which here is 3 October 20X3. Therefore no expense or liability should be recognised in the financial statements to 30 September 20X3.

1 + ½

However, Delta should consider whether the planned termination and the termination benefit payable on 31 January 20X4 of $450,000 ($15,000 × 30) is material information for users of the financial statements. If so, it should disclose the issue in the notes to the financial statements at 30 September 20X3.

1 + ½

$$\frac{6}{25}$$

42 Delta (December 2020)

Top tips. In this question, you were required to explain, including calculations, the accounting treatment of three issues:

(1) A share-based payment scheme which was modified in the current accounting period.

(2) The sale of two properties.

(3) The sale of two business units.

As the requirement was to 'explain', simply providing calculations is not enough, they must be accompanied by adequate explanation.

The modification of the share-based payment in part (a) was difficult and you might not have known how to approach it. However, don't let this put you off as you could still have scored well on this part of the question by explaining the basic principles (with relevant calculations) for accounting for share-based payments, such as spreading costs over the vesting period and explaining that the total amount is accumulated in equity and the movement in the year is an expense in the period.

Part (b) required knowledge and application of IFRS 5 *Non-Current Assets Held for Sale and Discontinued Operations* in two different scenarios. Exhibit 2 required the application of the 'held for sale' criteria of IFRS 5. One of the properties met these criteria, while the other did not. Exhibit 3 required the application of the discontinued operations criteria of IFRS 5. One business unit met these criteria, whereas the other remained part of continuing operations.

Remember to appropriately allocate your time when faced with a question such as this in the DipIFR exam. Part (b) was worth 15 marks, so you should have spent around 29 minutes (15 marks × 1.95 minutes per mark) on it. Around 19 of those minutes should have been spent explaining how the sale of the properties should be accounted for, and only 10 minutes on the sale of the business units.

Examining team's comments.

Some common errors identified in this question included the following:

• A minority of candidates treated the share-based payment scheme as a cash settled (as opposed to equity settled) share based payment scheme.

• A significant minority of candidates incorrectly stated that 'held for sale' assets are always measured at 'fair value less costs to sell' (rather than the lower of current carrying amount and fair value less costs to sell). Additionally a significant minority of candidates were unable to distinguish between property 1 (that satisfied the 'held for sale' criteria) and property 2 (that did not).

• Answers to the issue in Exhibit 3 were on the whole unsatisfactory. Only a minority of candidates were able to identify the first unit sold to be a discontinued operation and the second to be part of continuing operations. Consequently many candidates simply stated that the profits on sale would be included in the statement of profit or loss.

Marks

Exhibit 1 – Share-based payment

Under the principles of IFRS 2 *Share-based payment* – equity settled share-based payment obligations are measured using the fair value of the equity instruments to be issued at the **grant** date. In this case, therefore, the relevant fair value is **$2.50** per option.

½ + ½

Where vesting conditions apply (as is the case here) then, in the case of non-market conditions, the number of options expected to vest is adjusted to latest estimates at the end of the reporting period.

½

Therefore, for the year ended 30 September 20X4, the expected total cost of the arrangement is $300,000 (3,000 × 40 × $2.50).

1

The cost is recognised in profit or loss over the vesting period. Therefore the amount recognised in profit or loss for the year ended 30 September 20X4 is $100,000 ($300,000 × 1/3).

½ + ½

The expected total cost of the arrangement at 30 September 20X5 would be $285,000 (3,000 × (50 – 12) × $2.50).

1

Therefore the cumulative amount recognised in profit or loss up to 30 September 20X5 in respect of the original arrangement will be **$190,000** ($285,000 × 2/3) and the actual amount recognised for the year ended 30 September 20X5 will be **$90,000** ($190,000 – $100,000). This will be shown as an **employment expense** under operating expenses.

½ + ½ + ½

The modification to the terms of the arrangement which takes place on 1 April 20X5 will be an **additional cost which will be recognised over the remaining vesting period**. This additional cost will be based on the increase in the fair value of an option caused by the modification.

½ + ½

In this case, the additional cost which will be recognised over the remaining vesting period will be $68,400 (3,000 × 38 × ($2.70 – $2.10)).

1

The amount which will be recognised in the year ended 30 September 20X5 will be **$22,800** ($68,400 × 6/18) and so the total charge to profit or loss for the year ended 30 September 20X5 in respect of the arrangement will be **$112,800** ($90,000 + $22,800).

½ + ½

The cumulative total cost recognised to date of **$212,800** ($190,000 + $22,800) will be shown in the equity section of the statement of financial position at 30 September 20X5.

½ + ½

10

Marks

Exhibit 2 – Sale of two properties

Under the principles of *IFRS 5 – Non-current Assets Held for Sale and Discontinued Operations* – property 1 would be classified as 'held-for-sale' from 1 September 20X5. This is **because** the property is available for immediate sale in its current condition, is being actively marketed at a reasonable price, and a sale is expected in less than 12 months.

½ + ½

Property 1 is removed from non-current assets (PPE) and separately classified as a current asset on the statement of financial position as a 'held for sale' asset.

1

When an asset is classified as held-for-sale, it is **measured at the lower of its current carrying amount and its fair value less costs to sell**. Held-for-sale assets are **not** depreciated after classification.

1 + ½

The fair value less costs to sell for property 1 is $57 million (95% × $60m). Therefore property 1 will be measured at $50 million.

1

Property 2 cannot be classified as held-for-sale because it is not available for immediate sale in its current condition. Therefore it will continue to be presented in PPE.

1

Based on the information available in the question, it would appear that property 2 has suffered impairment.

½

An asset has suffered impairment if its recoverable amount is lower than its carrying amount. Recoverable amount is the higher of value-in-use and fair value less costs to sell.

1

Since property 2 is not able to generate any future income for Delta other than through sale, then in this case the recoverable amount of the property is its fair value less costs to sell.

½

The fair value less costs to sell of property 2 is $32.75 million ($45m × 95% – $10m). The repair costs of $10 million are necessarily incurred in getting the property into a saleable condition and so are deducted in computing its fair value less costs to sell.

1 + ½

Property 2 will therefore be recognised in PPE at $32.75 million.

½

An impairment loss of $7.25 million ($40m – $32.75m) will be recognised as an operating expense in the statement of profit or loss and other comprehensive income.

½

10

Exhibit 3 – Sale of two business units during the year

Under the principles of IFRS 5, the segment would be regarded as a discontinued operation because it is a separate line of business which has been disposed of in the period.

1

This means that, in the statement of profit or loss and other comprehensive income, the results and post-tax gain or loss on sale would be presented as a single amount below the profit after tax from continuing operations and described as profit or loss on discontinued operations.

1

In this case, the amount would be $8.2 million ($5m + (($54m – $50m) × 80%)).

1

The sale of the distribution centres is not separately presented as it is not a discontinued operation – the distribution operations of Delta are being reorganised, not discontinued.

1

Marks

The profit on disposal of the distribution centre of $2 million ($12m − $10m) would be
recognised as part of its pre-tax profit for the year.

1

5

25

43 Omega (December 2020) (amended)

Top tips. This is typical of the style of question that you should expect to see in Question 4 of the DipIFR exam – questions from a director on several accounting issues. This question included knowledge and application of IFRS 6 *Exploration for and Evaluation of Mineral Resources,* as well as IFRS Sustainability Disclosure Standards both of which you may have considered to be peripheral to the syllabus. Note that all areas of the syllabus could feature in an exam, none are peripheral, so you should make sure you are adequately prepared for all aspects of the syllabus to be tested.

Time management is also a common issue in the DipIFR exam (an especially so in Question 4). Make sure you practice a full range of questions to improve your time management across the whole exam paper.

This question also tested IAS 10 *Events After the Reporting Period.*

Examining team's comments.

The examiner's report stated that 'A general observation regarding question four is that candidates should make sure they answer the exact questions the directors is asking. The form of these questions often provides a useful structure for the candidate's answer and should help to prevent a candidate from producing irrelevant material.' (Examiner's report – December 2020)

Exhibit 1 – Sale of two business units during the year

IFRS 6 – *Exploration for and Evaluation of Mineral Resources* – specifies financial reporting in this area.

½ (principle)

IFRS 6 does not specifically prescribe what expenditures should be included as exploration and evaluation assets. Relevant entities are allowed to determine an accounting policy which specifies which expenditures should be included as exploration and evaluation assets and must apply it consistently. (Exact wording not needed – just the overall sense of the point.)

2

IFRS 6 states that, in making this determination, entities should consider the degree to which the expenditure can be associated with finding the specific mineral resources it is seeking.

1

Therefore it is quite possible that two entities in fairly similar sectors might make a different assessment of their accounting policies given very specific criteria which might apply to one entity or another. (Exact wording not needed – just the overall sense of the point.)

1

IFRS 6 does, however, **specifically prohibit** the inclusion of the costs of developing mineral resource in the exploration and evaluation assets figure. Such expenditures should be accounted for in accordance with **IAS 38** *Intangible Assets.*

1 + ½

IFRS 6 allows exploration and evaluation assets to be measured under either the cost model or the revaluation model.

1

7

Exhibit 2 – Events occurring after 30 September 20X5

The accounting treatment of events occurring after the year-end date is set out in IAS 10 – *Events after the Reporting Period.*

½ (principle)

IAS 10 defines events after the reporting period as being those events occurring after the end of the reporting period up to the date the financial statements are authorised for issue (15 November 20X5).

1

IAS 10 classifies events after the reporting period into two types – adjusting and non-adjusting.

½ (principle)

Adjusting events provide additional evidence of conditions existing at the reporting date. (Exact wording not needed – just the overall sense of the point.)

1

The information about the legal case provides additional evidence about the final liability and so is an adjusting event, so it is proper to recognise the correct amounts ($5.5m) in the financial statements. (Exact wording not needed – just the overall sense of the point.)

2

The fire at the factory does not relate to conditions at the reporting date and so is non-adjusting.

1

IAS 10 requires **disclosure** of the impact of non-adjusting events in the notes to the financial statements. The only exception to this rule would be if the event impacted on the **going concern** status of Omega. This is not the case based on the information provided.

1 + 1

The insolvency of the customer occurred after the financial statements were authorised for issue so it is not reportable in the financial statements for the year ended 30 September 20X5. (Exact wording not needed – just the overall sense of the point.)

$\underline{2}$

$\underline{10}$

Exhibit 3 – Sustainability disclosures

The principles underpinning IFRS Accounting Standards sustainability disclosures are set out in IFRS S1 General Requirements for Disclosure of Sustainability-related Financial Information and IFRS S2 Climate-related disclosures.

1

The objective of IFRS S1 is to require an entity to disclose information about its sustainability-related risks and opportunities that is useful to investors when making decisions relating to providing resources to the entity.

1

IFRS S1 requires disclosure of all sustainability-related risks and opportunities that could reasonably be expected to affect the entity's cash flows, its access to finance or its cost of capital over the short, medium or long term (referred to as the entity's 'prospects')

1

Sustainability-related risks and opportunities arise through an entity's **dependencies** on certain relationships (with stakeholders and society) and resources (the economy and the natural environment) and the entity's **impacts** on those relationships and resources.

1 + ½

Dependencies are the reliance an entity has on its stakeholders, society, the economy, and the natural environment through the resources it uses and the relationships it has. For example: worker health, diversity, climate risks, resource availability, consumer expectations, regulatory risks.

1

Impacts are the effect that an entity has on its stakeholders, society, the economy, and the natural environment, through the resources it uses and the relationships it has. For example: worker rights, human rights, waste generation, greenhouse gas emissions, water usage.

1

For **Omega**, dependencies could include the continued availability of mineral resources, consumer expectations regarding mining activities and regulatory risks which could place restrictions on its activities (any relevant application accepted).

1

For **Omega**, impacts could include the waste generated through exploration for and extraction of mineral resources, workers rights in terms of conditions under which employees work and water usage in the extraction process (any relevant application accepted).

1

<u>8</u>

<u>25</u>

44 Townsend

(a) (i) Potential ordinary shares are financial instruments or other contracts which may entitle the holder to ordinary shares.

Examples of potential ordinary shares include convertible preference shares, share options and contingently issuable shares.

Tutorial note. Only one example was required to gain the marks.

(ii) The diluted earnings per share is calculated by computing what the earnings per share figure would have been if the potential ordinary shares had been converted into ordinary shares on the first day of the accounting period, or from their date of acquisition by the holder, if the potential ordinary shares were acquired during the current accounting period.

The diluted earnings per share figure only needs to be disclosed if it is lower than the basic earnings per share figure.

(iii) **Basis of basic EPS**

Some might say that it is misleading to calculate basic EPS without taking into account **financial instruments** that will enable their holder to become a shareholder. Because of the 'quasi-equity' nature of these financial instruments and the likelihood that holders of such securities will exercise their right to convert, basic EPS might be said to be a meaningless statistic if it is not adjusted for these elements.

One potential problem with this method is that the definitions of 'share equivalents' would need to be quite precise. If this was not the case then the basic EPS would not be comparable between companies. This method also assumes that the likelihood of the conversion of the **share equivalent** is the same for all companies. The key test would probably be whether the holder of the financial instrument has an expectation of sharing in any increase in the value of the shares. A fall in the value of the shares might affect the likelihood of conversion and thus cause the EPS in this event to be unrealistic.

A problem with this approach is that the basic undiluted EPS will not be shown. It is probably most useful to users if **several statistics** are shown, eg the basic EPS, the diluted EPS showing maximum dilution and the diluted EPS showing the effects of all dilution.

(b) **Year ended 31 March 20X4**

Date	Narrative	Shares	Time	Bonus fraction	Weighted average
1.4.X3	Opening	40,000,000	$\times \, ^3/_{12}$	$\times \, ^5/_4$	12,500,000
1.7.X3	Full market price	8,000,000			
		48,000,000	$^6/_{12}$	$\times \, ^5/_4$	30,000,000
1.1.X4	Bonus issue ($^1/_4$)	12,000,000			
		60,000,000	$^3/_{12}$		15,000,000
					57,500,000

Earnings $13.8m, therefore EPS = 13.8/57.5 = 24c

Comparative

The EPS for 20X3 would be restated to allow for the effect of the bonus issue as follows:

25c $\times$ 48/60* = 20c

* Existing shares + new issue = 48

Existing shares + new issue + bonus issue = 60

Year ended 31 March 20X5

'2 for 5' rights issue takes place halfway through the year and results in 24 million additional shares.

Weighted average number of shares calculated as follows:

Date	Narrative	Shares	Time	Bonus fraction	Weighted average
1.4.X4	Opening	60,000,000	$^6/_{12}$	$^{2.4}/_2$ (W)	36,000,000
30.9.X4	Rights issue ($^2/_5$)	24,000,000			
		84,000,000	$^6/_{12}$		42,000,000
					78,000,000

Earnings $19.5m, therefore EPS = 19.5/78 = 25c

Comparative

The EPS for 20X4 is now restated following the rights issue in October 20X4 as follows:

24c $\times$ Theoretical ex-rights price (W)/Market price = 24c $\times$ 2/2.40 = 20c

Working:

		$
Theoretical ex-rights price		
5 shares at market price (5 $\times$ 2.4)	5 @ $2.4	12
2 shares at $1	2 @ 1	2
	7	14

∴ Theoretical ex-rights price = $14/7 = $2

(c) Basic EPS = $25.2m/84m = 30c

We must decide which, if any, of the potential ordinary shares are dilutive:

Loan stock

Incremental EPS: 1.8m (W1)/5.0m = 36c; this is higher than basic EPS therefore the loan stock is not dilutive and is not included in the calculation of diluted EPS.

Share options

Shares issued will be 12m @ $1.50 = $18m.

At market price of $2.50 the value would be $30 million.

The shortfall is $12 million, which is equivalent to 4.8 million shares at market price. The share options are dilutive as 4.8 million shares are deemed to have been issued for no consideration.

Diluted EPS = 25.2/(84.0 + 4.8) = 28.4c

Working:

1   *Loan stock*

	$m
When conversion takes place there will be a saving of:	
Interest (20m × 10%)	2.0
Less tax (2.0 × 20%)	(0.4)
	1.8

45 Gamma (June 2021)

Lease of machine

Under the principles of IFRS 16 *Leases* lessees need to create a 'right of use asset' and lease liability in respect of all leased assets, other than those leased on short-term leases or on 'low value' leases. Neither exception applies here.	(explanation of principle up to) 1
The initial carrying amount of the right of use (RoU) asset and lease liability will be the present value of the lease payments not yet paid using the rate of interest implicit in the lease (8% in this case) with the RoU asset adjusted by the initial payment of $200,000.	½
This initial carrying amount of the asset will be $862,400 ($200,000 + ($200,000 × 3.312 = 662,400)).	½ + 1
The RoU asset will be depreciated over the shorter of lease term and the useful life of the leased assets. In this case, this means over five years from 1 October 20X4 so the depreciation charge for the year ended 31 March 20X5 will be $86,240 ($862,400 × 1/5 × 6/12).	½ + 1
The RoU asset at 31 March 20X5 will have a carrying amount of $776,160 ($862,400 – $86,240). This amount will be presented under non-current assets.	½ + ½
The incorrect debiting of $200,000 to profit or loss should be corrected by debiting to the RoU asset (see above) to calculate the correct depreciation charge.	½
The lease liability will attract a finance cost of $26,496 ($662,400 × 8% × 6/12).	½ + 1
The lease liability at 31 March 20X5 will be $688,896 ($662,400 + $26,496). $173,504 of this amount will be presented as a current liability ($200,000 less 6 months finance charge $26,496), with the balance of $515,392 being non-current.	½ + ½ + ½
	9

Purchase of property

Under the principles of IAS 21 *The Effects of Changes in Foreign Exchange Rates* the property will initially be recorded using the rate of exchange in force at the date of purchase.	(principle) 1
Therefore the property will be recorded at an initial carrying amount of $2.2 million (4.4 million crowns/2). A liability of $2.2 million will also be recorded.	½ + ½
When the liability is settled on 30 June 20X4, a payment of $2.5 million will be required (4.4 million crowns/1.76). This will create an exchange loss of $300,000 which will be debited to profit or loss.	½ + ½ + ½

Under the principles of IAS 16 *Property, Plant Equipment* the buildings element of the property will be deprecated over its useful life of 40 years. This means that depreciation of $33,000 ($2.2m × 60% × 1/40) will be required for the year ended 31 March 20X5.   ½ + 1

Since the property is measured using the revaluation model, the closing carrying amount will be its fair value in crowns translated into $ using the rate of exchange in force at the year end. In this case, the closing $ carrying amount will be $3 million (4.8m crowns/1.60).   1

The valuation gain of $833,000 ($3m – ($2.2m – $33,000)) will be recognised in other comprehensive income under the principles of IAS 16.   1 + ½

The property will be presented as a non-current asset in the statement of financial position at its closing carrying amount of $3 million.   ½
     8

Computation of earnings per share

$10,254,264 (W1)/81,250,000 (W2)   4 (W1) + 3½ (W2)
So EPS equals 12.6 cents.   ½
     8
     25

Working 1 – Earnings for EPS purposes

	$	
Profit as per draft financial statements	10,000,000	½
Adjustments due to exhibits 1 and 2 (where figures have been incorrectly calculated earlier in the question but appropriately used as an adjustment then marks will be awarded here under the 'own figure' rule):		
Lease rental (exhibit 1)	200,000	½
Depreciation of right of use asset (exhibit 1)	(86,240)	½
Finance cost re: right of use asset (exhibit 1)	(26,496)	½
Payment for property incorrectly charged to P/L (exhibit 2)	2,500,000	½
Exchange loss on property (exhibit 2)	(300,000)	½
Depreciation of property (exhibit 2)	(33,000)	½
Dividend paid to preference shareholders	(2,000,000)	½
Earnings for EPS purposes	10,254,264	4

Working 2 – Number for EPS purposes

70 million × 6/12 × $1.50/$1.40 (W3) + 70 million × 5/4 × 6/12   ½ + 1½ (W3)
So number equals 81.25 million.   + 1 + ½
     3½

Working 3 – Theoretical ex-rights price

	Number	$	
Pre-rights	4	6.00	½
Rights issue	1	1.00	½
Post-rights	5	7.00	
So theoretical ex-rights price is $1.40.			½
			1½
			⇒ W2

46 Gamma (December 2022)

Top tips. This question required candidates to identify the appropriate financial reporting treatment for two complex issues, compute the EPS and explain the ethical issue they faced as a result of the scenario.

The first issue was based on IFRS 15 *Revenue from Contracts with Customers*. It is important to learn the five step approach, but to score good marks in the exam you also need to be able to apply your knowledge to the scenario. Very few marks are available for simply copying out the approach from the standard.

Always pay close attention to the requirements. For EPS candidates were only required to calculate, not explain. No marks were gained for providing any explanations for EPS meaning time was wasted here.

Make sure you attempt all parts of the question – missing out on one of the requirements altogether means potentially achievable marks are missed.

Examining team's comments.

The examiner's report stated that generally there was insufficient explanation of the accounting required, meaning marks were lost by many candidates. However in the ethical requirement, marks were generally satisfactory where attempt was made to relate the scenario to the ethical guidance.

Attachment 1 to email

The relevant standard is IFRS 15 *Revenue from Contracts with Customers*. Under IFRS 15, the sale of goods with an after-sales service must be considered as two separate performance obligations. **1 mark**

Where the transaction price is a single amount, then it needs to be allocated to the individual performance obligations based on the relative stand-alone selling prices of the individual components. **1 mark**

In this case, the sum of the selling prices of the individual components is $960,000 [$800,000 (the stand-alone selling price of the machine) + 2 × $80,000 (the stand-alone selling price of a two-year repair contract)]. **1 mark**

Given that the agreed price payable for the 'bundle' is $840,000, then the revenue from the sale of the machine would be measured at **$700,000** ($840,000 × 800,000/960,000). **1 mark** This would be recognised in full in the year ended 30 September 20X5 as delivery of the machine means the performance obligation has been satisfied. **1 mark**

Therefore the revenue from the after-sales repair service would be **$140,000** ($840,000 – $700,000). This revenue needs to be recognised over the two-year period from 1 April 20X5 – the period in which Gamma provides the service to the customer. **1 mark**

This means that the revenue recognised from this source in the year ended 30 September 20X5 is $35,000 (140,000 × 6/24). The difference of $105,000 between the amount received from the customer ($840,000) and the amount recognised as revenue in the year ended 30 September 20X5 ($700,000 + $35,000 = $735,000) will be shown as a contract liability (deferred income) in the statement of financial position of Gamma. **2 marks**

The contract liability will be split between current and non-current (principle). **$70,000** ($105,000 × 12/18) will be shown as a current liability and **$35,000** as a non-current liability. **1 mark**

IFRS 15 requires that the costs of fulfilling a contract (the repair service) should initially be recognised as assets and taken to profit or loss on a systematic basis as goods or services are transferred to the customer. **1 mark**

In this case, it would appear that the costs incurred to date ($20,000) of fulfilling the repair service should be shown as a cost in profit or loss rather than as an asset in the statement of financial position. **1 mark**

Given that the total costs of fulfilling the contract are estimated to be $50,000 per annum, there is a case for arguing that $25,000 (50,000 × 6/12) should be recognised in profit or loss (not just the $20,000 incurred) as a cost in the year ended 30 September 20X5 with a liability of $5,000 (25,000 – 20,000) recognised in current liabilities. **1 mark**

Workings

1 *Spreadsheet workings: computation of revenue recognised*

	Machine	Repair service	Total
	$	$	$
Stand-alone selling price	800,000	160,000	960,000
'Bundle' price			840,000
Allocation of 'bundle price' in relevant proportions	700,000	140,000	840,000
Revenue recognised in the period	700,000	35,000	735,000
Amount received from customer in the period	(700,000)	(140,000)	(840,000)
So contract liability at year end equals	n/a	(105,000)	(105,000)
Settled within 12 months (12/18)	n/a	70,000	70,000
Settled after more than 12 months (6/18)	n/a	35,000	35,000

Attachment 2 to email

The relevant standard is IAS 36 *Impairment of Assets*. IAS 36 requires that assets are reviewed for impairment whenever indicators of impairment are present. **0.5 mark** The fact that there is currently a surplus of properties available for rental is prima-facie evidence that indicators are present in this case. **1 mark**

An impairment review involves comparing the carrying amount of an asset with its recoverable amount. The recoverable amount of an asset is the higher of its value in use and its fair value less costs of disposal. **1 mark**

The value in use of the asset in this case is **$1 million**. IAS 36 requires that value in use be computed based on the existing use to which the asset is being put, with no account taken of potential changes in use due to possible future restructurings (principle). The fair value less costs of disposal is $900,000 which is lower than the value in use. **1 mark**

Therefore the property has suffered impairment of **$200,000** ($1.2 million – $1 million). This amount will be taken to **profit or loss** as an operating cost. **1 mark**

The revised carrying amount of the asset will be $1 million. This will be shown as a non-current asset in the statement of financial position. **0.5 mark**

2 *Spreadsheet workings: calculation of earnings per share (1 mark for corrected earnings, 1 for weighted average shares, 1 for calculation of EPS OF)*

	$
Earnings as per draft financial statements (exhibit 1)	1,800,000
Adjustments to revenue and for repair service costs ($105,000 + $20,000 – OF rule applies here. Adjustment of $20,000 could alternatively have been $25,000)	(125,000)
Impairment of property	(200,000)
Earnings as corrected	1,475,000
Weighted average number of shares = 4,500,000 × 4/12 + 6,000,000 × 8/12	5,500,000
Therefore earnings per share equals (1,475,000/5,500,000)	26.8 cents

Ethical issue – Email from FD

You are in danger of breaching the fundamental ethical principle of objectivity. **0.5 mark** You have a personal interest in reporting a favourable profit because of the fact that you own shares in Gamma and a favourable profit could result in enhanced dividends and shareholder value. **1 mark**

You face a further danger of breaching the principle of objectivity **0.5 mark** because of the way the FD has linked your complying with this instructions to your upcoming staff appraisal (candidates who refer to an intimidation threat here will receive appropriate credit). **1 mark**

You also may be breaching the fundamental ethical principle of professional competence and due care. The treatments suggested by the FD are clearly inappropriate and not in compliance with IFRS Accounting Standards. **1 mark** Were you to implement them, you would be in breach of your professional duty to conduct yourself in a competent manner. **1 mark**

47 Ontario

Marking scheme

	Marks

Exhibit 1 – Impairment of financial assets

A financial asset is impaired when its carrying amount cannot be reasonably expected to be recovered through future generation of income or sale proceeds. — 1

IFRS 9 *Financial Instruments* – classifies financial assets into three types. One of these types is 'fair value through profit and loss'. Where financial assets are measured on this basis, any impairment of the asset is automatically reflected in the measurement basis so no further action is required. — 1

As far as other financial assets are concerned, the general rule is that we should recognise **a loss allowance** for 'expected credit losses'. The loss allowance should be recognised in **profit or loss** and **deducted from the carrying amount** of the financial asset in the statement of financial position. — ½ + ½ + ½ + ½

A credit loss is the difference between the cash flows we are contractually entitled to receive in respect of a financial asset and the cash flows which are expected based on current circumstances. — 1

Unless the credit risk attaching to the financial asset has increased significantly since initial recognition, the loss allowance should be based on expected credit losses in the next 12 months. — 1

Where the credit risk has increased significantly since initial recognition, the loss allowance should be based on lifetime expected credit losses. — 1

As far as trade receivables are concerned, as a simplifying measure IFRS 9 allows the loss allowance to always be measured based on the lifetime expected credit losses. — 1 / 8

Marks

Exhibit 2 – Accounting policies

IAS 8 *Accounting Policies, Changes in Accounting Estimates and Errors* defines an accounting policy as 'the specific principles, bases, conventions, rules and practices applied by an entity in preparing and presenting financial statements'.

1½

An example of an accounting policy would be the decision to apply the cost model or the fair value model when measuring investment properties.

1

When an entity changes an accounting policy, the change is applied **retrospectively**. This means that the **comparative** figures are based on the new policy (rather than last year's actual figures). The **opening balance of retained earnings is restated** in the **statement of changes in equity**.

½ + ½ +
½ + ½

Accounting estimates are monetary amounts in financial statements that are subject to measurement uncertainty. They are made in order to implement accounting policies. An example of an accounting estimate would be (consistent with the above given example) the fair value of an investment property at the reporting date (where the fair value model was being applied).

1½

Changes in accounting estimates are made **prospectively**. This means applying the new estimates **from the date of the change**, without amending any previously published amounts.

½
½
‾‾
7

Exhibit 3 – Segment reporting

A reportable segment is an operating segment that satisfies certain materiality criteria.

½

An operating segment is a component of an entity:

- That engages in business activities from which it may earn revenues and incur expenses.

½ + ½

- Whose operating results are regularly reviewed by the Chief Operating Decision Maker (CODM).

½ + ½

- For which discrete financial information is available.

½

- The CODM is a **function**, not a title. The function is to make decisions about **allocating resources** and **assessing performance**.

½ + ½ +
½

The materiality criteria are any one of the following:

½

- Reported revenue is 10% or more of the total revenue of all operating segments.

½

- The **absolute amount of its reported profit or loss** is 10% or more of the greater of the **combined reported profit** of all the profit making segments and the **combined reported loss** of all the segments that reported a loss.

½ + ½ + ½

- Total assets are 10% or more of the total assets of all operating segments.

½

Two or more operating segments that exhibit **similar economic characteristics** can be combined into a **single operating segment** for reporting purposes.

½ + ½

Even if an operating segment does not meet any of the quantitative thresholds, it can be considered reportable if management believes that information about that segment would be useful to users of the financial statements.

½

As a minimum, the total external revenue of reportable segments should be at least 75% of total entity revenue. If this is not achieved by applying the size criteria to individual segments, **additional reportable segments need to be added until this threshold is achieved**.

½ + ½
‾‾
10
‾‾
25

48 Omega (December 2014) (amended)

Top tips. This was a typical discursive question, requiring you to explain three different issues to a non-accountant. Exhibit 1 (possibly the most difficult, if you had not prepared this topic) concerned segment reporting (IFRS 8).

Exhibit 2 asked you to explain the way in which equity settled share-based payments are treated in the financial statements. Here it was important not to waste time explaining **why** there is a charge to profit or loss. Read the query carefully to see what the managing director actually wants to know.

Exhibit 3 focuses on the basic requirements of IFRS 5.

Exhibit 4 tests your understanding of IAS 36 and specifically testing cash generating units rather than individual assets for impairment losses.

Easy marks. You should have been able to score almost full marks on Exhibit 3, and if you had revised that topic, there were also some easy marks for stating the basic requirements of IFRS 2 regarding the treatment of equity settled share based payment.

Examining team's comments. Candidates did not answer Exhibit 1 very well. A significant number of candidates were unaware of any of the requirements of the IFRS Accounting Standards on segment reporting – IFRS 8. Another factor in Exhibit 1 was that many candidates did not address the requirements of the question specifically enough. The question asked why the segment reports of two apparently similar entities could be so different. A number of candidates did not really attempt to address this issue, but simply defined the meaning of an operating segment and (in some cases at least) the relevant requirements of IFRS 8. Answers to Exhibit 2 were generally of a satisfactory standard but a significant minority of candidates wasted time by making references to cash-settled share-based payments. These were not part of the requirement so, whilst the comments were in many cases correct, they did not score marks. Once again the message here is that candidates must focus carefully on the exact requirements of each question. Answers to Exhibit 3 were generally satisfactory.

[References: IFRS 2: paras. 2, 7–8, 14; IFRS 5: paras. 6–8, 15, 18, 20–22, 25, 38; IFRS 8: paras. 5, 7, 23; IAS 36 paras. 6, 9, 18)

Marking guide

	Marks
IFRS 8 general definition	1½
CODM	2½
Differences	4
SBP explanation	2½
SBP accounting	5½
HFS definition	1
HFS accounting	3
CGU definition	2
Impairment definition	1
Reason for CGU	2
Total	**25**

	Marks

Exhibit 1 – Operating segments

It is true that the there is an International Financial Reporting Standard (IFRS) which deals with operating segments and lays down the content of segmental reports. The relevant standard is IFRS 8 *Operating Segments*. — ½

However, differences between the segment reports of organisations will arise from how segments are identified and what exactly is reported for each segment. — ½ + ½

IFRS 8 defines an operating segment as a component of an entity which engages in revenue earning activities and whose results are regularly reviewed by the **chief operating decision maker (CODM)**. — ½ + ½

The CODM is the **individual, or group of individuals**, who makes decisions about **segment performance** and **resource allocation**. — ½ + ½ + ½

This definition means that the operating segments of apparently similar organisations could be identified very differently, with a consequential impact on the nature of the report. — ½

As stated above, differences also arise due to the reporting requirements for each segment. IFRS 8 requires that 'a measure' of profit or loss is reported for each segment. However, the **measurement of revenues and expenses which are used in determining profit or loss is based on the principles used in the information the CODM sees**. This is so, **even if these principles do not correspond with IFRS**. This could **clearly cause differences** between reports from apparently similar organisations. — ½ + ½ + ½ + ½

Additionally, IFRS 8 requires a measure of total **assets** and **liabilities** by operating segment if the **CODM sees this information**. Since **some CODMs may see this information and some may not**, this could once again cause differences between the reports of apparently similar organisations. — ½ + ½ + ½

8

Exhibit 2 – Share based payments

An equity-settled share-based payment transaction is one in which an entity receives goods or services in exchange for a right over its equity instruments. — ½

Where the payments involve the granting of share options, IFRS 2 *Share-based Payment* requires that the payments are measured at the **fair value** of the options at the **grant date**. No change is made to this measurement when the fair value **changes after the grant date**. — ½ + ½ + ½

Unless the entity has traded options which have exactly the same terms and conditions as those granted to employees (unlikely), then fair value is estimated using an option pricing model. — ½

The first step in accounting for such payments is to estimate the total expected cost of the share-based payment. — ½

This estimate takes account of any **conditions** attaching to the options vesting (**the employees becoming unconditionally entitled to exercise them**) other than **market** conditions (those based on the future share price, which are taken account of in estimating the fair value of the option at the grant date). — ½ + ½ + ½

Marks

The total expected cost is recognised in the financial statements over the vesting period (ie the period from the grant date to the vesting date).

½

In the case of options granted to employees, the debit entry would be recorded as **remuneration** expense. Normally this would mean the debit entry being shown in the statement of **profit or loss** but in theory the debit entry could be an asset depending on the work of the employee involved.

½ + ½

The credit entry is taken to **equity**. IFRS 2 is **silent** as to which component of equity this should be – normally it would be to an option reserve.

½ + ½

The above treatment is **unaffected** by whether or not employees subsequently exercise vested options. **If they do**, then the entity debits cash and credits equity with the cash proceeds.

½ + ½
8

Exhibit 3 – Non-current assets held for sale

A non-current asset is classified as held for sale when its carrying amount will be recovered principally through a sale transaction, rather than through continuing use.

1

Such assets are measured at the lower of their **carrying amount** and **fair value less costs to sell**. Any write downs arising out of this process are treated as **impairment losses**.

½ + ½ + ½

The 'held for sale' definition can apply to **groups of assets** as well as single assets where the group of assets is to be sold as a **single unit**. It is in situations **such as this** that liabilities associated with such groups of assets are separately identified.

½ + ½ + ½
4

Exhibit 4 – Cash generating units

1 + 1

A cash generating unit is defined as the smallest possible identifiable group of assets that generates cash inflows that are largely independent of the reporting entity's other cash-generating units. Identifying the smallest possible group of assets is important as this means there will be fewer assets within each cash generating unit.

To determine whether impairment of a cash generating unit has incurred, it is necessary to compare the carrying amount of the asset with its **recoverable amount**. The recoverable amount is the **higher of fair value less costs of disposal and value in use**.

1

It is not always easy to estimate value in use. In particular, it is not always practicable to identify cash flows arising from an individual non-current asset. For example, the individual assets in a supermarket are unlikely to generate cash flows in their own right, but when combined (as a cash generating unit), it is possible to identify the cash flows. If this is the case, value in use should be calculated at the level of **cash generating units**.

1+1

5
25

49 Omega (June 2022)

Top tips. This question required candidates to answer questions on five specific issues in the context of preparing consolidated financial statements.

It is important to plan your answers to a question such as this where there are a range of different issues to deal with. Start by setting up sub-headings for each of the issues and note down the relevant guidance and one or two key things that you need to say. You can then build up your answer by bringing in calculations as necessary and additional points linking your answer to the scenario.

Easy marks. You should have been able to score marks for the first three issues by using your knowledge of accounting standards and consolidation principles.

Examining team's comments. Candidates should make sure they answer the exact questions the director is asking. The form of these questions often provides a useful structure for the candidate's answer.

Exhibit 1

Query 1

IFRS 10 *Consolidated Financial Statements* deals with the procedures to be followed when preparing such statements.

IFRS 10 states that the financial information relating to any subsidiary entity should normally be prepared to the same reporting date as the reporting date of the parent entity. **1 mark**

Where a subsidiary has a reporting date which differs from that of the parent, then it is normally necessary to prepare additional financial information relating to that subsidiary as of the same date as the reporting date of the parent. **1 mark**

If this is not practicable, then IFRS 10 allows the parent to prepare consolidated financial statements which incorporate financial information for the subsidiary drawn up to the most recent reporting date of the subsidiary. **1 mark**

In such circumstances, IFRS 10 requires adjustments to be made for 'significant' transactions which occur between the reporting date of the subsidiary and the reporting date of the parent. **0.5 mark**

The above facility is only possible where the reporting dates of the subsidiary and the parent differ by three months or less. **0.5 mark**

Therefore it would be possible to use the financial statements of NewSub for the year ended 31 December 20X4 to prepare the consolidated financial statements of Omega for the year ended 31 March 20X5. **1 mark**

There is no requirement for NewSub to change its year end following its acquisition by Omega but this might make the consolidation process more straightforward in the future. **1 mark**

Query 2

Segmental disclosures are required by IFRS 8 – Operating Segments.

IFRS 8 only applies to listed entities, so it is not necessary for NewSub to give such disclosures in its own individual financial statements. **1 mark**

Given that NewSub is now part of the Omega group, then disclosures relating to its operating segments would be required in theory in the consolidated financial statements of Omega. **1 mark**

In practice, the operating segments of NewSub would need to meet the criteria for them to be reportable in the consolidated financial statements of Omega. **0.5 mark**

These criteria are that the operating segments would be regularly reviewed by the Omega group management (chief operating decision maker) and they are material in the context of the Omega group. **1 mark**

In this context, 'material' means that the reported revenues, profits or assets of the segment are 10% or more of the combined reported revenues, profits or assets of all of the operating segments of the Omega group, ie exceeds the quantitative thresholds in IFRS 8. **1 mark**

Notwithstanding the quantitative thresholds, however, IFRS 8 permits entities to disclose information about operating segments if, in the judgement of management, such information would be useful to users. **0.5 mark**

Query 3

Accounting for investment properties is set out in IAS 40 *Investment Property.*

IAS 40 states that investment properties are initially accounted for at cost. **1 mark**

IAS 40 allows an accounting policy choice for subsequent measurement of investment properties. **1 mark**

IAS 40 allows either the cost model or the fair value model but requires a consistent choice of measurement model for all investment property. **1 mark**

On the date when Omega acquires NewSub, the 'cost' of NewSub's investment properties from the perspective of the consolidated financial statements would be their fair value at the date of acquisition of NewSub. **1 mark**

This means that, for the purposes of the Omega group consolidation, NewSub's investment properties will need to be measured using the fair value model. This will require on-going adjustments to be made at group consolidation level. **1 mark**

It is not necessary for NewSub to adjust its accounting policy in its own financial statements but for practical purposes this might be the preferred option going forward. **1 mark**

Exhibit 2 – Statement of profit or loss and other comprehensive income

Query 1

The overall requirements for presentation of financial statements are set out in IAS 1 *Presentation of Financial Statements.*

IAS 1 requires that the statement of profit or loss and other comprehensive income discloses certain key elements, for example, revenue and income tax expense. **0.5 mark**

As far as other detailed line items are concerned, IAS 1 states that they should be presented in a manner that is relevant to an understanding of the financial performance of the reporting entity. **0.5 mark**

In particular, IAS 1 states that operating expenses should be presented based on either their nature or their function, whichever provides financial information which is more reliable or relevant. **1 mark**

Therefore it is perfectly possible that the detailed line items in the respective statements of Omega and Rival could be quite different while still complying with full IFRS Accounting Standards. **1 mark**

Query 2

As far as the allocation of items between profit or loss and other comprehensive income is concerned, IAS 1 states that all items of income and expense should be presented in profit or loss unless another IFRS Accounting Standards requires or permits otherwise. **1 mark**

There is no theoretical distinction between 'profit or loss items' and 'other comprehensive income items'. However, it is more likely for gains, rather than losses, to be recognised in other comprehensive income (for example, revaluation gains on re-measurement of property, plant and equipment are usually recognised in other comprehensive income whereas revaluation losses are unusually recognised in profit or loss). **1 mark**

Gains or losses which are recognised in profit or loss contribute to the computation of earnings per share (EPS). Those recognised in other comprehensive income do not. **1 mark**

EPS is a key performance indicator for listed entities which must be disclosed in the published financial statements. **1 mark**

This would therefore matter for both Omega and Rival. **1 mark**

50 Whitebirk

> **BPP Study Text reference.** Small and medium-sized entities are covered in Chapter 19 of your BPP Study Text.
>
> **Top tips.** Part (a) on the different approaches which could have been used and the main differences between the IFRS for SMEs Accounting Standard (SMEs Accounting Standard) and full IFRS Accounting Standards, was reasonably straightforward. Part (b) required you to apply the standard to specific areas: goodwill, research and development expenditure, investment property and intangible assets.
>
> **Easy marks.** This was a rich source of easy marks for the well-prepared candidate.

(a) (i) **Approaches which the IASB could have taken in developing the *SMEs* Accounting Standard**

There were three main approaches which the IASB could have taken in developing the SMEs Accounting Standard

(1) **National GAAP for SMEs and IFRS Accounting Standards for listed companies**

It could be argued that small and medium-sized entities have little in common with larger listed entities and that listed entities have more in common with listed entities in other developed countries. It would therefore be appropriate for listed companies to use IFRS Accounting Standards and for smaller entities to have their own national 'little GAAP'.

The **disadvantage** of this approach is the **inconsistency** within countries between 'big GAAP' and 'little GAAP'. This would make comparability difficult. Further, if an SME, having applied national GAAP for SMEs for some time, wished to list its shares on a capital market, the **transition to IFRS Accounting Standards** would be even more **onerous** than it is currently.

(2) **Exemptions for SMEs within existing standards**

Another approach would be exemptions for smaller companies from some of the requirements of existing standards, and for these exemptions to be contained within IFRS Accounting Standards, probably as an appendix.

This approach has the **disadvantage** that preparers of small company financial statements would still need to look through mainstream IFRS Accounting Standards to determine what they did not need to do. Arguably this is **far less convenient** than having a 'stand-alone' standard designed for SMEs.

(3) **A separate set of standards only relevant for SMEs**

This is closest to what actually happened, but it is not as convenient as having one standard as a one-stop shop. It would have resulted in a proliferation of accounting standards, adding to an already complex picture.

In the event, none of the above approaches was followed. Instead the SMEs Accounting Standard, published in July 2009, is a self-contained document. It is the first set of international accounting requirements developed specifically for small and medium-sized entities. Although it has been **prepared on a similar basis to IFRS Accounting Standards**, it is a **stand-alone product** and will be updated on its own timescale.

(ii) **Modifications to reduce the burden of reporting for SMEs**

The SMEs Accounting Standard has **simplifications** that reflect the needs of users of SMEs' financial statements and cost-benefit considerations. It is designed to facilitate financial reporting by small and medium-sized entities in a number of ways:

(1) It provides significantly **less guidance** than full IFRS Accounting Standards. A great deal of the guidance in full IFRS Accounting Standards would not be relevant to the needs of smaller entities.

(2)   Many of the **principles** for recognising and measuring assets, liabilities, income and expenses in full IFRS Accounting Standards are **simplified**. For example, goodwill and intangibles are always amortised over their estimated useful life (or ten years if it cannot be estimated). Research and development costs must be expensed. Government grants are recognised as income in full when receivable.

(3)   Where full IFRS Accounting Standards allow accounting policy choices, the SMEs Accounting Standard **allows only the easier option**. Examples of alternatives not allowed in the SMEs Accounting Standard include: revaluation model for intangible assets and choice between cost and fair value models for investment property.

(4)   **Topics not relevant** to SMEs are **omitted**: earnings per share, interim financial reporting, segment reporting, and insurance.

(5)   Significantly **fewer disclosures** are required.

(6)   The standard has been written in **clear language** that can easily be translated.

The above represents a considerable reduction in reporting requirements – perhaps as much as 90% – compared with listed entities. Entities will naturally wish to use the SMEs Accounting Standard if they can, but **its use is restricted**.

The restrictions are **not related to size**. There are several disadvantages of basing the definition on size limits alone. Size limits are **arbitrary** and **different limits are likely to be appropriate in different** countries. Most people believe that SMEs are **not simply smaller versions of listed entities**, but differ from them in more fundamental ways.

The most important way in which SMEs differ from other entities is that they are **not usually publicly accountable**. Accordingly, there are **no quantitative thresholds** for qualification as a SME; instead, the scope of the SMEs Accounting Standard is determined by a **test of public accountability**. The SMEs Accounting Standard is suitable for all entities except those whose securities are publicly traded and financial institutions such as banks and insurance companies.

Another way in which the use of the SMEs Accounting Standard is restricted is that **users cannot cherry pick** from the SMEs Accounting Standard and full IFRS Accounting Standards. If an entity adopts the SMEs Accounting Standard, it **must adopt it in its entirety**.

(b)   (i)   **Acquisition of Close**

IFRS 3 *Business Combinations* allows an entity to adopt the full or partial goodwill method in its consolidated financial statements. The SMEs Accounting Standard **only allows the partial goodwill method**. This avoids the need for SMEs to determine the fair value of the non-controlling interests not purchased when undertaking a business combination.

In addition, IFRS 3 *Business Combinations* requires goodwill to be tested annually for impairment. The SMEs Accounting Standard **requires goodwill to be amortised instead**. This is a much simpler approach and the SMEs Accounting Standard specifies that if an entity is unable to make a reliable estimate of the useful life, it is presumed to be ten years, simplifying things even further.

Goodwill on Whitebirk's acquisition of Close will be calculated as:

	$'000
Consideration transferred	5,700
Non-controlling interest: 10% × $6m	600
	6,300
Less fair value of identifiable net assets acquired	(6,000)
Goodwill	300

This goodwill of $0.3 million will be amortised over ten years, that is $30,000 per annum.

(ii)   **R&D expenditure**

The SMEs Accounting Standard requires all internally generated research and development expenditure to be **expensed through profit or loss**. This is simpler than IFRS Accounting Standards – IAS 38 *Intangible Assets* requires internally generated assets to be capitalised if certain criteria (proving future economic benefits) are met, and it is often difficult to determine whether or not they have been met.

Whitebirk's total expenditure on research ($0.5m) and development ($1m) must be written off to profit or loss for the year, giving a charge of $1.5 million.

(iii) **Investment properties**

Investment properties must be held at fair value through profit or loss under the SMEs Accounting Standard, where their fair value can be measured without undue cost or effort, which appears to be the case here, given that an estate agent valuation is available. Consequently a gain of $0.2 million ($1.9m – $1.7m) will be reported in Whitebirk's profit or loss for the year.

(iv)   **Intangible asset**

IAS 36 *Impairment of Assets* requires annual impairment tests for indefinite life intangibles, intangibles not yet available for use and goodwill. This is a complex, time-consuming and expensive test.

The SMEs Accounting Standard only requires impairment tests where there are indicators of impairment. In the case of Whitebirk's intangible asset, there are no indicators of impairment, and so an impairment test is not required.

In addition, IAS 38 *Intangible Assets* does not require intangible assets with an indefinite useful life to be amortised. In contrast, under the SMEs Accounting Standard, all intangible assets must be amortised. If the useful life cannot be established reliably, it must not exceed ten years.

51 Epsilon (June 2021)

Top tips. This question was a standard Question 4 in that it presented several queries from a director which you were required to answer. It is important that you respond to the exact questions that the director is asking, as there will not be marks available for providing information that is not relevant to the questions asked, even if it is technically correct. In this question, the director's questions were very clearly laid out and it is recommended that you follow this structure when preparing your answer.

Examining team comments.

The examining team report commented that many candidates presented very short answers to this question, indicating poor time management. It is important that you work out how many minutes you should be spending on each question, and on each part of each question and then stick to that when preparing your answers. You can calculate the amount of time by multiplying the number of marks by 1.95 minutes per mark. Each question in DipIFR is worth 25 marks, so you should spend no more than 48 minutes on each. For this question, you should split this time as approximately 15 minutes each on Exhibits 1 and 3 and slightly more (18 mins) on Exhibit 2.

	Marks

Newby

Because Newby was previously owned by three private shareholders and does not operate in the banking or finance sector, it is regarded as an entity which is not publicly accountable.

1 + 1

In these circumstances, Newby is permitted, but not required, to adopt the simplified form of financial reporting set out in the IFRS Accounting Standard for Small and Medium Sized Entities (the IFRS for SMEs Accounting Standard).

1 + 1

The IFRS for SMEs Accounting Standard restricts the recognition of assets and liabilities in certain circumstances (eg borrowing costs are always expensed under the IFRS for SMEs Accounting Standard). In addition, the disclosure requirements of the IFRS for SMEs Accounting Standard are less than for full IFRS Accounting Standards.

1 + 1

Even though Newby is now part of a group which will use full IFRS in its consolidated financial statements, Newby would still be able to use the IFRS for SMEs Accounting Standard in its own individual financial statements. Adjustments would of course be required at consolidation level to make the consolidated financial statements fully IFRS Accounting Standards compliant.

1 + 1

8

New investment

Under the principles of IFRS 10 *Consolidated Financial Statements* Sandy would be a subsidiary if we were in a position to control its operating and financial policies.

1

In this case, whilst the investment is long term and substantial, it does not give us control, so consolidation is inappropriate.

1

Under the principles of IAS 28 *Investments in Associates and Joint Ventures* the 40% shareholding in Sandy, being greater than 20%, would be presumed to give us significant influence over the operating and financial policies of Sandy.

1 + 1

Given the fact that we are able to appoint four of the ten members of Sandy's board of directors, and there is no evidence that the other shareholders or board members are acting in concert to prevent us from exercising this influence, then the presumption of significant influence would appear to be appropriate in this case.

1 + 1

Therefore IAS 28 would regard Sandy as an associate.

1

IAS 28 requires that investments in associates are measured using the equity method. This method initially measures the investment at cost, but then adjusts the carrying amount by the investing entity's share (40% in this case) of the post-acquisition change in net assets of the investee entity (Sandy in this case). This amount is not necessarily the same as the fair value of the investment at any given date.

½ + 1 + ½

9

Measurement change

The decision to measure raw materials inventory using the weighted average cost formula rather than the first in first out formula represents a change in accounting policy. This is because it represents a change in the principles under which assets are measured. 1

Under the principles of IAS 8 *Accounting Policies, Changes in Accounting Estimates and Errors* accounting policy changes are appropriate if the new policy would result in the financial statements providing reliable and more relevant information about the effects of

transactions, other events or conditions on the entity's financial position, performance of cash flows. ½ +1

Under the principles of IAS 2 *Inventories* decisions about the more relevant measurement formula for inventories are made for categories of inventory having a similar nature and use to the entity. Raw materials inventory would be regarded as having a different nature and use to other types of inventory, so it is theoretically appropriate that they could be measured using the weighted average cost formula whilst other types of inventory are measured using the first in first out formula. 1 + 1

Where an entity changes its accounting policies in any financial period, comparability is ensured by re-stating prior year figures which are presented as comparatives. The comparatives are presented as they would have been had the previous financial statements been presented using the new accounting policy. ½ + 1

The difference between the opening and closing equity as presented in the previous year's financial statements and the equivalent figures measured using the new accounting policy is shown as an adjustment to the opening equity for the current period and the opening equity in the previous period. These differences are presented in the statement of changes in equity (and its comparative) and do not affect reported profit or loss.

(exact wording not required – up to) 2

8

25

52 Alpha (December 2019)

Tutorial note. In Q1 of the DipIFR exam will always be a consolidation question. This question should be answered using the spreadsheet response option (only the spreadsheet response option will be available to you). The spreadsheet response option will be pre-populated with an exact copy of the draft financial statements provided in exhibit 1 of the question. You should manipulate this data in order to produce the consolidated financial statement required by the question. If you accidentally delete any of the information in the pre-populated spreadsheet, you can refer back to exhibit 1 to find the relevant information.

Good exam technique for a question such as this is to layout a proforma consolidated statement of financial position (using the data provided in the pre-populated spreadsheet response option). Once you have done that, you can start working through the adjustments, setting up a new working as required. Transfer your adjustments to the proforma when you have completed each working. Make sure you include all your calculations in your answer, as the marker can then award you 'own figure' marks where possible, should you make a mistake in your calculations.

We recommend that you practise the consolidation questions in this Kit using a spreadsheet. This is so that you can plan how to layout your consolidated financial statement and your workings.

Note that no explanations are required in question 1 so do not waste time providing them. The examiner is looking for application of techniques for consolidation, not explanations of the principles involved.

CONSOLIDATED STATEMENT OF FINANCIAL POSITION OF ALPHA AT 30 SEPTEMBER 20X7

	$'000	Marks
Assets		
Non-current assets		
Property, plant and equipment (966,500 + 546,000 + 35,000 (W1))	1,547,500	½ + ½
Goodwill (W2)	62,000	3½ (W2)
Intangible assets (20,000 + 10,000 (W1))	30,000	½ + ½
	1,639,500	
Current assets		
Inventories (165,000 + 92,000 – (30,000 × 1/3 × 25/125%))	255,000	½ + 1
Trade receivables (99,000 + 76,000)	175,000	½
Cash and cash equivalents (18,000 + 16,000)	34,000	½
	464,000	
Total assets	2,103,500	
Equity and liabilities		
Equity attributable to equity holders of the parent		
Share capital ($1 shares)	360,000	½
Retained earnings (W4)	571,310	7 (W4)
Other components of equity (W8)	113,380	4 (W8)
	1,044,690	
Non-controlling interest (W3)	156,000	1 (W3)
Total equity	1,200,690	
Non-current liabilities		
Long-term borrowings (W10)	365,210	1½ (W10)
Deferred tax (W11)	131,600	1½ (W11)
Pension liability	205,000	½
Total non-current liabilities	701,810	
Current liabilities		
Trade and other payables (70,000 + 59,000)	129,000	½
Short-term borrowings (40,000 + 32,000)	72,000	½
Total current liabilities	201,000	
Total equity and liabilities	2,103,500	25

WORKINGS

1   *Net assets table for Beta*

	1 April 20X7 $'000	30 September 20X7 $'000	For W2	For W4
Share capital	160,000	160,000	½	
Retained earnings:				
Per financial statements of Beta	340,000	360,000	½	½
Fair value adjustments:				
Plant and equipment	40,000	35,000	½	1
Development project	10,000	10,000	½	½
Deferred tax on fair value adjustments:				
Date of acquisition (20% × (40,000 + 10,000))	(10,000)		½	
Year end (20% × (35,000 + 10,000))		(9,000)		½
Net assets for the consolidation	540,000	556,000	2½ ⇒ W2	2½ ⇒ W2
Increase in net assets post-acquisition (556,000 – 540,000)	16,000			

2 *Goodwill on acquisition of Beta*

	$'000	
Cost of investment:		
Cash paid	450,000	½
Non-controlling interest at date of acquisition (40,000 × $3.80)	152,000	½
Net assets at date of acquisition (W1)	(540,000)	2½ (W1)
	62,000	3½

3 *Non-controlling interest in Beta*

	$'000	
At date of acquisition (W2)	152,000	½
25% of post-acquisition increase in net assets of 16,000 (W1)	4,000	½
	156,000	1

4 *Retained earnings*

	$'000	
Alpha – per draft SOFP	570,000	½
Adjustment for unrealised profit on unsold inventory		
(2,000 less 20% (deferred tax))	(1,600)	½
Adjustment for finance cost of loan (W6)	(4,090)	1 (W6)
Adjustment re: defined benefit retirement benefit plan (W7)	(5,000)	2 (W7)
Beta – 75% × 16,000 (W1)	12,000	½ + 2½ (W1)
	571,310	7

5 *Equity component of long-term loan*

	$'000	
Total proceeds of compound instrument	300,000	½
Debt component:		
– Interest stream – 300,000 × 6% × $3.99	(71,820)	½
– Principal repayment – 300,000 × $0.681	(204,300)	½
So equity component equals	23,880	1½

6 *Adjustment for finance cost of loan*

	$'000	
Actual finance cost – 8% (300,000 – 23,880 (W5))	22,090	½
Incorrectly charged by Alpha (300,000 × 6%)	(18,000)	½
So adjustment equals	4,090	1

7 *Adjustment re: defined benefit retirement benefit plan*

	$'000	
Current service cost	60,000	½
Interest cost (8% × 187,500)	15,000	1
Contributions incorrectly charged to profit or loss	(70,000)	½
So adjustment equals	5,000	2

8 *Other components of equity*

	$'000	
Alpha – per draft financial statements	102,000	½
Equity element of convertible loan (W5)	23,880	1½
Actuarial gain/(loss) on defined benefit retirement benefits plan (W9)	(12,500)	2
	113,380	4

9 *Actuarial gain/(loss) on defined benefit pension plan*

	$'000	
Opening liability	187,500	½
Current service cost	60,000	½
Interest cost (principle mark already awarded)	15,000	
Contributions paid into plan	(70,000)	½
	192,500	
Actuarial loss on re-measurement (balancing figure)	12,500	½
Closing liability (principle mark already awarded)	205,000	
		2

10 *Long-term borrowings*

	$'000	
Opening loan element (300,000 – 23,880 (W5))	276,120	½
Finance cost less interest paid (W6)	4,090	½
So closing loan element for Alpha equals	280,210	
Long-term borrowings of Beta	85,000	½
So consolidated long-term borrowings equals	365,210	1½

11 *Deferred tax*

	$'000	
Alpha + Beta – per draft SOFP (69,000 + 54,000)	123,000	½
On closing fair value adjustments in Beta (W1)	9,000	½
On unrealised profits in inventory (2,000 × 20%)	(400)	½
	131,600	1½

53 Alpha (December 2020)

Top tips. This is a typical consolidation question which will feature as question 1 of the DipIFR exam. In this question you were required to prepare the consolidated statement of financial position (CSOFP) for Alpha, a parent with one subsidiary acquired at the start of the reporting period. The acquisition of Beta included contingent consideration and fair value adjustments. There was also some intra-grouping trading and an impairment review to address for Beta as well as a retirement benefit plan for Alpha.

Good exam technique for a question such as this is to layout a proforma consolidated statement of financial position (using the data provided in the pre-populated spreadsheet response option). Once you have done that, you can start working through the adjustments, setting up a new working as required. Transfer your adjustments to the proforma when you have completed each working. Make sure you include all your calculations in your answer, as the marker can then award you 'own figure' marks where possible, should you make a mistake in your calculations.

We recommend that you practise the consolidation questions in this Kit using a spreadsheet. This is so that you can plan how to layout your consolidated financial statement and your workings.

Note that no explanations are required in question 1 so do not waste time providing them. The examiner is looking for application of techniques for consolidation, not explanations of the principles involved.

Examining team's comments.

The examining team stated that 'on the whole, this question was answered satisfactorily. ... a clear majority of candidates achieved a pass in this question'

Some common errors were identified, including the following:

- Including the costs incurred by Alpha when acquiring Beta as part of the goodwill calculation rather than showing them as an expense.

- Incorrectly dealing with the contingent consideration on acquisition of Beta; some candidates ignored the change in the fair value of the contingent consideration since the date of acquisition (from $60 million to $50 million). Others used $50 million (rather than $60 million) to compute the goodwill figure. Still others used the correct figure to compute the goodwill figure and included the appropriate liability in the consolidated statement of financial position, but did not adjust for the change in the fair value of the contingent consideration since the date of acquisition ($60 million – $50 million) as a movement in consolidated retained earnings.

- Grossing up the goodwill on acquisition of Beta when performing the impairment review. This is only necessary when the non-controlling interest at the date of acquisition is measured using the proportionate method.

- Failing to allocate part of the goodwill impairment loss to the non-controlling interest. (Examiner's report – December 2020)

CONSOLIDATED STATEMENT OF FINANCIAL POSITION OF ALPHA AT 30 SEPTEMBER 20X5

	$'000	Marks
Assets		
Non-current assets		
Property, plant and equipment (250,000 + 170,000 + 44,000 (W1))	464,000	½
Goodwill (W2)	34,520	6½ (W2)
	498,520	
Current assets		
Inventories (80,000 + 60,000 – (20,000 × 25%))	135,000	½ + 1
Trade receivables (90,000 + 55,000)	145,000	½
Cash and cash equivalents (30,000 + 25,000)	55,000	½
	335,000	
Total assets	833,520	
Equity and liabilities		
Equity attributable to equity holders of the parent		
Share capital ($1 shares)	160,000	½
Retained earnings (W5)	138,540	6½ (W5)
Other components of equity (W7)	52,500	3 (W7)
	351,040	
Non-controlling interest (W4)	58,680	2 (W4)
Total equity	409,720	
Non-current liabilities		
Long-term borrowings (90,000 + 15,000)	105,000	½
Deferred tax (20,000 + 15,000 + 8,800 (W1))	43,800	½ + ½
Contingent consideration payable	50,000	½
Pension liability (160,000 – 105,000)	55,000	½
Total non-current liabilities	253,800	
Current liabilities		
Trade and other payables (70,000 + 50,000)	120,000	½
Current tax payable (30,000 + 20,000)	50,000	½
Total current liabilities	170,000	
Total liabilities	423,800	
Total equity and liabilities	833,520	25

Workings

1 **Net assets table for Beta**

	1 October 20X4 $'000	30 September 20X5 $'000	For W2	For W5
Share capital	80,000	80,000	½	
Retained earnings:				
Per financial statements of Beta	80,000	85,000	½	½
Fair value adjustments (post-acquisition additional depreciation 55,000 × 1/5 = 11,000)	55,000	44,000	½	½
Deferred tax on fair value	(11,000)	(8,800)	½	½
Unrealised profit on intra-group sales by Beta (25% × 20,000)		(5,000)		½
Other components of equity	45,000	45,000	½	½
Net assets for the consolidation	249,000	240,000	2½	2½
			→W2	→W5

Decrease in net assets (249,000 – 240,200) = 8,800

Marks

2 **Goodwill on acquisition of Beta**

	$'000	
Cost of investment:		
Cash paid	175,000	½
Fair value of contingent consideration at date of acquisition	60,000	½
Non-controlling interest at date of acquisition	65,000	½
Net assets at date of acquisition (W1)	(249,000)	2½ (W1)
Goodwill at date of acquisition	51,000	
Impairment at 30 September 20X5 (W3)	(16,480)	2½ (W3)
Goodwill at 30 September 20X5	34,520	6½

3 **Impairment of goodwill at 30 September 20X5**

	Unit A $'000	Unit B $'000	Unit C $'000	Total $'000	
Fair value of identifiable net assets of Beta at 30 September 20X5 (40:35:25)	96,080	84,070	60,050	240,200	½
Goodwill on acquisition (W2) (40:35:25)	20,400	17,850	12,750	51,000	½
	116,480	101,920	72,800	291,200	
Recoverable amounts of CGUs	(100,000)	(110,000)	(80,000)		½
Impairment	16,480	Nil	Nil		1
					2½
					→W2

4 **Non-controlling interest in Beta**

	$'000	
At date of acquisition	65,000	½
25% of post-acquisition decrease in net assets (25% × 8,800 (W1))	(2,200)	½ + ½
25% of impairment of goodwill of (25% × 16,480 (W3))	(4,120)	½
	58,680	2

  BPP LEARNING MEDIA

5   Retained earnings

	$'000	
Alpha – per draft SOFP	150,000	½
Adjustment re: defined benefit retirement plan (W6)	2,500	1 (W6)
Reduction in fair value of contingent consideration (60,000 – 50,000)	10,000	1
Acquisition costs of Beta	(5,000)	½
75% of post-acquisition share of Beta (75% × 8,800 (W1))	(6,600)	½ + 2½ (W1)
75% of impairment of goodwill of (75% × 16,480 (W3))	(12,360)	½
	138,540	6½

6   Adjustment re: defined benefit retirement plan

	$'000	
Current service cost and net interest cost	(27,500)	½
Contributions incorrectly charged to retained earnings	30,000	½
Adjustment to retained earnings	2,500	1
		→W5
		Marks

7   Other components of equity

	$'000	
Alpha – per draft financial statements	60,000	½
Actuarial gain/(loss) on defined benefit retirement plan (W8)	(7,500)	2½ (W8)
	52,500	3

8   Actuarial gain/(loss) on defined benefit retirement plan

	$'000	
Opening liability	50,000	½
Current service cost and net interest cost	27,500	½
Contributions paid into plan	(30,000)	½
	47,500	
Actuarial loss on re-measurement (balancing figure)	7,500	½
Closing liability ($160,000 – $105,000)	55,000	½
		2½
		→W7

54 Alpha (June 2021)

Top tips. Question 1 of the exam always requires the preparation of a consolidated statement. In June 2021, it was a consolidated statement of financial position.

Note that you will only have the spreadsheet response option available to answer question 1 of the exam. The spreadsheet response option will contain an exact copy of the financial statement information provided in exhibit 1. You should manipulate this information figures easily to prepare your consolidated financial statement proforma. When preparing your answer in the exam, you should make sure that it is clear to the marker what you have done. You must ensure that where you have calculated the number in a particular cell, you either use spreadsheet formula or type out your calculation separately, so that the marker can see exactly what you have done and can then award own figure marks if you have made any mistakes.

Before your exam, you should spend some time getting familiar with the functionality available in the CBE. You can do this by accessing the CBE specimen exam and past exams on the DipIFR Study Support Resources section of the ACCA website.

Easy marks. There are marks available for transferring your figures from your workings to the correct place on the face of the consolidated statement of financial position.

ANSWERS

> **Examining team's comments.** Two relatively common errors were noted:
>
> • Incorrect treatment of the costs of acquiring Beta in the consolidated financial statements. The costs of issuing Alpha shares (issued to the former shareholders of Beta) should have been deducted from other components of equity. A number of candidates either deducted these costs from consolidated retained earnings or used them to increase the goodwill figure by including them as part of the fair value of the consideration given. The due diligence costs should have been deducted from consolidated retained earnings but a number of candidates used them to increase the goodwill figure (in the same way as the share issue costs already described).
>
> • Incorrect treatment of the loan asset due from a customer who was in financial difficulty. Two fairly common errors were noted in this regard. The first was incorrect computation of the measurement of the loan asset at 1 April 20X4, immediately before the customer began to face financial difficulty. A number of candidates deducted the issue costs of the loan from the initial carrying amount of the loan rather than adding these costs on. This suggests a 'rote learning' of the fact that issue costs of a loan are deducted in computing the initial carrying amount. This would of course be true if Alpha was receiving the loan proceeds and it was a financial liability. A substantial number of candidates incorrectly computed the recoverable amount of the loan asset on 31 March 20X5 (the present value of $30 million receivable in one year using a discount rate of 7% per annum). Many ignored the time value of money altogether and worked with a recoverable amount of $30 million. Candidates should note that discounting is relatively important in financial reporting. Many candidates clearly need to give the topic of discounting some more attention.

Marking scheme

Marks

CONSOLIDATED STATEMENT OF FINANCIAL POSITION OF ALPHA AT 31 MARCH 20X5

(**Note.** all figures below in $'000)

	$'000	
Assets		
Non-current assets		
Property, plant and equipment (240,000 + 140,000 + 12,000 (W1))	392,000	½ + ½
Brand (W1)	12,000	½
Goodwill (W2)	27,400	5 (W2)
	431,400	
Current assets:		
Inventories (70,000 + 50,000 – 4,000 (W4))	116,000	½ + ½
Trade receivables (80,000 + 45,000 – 15,000)	110,000	½ + ½
Financial asset (W5)	28,037	½ + ½
Cash and cash equivalents (19,360 + 20,000 + 15,000 (cash in transit))	54,360	½ + ½
	308,397	
Total assets	739,797	
Equity and liabilities		
Equity attributable to equity holders of the parent		
Share capital ($1 shares)	140,000	½
Retained earnings (W4)	114,257	9 (W4)
Other components of equity (W6)	49,700	1
	303,957	
Non-controlling interest (W3)	36,840	1 (W3)
Total equity	340,797	
Non-current liabilities		
Long-term borrowings (120,000 + 30,000)	150,000	½
Deferred tax (W7)	79,000	1½ (W7)
Total non-current liabilities	229,000	
Current liabilities		

BPP
LEARNING
MEDIA

Trade and other payables (70,000 + 55,000)	125,000	½
Current tax payable (30,000 + 15,000)	45,000	½
Total current liabilities	170,000	
Total liabilities	399,000	
Total equity and liabilities	739,797	25

WORKINGS. ALL NUMBERS ARE IN $000 UNLESS OTHERWISE STATED.

Marks

Workings

1 *Net assets table for Beta*

	1 April 20X3 $'000	31 March 20X5 $'000	For W2	For W4
Share capital	60,000	60,000	½	
Retained earnings:				
Per financial statements of Beta	25,000	45,000	½	½
Fair value adjustment to PPE	20,000	12,000	½	½
Fair value adjustment to Brand	15,000	12,000	½	½
Fair value adjustment to contingent liability	(10,000)	Nil	½	½

Marks

	1 April 20X3 $'000	31 March 20X5 $'000	For W2	For W4
Deferred tax on fair value adjustments:	(5,000)	(4,800)	½	½
Other components of equity	35,000	35,000	½	
Net assets for the consolidation	140,000	159,200	3½	2½
			⇒ W2	⇒ W4

Post-acquisition increase in net assets (159,200 – 140,000) = 19,200

2 *Goodwill on acquisition of Beta*

	$'000	
Cost of investment:		
Shares issued by Alpha – 48 million × 2/3 × $4.20	134,400	1
Non-controlling interest at date of acquisition	33,000	½ Net
assets at date of acquisition (W1)	(140,000)	3½ (W1)
Goodwill at date of acquisition	27,400	5

3 *Non-controlling interest in Beta*

	$'000	
At date of acquisition	33,000	½
20% of post-acquisition increase in net assets (20% × 19,200 (W1))	3,840	½
	36,840	1

4 *Retained earnings*

	$'000	
Alpha – per draft SOFP	120,000	½
Impairment of financial asset (W5)	(14,403)	3½ (W5)
Due diligence costs re: acquisition of Beta	(3,500)	½
80% of post acquisition share of Beta' profits (80% × 19,200 (W1))	15,360	½ + 2½ (W1)
Unrealised profit on sales to Beta (33.33/133.33 × 16,000)	(4,000)	½
Deferred tax on unrealised profit (20% × 4,000)	800	½ + ½
	114,257	9

209

5 *Impairment of financial asset*

	$'000	
Original loan amount	40,000	½
Costs of issuing loan	2,000	½ + ½
	42,000	
Finance income recognised in the year ended 31 March 20X4 (7% × 42,000)	2,940	½
Interest payment received on 31 March 20X4	(2,500)	½
	42,440	
Recoverable amount at 31 March 20X5 (30,000/(1.07))	(28,037)	½ + ½
So impairment equals	14,403	3½
		⇒ W4

6 *Other components of equity*

	$'000	
Alpha – per draft SOFP	52,200	½
Cost of issuing shares to acquire Beta	(2,500)	½
	49,700	1

7 *Deferred tax*

	$'000	
Alpha + Beta (60,000 + 15,000)	75,000	½
Deferred tax on fair value adjustments (W1)	4,800	½
Deferred tax on unrealised profit adjustment (W4)	(800)	½
	79,000	1½

55 Alpha (June 2022)

Top tips. Question 1 of the exam always requires the preparation of a consolidated statement. In June 2022, it was a consolidated statement of financial position.

Note that you will only have the spreadsheet response option available to answer question 1 of the exam. The spreadsheet response option will contain an exact copy of the financial statement information provided in exhibit 1. You should manipulate this information to prepare your consolidated financial statement proforma. When preparing your answer in the exam, you should make sure that it is clear to the marker what you have done. You must ensure that where you have calculated the number in a particular cell, you either use spreadsheet formula or type out your calculation separately, so that the marker can see exactly what you have done and can then award own figure marks if you have made any mistakes.

Before your exam, you should spend some time getting familiar with the functionality available in the CBE. You can do this by accessing the CBE specimen exam and past exams on the DipIFR Study Support Resources section of the ACCA website.

Easy marks. There are easy marks available for producing standard workings for balances such as goodwill. Ensure you are comfortable with producing the standard workings

Examining team's comments. On the whole this question was answered reasonably satisfactorily. The relatively common errors were:

- Incorrect treatment of the deferred consideration on acquisition of a subsidiary. A significant minority failed to appreciate that this remained a liability at the reporting date.

- Incorrect computation of the carrying amount of the constructed asset, especially failing to depreciate the asset from when it was available for use (rather than the date it was actually brought into use) and failing to appreciate that borrowing costs could only be capitalised for the period in which both borrowings had been taken out and construction activities were being carried out.

- Incorrect treatment of the convertible loan. Most candidates realised that the loan contained both equity and liability components, but the calculation of the liability component was of variable quality.

Consolidated statement of financial position of Alpha at 31 March 20X5

[**Note.** All figures below in $'000]

	$'000	Marks
Assets		
Non-current assets		
Property, plant and equipment (380,000 + 185,000 + 18,000 (W1) − 2,463 (W5))	580,537	½ + ½
Goodwill (W2)	46,800	6 (W2)
	627,337	
Current assets		
Inventories (90,000 + 65,000 − 4,000 (W4))	151,000	½
Trade receivables (100,000 + 50,000)	150,000	½
Cash and cash equivalents (35,000 + 20,000)	55,000	½
	356,000	
Total assets	983,337	
Equity and liabilities		
Equity attributable to equity holders of the parent		
Share capital ($1 shares)	200,000	½
Retained earnings (W4)	140,216	5½ (W4)
Other components of equity (W8)	76,560	1 (W8)
	416,776	
Non-controlling interest (W3)	42,880	1 (W3)
Total equity	459,656	
Non-current liabilities		
Long-term borrowings (200,000 + 20,000 − 5,419 (W6))	214,581	½ + ½
Deferred tax (20,000 + 10,000 + 3,600 (W1))	33,600	½ + ½
Total non-current liabilities	248,181	
Current liabilities		
Trade and other payables (85,000 + 60,000)	145,000	½ + ½
Current tax payable (40,000 + 30,000)	70,000	½ + ½
Deferred consideration payable to former shareholders of Beta (W7)	60,500	2 (W7)
Total current liabilities	275,500	
Total liabilities	523,681	
Total equity and liabilities	983,337	

Workings

1   *Net assets table for Beta*

	1 April 20X3 $'000	31 March 20X5 $'000
Share capital	100,000	100,000
Retained earnings:		
Per financial statements of Beta	60,000	80,000
Fair value adjustment to PPE (post-acquisition additional depreciation = 30,000 × 2/5 = 12,000)	30,000	18,000
Deferred tax on fair value adjustment	(6,000)	(3,600)
Other components of equity	20,000	20,000
Net assets for the consolidation	204,000	214,400
Post-acquisition increase in net assets (214,400 − 204,000) = 10,400		
	½ each item = total 2½ to W2	½ each item = total 2 to W4

2   *Goodwill on acquisition of Beta*

	$'000	**Marks**
Cash cost of shares purchased	160,000	½
Deferred consideration (66,500 × 0.75132)	50,000	½
Non-controlling interest at date of acquisition (204,000 (W1) × 20%)	40,800	½
Net assets at date of acquisition (W1)	(204,000)	2½ from W1
Goodwill on acquisition equals	46,800	

3   *Non-controlling interest in Beta*

	$'000	**Marks**
At date of acquisition (W2)	40,800	½
20% of post-acquisition increase in net assets (20% × 10,400 (W1))	2,080	½
	42,880	

4   *Retained earnings*

	$'000	**Marks**
Alpha – per draft SOFP	160,000	½
Adjustment to carrying amount of PPE (W5)	(2,463)	½
Adjustment to finance cost of convertible loan (5,141 (W6) – 4,000)	(1,141)	½
Acquisition costs	(10,000)	½
Finance costs of deferred consideration on acquisition of Beta (5,000 + 5,500 (W7))	(10,500)	½
80% of post-acquisition share of Beta profits (80% × 10,400 (W1))	8,320	½ + 2 (W1)
Unrealised profit on sales to Beta (20/120 × 24,000)	(4,000)	½
	140,216	

5   *Adjustment to carrying amount of PPE*

	$'000	**Marks**
Construction cost	60,000	
Finance cost eligible for capitalisation (60,000 × 8% × 4/12)	1,600	½
	61,600	
Depreciation (61,600 × 1/10 × 4/12)	(2,053)	½
Correct carrying amount	59,547	
Carrying amount per draft financial statements of Alpha	(62,010)	
Adjustment to carrying amount equals	(2,463)	½

6   *Adjustment to carrying amount of convertible loan*

	$'000	**Marks**
Carrying amount on 1 April 20X4 (4,000 × 4.10 + 80,000 × 0.713)	73,440	½
Finance cost for year ended 31 March 20X5 (73,440 × 7%)	5,141	½
Cash interest paid on 31 March 20X5	(4,000)	½
Carrying amount on 31 March 20X5	74,581	
Carrying amount in draft financial statements of Alpha	(80,000)	
Adjustment to carrying amount equals	(5,419)	½

7   *Deferred consideration payable to former shareholders of Beta*

	$'000	**Marks**
At 1 April 20X3 (W2)	50,000	½
Finance cost for year ended 31 March 20X4 (50,000 × 10%)	5,000	½
	55,000	
Finance cost for year ended 31 March 20X5 (55,000 × 10%)	5,500	½
At 31 March 20X5	60,500	½

8   *Other components of equity*

	$'000	**Marks**
Alpha – per draft SOFP	70,000	½
Equity component of convertible loan (80,000 – 73,440 (W6))	6,560	½
	76,560	

56 Alpha (December 2022)

Top tips. Question 1 of the exam always requires the preparation of a consolidated statement. In December 2022, it was a consolidated statement of financial position.

Note that you will only have the spreadsheet response option available to answer question 1 of the exam. The spreadsheet response option will contain an exact copy of the financial statement information provided in exhibit 1. You should manipulate this information to prepare your consolidated financial statement proforma. When preparing your answer in the exam, you should make sure that it is clear to the marker what you have done. You must ensure that where you have calculated the number in a particular cell, you either use spreadsheet formula or type out your calculation separately, so that the marker can see exactly what you have done and can then award own figure marks if you have made any mistakes.

Before your exam, you should spend some time getting familiar with the functionality available in the CBE. You can do this by accessing the CBE specimen exam and past exams on the DipIFR Study Support Resources section of the ACCA website.

Easy marks. There are marks available for standard workings for balances such as goodwill. Ensure you are comfortable with producing the standard workings

Examining team's comments. On the whole this question was answered reasonably satisfactorily. Relatively common errors that were noted:

- Incorrect treatment of restoration costs required at the end of the extraction process. Candidates should have recognised a provision and an associated asset at the PV of the future restoration costs. A finance cost on the provision and depreciation (or amortisation) on the associated asset should then have been recognised. The suggested answer shows the asset as an intangible, but full credit was given if candidates included this as part of property, plant and equipment.

- Some candidates were unable to correctly calculate the impairment of goodwill on acquisition of Beta. Since the non-controlling interest in Beta was initially measured using the fair value method, there was no need to gross up the goodwill figure prior to performing the impairment review. Having calculated the impairment, some omitted to then allocate this amount between consolidated retained earnings and the non-controlling interest. It is important not to 'rote learn' adjustments as this can cause confusion when attempting to apply to the scenario.

- Computations of the unrealised profit on intra-group trading were disappointing. Errors included computation and incorrect adjustment (20/120 in this case), applying this to all intra-group sales in the period, and getting the adjustment to inventories and retained earnings the wrong way round.

Consolidated statement of financial position of Alpha as at 30 September 20X2

	$000	Marks
Assets		
Non-current assets		
Property, plant and equipment (680,000 + 430,000 + 20,000 (W1) − 8,000 (W1))	1,122,000	½ + ½
Intangible assets (3,000 + 1,600 (W1) − 800 (W1) + 2,484 (W8) − 497 (W8))	5,787	½ + ½ + ½
Investment in associate (W5)	20,250	1½ (W5)
Goodwill (W2)	49,760	
	1,197,797	
Current assets		
Inventories (30,000 + 28,000 − 625 (W6))	57,375	½
Trade receivables (16,700 + 9,800)	26,500	½
Cash and cash equivalents (12,000 + 6,450)	18,450	½
	102,325	
Total assets	1,300,122	
Equity and liabilities		
Equity		

	$000	Marks
Share capital ($1 shares)	380,000	½
Retained earnings (W4)	720,505	5½ (W4)
Non-controlling interest (W3)	103,500	1½ (W3)
Total equity	1,204,005	
Non-current liabilities		
Provision (2,484 (W8) + 248 (W8))	2,732	½ + ½
Long-term borrowings (4,200 + 8,900)	13,100	½
Deferred tax (3,750 + 4,500 + 2560 (W1) – 125 (W6))	10,685	½ + ½ + ½
Total non-current liabilities	26,517	
Current liabilities		
Trade and other payables (18,960 + 11,400)	30,360	½
Short-term borrowings (29,790 + 9,450)	39,240	½
Total current liabilities	69,600	
Total equity and liabilities	1,300,122	

Workings

1 *Net assets – Beta*

	Acquisition $000	Year end $000	Movement $000
Share capital	100,000	100,000	
Retained earnings	275,000	340,000	
FV adjustment: PPE	20,000	20,000	
FV depreciation ($20 million/5 years × 2)		(8,000)	
Contingent liability	(4,000)	nil	
Customer list	1,600	1,600	
Amortisation of customer list ($1.6m/4 years × 2)		(800)	
Deferred tax on fair value adjustment	(3,520)	(2,560)	
Net assets for consolidation	389,080	450,240	
Post-acquisition increase in net assets ($450,240 – $389,080)			61,160
Marks	½ each line = 3 to W2	½ each new line = 3 to W4	

2 *Goodwill – Beta*

	$000	Marks
Cost of investment	380,000	½
NCI at acquisition	98,000	½
	478,000	
Less net assets (W1)	(389,080)	3 (from W1)
Goodwill at acquisition	88,920	
Less impairment (W7)	(39,160)	½
Goodwill at 30 September 20X2	49,760	

3 *Non-controlling interest in Beta*

	$000	Marks
At acquisition (W2)	98,000	½
NCI share of movement (25% × $61,160 (W1))	15,290	½
Impairment (25% × $39,160 (W7))	(9,790)	½
	103,500	

4   *Retained earnings*

	$000	**Marks**
Alpha	703,000	
Alpha % of Beta post-acquisition profits (75% × $61,160 (W1))	45,870	½ + 3 (W1)
Alpha % of associate (Drax) post acquisition (W5)	2,250	½
PURP (W6)	(500)	½
Impairment (75% × $39,160) (W7)	(29,370)	½
Adjustments re provision (W8)	(745)	½
	720,505	

5   *Investment in associate (Delta)*

	$000	**Marks**
Cost	18,000	½
25% of post-acquisition profits ($79,000 – $70,000 (W4))	2,250	½
Carrying amount at 30 September 20X2	20,250	½

6   *PURP*

	$000	**Marks**
Sales in inventory ($15m × 25%)	3,750	½
Unrealised profit ($3,750 × 20/120)	625	½
Deferred tax asset ($625 × 20%)	125	½
Adjustment to retained earnings	500	

7   *Impairment of Beta as at 30 September 20X2*

	$000	**Marks**
Net assets of Beta	450,240	
Goodwill on acquisition	88,920	½
	539,160	
Recoverable amount of Beta as a CGU	500,000	½
Impairment	39,160	½

8   *Adjustment re provision:*

	$000	**Marks**
Provision recognised on 1 October 20X1 (4,000 × 0.621)	2,484	
Unwind discount on 30 September 20X2 (2,484 × 0.1)	248	½
	2,732	
Amortisation at 30 September 20X2 (2,484/5)	497	½
Retained earnings adjustment (W4) (248 + 497)	745	

57 Alpha (December 2012) (amended)

Top tips. The group accounting question is always a tough one, covering a number of different topics, and with a lot of adjustments to keep track of. This can be off-putting when you first read the question, so make sure you have a plan to get started. In question 1 of your exam, only the spreadsheet response option will be available and will contain an exact copy of the financial statement information in exhibit 1. You should, then manipulate this information to produce a proforma for your consolidated SPLOCI. You can then work through the adjustments in the question. Reference your calculations and show your workings clearly. This is for your benefit as well as for the marker. You will probably find that if you take each issue individually, you know how to deal with each one:

- Treatment of acquisition costs
- Non-controlling interest
- Joint arrangement
- Foreign currency
- Fundamental accounting requirements for consolidation of subsidiaries and associates

We recommend that you practise the consolidation questions in this Kit using a spreadsheet. This is so that you can plan how to layout your consolidated financial statement and your workings.

Easy marks. As with most groups questions, there are easy marks for slotting the simpler figures into the statement of profit or loss and other comprehensive income.

Examining team's comments. On the whole this question was answered reasonably well although the standard of the workings varied considerably. It is very important that candidates show clear workings to support the figures that are being produced in a question like this.

Areas showing good knowledge:

- Most candidates correctly consolidated the parent and subsidiary (Beta) with only a small number attempting to proportionally consolidate Beta.

- Most candidates used good standard formats although some did not split the total comprehensive income between the group and the non-controlling interest (NCI). It was also pleasing to see that most made an attempt to calculate the profit relating to the NCI.

- Most candidates were able to correctly account for the unrealised profits on inter-company trading, although a reasonable number did not adjust for only the group share of the unrealised profit with the joint venture (Gamma).

Areas where mistakes were common:

- The share based payment was often incorrect. Many thought this was the second year of the scheme so deducted a charge for last year. In addition it was placed in some strange sections of the statement, eg other comprehensive income (OCI) instead of cost of sales or administrative expenses.

- Some added the adjustments for investment income and finance cost instead of deducting them.

- Calculations of the gain on investment at FVTOCI and the reclassification of the cash flow hedge were rarely done correctly. The figure most commonly added to OCI for the former was $100,000 (rather than $50,000). Few candidates were aware that the gain on re-measurement of the hedging derivative was taken initially to OCI and then reclassified to profit or loss.

Marking scheme

		Marks
CONSOLIDATED STATEMENT OF PROFIT OR LOSS AND OTHER COMPREHENSIVE INCOME OF ALPHA FOR THE YEAR ENDED 30 SEPTEMBER 20X2		
	$'000	
Revenue (W1)	365,000	1½
Cost of sales (balancing figure)	(282,000)	½
Gross profit (W2)	83,000	3½
Distribution costs (7,000 + 6,000)	(13,000)	½
Administrative expenses (W3)	(26,000)	5
Investment income (W4)	200	2½
Finance cost (W5)	(10,850)	2
Other income (re-classified gains on cash flow hedge)	5,000	1
Share of profit of joint venture (W6)	4,600	3
Profit before tax	42,950	
Income tax expense (10,100 + 6,000)	(16,100)	½
Net profit for the period	26,850	
Other comprehensive income (W8)	(950)	2
Total comprehensive income	25,900	
Net profit attributable to:		
Non-controlling interest (W9)	2,020	1½
Controlling interest	24,830	½
	26,850	

Total comprehensive income attributable to:		
Non-controlling interest	2,020	½
Controlling interest	23,880	½
	25,900	25

Workings

1 *Revenue*

	$'000	
Alpha + Beta	390,000	½
Intra-group sales – to Beta	(25,000)	½ + ½
	365,000	1½

2 *Gross profit*

	$'000	
Alpha + Beta	90,000	½
Unrealised profit Beta (20% × $5m)	(1,000)	1
Extra depreciation ($4m × ½)	(2,000)	1
Extra amortisation ($6m × 12/18)	(4,000)	1
	83,000	3½

3 *Administrative expenses*

	$'000	
Alpha + Beta	17,000	½
Increase in fair value of contingent consideration	2,000	1
Beta acquisition costs	1,000	1½
Charge for share based payment award (2,500 × 960 × $5 × ½)	6,000	2
	26,000	5

Tutorial note. The above costs would, if sensibly included elsewhere in the statement, have also been awarded credit.

4 *Investment income*

	$'000	
Per accounts of Alpha	15,300	½
Dividend received from Beta (10,000 × 80%)	(8,000)	½
Interest received from Beta (40,000 × 5%)	(2,000)	½
Dividend received from Gamma (10,000 × 50%)	(5,000)	½
Increase in fair value of investment in Zeta	(100)	½
Residue in consolidated profit or loss	200	2½

5 *Finance cost*

	$'000	
Alpha + Beta	12,900	½
Interest paid by Beta to Alpha (W4)	(2,000)	½
Transaction costs of investment in Zeta	(50)	1
Residue in profit and loss	10,850	2

6 *Share of profits of Gamma*

	$'000	
Share of profit ($20m × 50% × 9/12)	7,500	1
Impairment (W7)	(2,500)	2 (W7)
Unrealised profit on sales from Alpha (20% × $4m × 50%)	(400)	1
	4,600	4

7   *Impairment of investment in Gamma*

	$'000	
Cost	50,000	½
Share of profit ($20m × 50% × 9/12)	7,500	½
Dividend received	(5,000)	½
Carrying amount	52,500	
Recoverable amount	(50,000)	½
So impairment equals	2,500	2
		⇒ W6

8   *Other comprehensive income*

	$'000	
Gain on cash flow hedge	4,000	½
Reclassification of gain on cash flow hedge	(5,000)	½
Gain on investment at FVTOCI ((100,000 × ($11 – $10)) – $50,000)	50	1
	(950)	2

9   *Non-controlling interest in Beta*

	$'000	
Profit for the year	16,100	½
Fair value adjustments (2,000 + 4,000)	(6,000)	½
	10,100	
Non-controlling interest (20%)	2,020	½
		1½
		25

58 Abiola (June 2016) (amended)

Top tips. This is a typical group accounting question and at first sight it may look difficult. As usual, you should work methodically, taking each issue in turn. Remember that you will only have the spreadsheet response option available to use in question 1 in your exam. The spreadsheet will contain an exact copy of the information available in exhibit 1.

We recommend you practise completing the rest consolidation questions in this Kit in a spreadsheet to get used to preparing your answer using a spreadsheet. Always provide full and clear workings and reference each working to your main answer. The more simple workings can be done on the face of the statement of profit or loss. If you have practised similar questions, you should be able to make a good attempt at this one. In this question, the main issues are:

- Impairment of goodwill (Busayo)
- Acquisition of a subsidiary during the year (Cuca)
- Inter-group trading
- Revenue from a service contract
- Issue of a convertible bond

Easy marks. As usual, there are easy marks for slotting the simpler figures into the statement.

Examining team's comments.

Common errors highlighted in the examining team's report include:

- Incorrectly calculating the impairment of Busayo's goodwill due to not grossing up the goodwill in order to compare it to the recoverable amount of Busayo. The examining team commented that this is tested frequently in the DipIFR exam.

- Failing to show the non-controlling interest in profits and total comprehensive income.

- Incorrectly calculating the liability element of the convertible loan by discounting the amount upon issue rather than the amount on redemption.

- Incorrectly using mark-up, rather than margin in calculating the unrealised profit.

Marking scheme

		Marks
CONSOLIDATED STATEMENT OF PROFIT OR LOSS AND OTHER COMPREHENSIVE INCOME OF ABIOLA FOR THE YEAR ENDED 31 MARCH 20X6		
	$'000	
Revenue (W1)	639,200	3½ (W1)
Cost of sales (W3)	(381,955)	8 (W3)
Gross profit	257,245	
Distribution costs (20,000 + 16,000 + 15,000 × 6/12)	(43,500)	½
Administrative expenses (30,000 + 19,000 + 18,000 × 6/12)	(58,000)	½
Investment income (W5)	3,600	1½ (W5)
Finance costs (W6)	(61,000)	4 (W6)
Profit before tax	98,345	
Income tax expense (15,000 + 12,000 + 6/12 × 11,000)	(32,500)	½
Profit for the year	65,845	
Other comprehensive income		
Items that will not be reclassified to profit and loss		
Losses on financial assets designated at fair value through other comprehensive income (40,000 – 37,000)	(3,000)	1
Gains on derivatives classified as effective fair value hedges (8,700 – 6,000)	2,700	1
Total comprehensive income for the year	65,545	

		Marks
Profit attributable to:		
Owners of Abiola (balancing figure)	52,595	½
Non-controlling interest (W9)	13,250	3 (W9)
	65,845	
Total comprehensive income attributable to:		
Owners of Abiola (balancing figure)	52,295	½
Non-controlling interest (as above)	13,250	½
	65,545	
		25

Workings

1   *Revenue*

	$'000	
Abiola + Busayo + 6/12 × Cuca	665,000	½
Intra-group revenue (15,000 + 8,000)	(23,000)	½
Deferred service revenue (W2)	(2,800)	2½ (W2)
	639,200	3½

2   *Deferred service revenue*

	$'000	
Actual price of 'package' (A)	51,200	½
Sum of fair values of individual components (60,000 + 4 × 1,000) (B)	64,000	½
A/B	80%	½
So 'service revenue' (4 × 1,000 × 80%)	3,200	½
Amount deferred (42/48)	2,800	½
		2½
		⇒W1

3   *Cost of sales*

	$'000	
Abiola + Busayo + 6/12 × Cuca	400,000	½
Intra-group purchases (as W1)	(23,000)	½
Unrealised profit:		
Closing inventory (10% × (3,000 + 2,800))	580	1
Opening inventory (10% × 2,000)	(200)	½ + ½
Impairment of Busayo goodwill (W4)	3,200	3 (W4)
Extra depreciation on fair value adjustments:		
Property ((25,000 − 10,000) × 1/20 × 6/12)	375	1
Plant and equipment (8,000 × 1/4 × 6/12)	1,000	1
	381,955	8

4   *Impairment of Busayo goodwill*

	$'000	
Net assets at 31 March 20X6	174,000	½
Grossed up goodwill (8,000 × 100/80)	10,000	½ + ½
	184,000	
Recoverable amount	(180,000)	½
So gross impairment	4,000	½
Recognise group share (80%)	3,200	½
		3
		⇒ W3
		Marks

5   *Investment income*

	$'000	
Abiola	19,800	½
Intra-group dividends eliminated:		
– Busayo (80% × 12,000)	(9,600)	½
– Cuca (paid post-acquisition – 60% × 11,000)	(6,600)	½
	3,600	1½

6   *Finance cost*

	$'000	
Abiola + Busayo + 6/12 × Cuca	35,500	½
Change in fair value of contingent consideration (42,000 − 40,000)	2,000	1
Finance cost on deferred consideration (W7)	1,000	1 (W7)
Finance cost on convertible bond (W8)	22,500	1½ (W8)
	61,000	4

> **Tutorial note.** It would be acceptable to show the change in fair value of the contingent consideration under a reasonable alternative expense heading, such as administrative expenses.

7   *Finance cost on deferred consideration*

	$'000	
$24,200/(1.10)^2 \times 10\% \times 6/12$	1,000	1
		⇒ W6

> **Tutorial note.** Deferred consideration of $24.2 million is payable on 30 September 20X7. At the acquisition date, Abiola should recognise a liability, measured at the amount payable discounted at a rate of 10% ($24,200/(1.10)^2$. At the year end, six months have passed, and therefore six months' worth of the discount should be unwound and charged to finance costs.

8   *Finance cost on convertible bond*

	$'000	
Liability element of convertible loan (362,320 × 0.621)	225,000	1
So appropriate finance cost = 10% × 225,000	22,500	½
		1½
		⇒ W6

9   *Non-controlling interest in profit*

	Busayo	Cuca (6/12)	Total	
	$'000	$'000	$'000	
Profit after tax	36,000	16,500		1
Extra depreciation – Cuca (375 + 1,000 (W3))		(1,375)		½ + ½
Relevant profit	36,000	15,125		
Non-controlling interest (20%/40%)	7,200	6,050	13,250	½ + ½
				3

59 Alpha (September 2020)

> **Top tips.** This is a typical consolidation question which will feature as question 1 of the DipIFR exam. In this question you were required to prepare the consolidated statement of profit or loss and other comprehensive income for Alpha, a parent with one subsidiary. As well as accounting for the subsidiary (including deferred consideration) and some intra-grouping trading, there were three additional financial reporting issues to deal with including the fair value of equity investments, revaluation of PPE, and an equity-settled share-based payment scheme.
>
> You will only have the spreadsheet option available to answer question 1 of the exam. The spreadsheet response option will be pre-populated will the financial information from exhibit 1. You can manipulate this information to prepare your consolidated financial statement. Make sure you spend some time before the exam practising in a spreadsheet how you will lay out your answer to a consolidation question, including workings and making use of spreadsheet functions (such as 'sum') to speed up calculations. We recommend you practise the consolidation questions in this Kit using a spreadsheet.
>
> You should remember that no explanations are required in question 1. The examiner is looking for the application of consolidation techniques, not explanations of the principles involved.
>
> **Examining team's comments.**
>
> The examiner's report identified some common errors, which included the following:
>
> * Deducting the full subsidiary dividend of $5,000 from the investment income instead of the parent's share of 90%.

- Including the gain on re-measurement of the investment portfolio in other comprehensive income and not in the statement of profit or loss.

- Making an additional overall adjustment on the revaluation of PPE. All that was required was to reclassify $3.5 million of the current year revaluation gain from other comprehensive income to profit or loss.

- Not attributing the profit and total comprehensive income between the shareholders of Alpha and the non-controlling interest.

CONSOLIDATED STATEMENT OF PROFIT OR LOSS AND OTHER COMPREHENSIVE INCOME OF ALPHA FOR THE YEAR ENDED 31 MARCH 20X5

	$'000	Marks
Revenue (W1)	93,800	1
Cost of sales (W2)	(28,750)	4½
Gross profit	65,050	½
Distribution costs (5,000 + 2,000)	(7,000)	½
Administrative expenses (W3)	(13,076)	4
Investment income (W5)	2,000	4
Finance costs (W6)	(6,700)	4
Profit before tax	40,274	½
Income tax expense (7,000 + 4,000)	(11,000)	½
Profit for the year	29,274	½
Other comprehensive income:		
Items that will not be reclassified to profit or loss:		
Gains on property valuation (W8)	4,500	1½
Other comprehensive income for the year:		
Total comprehensive income for the year	33,774	½
Profit for the year attributable to:		
Shareholders of Alpha (balancing figure)	28,174	½
Non-controlling interest in Beta (10% × 11,000)	1,100	1
	29,274	
	$'000	Marks
Total comprehensive income for the year attributable to:		
Shareholders of Alpha (balancing figure)	32,374	½
Non-controlling interest in Beta (W9)	1,400	1
	33,774	25

Workings

1   *Revenue*

	$'000	
Alpha + Beta (64,800 + 39,000)	103,800	½
Intra-group sales	(10,000)	½
	93,800	1

2   *Cost of sales*

	$'000	
Alpha + Beta (26,000 + 16,000)	42,000	½
Intra-group purchases	(10,000)	½
Unrealised profit on closing Beta inventory (33/133 × 3,000)	750	½ + ½ + ½
Unrealised profit on opening Beta inventory (33/133 × 2,000)	(500)	½ + ½
Cumulative prior year revaluation deficit written back due to current year revaluation gain	(3,500)	1
	28,750	4½

3   *Administrative expenses*

	$'000	
Alpha + Beta (9,000 + 3,500)	12,500	½
Charge for equity settled share-based payment (W4)	576	3½
	13,076	4

4   *Charge for equity settled share-based payment*

	$'000	
Cumulative charge for the two years to 31 March 20X5 (450 × 4,000 × $1.20 × 2/4)	1,080	2
Charged in the year ended 31 March 20X4 (420 × 4,000 × $1.20 × ¼)	(504)	1
So charge for the year ended 31 March 20X5 equals	576	½
		3½
		⇒W3

5   *Investment income*

	$'000	
Alpha + Beta	7,000	½
Intra-group interest eliminated (25,000 × 8%)	(2,000)	1
Intra-group dividend eliminated (5,000 × 90%)	(4,500)	1
So dividend income from investment portfolio equals	500	½
Gain on re-measurement of investment portfolio (33,500 – 32,000)	1,500	1
	2,000	4

6   *Finance costs*

	$'000	
Alpha + Beta (4,000 + 2,500)	6,500	½
Intra-group interest eliminated (give OF credit here)	(2,000)	½
Finance cost on deferred consideration (W7)	2,200	3 (W7)
	6,700	4
		Marks

7   *Finance cost on deferred consideration*

	$'000	
Deferred consideration on 1 April 20X3 (26,620 × 0.7513)	20,000	1
Finance cost for y/e 31 March 20X4 (20,000 × 10%)	2,000	1
Deferred consideration at 31 March 20X4	22,000	½
So finance cost for y/e 31 March 20X5 equals (22,000 × 10%)	2,200	½
		3
		⇒W6

8   *Revaluation gains*

	$'000	
Alpha + Beta (5,000 + 3,000)	8,000	½
Portion of Alpha gain credited to profit or loss	(3,500)	1
So adjustment equals	4,500	1½

9   *Total comprehensive income attributable to NCI*

	$'000	
NCI in profit (give OF credit here)	1,100	½
NCI in Beta's revaluation gain (3,000 × 10%)	300	½
	1,400	1

60 Alpha (December 2021)

Tutorial note. In Q1 of the DipIFR exam will always be a consolidation question. This question should be answered using the spreadsheet response option (only the spreadsheet response option will be available to you). The spreadsheet response option will be pre-populated with an exact copy of the draft financial statements provided in exhibit 1 of the question. You should manipulate this data in order to produce the consolidated financial statement required by the question. If you accidentally delete any of the information in the pre-populated spreadsheet, you can refer back to exhibit 1 to find the relevant information.

Good exam technique for a question such as this is to layout a proforma consolidated statement of profit or loss (using the data provided in the pre-populated spreadsheet response option). Once you have done that, you can start working through the adjustments, setting up a new working as required. Transfer your adjustments to the proforma when you have completed each working. Make sure you include all your calculations in your answer, as the marker can then award you 'own figure' marks where possible, should you make a mistake in your calculations.

We recommend that you practise the consolidation questions in this Kit using a spreadsheet. This is so that you can plan how to layout your consolidated financial statement and your workings.

Note that no explanations are required in question 1 so do not waste time providing them. The examiner is looking for application of techniques for consolidation, not explanations of the principles involved.

Marking scheme

		Marks

CONSOLIDATED STATEMENT OF PROFIT OR LOSS AND OTHER COMPREHENSIVE INCOME OF ALPHA FOR THE YEAR ENDED 30 SEPTEMBER 20X5

	$'000	
Revenue (290,000 + 240,000 – 20,000)	510,000	½ + ½
Cost of sales (W1)	(253,840)	12½ (W1)
Gross profit	256,160	
Other income (W6)	6,100	2½ (W6)
Distribution costs (15,000 + 12,000)	(27,000)	½
Administrative expenses (55,000 + 50,000 – 6,000 (management charge))	(99,000)	½ + ½
Finance costs (30,000 + 28,000)	(58,000)	½
Other expenses	(1,000)	½
Profit before tax	77,260	
Income tax expense (W7)	(17,700)	1½ (W7)
Profit for the year	59,560	
Other comprehensive income:		
Items that may be reclassified subsequently to profit or loss:		
Cash flow hedges (W8)	29,300	1½ (W8)
Total comprehensive income for the year	88,860	
Profit for the year attributable to:		
Shareholders of Alpha (balancing figure)	57,800	½
Non-controlling interest (W9)	1,760	2 (W9)
	59,560	
Total comprehensive income for the year attributable to:		
Shareholders of Alpha (88,860 – 1,760)	87,100	½
Non-controlling interest	1,760	½
	88,860	25

DO NOT DOUBLE COUNT MARKS. ALL NUMBERS IN $'000 UNLESS OTHERWISE STATED.

Workings

1   *Cost of sales*

	$'000	
Alpha + Beta (130,500 + 132,000)	262,500	½
Intra-group purchases	(20,000)	½
Unrealised profit (25% × 3,200)	800	½
Fair value adjustments:		
Plant (18,000 × 1/6)	3,000	½
Patent (20,000 × 1/10)	2,000	½
Inventory	1,500	½
Impairment of goodwill (W2)	4,040	9½ (W2)
	253,840	12½

2   *Impairment of Beta goodwill*

	$'000	
Net assets of Beta on 30 September 20X5 (W3)	210,400	3 (W3)
Grossed up goodwill (15,720 (W5) × 100/80)	19,650	4 (W5) + 1
	230,050	
Recoverable amount	(225,000)	½
So gross impairment equals	5,050	½
Only recognise group share (80%)	4,040	½
		9½
		⇒ W1

3   *Net assets of Beta at 30 September 20X5*

	$'000	
Net assets of Beta per own financial statements (W4)	184,000	1½ (W4)
Closing fair value adjustments:		
Plant (18,000 × 5/6)	15,000	½
Patent (20,000 × 9/10)	18,000	½
Related deferred tax (20% × (15,000 + 18,000))	(6,600)	½
Net assets of Beta per consolidated financial statements	210,400	3
		⇒ W2

4   *Net assets of Beta per own financial statements*

	$'000	
Net assets at 30 September 20X4 (given)	180,000	½
Profit for the year to 30 September 20X5 per own financial statements	14,000	½
Dividend paid during the year ended 30 September 20X5	(10,000)	½
Net assets at 30 September 20X5	184,000	1½
		⇒ W3

5   *Goodwill of Beta*

	$'000	$'000	
Cost of investment:			
Immediate cash payment		185,000	½
Non-controlling interest at the date of acquisition:			
20% × 211,600 (see below)		42,320	½ + ½
Net assets at the date of acquisition:			
As per financial statements of Beta	180,000		½
Fair value adjustments:			
PPE	18,000		½
Patent	20,000		½
Inventory	1,500		½
Related deferred tax (20% × (18,000 + 20,000 + 1,500))	(7,900)		½
		(211,600)	
		15,720	4
			⇒ W2

6   *Other income*

	$'000	
Alpha + Beta	20,000	½
Dividend received by Alpha from Beta (10,000 × 80%)	(8,000)	½
Management charge from Alpha to Beta	(6,000)	½
Ineffective portion of cash flow hedge on Contract A (5,600 – 5,500)	100	1
	6,100	2½

7   *Income tax expense*

	$'000	
Alpha + Beta	19,000	½
Deferred tax on fair value adjustments (20% × (3,000 + 2,000 + 1,500 (W1)))	(1,300)	1
	17,700	1½

8   *Cash flow hedges*

	$'000	
Alpha – per draft financial statements	18,000	½
Gain on effective portion of hedging derivative for commitment due on:		
Contract A	5,500	½
Contract B	5,800	½
	29,300	1½

> **Tutorial note.** The portion of the gain or loss on the derivative contract which is effective (up to the value of the loss or gain on the future commitment cash flow) is recognised in other comprehensive income (cash flow hedge reserve). Any excess which is ineffective is recognised immediately in profit or loss (other income) – Contract A ($5,600 – $5,500 = $100 (W6)).

9   *Non-controlling interest*

	$'000	
Profit of Beta – per draft financial statements	14,000	½
Fair value adjustments to profit before tax (3,000 + 2,000 + 1,500 (W1))	(6,500)	½
Related deferred tax (20%)	1,300	½
	8,800	
Non-controlling interest (20%)	1,760	½
		2

ACCA Diploma in International Financial Reporting

Mock Exam 1

(June 2023 exam)

Questions	
Time allowed	3 hours and 15 minutes
ALL FOUR questions are COMPULSORY and must be attempted	

DO NOT OPEN THIS EXAM UNTIL YOU ARE READY TO START UNDER EXAMINATION CONDITIONS

ALL FOUR questions are compulsory and MUST be attempted

1 Alpha (June 2023)

Alpha, a parent with two subsidiaries, Beta and Gamma, is preparing the consolidated statement of profit or loss for the year ended 31 December 20X9.

The following **exhibits** provide information relevant to the question:

(1)   Draft financial statements – draft statements of profit or loss and summarised statements of changes in equity for Alpha, Beta and Gamma for the year ended 31 December 20X9

(2)   Alpha's investment in Beta – details of Alpha's investment in Beta

(3)   Alpha's investment in Gamma – details of Alpha's investment in Gamma

(4)   Other information – details of intra-group trading and information on the investment income

This information should be used to answer the requirement.

Requirement

Using exhibits 1 to 4, prepare the consolidated statement of profit or loss of Alpha for the year ending 31 December 20X9. You do not need to consider the deferred tax effects of any adjustments you make. No explanations of consolidation adjustments are required.   **(25 marks)**

Exhibit 1 Draft financial statements

Statements of profit or loss for the year ending 31 December 20X9

	Alpha	Beta	Gamma
	$000	$000	$000
Revenue (exhibit 4)	1,935,000	280,000	900,000
Cost of sales (exhibits 2–4)	(495,000)	(132,000)	(540,000)
Gross profit	1,440,000	148,000	360,000
Operating expenses	(679,000)	(59,000)	(156,000)
Profit from operations	761,000	80,000	204,000
Investment income (exhibit 4)	128,000		
Finance costs	(30,000)	(8,000)	(36,000)
Profit before tax	859,000	81,000	168,000
Income tax expense	(280,000)	(19,000)	(42,000)
Profit for the year	579,000	62,000	126,000

Summarised statements of changes in equity for the year ending 31 December 20X9

	Alpha	Beta	Gamma
	$000	$000	$000
Total equity on 1 January 20X9	840,000	180,000	211,000
Profit for the year	579,000	62,000	126,000
Dividends paid on 30 June 20X9	(143,000)	(51,000)	(67,000)
Total equity on 31 December 20X9	1,276,000	191,000	270,000

Exhibit 2 Alpha's investment in Beta

On 1 April 20X4, Alpha acquired 80 million of the 100 million equity shares of Beta and gained control of Beta. Alpha acquired the equity shares in Beta by issuing one new share in Alpha for every two acquired in Beta. On 1 April 20X4, the fair value of an equity share in Alpha was $3.20 and the fair value of an equity share in Beta was $1.60. On 1 April 20X4, the net assets of Beta had a fair value of $100 million and this was equal to the carrying amount of the net assets on this date. Alpha used the proportionate share of net assets method for measuring the non-controlling interest.

No impairments of goodwill on acquisition of Beta have been necessary in the consolidated financial statements of Alpha up to and including 31 December 20X8. Beta is a single cash generating unit. On 31 December 20X9, the annual impairment review of goodwill indicated that the recoverable amounts of the net assets, including goodwill, of Beta at that date were $235 million. Any impairments of goodwill are charged as part of cost of sales in the consolidated statement of profit or loss.

Exhibit 3 Alpha's investment in Gamma

Details of acquisition

On 1 January 20X6, Alpha acquired 7.5 million of the 10 million equity shares in Gamma and gained control of Gamma. Alpha paid $95 million in cash for the equity shares. On 1 January 20X6, the carrying amount of the identifiable net assets of Gamma in its individual financial statements were $70 million and their fair values were $85 million. The difference was due to property whose fair value exceeded the carrying amount by $15 million. $11.4 million of this difference referred to the depreciable component of this property. The estimated useful life of the depreciable component of the property at 1 January 20X6 was eight years. All depreciation of property, plant and equipment is charged to cost of sales.

Alpha used the fair value method for measuring the non-controlling interest when recognising the goodwill on the acquisition of Gamma. The fair value of an equity share in Gamma on 1 January 20X6 was $4.20 which can be used to measure the fair value of the non-controlling interest. No impairments of the goodwill in Gamma have occurred.

Details of disposal

On 31 August 20X9, Alpha disposed of its entire equity shareholding in Gamma for a cash consideration of $330 million. Income tax payable on this disposal is expected to be $38 million. On 31 August 20X9, Alpha credited the disposal proceeds to a suspense account. Gamma represented a separate major line of business which the Alpha Group was withdrawing from. You can assume that the profits of Gamma for the year ended 31 December 20X9 accrued evenly.

Exhibit 4 Other information

Intra-group trading

Beta has purchased goods from Alpha during the year. This is the first year in which intra-group trading took place. Alpha applies a mark-up of one-third to the cost of these goods when computing the sales price.

Alpha sold goods with an invoice value of $42 million to Beta during the year to 31 December 20X9. At the year end, Beta still held some of these goods with an invoice value of $19.2 million in inventory.

2 Theta (June 2023)

Theta, a listed entity, prepares financial statements to 30 June each year. You are a trainee accountant employed by Theta and report to the finance director (FD) of Theta. One of your key responsibilities is to prepare the first draft of Theta's published financial statements. You have recently received an email from the FD regarding the financial statements for the year ended 30 June 20X5. You are unsure how to respond to this email and have asked a friend of yours for advice. This friend is a qualified accountant who is not employed by Theta.

The following exhibits provide information relevant to the question.

(1)   An email from the FD

(2)   Attachment to the email – details information relating to the construction of new plant, a loan to finance the construction, and environmental damage.

This information should be used to answer the requirements.

Requirements

(a)   Using the information in exhibit 2, explain and show how the transactions described there should be accounted for in the financial statements of Theta for the year ended 30 June 20X5.

Notes:
*   Marks will be awarded for BOTH figures AND explanations
*   Ignore taxation
*   Your answer to this part should NOT discuss any ethical issues

(21 marks)

(b)   Using the information in exhibit 1, identify and explain the ethical issues which confront you as a result of the email sent to you from the finance director and whether you should ask advice from your friend who is not employed by Theta.   **(4 marks)**

Total 25 marks

Exhibit 1 Email

To:	Trainee accountant
From:	Finance director
Subject:	Financial statement preparation
Date:	30 June 20X5

As you will know, we are just about to begin the preparation of the published financial statements for the year ended 30 June 20X5. It is very important that the upcoming set of financial results show a favourable financial performance. This will reflect well on the whole finance department including you. I want these statements to report as high a profit as possible to satisfy the shareholders and boost the share price. I understand that you do not currently own any shares in Theta. It would be advantageous for you to purchase some shares immediately, before the latest results are published. If the results show a high profit, then the share price is likely to rise.

I would like you to prepare a draft of the financial statements for my review and approval. There is a relatively complex set of transactions which have occurred in the year ended 30 June 20X5 which you may be unsure how to deal with. These transactions are described in the attachment to this email. I have also included the way in which I would like you to deal with them in the financial statements. You should be aware that your annual performance appraisal, which I am responsible for, is due shortly.

Exhibit 2 Attachment to the email

We have constructed a plant and I have provided details of the costs of construction, a loan taken to finance the costs of construction and some details of environmental damage arising from the construction.

Cost of plant

On 1 January 20X5, we began to construct a plant which will produce fertiliser. This fertiliser can be sold to entities in the agricultural industry. We completed construction of the plant on 1 March 20X5 and then provided relevant employees with a comprehensive training course on the plant's operating method.

We could have begun to operate the plant from 1 April 20X5 but prior to beginning operations, we held an opening ceremony in late April 20X5 and invited a large number of potential customers to demonstrate that the plant was ready for production.

Although we started production on 15 May 20X5, this was only at a small fraction of the plant's operating capacity. We will begin to operate the plant at full capacity from 1 July 20X5.

The costs which we have incurred on this construction project to date and which I want you to include as part of property, plant and equipment (PPE) in the statement of financial position at 30 June 20X5 are as follows:

	$000
Materials used in the construction of the plant	4,000
Production overheads directly related to the construction of the plant	2,000
Allocation of general administrative overheads to the construction cost (using our normal overhead allocation model)	1,000
Salaries of construction staff from 1 January 20X5 to 30 June 20X5 ($500,000 per month)	3,000
Costs of training staff in the use of the new plant	600
Cost of testing the plant's operating systems to ensure they are fit for purpose	200
Costs associated with opening ceremony in April 20X5	250
Total	**11,050**

The estimated useful life of the plant is 20 years, and we should start to depreciate it on 1 July 20X5 when it is operating at full capacity.

Loan

On 1 December 20X4, we borrowed $8 million to partly finance construction of the plant. The lender charged a lending fee of $200,000 so we actually received a net sum of $7.8 million on 1 December 20X4. There is no interest payable on this borrowing, but we will repay $8.52 million on 30 November 20X5. I want you to show a loan figure of $8 million in the statement of financial position as at 30 June 20X5, and the lending fee of $200,000 as an additional component of PPE. Do not account for the extra amount repayable on 30 November 20X5.

Environmental damage

The construction of the plant caused some environmental damage. When we stop using the plant in 20 years' time, the cost of rectifying this damage is estimated to be $10 million. There is no legal obligation for us to rectify this damage. However, we have a reputation for rectifying all environmental damage we have caused. Since there is no legal obligation, you can forget about it from the point of view of the financial statements for the current year. A colleague of yours has stated that an annual discount rate appropriate to the risks associated with this construction project is 10% and therefore the present value of $1 payable in 20 years' time is approximately 15 cents. However, ignore all this – I do not want any recognition of this potential future cost at all.

3 Delta (June 2023)

Delta prepares financial statements to 30 June each year.

The following exhibits provide information relevant to the question:
(1) Construction contract – information regarding the construction and installation of complex machinery
(2) Joint arrangement – information regarding an arrangement with another entity, Drax.

This information should be used to answer the requirements.

Requirement:

Using the information in exhibits 1 and 2, explain and show how the transactions described there should be accounted for and reported in the financial statements of Delta for the year ended 30 June 20X5. No marks will be awarded for simply stating the five-step revenue recognition model without appropriate application to the scenario.

Notes:

*   The mark allocations are indicated in each exhibit
*   Marks will be awarded for BOTH figures and explanations

Total 25 marks

Exhibit 1

Construction contract

On 1 March 20X5, Delta signed a contract for the construction and installation by Delta of complex machines. All work was to take place at the customer's business premises. Work began on the construction on 1 April 20X5. The terms of the contract are that all work is due to be completed by 30 September 20X5.

When the work is fully completed, the machines will be subject to an independent third-party inspection and the quality of the machines will be given a rating as: unsatisfactory, satisfactory or premium. If the rating is satisfactory or premium, the Delta will have fulfilled its obligations under the contract. The costs of the inspection will be borne by the customer.

The total basic price payable by the customer for the construction and installation of the machines was $12 million. However, this basic price is subject to the following conditions:

(i)   The contract price increases by $100,000 for every full week that the work is satisfactorily completed and inspected **before** 30 September 20X5, subject to a minimum additional payment of $800,000.

(ii)   The contract price reduces by $100,000 for every full week that there is a delay in satisfactory completion and inspection of the work **after** 30 September 20X5, subject to a maximum reduction in the total payment of $800,000.

(iii)   If the third-party inspection rates the quality of the suite of machines as premium, then the contract price increases by $600,000. This increase applies irrespective of when the inspection is carried out.

At 30 June 20X5, the directors of Delta reasonably estimated that the work would be completed four weeks after 30 September 20X5 and that the work would be given a premium rating by the inspector.

Delta uses input methods to estimate the stage of completion of its construction contracts. Delta's latest estimate of the total costs of completing the work was $9.5 million. The costs incurred up to 30 June 20X5 were $5.33 million. Details are given below:

Total estimated costs and costs incurred to date

	Total estimated costs $000	Costs incurred to 30 June 20X5 $000
Commission payable to a third party re: contract negotiation	300	300
Materials used on the contract	4,200	2,200
Direct labour used on the contract (Note 1)	2,000	1,100
Costs of wasted materials (Note 1)	Nil	250
Depreciation of assets of Delta used on the contract	1,200	600
Amounts paid to sub-contracted labour	800	400
Allocation of general overheads of Delta to the contract	1,000	480
Totals	**9,500**	**5,330**

Note 1

In May 20X5, inefficient working practices meant materials, which cost Delta $250,000, were wasted, and had to be disposed of. These inefficient working practices also resulted in additional direct labour costs of $100,000. These costs have been included in costs incurred to 30 June 20X5 but have not been included in the total estimated costs.

On 30 June 20X5, Delta sent an invoice to the customer for $6 million. This amount is payable on 31 July 20X5 and there is no reason to doubt that it will be paid.   **(15 marks)**

Exhibit 2

Joint arrangement

On 1 April 20X5, Delta entered into a contractual arrangement with another entity, Drax, to jointly manufacture and distribute a product for sale. The manufacturing process for the product has two distinct stages. Both stages require particular specialised skills. The employee of Delta have the necessary skills to perform stage 1 of the manufacturing process and the employees of Drax have the necessary skills to perform stage 2.

Under the terms of the arrangement, Delta purchases the raw materials and performs stage 1 of the manufacturing process. The partly completed products are then transferred to Drax at their cost of manufacture to date. Drax completes the manufacturing process and sells the products.

All the costs and revenues associated with this arrangement are shared equally by Delta and Drax irrespective of who initially incurs them. Settlement of amounts owed by Drax to Delta or vice-versa, including Delta's share of cash collected from customers, will be made every three months. All decisions regarding the manufacture and distribution of the product and the collection of revenues need to be agreed by both delta and Drax.

Details of costs associated with the arrangement for the first three months were as follows:

	Delta	Drax
	$000	$000
Purchase of raw materials	6,500	14,000 (Note 1)
Manufacturing costs	8,500	14,500
Cost of sales		(26,000)
Advertising and distribution costs	400	1,000

Note 1: The 'purchase' of raw materials by Drax is the cost of partly completed goods transferred from Delta to Drax.

During the three-month period from 1 April 20X5 to 30 June 20X5, Drax sold products for a total invoiced price of $40 million. In that period, Drax received $32 million from customers relating to the sale of these products.

(10 marks)

4 Omega (June 2023)

You are the financial controller of Omega, a listed entity with a number of subsidiaries. Omega prepares financial statements to 30 June each year. One of Omega's directors, who is not an accountant, has reviewed the first draft of the consolidated financial statements of Omega for the year ended 30 June 20X5. She has raised some queries as a result of her review.

The following exhibits provide information relevant to the question:
(1)   Disclosures – details of transactions between group and non-group companies
(2)   Investment in Newco – details of an investment made in the year ended 30 June 20X5
(3)   Financial statements of Tiny and Minor – details different consolidation adjustments required for two subsidiaries.

This information should be used to answer the requirement.

Requirement:

Provide answers to the queries raised by the director relating to the consolidated financial statements for the year ended 30 June 20X5. The queries you need to address appear in exhibits 1 to 3. You should justify your answers with reference to relevant IFRS Accounting Standards.
Note: The mark allocations are indicated in each exhibit.   **(Total 25 marks)**

Exhibit 1 Disclosures

You will be aware that most of our group companies engage the same non-group entity (Dixon) to distribute their products to customers. Transactions with, and outstanding balances owing to, Dixon are quite significant in the context of the group as a whole.

However, one of our subsidiaries (Apex) uses another distributor (Gower). Gower is a company which is controlled by the spouse of the managing director (MD) of Apex. The MD of Apex is also a director of Omega. Transactions with Gower are quite significant to Apex as a single entity but not to the Omega group as a whole.

I am very surprised, therefore, to see details of the transactions with Gower disclosed in the consolidated financial statements but not those with Dixon. Surely this should be the other way round. Please explain this to me. What details should I expect to see in any disclosures of this nature?

(7 marks)

Exhibit 2 Investment in Newco

During the last year, we acquired a 35% shareholding in Newco. We paid $60 million for this investment. There are two other shareholders in Newco, one holding 28% of the shares and the other 37% of the shares. Each shareholder, including Omega, is allowed to appoint two of Newco's six directors. Decisions at board level are made based on a simple majority of votes cast.

Newco has not paid a dividend since we acquired our shareholding because Newco needs to invest cash generated during the period to expand the business. Our draft consolidated financial statements show a figure of $63.5 million for the investment in Newco.

I do not understand why this single figure appears in our consolidated financial statements as a non-current asset. I thought that the consolidated financial statements showed the underlying assets and liabilities of subsidiaries rather than an investment figure.

Surely Newco is a subsidiary given our significant shareholding? Even if we did show a figure for the investment in Newco in Omega's consolidated financial statements, I would have expected it to be $60 million, the amount we paid for the shares. Is the $63.5 million figure based on the value of the shares at the year end? Please explain this financial reporting treatment to me. **(8 marks)**

Exhibit 3 Financial statements of Tiny and Minor

You may be aware that we acquire control of a new subsidiary, Minor, during the year ended 30 June 20X5 and have included its results in the draft consolidated financial statements for the first time. I noticed that various adjustments were made to the figures which were shown in Minor's own individual financial statements when including them in the consolidated financial statements of Omega.

One example of an adjustment is that development expenditure incurred by Minor and charged as an expense in Minor's own financial statements, appears to be treated as an intangible asset in the consolidated financial statements.

When I examine the individual financial statements of Tiny, an unlisted and even smaller subsidiary which was acquired some years ago, it appears that development expenditure is treated as an intangible asset in Tiny's own financial statements. In this case, no adjustments are necessary in order to include the intangible asset in the consolidated financial statements.

Please explain this apparent inconsistency to me. It would seem to me that all research and development expenditure should be treated as an intangible asset, since it is likely to produce future benefits. Surely development expenditure should be treated consistently in financial statements. Is the different treatment caused by the fact that Minor is a relatively small unlisted company using a simplified version of IFRS Accounting standards and are all small companies required to use them? **(10 marks)**

Answers

1 Alpha (June 2023)

Marking guide

	Marks
Statement of profit or loss	
Revenue	1
Cost of sales	2
Impairment of Beta goodwill	5.5
Investment income	1.5
Operating expenses, finance costs, income tax	1.5
	11.5
Profit from discontinued operations	
Gain on disposal of Gamma	7
Profit share, fair value adjustment, tax	3.5
	10.5
Profit for the year	
Shareholders of Alpha	0.5
Non-controlling interest	2.5
	3
Total	25

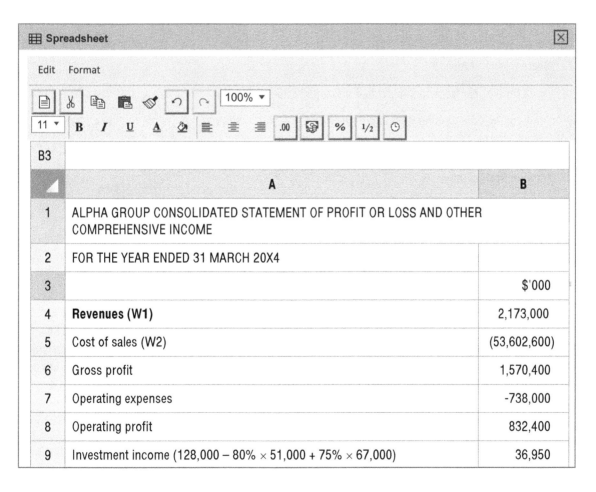

	A	B
1	ALPHA GROUP CONSOLIDATED STATEMENT OF PROFIT OR LOSS AND OTHER COMPREHENSIVE INCOME	
2	FOR THE YEAR ENDED 31 MARCH 20X4	
3		$'000
4	**Revenues (W1)**	2,173,000
5	Cost of sales (W2)	(53,602,600)
6	Gross profit	1,570,400
7	Operating expenses	-738,000
8	Operating profit	832,400
9	Investment income (128,000 − 80% × 51,000 + 75% × 67,000)	36,950

	Spreadsheet	☒

Edit   Format

B3

	A	B
10	Finance costs (30,000 + 8000)	-38,000
11	Profit before tax	831,350
12	Income tax expense (280,000 + 19,000)	-299,000
13	Profit for the year from continuing operations	532,350
14	Profit from discontinued operations (W5)	165,469
15		
16	**Profit for the year**	697,819
17		
18	**Profit attributable to:**	
19	Owners of the parent (balancing figure)	664,656
20	Non-controlling interests (W10)	33,163
21		697,819
22	Shareholders of Alpha:	
23	Profit for the year from continuing operations (532,350 – 12,400)	519,950
24	Profit for the year from discontinuing operations (165,469 – 20,763)	144,706
25		664,656
26	**Non-controlling interests**	
27	Profit for the year from continuing operations (62,000 × 20%)	12,400
28	Profit for the year from discontinuing operations (84,000 – 950 (w5) × 25%)	20,763
29		33,163

Tutorial note. The answer above has been presented in a spreadsheet to replicate how you might present your answer in the spreadsheet response option in your computer-based exam. The information in Exhibit 1 will be prepopulated in the spreadsheet response option. It is important that you get familiar with the exam software and the features available within it. You can do this by accessing the past exams available in the DipIFR Study Support Resources section of the ACCA website. In preparing for the exam, you should practice your answers using a spreadsheet so you know how to set out your workings. Make sure that in the exam you make full use of the pre-populated spreadsheet response option to answer Question 1.

Consolidated statement of financial position of Alpha at 31 March 20X5

Workings

	$'000
Working 1 – Revenue	
Alpha + Beta ($1,935,000 + $280,000)	2,215,000
Intra-group revenue	(42,000)
	2,173,000
Working 2 – Cost of sales	
Alpha + Beta ($495,000 + $132,000)	627,000
Intra-group purchases	(42,000)
Unrealised profit (1/4 × $19,200)	4,800
Impairment of Beta goodwill (W4)	12,800
	602,600
Working 3 – Goodwill on acquisition of Beta	
Cost of investment (80m/2 = 40m × $3.20)	128,000
NCI (20% × $100m)	20,000
Less fair value of net assets at date of acquisition	(100,000)
Goodwill on acquisition	48,000
Working 4 – Impairment of goodwill in Beta	
Net assets at 31 December 20X9	191,000
Add goodwill (grossed up $48 million (W3) × 100/80)	60,000
Total	251,000
Recoverable amount	235,000
Group share (80%)	12,800
Working 5 – Profit from discontinued operation	
Profit of Gamma to 31 August 20X9 ($126,000 × 8/12)	84,000
Fair value adjustment to profit ($11.4m × 1/8 × 8/12)	(950)
Gain on disposal of Gamma (W6)	120,419
Tax on gain on disposal	(38,000)
Profit from discontinued operation	165,469
Working 6 – Gain or loss on disposal of Gamma	
Disposal proceeds	330,000
Less net assets at date of disposal (W7)	(237,775)
Less goodwill at date of disposal (W8)	(20,500)
Add NCI at date of disposal (W9)	48,694
	120,419
Working 7 – Net assets of Gamma on date of disposal	
At 1 January 20X9	211,000
Profit to date of disposal ($126,000 × 8/12 – OF rule applies from W5)	84,000
Dividend paid 30 June 20X9	(67,000)

	$'000
Fair value adjustment to property:	
Depreciable component ($11.4m × 52/96	6,175
Non-depreciable component ($15m − $11.4m)	3,600
	237,775

Working 8 – Goodwill of Gamma at date of disposal

Cost of investment	95,000
NCI in Gamma at date of acquisition (2.5m × $4.20)	10,500
Less fair value of net assets of Gamma at date of acquisition	(85,000)
	20,500

Working 9 – NCI in Gamma at date of disposal

NCI at date of acquisition (W8)	10,500
25% of movement since acquisition ($237,775 (W7) − $85,000)	38,194
	48,694

Working 10 – Non-controlling interest

Beta – 20% × $62,000	12,400
Gamma – 25% × ($84,000 − $950) (W5 – OF rule applies here)	20,763
	33,163

2 Gamma (June 2023)

Marking guide

	Marks
Attachment 1	
Explanations per IAS 16 Property, plant and equipment	5.5
Calculations	1
Explanations per IFRS 9 Financial Instruments	3
Calculations	2.5
Explanations per IAS 23 Borrowing Costs	1
Calculations	0.5
Explanations per IAS 37 Provisions	5
Calculations	2.5
	21
Ethics	4
Total	25

Attachment 1 to email

The relevant standard is **IAS 16** – *Property, Plant and Equipment* (PPE). IAS 16 states that the cost of an item of PPE should be its purchase price plus any costs directly attributable to bringing the asset to the location and condition for it to be capable of operating in the manner intended by management (**principle**).

Under this principle, the **materials** used in the construction of the plant should be included in the cost of PPE and also the **production overheads** directly related to its construction.

However, IAS 16 does **not allow general administrative overheads** to be included as part of PPE. Such overheads ($1 million in this case) should be recognised in the statement of profit or loss as an **operating expense**.

IAS 16 **allows** the cost of employee benefits payable to construction staff to be included in the cost of PPE, but **only** those costs incurred during the construction period, which is January and February 20X5. Therefore **$1 million** (2 × $500,000) will be included in PPE whilst the other $2 million will be recognised in the statement of profit or loss as an **operating expense**.

The costs of training staff to operate the new plant **cannot be recognised in PPE since** they are specifically disallowed by IAS 16. These costs ($600,000) should be recognised in the statement of profit or loss as an **operating expense**.

The cost of $200,000 to test the operating systems to ensure they are fit for purpose are necessary to enable the plant to be used and should be recognised in PPE.

The costs of an opening ceremony **cannot** be recognised in PPE and should be recognised in the statement of profit or loss as an **operating expense**.

Under the principles of IFRS 9 – *Financial Instruments* – the borrowing is a **financial liability** measured using the **amortised cost** method.

The initial carrying amount of the financial liability should be the **net proceeds** received from the lender of $7.8 million. The borrowing fee should **not** be included in PPE (principle).

The difference of $720,000 ($8.52 million – $7.8 million) between the initial carrying amount of the borrowing and the final repayment will be a finance (borrowing) cost (**principle**). In this case, the finance cost for the year ended 30 June 20X5 will be **$420,000** ($720,000 × 7/12).

Under the principles of IAS 23 – *Borrowing Costs* – costs of borrowings taken out to finance the construction of an asset are recognised in PPE during the period in which activities are taking place in order to get the asset ready for use (**principle**). In this case, the borrowing (finance) costs which are recognised in this way will be those incurred in the three-month period from 1 January 20X5 to 1 April 20X5 of **$180,000** ($720,000 × 3/12).

The remaining borrowing costs of **$240,000** ($420,000 – $180,000) will be recognised in the **statement of profit or loss as a finance cost**.

The closing borrowings balance will be **$8,220,000** ($7.8 million + $420,000). This will be recognised in the statement of financial position as a **current liability**.

Under the principles of **IAS 37** – *Provisions, Contingent Liabilities and Contingent Assets* – a provision for the environmental rectification cost is required **if** there is an obligation arising out of a past event which can be reliably measured.

Although there is no legal obligation to rectify the damage, Theta has, by its reputation, created a constructive obligation and will undertake this expenditure, so a provision is required – sense of the point.

Where the time value of money is material, IAS 37 requires that the provision be measured at the present value of the expected future expenditure (**principle**). Therefore the provision which should be recognised from **1 March 20X5** (the date construction is completed and the environmental damage caused) and measured at **$1.5 million** ($10 million × 0.15).

Under the **principles** of IAS 16 this recognition provision is included as part of the cost of PPE, so an additional **$1.5 million** is included in PPE.

Therefore the total amount included in the cost of PPE at 30 June 20X5 is $8,880,000 (W1).

Depreciation should be charged from 1 April 20X5, the date the asset is available for use (principle).

Therefore depreciation for the year ended 30 June 20X5 will be $111,000 ($8,880,000 × 1/20 × 3/12).This will be recognised in the **statement of profit or loss** as an operating expense.

The closing balance of PPE will be **$8,769,000** ($8,880,000 – $111,000). This will be recognised as a **non-current asset** in the statement of financial position.

As the date for payment of the $10 million rectification cost gets closer, the discount unwinds and the unwinding amount is added to the recognised provision (principle).

For the year ended 30 June 20X5, the amount of the unwinding is **$50,000** ($1.5 million × 10% × 4/12). $50,000 will be recognised in the statement of profit or loss as a **finance cost**.

The closing provision will be **$1,550,000** ($1.5 million + $50,000). This will be recognised as a **non-current** liability in the statement of financial position.

W1 – Spreadsheet workings: total cost of PPE at 30 June 20X5

	$'000
Material cost	4,000
Production overheads	2,000
Construction staff salaries	1,000
Costs of testing the operating systems	200
Attributable finance costs	180
Environmental rectification provision	1,500
	8,800

Ethical issue – Email from FD

Spreadsheet

	A	B
1	ALPHA GROUP CONSOLIDATED STATEMENT OF FINANCIAL POSITION	
2	AS AT 31 DECEMBER 20X9	
3		$'000
4	**Assets**	
5	Non-current assets	
6	Property, plant and equipment (350,000 + 225,000 + 12,000 (W1))	587,000
7	Goodwill (W2)	76,000
8	Investment in associate	45,400
9	Financial assets	36,000
10		744,400
11	**Current assets**	
12	Inventories (105,000 + 80,000 – 5,000)	180,000
13	Trade receivables (95,000 + 70,000 – 10,000 cash in transit)	155,000
14	Cash and cash equivalents (30,000 + 35,000 + 10,000 cash in transit)	75,000
15		410,000
16	**Total assets**	**1,154,400**

	Spreadsheet	

Edit   Format

| 11 ▾ | **B** | *I* | U | **A** | | | | | .00 | | % | ½ | |

B3

	A	B
17	**Equity and liabilities**	
18	Equity attributable to equity holders of the parent	
19	Share capital ($1 shares)	200,000
20	Retained earnings (W4)	204,700
21	Other components of equity	107,000
22		511,700
23	Non-controlling interest	50,400
24	Total equity	562,100
25	**Non-current liabilities**	
26	Long-term borrowings (W7)	192,300
27	Deferred tax (110,000 + 25,000)	135,000
28		327,300
29	**Current liabilities**	
30	Trade and other payables (100,000 + 90,000)	190,000
31	Current tax payable (50,000 + 25,000)	75,000
32		265,000
33	**Total liabilities**	**592,300**
34	**Total equity and liabilities**	**1,154,400**

Tutorial note. The answer above has been prepared in the ACCA exam word processing software to replicate how you might present your answer in the word processing response option in your computer-based exam. It is important that you get familiar with the exam software and the features available within it. You can do this by accessing the past exams available in the DipIFR Study Support Resources section of the ACCA website.

3 Delta (June 2023)

Marking guide

	Marks
Exhibit 1	
Explanations per IFRS 15	8
Calculations	7
	15
Exhibit 2	
Explanations per IFRS 11	5
Calculations	5
	10
Total	25

Exhibit 1 – Construction contract

The financial reporting treatment of this contract is governed by **IFRS 15** – *Revenue from Contracts with Customers*.

Delta has a single performance obligation, to construct and install a machines.

Delta must establish the timing of recognition of revenue as to **when the performance obligation is satisfied**. IFRS 15 allows for two scenarios, the performance obligation being satisfied **over time** or the performance obligation being satisfied **at a point in time**.

IFRS 15 states that a performance obligation is satisfied when control of the goods (or services) is transferred to the customer. In the current circumstances, given that Delta is constructing and installing the machines at the customer's premises, then 'control' of the machines is being transferred to the customer as they are being constructed. Therefore the performance obligation is being satisfied over time and the revenue is recognised on this basis – sense of the point.

Given that the performance obligation is being satisfied over time, it is necessary to measure the extent of its completion at the reporting date. The question tells us that Delta uses input methods to measure the extent of completion. This involves computing the costs incurred up to 30 June 20X5 as a proportion of the total expected costs of the project – sense of the point.

IFRS 15 states that costs which were **not originally envisaged** when the contract was planned, and are caused by inefficiencies or similar issues, should be charged to **profit or loss** as incurred rather than being included as a 'contract cost'. The **same applies** to any general or administrative overheads.

In this case, the cost of wasted materials and labour costs of disposal of wasted material of **$350,000** ($250,000 + $100,000) as well as the 'allocated general overheads' of **$480,000** should be charged to the statement of profit or loss for the year ended 30 June 20X5.

At 30 June 20X5, the performance obligation would be regarded as being 52.9% satisfied (W1).

The consideration for the contract includes a variable component (based on completion dates). Where this occurs, IFRS 15 states that the revenue should be based upon the estimated amount receivable from the customer in exchange for the promised goods.

The total revenue will be estimated as $12.2 million (W2).

Therefore the revenue which will be recognised in the statement of profit or loss will be $6,453,800 ($12.2 million × 52.9%).

Costs associated with the contract which will be recognised in the statement of profit or loss will be $4.5 million (W1).

The statement of financial position at 30 June 20X5 will show, as a **current asset**, a contract asset of **$453,800** (W3).

Workings

W1 – % age of completion calculation

	Total estimated cost	Cost to date
	$'000	$'000
Commission	300	300
Materials	4,200	2,200
Direct labour	2,000	1,000 *
Depreciation	1,200	600
Sub-contractors	800	400
Total cost for completion calculation	8,500	4,500

* This represents the $1.1 million labour costs incurred to date less the labour costs ($100,000) relating to the inefficient working which are taken straight to profit or loss.

Thus the contract is regarded as 52.9% complete ((4,500/8,500) × 100%).

W2 – Estimate of total revenue on the contract

	$'000
Original contracted price	12,000
Reduction for expected four-week overrun (4 × $100,000)	(400)
Expected additional amount due to premium quality of the work	600
Total expected revenue	12,200

W3 Contract asset at 30 June 20X5

	$'000
Revenue recognised by Delta (52.9% × $12.2m)	6,453·8
Less: invoiced by 30 June 20X5	(6,00)
Contract asset	453·8

Exhibit 2 – Joint arrangement

The financial reporting treatment of this arrangement is governed by **IFRS 11 – *Joint Arrangements***. IFRS 11 states that a joint arrangement is one of which two or more parties have joint control.

The arrangement between Delta and Drax is a joint arrangement because all the decisions relating to the product must be agreed by both parties, so they have joint control (sense of the point).

An arrangement is a joint operation **when the parties to the arrangement have rights to the assets and obligations for the liabilities** of the arrangement. This is the type of arrangement which Delta and Drax have entered into.

When accounting for a joint operation, each operator includes its share of the assets, liabilities, revenues and expenses of the operation (sense of the point).

This means that Delta will recognise the following amounts in the **statement of profit or loss** for the year ended 30 June 20X5:

Revenue of **$20 million** ($40 million × **50%**).

Cost of sales of **$13 million** ($26 million × 50%).

Advertising and distribution costs of **$700,000** (50% × ($400,000 + $1 million)).

Delta will recognise the following amounts under **current assets** in the **statement of financial position** at 30 June 20X5:

Trade receivables of **$4 million** (50% × ($40 million – $32 million)).

Inventories $1.75 million (W1).

An amount receivable from Drax of **$15.95** million (W2).

W1 – Inventories of Delta at 30 June 20X5

	Total	Delta share (50%)
	$'000	$'000
Raw materials purchased by Delta	6,500	3,250
Manufacturing costs incurred by Delta	8,500	4,250
Manufacturing costs incurred by Drax	14,500	7,250
Transferred to cost of sales	(26,000)	(13,000)
So closing inventories equals	3,500	1,750

W2 – Balance receivable from Drax on 30 June 20X5

	$'000	$'000
Raw materials purchased by Delta (Drax share)	3,250	
Manufacturing costs incurred by Delta (Drax share)	4,250	
Manufacturing costs incurred by Drax (Delta share)		7,250
Advertising and distribution costs incurred by Delta (Drax share)	200	
Advertising and distribution costs incurred by Drax (Delta share)		500
Cash collected from customers by Drax (Delta share)	16,000	
Balance carried forward (debit)		15,950
	23,700	23,700

4 Omega (June 2023)

	Marks
Exhibit 1	
Explanations per IAS 24	7
Exhibit 2	
Explanations per IFRS 10	1
Explanations per IAS 28	7
	8
Exhibit 3	
Explanations per IFRS 10	2
Explanations IFRS for SMEs	5
Explanations per IAS 38	3
	10
Total	**25**

Exhibit 1 – Disclosures

The transactions with Gower need to be disclosed because Gower is a **related party** of Omega (the reporting entity) according to IAS 24 – *Related Party Disclosures*.

IAS 24 states that a director of an entity is a member of the key management personnel (KMP) of that entity. Key management personnel are automatically related parties. Therefore the MD of Gower is a related party of Omega as he is a director of Omega.

IAS 24 further states that close family members of the related parties of an entity are themselves related parties. Therefore the spouse of the director would also be a related party of Omega.

Finally, IAS 24 states that because Gower is **controlled** by the spouse of a director of Omega, then Gower is itself a related party of Omega.

Disclosures required relating to Gower in the consolidated financial statements would be the nature of the related party relationship, the amount of transactions in the period, and the amount of any outstanding balances with Gower (likely to be payables) at the year end.

The nature of related party relationships is such that materiality is considered using qualitative measures as well as quantitative ones. Therefore despite their relatively small amounts, transactions with Gower might need to be disclosed in the consolidated financial statements of Omega to enable the users to assess their significance (sense of the point).

Dixon is not a related party of Omega, so disclosure of transactions and balances would only be necessary if this was considered relevant to the overall understanding of the consolidated financial statements (sense of the point).

Exhibit 2 – Investment in Newco

Newco is not a subsidiary of Omega. Based on the principles outlined in **IFRS 10** – *Consolidated Financial Statements* – a subsidiary entity is one which is **controlled** by the investor. The facts here indicate that Omega cannot exercise control over Newco, **based on** a shareholding of only 35% and an ability to appoint only two out of its six directors.

The ability to appoint two of the six directors, and the ownership of 35% of the shares would, however, given the rights of appointment of the other directors, and the ownership of the other shares, appear to give Omega the ability to exercise significant influence over Newco – sense of the point.

Under the principles of **IAS 28** – *Investments in Associates and Joint Ventures* – Newco would be regarded as an **associate** of Omega because of the ability of Omega to exercise significant influence. IAS 28 contains a rebuttable presumption that ownership of **20%** or more of the equity shares of an entity gives the investor the ability to exercise significant influence.

Where the investor prepares consolidated financial statements (the case for Omega), then IAS 28 requires the investor to account for the investment in the associate under the **equity method**. Under the equity method, the investment in the associate is shown at **cost plus the investor's share of the post-acquisition change in net assets of the associate**. The post-acquisition increase in the carrying amount of the investment is shown in **profit or loss or other comprehensive income**.

If there are transactions between the associate and the investor, then any profits made by either party are eliminated to the extent of the investor's share in the associate. If, at the year end, the investment in the associate has suffered impairment, then the investment should be written down to its recoverable amount.

The increase in the carrying amount of Omega's investment in Newco **implies** that, since acquisition, the net assets of Newco have increased by $10 million and Newco's share of this increase is $3.5 million.

This means that the carrying amount of $63.5 million for the investment in Newco is not necessarily the value of the shares at the year end. This value will be determined by market forces.

Exhibit 3 – Financial statements of Tiny and Minor

Based on the principles outlined in **IFRS 10** – *Consolidated Financial Statements* – all group entities should be reflected in the consolidated financial statements by applying uniform accounting policies. If individual group entities prepare their financial statements using accounting policies which differ from those of the parent, then appropriate adjustments should be made when reflecting their assets, liabilities, profits and losses in the consolidated financial statements.

It would suggest that due to the size of the company, Minor is preparing its financial statements using the IFRS for SMEs Accounting Standard (IFRS for SMEs Standard) while Tiny is applying the full IFRS Accounting Standards– sense of the point.

The ability to use the IFRS for SMEs Standard, however, does not depend on the size of the reporting entity, but on whether or not the entity is 'publicly accountable'. It is likely therefore that Minor is not 'publicly accountable'.

Entities which are not publicly accountable have the right, but not the obligation, to use the SMEs Standard rather than full IFRS Accounting Standards. This could explain why Minor is using the IFRS for SMEs Standard but Tiny is not.

The IFRS for SMEs Standard contains less detailed reporting requirements than full IFRS Accounting Standards and provides for more straightforward accounting treatments in certain cases – sense of the point.

A specific example of the above is that under the IFRS for SMEs Standard, all research and development costs are charged as an expense in the statement of profit or loss in all circumstances.

Accounting for research and development costs under full IFRS Accounting Standards is governed by **IAS 38** – *Intangible Assets*. IAS 38 requires that development costs are recognised as an intangible asset once there is a separately defined project, with clearly identifiable expenditure, adequate resources to complete the project, and reasonable certainty that future economic benefits will exceed the capitalised costs. IAS 38 requires research costs to be charged as an expense to profit or loss in all circumstances because at the research stage there is no definite prospect of future benefit for the reporting entity – sense of the point.

In future periods it might be beneficial to require Minor to use full IFRS Accounting Standards in the preparation of its individual financial statements to make the consolidation process more straightforward as no adjustments would be required.

ACCA Diploma in International Financial Reporting

BPP Mock Exam 2

(December 2023 exam)

Questions	
Time allowed	3 hours and 15 minutes
ALL FOUR questions are COMPULSORY and must be attempted	

DO NOT OPEN THIS EXAM UNTIL YOU ARE READY TO START UNDER EXAMINATION CONDITIONS

BPP
LEARNING
MEDIA

1 Alpha (December 2023)

Alpha, a parent with one subsidiary, Beta, is preparing its consolidated statement of financial position (SOFP) as at 31 December 20X9.

The following exhibits provide information relevant to the question:

Financial statements – draft SOFP for Alpha and Beta as at 31 December 20X9
(1)   Alpha's investment in Beta – details of Alpha's investment in Beta
(2)   Alpha's other investments – a summary of Alpha's other investments, including the investment in Gamma
(3)   Inter-company trading – details of trading between Alpha and Beta, and Alpha and Gamma
(4)   Convertible loan – a convertible loan taken out by Alpha on 1 January 20X9

This information should be used to answer the requirement.

Requirement

Using exhibits 1 to 5 prepare the consolidated statement of financial position of Alpha as at 31 December 20X9.

Notes:

- No explanations of consolidation adjustments are required. Marks will not be awarded for explanations.
- You do not need to consider the deferred tax effects of any adjustments you make
- You should show all workings to the nearest $000

(25 marks)

Exhibit 1 Financial statements

Statements of financial position at 31 December 20X9

	Alpha $000	Beta $000
Assets		
Non-current assets		
Property, plant and equipment (Exhibit 2)	350,000	225,000
Financial assets (Exhibits 2 and 3)	290,000	Nil
	640,000	225,000
Current assets		
Inventories (Exhibit 4)	105,000	80,000
Trade receivables (Exhibit 4)	95,000	70,000
Cash and cash equivalents (Exhibit 4)	30,000	35,000
	230,000	185,000
Total assets	870,000	410,000
Equity and liabilities		
Share capital ($1 shares)	200,000	100,000
Retained earnings	170,000	65,000
Other components of equity	100,000	55,000
Total equity	470,000	220,000
Non-current liabilities		
Long-term borrowings (Exhibit 5)	140,000	50,000
Deferred tax	110,000	25,000
	250,000	75,000

Current liabilities

Trade and other payables	100,000	90,000
Current tax payable	50,000	25,000
	150,000	115,000
Total liabilities	**400,000**	**190,000**
Total equity and liabilities	**870,000**	**410,000**

Exhibit 2 Alpha's investment in Beta

On 1 January 20X8, Alpha acquired 80 million shares in Beta and gained control of Beta. Alpha acquired the shares in Beta by issuing one Alpha share for every two shares acquired in Beta. Alpha incurred costs of $2 million when issuing these shares. Alpha included these issue costs as part of the carrying amount of its investment in Beta in its own statement of financial position. On 1 January 20X8 the fair value of an Alpha share was $5.40.

On 1 January 20X8 the individual financial statements of Beta showed a balance on retained earnings and other components of equity of $30 million and $55 million respectively. On 1 January 20X8 the carrying amounts of the individual assets and liabilities of Beta in its own financial statements were the same as their fair values, with the exception of:

- Property, plant and equipment which had a carrying amount of $100 million and a fair value of $120 million. The estimated useful life of this property, plant and equipment at 1 January 20X8 was five years.

- A contingent liability which had a fair value of $25 million on 1 January 20X8. The contingent liability was resolved during 20X8 and did not exist at 31 December 20X8.

The directors of Alpha elected to measure the non-controlling interest in Beta on 1 January 20X8 using the fair value method. On 1 January 20X8 the fair value of a share in Beta was $2.00.

Exhibit 3 Alpha's other investments

On 1 January 20X8 Alpha purchased 20 million of Gamma's 50 million $1 Equity shares for a cost of $41 million. The purchase of these shares allowed Alpha to appoint two of Gamma's five directors. The other three directors of Gamma act independently of each other.

On 1 January 20X8 the individual financial statements of Gamma showed a balance on retained earnings of $20 million. On 1 January 20X8 the carrying amounts of the individual assets and liabilities of Gamma in its own financial statements were the same as their fair values. The balance of retained earnings of Gamma in its own financial statements at 31 December 20X9 was $35 million.

The remaining financial assets of Alpha consist of a portfolio of equity investments. These investments are held for trading purposes. The carrying amount of the portfolio in the individual financial statements of Alpha represents the fair value of the portfolio at 1 January 20X9, adjusted for purchases into and sales out of the portfolio during 20X9. On 31 December 20X9 the fair value of the portfolio was $36 million.

Exhibit 4 Inter-company trading

Alpha sells products to both Beta and Gamma. Alpha applies a mark-up of 50% to the cost of these products when invoicing them to Beta and Gamma. On 31 December 20X9 the inventories of Beta and Gamma included goods purchased from Alpha. The amounts included in inventories were:

- $15 million in the inventories of Beta
- $12 million in the inventories of Gamma

On 29 December 20X9 Beta and Gamma owed Alpha for some of these goods and sent payments of $10 million and $6 million respectively to Alpha in respect of amounts owing for the purchase of products from Alpha. Alpha received and recorded both payments **after** 31 December 20X9.

Exhibit 5 Convertible loan

On 1 January 20X9 Alpha took out a long-term loan of $100 million. The loan does not require any payment of interest but is repayable five years after 1 January 20X9 at an amount of $150 million. As an alternative to receiving this repayment, the lenders can elect to convert their loan asset to equity shares in Alpha.

Were the conversion option not available, the lenders would have required an annual return of 10%. At a discount rate of 10% per annum the present value of $1 receivable in 5 years' time is approximately 62 cents.

The individual statement of financial position of Alpha shows this loan within non-current liabilities at a carrying amount of $100 million.

2 Delta (December 2023)

Delta, a listed entity, prepares financial statements to 30 September each year. You are a trainee accountant employed by Delta and report to the finance director (FD) of Delta. One of your key responsibilities is to prepare the first draft of Delta's published financial statements. You have recently received an email from the FD regarding the financial statements for the year ended 30 September 20X9.

The following exhibits provide information relevant to the question:

(1)   Email – an email from the FD
(2)   Attachment 1 to the email – information relating to the treatment of a defined benefit pension plan
(3)   Attachment 2 to the email – information relating to the decline in the resale price of a product

This information should be used to answer the requirements.

Requirements:

(a)   Using the information in exhibits 2 and 3, explain and show how the transactions described there should be accounted for in the financial statements of Delta for the year ended 30 September 20X9.

Notes:

*   Marks will be awarded for BOTH figures AND explanations

*   The mark allocations are indicated in each exhibit

*   Ignore taxation

*   Where your proposed treatment differs from that suggested by the finance director you should specifically comment on the reasons for this

*   Your answer to this part should NOT discuss any ethical issues   **(16 marks)**

(b)   Using the information in exhibit 1 and your answer from part (a), compute the earnings per share of Delta for the year ended 30 September 20X9.   **(5 marks)**

(c)   Using the information in exhibit 1, identify and explain the ethical issues that confront you as a result of the email sent to you from the finance director.   **(4 marks)**

Total 25 marks

Exhibit 1 Email from FD

To: Trainee accountant
From: Finance director
Subject: Financial statement preparation
Date: 25 October 20X9

As you will know, we are just about to begin the preparation of the published financial statements for the year ended 30 September 20X9. They need to be approved and issued no later than 30 November 20X9. It is very important that the upcoming set of financial results show a favourable financial performance. If the earnings per share (EPS) for the year exceed 50 cents then all staff will receive a cash bonus.

I have made an initial assessment of our financial performance for the year ended 30 September 20X9 and this shows that our reported profit for the year is likely to be $42 million. Since we had 80 million equity shares in issue on 1 October 20X8, the start of the year, then the EPS will be 52.5 cents per share ($42m/80m). Therefore we will achieve the EPS target which triggers the payment of the bonus. We issued 20 million equity shares at full market value on 1 July 20X9 but that will no affect the computation of the EPS figure for the year ended 30 September 20X9 since these shares were only in issue for 3 months.

Since you are a trainee accountant there are certain transactions affecting Delta which you may be unsure how to report in the financial statements. I have therefore attached details of two separate transactions and the manner in which I would like you to report them in the financial statements. The initially computed draft profit figure of $42 million is computed based on my instructions.

I would like you to follow my instructions and not to discuss them with anyone else. You will then receive your share of the staff bonus which is dependent on the EPS. I will also be sure to remember this favourably when conducting your annual performance appraisal which is due before 31 December 20X9.

Exhibit 2 – Attachment 1 to the email

Delta operates a defined benefit pension plan, and all employees are eligible to join the plan. Delta pays contributions into the plan and the managers of the plan pay benefits to retired employees at the end of each financial year.

I have been provided with the following information relating to the defined benefit pension plan. You can assume that all of these numbers are accurate:

	$m
Present value of obligations at 30 September 20X8	60
Present value of obligations at 30 September 20X9	67
Fair value of plan assets at 30 September 20X8	54
Fair value of plan assets at 30 September 20X9	58
Amounts related to year ended 30 September 20X9:	
- Contributions paid into plan	11
- Current service cost	12.5
- Benefits paid	7

The statement of financial position at 30 September 20X8 showed a net defined benefit liability of $6 million ($60m − $54m). I do not believe the net liability should be in the financial statements of Delta at all – it is a net liability of the defined benefit pension plan, not of Delta.

Therefore in computing the draft profit of $42 million I have used $6 million of the $11 million contributions paid by Delta to debit the liability and charged the remaining $5 million of contributions as an operating cost in the statement of profit or loss and other comprehensive income. You can ignore the amounts paid out to retired employees completely – the plan pays these out not Delta. Other than my accounting for these contributions, nothing should appear in the financial statements of Delta.

You may have noticed that there is a note on the file of information relating to the pension plan which states that the annual rate of return on high quality corporate bonds has been 8% throughout the year ended 30 September 20X9. You can ignore this though – you do not need this information to carry out my instructions.   **(10 marks)**

Exhibit 3 – Attachment 2 to the email

You will know that two of our most popular inventory lines are product X and product Y. Relevant financial details are as follows:

	Product X	Product Y
Number of units held in inventory at 30 September 20X9	10 million	6 million
Manufacturing cost per unit	$2.00	$3.00
Advertised selling price at 30 September 20X9 per unit	$2.80	$3.60
Selling price at 3 October 20X9 per unit following entry of new competitor into the market (see below)	$1.80	$3.60
Selling costs per unit	$0.08	$0.10

On 28 September 20X9 a new competitor entered the market selling goods very similar to product X. This had a significant impact on our ability to sell our product X inventory and so on 3 October 20X9 we were forced to reduce our sales prices to stay competitive. Our sales of product X which have been made since 30 September 20X9 have all been made at this reduced price.

In computing the draft profit of $42 million I have not made any adjustments to the carrying amount of inventory at 30 September 20X9 in respect of this though because the price reduction did not occur until October 20X9 – after the year end. Any losses we might make on future sales of product X items are more than offset by potential gains on product Y items.

(6 marks)

3 Epsilon (December 2023)

Epsilon prepares financial statements to 30 June each year. You are Epsilon's financial controller and are responsible for preparing the financial statements for the year ended 30 June 20X5.

The following exhibits provide information relevant to the question:

(1) Memorandum – a memorandum from a trainee accountant requesting information about the recognition and measurement of deferred tax balances

(2) Tax transactions – provides details of transactions for which deferred tax balances need to be computed

This information should be used to answer the question requirements.

Requirements:

(a) Answer queries (i) to (v) in exhibit 1

(b) Using the information in exhibit 2, explain and show how the deferred tax impacts should be accounted for and presented in the financial statements of Epsilon for the year ended 30 June 20X5

Notes:

- The mark allocations are indicated in each exhibit
- In requirement (b) marks will be awarded for BOTH figures AND explanations

(25 marks)

Exhibit 1 Memorandum

There are a number of trainee accountants who report to you. One of these trainee accountants, trainee A, is learning about deferred tax. Trainee A knows that deferred tax is the tax on temporary differences but is unsure about how to compute deferred tax balances in the financial statements and has sent the following memorandum:

Memorandum

To: **Financial controller**

From: **Trainee accountant**

I know that deferred tax is the tax on temporary differences. However, I do not understand:

(i) How to compute temporary differences

(ii) How to compute deferred tax balances in the statement of financial position once those temporary differences are calculated

(iii) Whether there is any difference between the recognition criteria for deferred tax liabilities and deferred tax assets

(iv) Whether deferred tax liabilities and deferred tax assets can be netted off against each other in the statement of financial position

(v) What the impact will be on the statement of profit or loss and other comprehensive income when a deferred tax liability or asset is recognised in the statement of financial position

Please can you explain these to me?

(9 marks)

Exhibit 2 Tax transactions

On 1 July 20X3 Epsilon purchased a large machine for $60 million. The useful life of the machine was estimated to be five years from 1 July 20X3, after which its residual value would be zero. In the tax jurisdiction in which Epsilon is located, this machine purchase qualifies for a tax deduction of $30 million in the year of purchase, followed by a deduction of $15 million for each of the next two years.

(a) On 1 July 20X4 Epsilon borrowed $40 million. No annual interest is payable on the loan. Instead the loan is repayable on 30 June 20X8 at an amount of $58.564 million (cumulative PV of principal and interest). The cumulative interest will be allowed as a tax deduction when the loan is repaid during the year ended 30 June 20X8. This loan carries an effective interest rate of 10% per annum.

(b) Epsilon has a wholly owned subsidiary, Fred. Fred is located in the same tax jurisdiction as Epsilon. On 30 June 20X5 the carrying amount of the net assets of Fred in the consolidated financial statements of Epsilon was $100 million. This figure did not include goodwill arising on acquisition of Fred of $20 million.

On 30 June 20X5 the directors of Epsilon carried out an impairment review of the goodwill arising on acquisition of Fred. Fred was considered to be a single cash-generating unit. On 30 June 20X5 the directors of Epsilon estimated that the value in use of Fred was $105 million and its fair value less costs of disposal was $90 million. If Epsilon were to decide to sell Fred then the original cost of purchasing Fred would be allowed as a tax deduction in the year of sale.

The annual rate of income tax payable by Epsilon on its profits can be assumed to be 20%. Assume that Epsilon will generate taxable income in every accounting period for the foreseeable future.

(16 marks)

4 Omega (December 2023)

You are the financial controller of Omega, a listed entity with a number of subsidiaries. Omega prepares financial statements to 30 June each year. Omega's sales director, who is not an accountant, has reviewed the first draft of the consolidated financial statements of Omega for the year ended 30 June 20X5. The sales director raised some queries as a result of the review.

The following exhibits provide information relevant to the question:

(1)   Fair values – details of the use of fair values in Omega's financial statements
(2)   Properties – details of the measurement of properties in Omega's financial statements
(3)   Assets – details of the assets included in the financial statements of two subsidiaries

The information should be used to answer the question.

Requirement:

Provide answers to the queries raised by the sales director relating to the consolidated financial statements for the year ended 30 June 20X5. The queries you need to address are in exhibits 1 to 3. You should justify your answers with reference to relevant IFRS Accounting Standards.

Note: The mark allocations are indicated in each exhibit.

(25 marks)

Exhibit 1 Fair values

When I reviewed the financial statements, it appeared that the measurement of most of Omega's assets was based on historical cost – what we paid for them. However, it appears from the notes to the financial statements that some assets are measured at fair value. A specific example of such a practice is the portfolio of equity shares which Omega has in a number of listed entities. It seems very inconsistent to measure some assets based on historical cost and others based on fair value.

I know that, in the specific case of equity shares, there is a quoted price which must be paid to buy them in the market, but a different quoted price at which a current owner could sell them in the market, and they may be traded on a number of security exchanges. I am unsure which one to use when identifying 'market price'.

In summary I would like you to address the following queries:

–   How do we know when to use historical cost and when to use fair value?

–   When we do use fair value, how do we measure fair value?

–   How do we decide which of the quoted prices we should use for equity shares?

––   What do we do if there is no market price? For example, in the case of shares in a company which is not listed.

(8 marks)

Exhibit 2 Properties

I am very confused by the accounting for properties in Omega's financial statements. We appear to measure all our properties at fair value in the financial statements. Please explain:

–   How we work out the fair value of a property if we do not actually advertise it for sale and we have no intention of selling any of our properties in the foreseeable future?

There also seems to be a significant inconsistency in the frequency with which we compute fair value of properties and treat gains or losses on the re-measurement of properties in our financial statements. For example:

–   It appears that properties which we rent out to others are re-measured to fair value every year and that all gains and losses on their re-measurement are recognised in profit or loss;

–   When it comes to properties that we actually use ourselves, like our factories and warehouses, it appears that we re-measure to fair value less frequently, maybe once every three years or so; and

–   Gains or losses on the re-measurement of properties like this appear to be recognised in other comprehensive income most of the time, but occasionally in profit or loss.

This all seems very inconsistent – surely we should adopt one approach for all our properties?

Please explain the apparent inconsistencies in our approach to me.   **(10 marks)**

Exhibit 3 Assets

You will know that we have two subsidiaries, Aston and Bern, which have fairly similar business models and sell very similar products, albeit in different geographical markets. Aston is a subsidiary which the Omega Group created and incorporated ten years ago. The Omega Group only acquired a controlling interest in Bern a couple of years ago although it has been trading for about ten years.

The two subsidiaries have very similar asset profiles and I would have expected to see that their impact on the consolidated financial statements would be very similar, but there are significant differences:

–   The consolidated financial statements have a goodwill figure relating to Bern but not relating to Aston.

–   The Bern brand name is recognised in the consolidated financial statements but not the Aston brand name

–   The carrying amount of Bern's property, plant and equipment is significantly higher than that of Aston despite the underlying assets being very similar.

Please explain why there are these differences in the consolidated financial statements.

(7 marks)

Answers

DO NOT TURN THIS PAGE UNTIL YOU HAVE
COMPLETED THE MOCK EXAM

1 Alpha (Dec 2023)

	Marks
Non-current assets	
PPE and financial assets	1.5
Goodwill	4
Investment in associate	2.5
Current assets	2.5
Equity	
Share capital and other components of equity	2
Retained earnings	7
Non-controlling interest	1.5
Non-current liabilities	
Long-term borrowings	2.5
Deferred tax	0.5
Current liabilities	1
Total	**25**

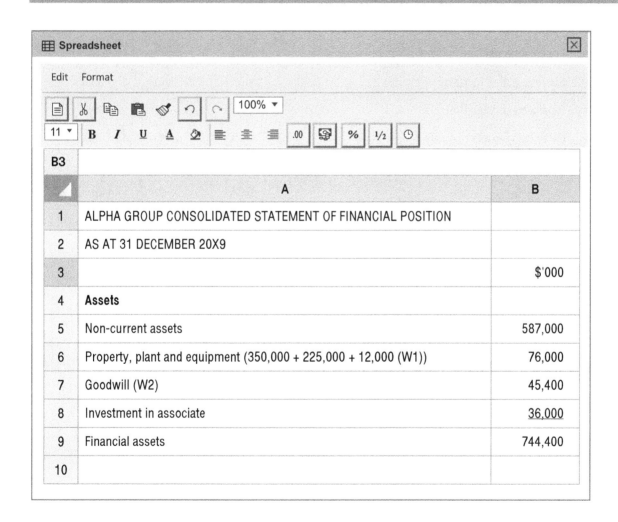

	A	B
	B3	
1	ALPHA GROUP CONSOLIDATED STATEMENT OF FINANCIAL POSITION	
2	AS AT 31 DECEMBER 20X9	
3		$'000
4	**Assets**	
5	Non-current assets	587,000
6	Property, plant and equipment (350,000 + 225,000 + 12,000 (W1))	76,000
7	Goodwill (W2)	45,400
8	Investment in associate	36,000
9	Financial assets	744,400
10		

Spreadsheet ⊠

Edit   Format

[toolbar icons] 100% ▾

11 ▾ **B** *I* U A ✏ ▤ ▤ ▤ .00 🔟 % ½ 🕐

B3		
	A	**B**
11	**Current assets**	
12	Inventories (105,000 + 80,000 – 5,000)	180,000
13	Trade receivables (95,000 + 70,000 – 10,000 cash in transit)	155,000
14	Cash and cash equivalents (30,000 + 35,000 + 10,000 cash in transit)	75,000
15		410,000
16	**Total assets**	**1,154,400**
17		
18	**Equity and liabilities**	
19	Equity attributable to equity holders of the parent	
20	Share capital ($1 shares)	200,000
21	Retained earnings (W4)	204,700
22	Other components of equity	107,000
23		511,700
24	Non-controlling interest	50,400
25	Total equity	562,100
26	**Non-current liabilities**	
27	Long-term borrowings (W7)	192,300
28	Deferred tax (110,000 + 25,000)	135,000
29		327,300
30	**Current liabilities**	
31	Trade and other payables (100,000 + 90,000)	190,000
32	Current tax payable (50,000 + 25,000)	75,000
33		265,000
34	**Total liabilities**	**592,300**
35	**Total equity and liabilities**	**1,154,400**

Tutorial note. The answer above has been presented in a spreadsheet to replicate how you might present your answer in the spreadsheet response option in your computer-based exam. The information in Exhibit 1 will be prepopulated in the spreadsheet response option. It is important that you get familiar with the exam software and the features available within it. You can do this by accessing the past exams available in the DipIFR Study Support Resources section of the ACCA website.

Working 1 – Net assets table for Beta

	1 January 20X8	31 December 20X9
	$'000	$'000
Share capital	100,000	100,000
Other components of equity	55,000	55,000
Retained earnings:		
Per financial statements of Beta	30,000	65,000
Fair value adjustments:		
Property, plant and equipment (post-acquisition additional depreciation 20,000/5 years × 2 = 8,000)	20,000	12,000
Contingent liability	(25,000)	–
Net assets for the consolidation	180,000	232,000

Increase in net assets (232,000 – 180,000) = 52,000

Working 2 – Goodwill on acquisition of Beta

	$'000
Fair value of shares issued (80,000 × ½ × $5.40)	216,000
Non-controlling interest at date of acquisition (20,000 × $2.00)	40,000
Net assets at date of acquisition (W1)	(180,000)
Goodwill at 1 January 20X9	76,000

Working 3 – Non-controlling interest in Beta

	$'000
At date of acquisition (W2)	40,000
20% of post-acquisition increase in net assets (20% × 52,000 (W1))	10,400
	50,400

Working 4 – Retained earnings

	$'000
Alpha – per draft SOFP	170,000
80% of post acquisition share of Beta (80% × 52,000 (W1))	41,600
Unrealised profit on sales to Beta (15,000 × 50/150)	(5,000)
Acquisition costs of Beta	(2,000)
Share of profits of Gamma (W5)	4,400
Finance cost of convertible loan (W7)	(9,300)
Gain on financial asset portfolio (W9)	5,000
	204,700

Working 5 – Investment in Gamma

	$'000
Cost of investment	41,000
Share of post-acquisition profits (W6)	4,400
	45,400

Working 6 – Share of post-acquisition profits of Gamma

	$'000
Per Gamma's own financial statements – 40% (35,000 – 20,000)	6,000
Unrealised profit in inventory – 40% × 12,000 × 50/150	(1,600)
	4,400

Working 7 – Long-term borrowings

	$'000
Loan element of convertible loan (150,000 × $0.62)	93,000
Finance cost (93,000 × 10%)	9,300
Alpha's remaining long-term borrowings (140,000 – 100,000)	40,000
Beta's long-term borrowings	50,000
	192,300

Working 8 – Other components of equity

	$'000
Alpha – per draft financial statements	100,000
Equity element of convertible loan (100,000 – 93,000 (W7))	7,000
	107,000

Working 9 – Gain on financial asset portfolio

	$'000
Carrying amount per draft financial statements of Alpha	290,000
Carrying amounts of investments in:	
Beta (216,000 (W3) + 2,000)	(218,000)
Gamma (W5)	(41,000)
Carrying amount of financial asset portfolio per draft financial statements of Alpha	31,000
Gain on revaluation of the portfolio (balancing figure)	5,000
Fair value of the portfolio at 31 December 20X9	36,000

2 Gamma (Dec 2023)

	Marks
Part a	
Explanations per IAS 19	5.5
Calculations	4.5
Explanations per IAS 2	3
Calculations	1.5
Explanations per IAS 10	1.5
	16
Part b EPS calculations	5
Part c Ethics	4
Total	25

(a)   **Attachment 1 to the email**

The relevant standard is IAS 19 – *Employee Benefits*. IAS 19 states that in the case of a defined benefit retirement plan, the contributing company should recognise the net defined benefit obligation/asset

(pension liability less pension asset) in its own statement of financial position. Therefore the treatment of this amount in the statement of financial position at 30 September 20X8 is correct but will need to be updated to reflect the position at 30 September 20X9 and cannot be ignored per the FD's suggestion. The net defined benefit obligation will be $9 million ($67 million – $58 million).

IAS 19 states that the current service cost (the increase in the defined benefit pension liability as a result of service in the current reporting period) should be recognised as an operating expense in the statement of profit or loss for the year. In the case of Delta, this expense is $12.5 million and not the $5 million presently charged to PL.

IAS 19 further requires that an interest charge on the net pension liability be shown as a finance cost in the statement of profit or loss. This charge should be based upon the opening net defined benefit liability using the rate of return on high quality corporate bonds at the start of the reporting period.

In this case, the finance cost for the year ended 30 September 20X9 will be $480,000 ($6 million × 8%).

The contributions payable by Delta to the defined benefit plan will be invested by the plan managers as plan assets and in effect reduce the closing amount of the net defined benefit liability. It cannot be used simply to reduce the liability as suggested by the FD or indeed expensed to profit or loss.

The benefits paid to retired plan members will reduce both the overall defined benefit liability and the assets of the plan, so will have no impact on the overall financial position of the net defined benefit obligation shown on Delta's statement of financial position.

Any difference between the opening and closing net liability and the impact of the transactions already described will be treated as an actuarial gain or loss. Any such gain or loss will be recognised in other comprehensive income.

In this case the actuarial loss will be $1.02 million (W1).

Attachment 2 to the email

Accounting for inventories is governed by IAS 2 – *Inventories*. IAS 2 states that inventories should be measured at the lower of cost and net realisable value.

IAS 2 states that the net realisable value of inventories should be determined for each category of inventory rather than for inventory as a whole. Therefore the fact that the net realisable value of product Y items is in excess of their cost is irrelevant in determining the net realisable of product X items.

The reduction in the selling price of product X items in October 20X9 is an event after the reporting period as defined in IAS 10 – *Events after the Reporting Period* – because it occurred after the reporting date but before the financial statements were authorised for issue.

The entry is an adjusting event because it provided more information about the likely sales proceeds (and therefore net realisable value) of inventory at the reporting date.

The net realisable value of an item of inventory is the anticipated sales proceeds net of selling costs.

Therefore the net realisable value of the product X items is $17.2 million (10 million × $1.72 [$1.80 – $0.08]). This amount should be shown as a current asset in the statement of financial position at 30 September 20X9. This requires a write down through profit of loss of $2.8 million ($20 million cost less NRV $17.2 million).

No adjustment is needed to product Y as cost ($3) is lower than NRV ($3.50).

(b)   Earnings (W2) = $31.22 million

Number = 80 million × 9/12 + 100 million × 3/12 = 85 million So EPS equals **36.7 cents** ($31.22 million/ 85 million shares).

Workings

Alternative working for separate obligation/asset column

	Asset $'000	Obligation $'000
Opening	54,000	60,000
Current service cost		12,500
Contributions paid	11,000	
Benefits paid	(7,000)	(7,000)
Interest	4,320	4,800
	62,320	70,300
Remeasurement loss/actuarial gain	(4,320)	3,300
Closing	58,000	67,000

Net to OCI (4,320 − 3,300) = 1,020

(c) **Ethical issue – Email from FD**

You are in danger of breaching the fundamental ethical principle of integrity. The FD has suggested that you collude in the reporting an inflated profit figure and, as a result, share in a profit related bonus (*candidates who referred to a self-interest threat here received appropriate credit*).

You could also be said to be potentially breaching the fundamental principle of integrity in these circumstances in the sense that colluding in the reporting of an inflated profit figure would present a misleading picture to the shareholders of Delta.

You face a danger of breaching the principle of objectivity because of the way the FD has linked your complying with these instructions to your upcoming staff appraisal (*candidates who referred to an intimidation threat received appropriate credit*).

You also may be breaching the fundamental ethical principle of professional competence and due care. The treatments suggested by the FD are clearly inappropriate and not in compliance with IFRS Accounting Standards. Were you to implement them, you would be in breach of your professional duty to conduct yourself in a competent manner.

3 Delta (Dec 2023)

Marking guide

	Marks
Exhibit 1	
Explanations per IAS 12	9
Exhibit 2	
Transaction a	
Explanations per IAS 12	1
Calculations	4
Transaction b	
Explanations per IFRS 9	1
Explanations per IAS 12	1
Calculations	2
Transaction c	
Explanations per IAS 36	2
Calculations per IAS 36	1
Calculations per IAS 12	1
Presentation	3
Total	25

Exhibit 1 – Memorandum

To: Trainee accountant

From: Financial controller

(i)   IAS 12 – *Income Taxes* requires us to compute temporary differences for **each** asset and liability. A temporary difference is the difference between the **carrying amount** of an asset or liability and its **tax base**.

The tax base of an asset or liability is the amount attributed to that asset or liability for tax purposes.

If the temporary difference is such that the subsequent settlement of the relevant asset or liability will generate taxable amounts, then the temporary difference is a taxable temporary difference.

If the temporary difference is such that the subsequent settlement of the relevant asset or liability will result in an allowable deduction for tax purposes, then the temporary difference is a deductible temporary difference.

(ii)   Deferred tax liabilities or assets should be measured by multiplying the relevant temporary difference by the **rate of corporate income tax which is expected to apply** when the relevant temporary difference generates taxable income or qualifies for a tax deduction. This rate should be computed with reference to **legislation which has been enacted or substantively enacted by the end of the reporting period**.

(iii)   With a very limited number of exceptions, deferred tax liabilities should be recognised on **all taxable temporary differences**.

Deferred tax assets should be recognised in respect of deductible temporary differences to the extent that it is probable that taxable profits will be available against which the deductible temporary difference can be utilised.

(iv)   Deferred tax liabilities and assets can be offset in the statement of financial position provided the relevant temporary differences relate to the same tax jurisdiction and the reporting entity intends to settle the relevant taxable amounts on a net basis.

(v)   The movement in a relevant deferred tax liability or asset from one reporting period to another would normally result in an **adjustment to the income tax charge in the statement of profit or loss**. However, if the movement in the relevant deferred tax amount was as a result of a transaction which is recognised directly in other comprehensive income (for example, most revaluations of property, plant and equipment), then the deferred tax consequences of the transaction would be recognised in other comprehensive income also.

Exhibit 2 – Transactions

Transaction (a)

The carrying amount of the asset on 30 June 20X5 is $36 million ($60 million × 3/5).

The tax base of the asset at 30 June 20X5 is $15 million ($60 million – $30 million – $15 million).

Therefore the **taxable** temporary difference is **$21 million** ($36 million – $15 million) and the relevant deferred tax liability is **$4.2 million** ($21 million × 20%).

The carrying amount of the asset on 30 June 20X4 would have been **$48 million** ($60 million × 4/5). Its tax base at that date would have been **$30 million** ($60 million – $30 million).

Therefore the taxable temporary difference on 30 June 20X4 would have been **$18 million** ($48 million – $30 million) and the relevant deferred tax liability would have been **$3.6 million** ($18 million × 20%).

The increase in the deferred tax liability of $0.6 million ($4.2 million – $3.6 million) will be charged to profit or loss.

Transaction (b)

Under the principles of IFRS 9 – *Financial Instruments* – the interest free loan would have incurred a finance cost **of $4 million ($40 million × 10%)**. This means that the carrying amount of the loan liability at 30 June 20X5 will be **$44 million ($40 million + $4 million)**.

The tax base of the loan will be $40 million as the entire interest is tax deductible but only when the loan is repaid in 20X8.

Therefore the **deductible** temporary difference will be **$4 million** ($44 million – $40 million) and the relevant potential deferred tax asset **$0.8 million** ($4 million × 20%). This asset **can be recognised because it is anticipated that Epsilon will generate sufficient taxable income in future periods to offset the potential future tax deduction**.

Transaction (c)

Under the principles of IAS 36 – *Impairment of Assets* – the goodwill on acquisition of Fred will be reviewed for impairment as **part of the overall cash-generating unit (CGU)**. The carrying amount of the CGU (including goodwill) will be **$120 million** ($100 million + $20 million).

An impairment review involves comparing the carrying amount of the unit with its recoverable amount. Recoverable amount is the **higher of value-in-use and fair value less costs of disposal**.

In this case, the recoverable amount of the CGU **is $105 million**. This means that the unit has suffered impairment of **$15 million** ($120 million – $105 million).

The impairment loss of $15 million will reduce the carrying amount of goodwill in Epsilon's consolidated financial statements but not its tax base. **Therefore the deductible temporary difference** will be $15 million and the associated potential deferred tax asset **$3 million ($15 million × 20%)**.

Overall presentation

The net deferred tax liability at 30 June 20X5 will be **$0.4 million** ($4.2 million – $0.8 million – $3 million). Offsetting of deferred tax liabilities and assets is justified because they relate to the **same** tax jurisdiction. The net liability will be shown as a non-current liability in the statement of financial position at 30 June 20X5.

The opening deferred tax position regarding these transactions would have been a liability of **$3.6 million** (see above). Therefore the reduction in the overall liability over the year will be **$3.2 million** ($3.6 million – $0.4 million). This amount will be shown as a **reduction in the tax charge in the statement of profit or loss** (since all the transactions which have generated these temporary differences affect profit or loss).

Tabular working – Deferred tax position at 30 June 20X5 and PL movement

Item	Carrying amount $'000	Tax base $'000	Taxable/(deductible) temporary difference $'000	Deferred tax liability/(asset) $'000
Machine – at 30 June 20X5	36,000	(15,000)	21,000	4,200
Loan – at 30 June 20X5	(44,000)	40,000	(4,000)	(800)
Goodwill – at 30 June 20X5	5,000	(20,000)	(15,000)	(3,000)
Overall position at 30 June 20X5				400
Machine – at 30 June 20X4	48,000	(30,000)	18,000	3,600

The credit to profit or loss in the year is the difference between the closing liability ($400,000) and the opening liability ($3.6 million). This difference is $3.2 million.

4 Omega (Dec 2023)

	Marks
Exhibit 1	
Explanations per IFRS 13	8
Exhibit 2	
Explanations per IFRS 13	2
Explanations per IAS 16	5
Explanations per IAS 40	3
Exhibit 3	
Explanations per IAS 38	2.5
Explanations per IFRS 3	4.5
Total	**25**

Exhibit 1 – Fair values

The use (or otherwise) of fair value as a measurement basis is covered by specific IFRS Accounting Standards. Overall, the requirements of specific IFRS Accounting Standards lead to a mixed measurement model being used.

The accounting standard which is relevant to the use of fair values is **IFRS 13** – *Fair Value Measurement*. As its title implies, IFRS 13 deals with the **measurement of fair value rather than when** fair value should actually be used as a measurement basis.

IFRS 13 states that the fair value of an asset is the **amount which could be expected to be received from its disposal in an orderly transaction between market participants**. Transaction costs are **not** deducted in computing fair value.

Therefore fair value is an exit measure rather than an entry measure. **In the case of shares in a listed entity, for which a 'buy' and a 'sell' price is quoted, it is the 'sell price' which is relevant for fair value measurement**.

Where possible, fair value should be based on **observable** market prices. If there is **more than one** 'market' on which the asset is traded (which could easily be the case for equity shares in a listed entity), then fair value measurement should be based on the **principal market** in which the asset is traded.

Where no specific market prices are available for an individual asset, then IFRS 13 requires that fair values are **estimated** using a range of possible approaches. In the case of shares in an unquoted entity, these **could include** basing fair value on the market prices of the shares of a similar listed entity, discounted for relative lack of marketability, or basing fair value on the projected future earnings, discounted at an appropriate discount rate.

Exhibit 2 – Properties

The fair value of a property would be computed using the **principles set out in IFRS 13**.

In the specific case of properties, fair values could almost certainly be estimated based on the market prices of similar properties which had recently been sold on the open market in the same location.

This estimate would need to reflect **alternative uses** to which the property could be put compared with its current usage. This is **because IFRS 13 requires us to base fair value measurement on the highest and best use** to which the property could be put and which 'market participants' would consider in making a decision to acquire the property.

There are **two separate** IFRS Accounting Standards dealing with the recognition and measurement of properties. These are **IAS 40** – *Investment Properties* and **IAS 16** – *Property, Plant and Equipment* (PPE).

IAS 40 **defines** an investment property as one which is held to earn rentals and/or capital appreciation. The properties which we rent out clearly meet this definition.

IAS 40 requires that investment properties are measured using **either** the cost model **or** the fair value model. It **appears** that Omega uses the fair value model to measure its investment properties.

Under the fair value model as set out in IAS 40, investment properties are revalued **annually** to fair value, with gains or losses recognised in **profit or loss**.

Owner occupied properties are dealt with under IAS 16. IAS 16 states that a particular class of PPE is measured using **either** the cost model **or** the revaluation model. Therefore it is **perfectly possible** that owner occupied properties are measured using fair value.

Under the revaluation model, properties are revalued with sufficient regularity to ensure that their year-end carrying amount does not differ significantly from their year-end fair value. This does not necessarily have to mean a new revaluation every year.

Where the revaluation of an owner occupied property results in a **surplus**, then the surplus is recognised in **other comprehensive income** unless it is reversing a revaluation deficit on the same asset which was **previously** recognised in profit or loss.

Where the revaluation results in a **deficit**, then the deficit is recognised in **profit or loss** unless it is reversing a revaluation surplus on the same asset which was **previously** recognised in other comprehensive income.

Exhibit 3 – Assets

The reason for the different treatment of the assets of Aston and Bern in the consolidated financial statements is due to the way the subsidiaries joined the group.

The assets of Aston arose as a result of the internal development of the company as part of the Omega group.

The goodwill attaching to Aston and its brand name are internally developed intangible assets. Recognition and measurement of such assets is dealt with in accordance with the requirements of IAS 38 – *Intangible Assets*.

IAS 38 prohibits the recognition of internally developed intangible assets unless they arise as part of a research and development project. Therefore it is inappropriate to recognise the goodwill attaching to Aston and its brand name in the consolidated financial statements of Omega.

The subsidiary Bern was acquired as a business combination. Accounting for business combinations is dealt with by IFRS 3 – *Business Combinations*.

IFRS 3 requires that, in the case of a business combination, the difference between the fair value of the consideration given and the fair values of the net assets acquired be recognised as goodwill arising on acquisition.

IFRS 3 requires that the assets and liabilities of a newly acquired subsidiary are separately identified and measured at fair value.

Therefore, provided the brand name attaching to Bern can be reliably fair valued, it would be recognised as an intangible asset in the consolidated financial statements of Omega.

The carrying amount of Bern's property, plant and equipment in the consolidated financial statements of Omega would be based on its fair value at the date of acquisition by Omega, whereas the carrying amount of Aston's property, plant and equipment in the consolidated financial statements of Omega would be based on its historical cost to Aston (and the group), presumably a lower figure.

ACCA Diploma in International Financial Reporting

BPP Mock Exam 3

(adapted from the specimen exam)

Questions	
Time allowed	3 hours and 15 minutes
ALL FOUR questions are COMPULSORY and must be attempted	

DO NOT OPEN THIS EXAM UNTIL YOU ARE READY TO START UNDER EXAMINATION CONDITIONS

Question 1

Alpha, a parent with two subsidiaries Beta and Gamma, is preparing the consolidated statement of profit or loss and other comprehensive income of the Alpha Group for the year ended 31 March 20X4. Information required to answer the question is provided in the Exhibits.

Exhibit 1 – Statements of profit or loss and other comprehensive income

	Alpha	Beta	Gamma
	$'000	$'000	$'000
Revenue (Exhibit 4)	420,000	335,000	292,000
Cost of sales (Exhibit 4)	(240,000)	(192,000)	(168,000)
Gross profit	180,000	143,000	124,000
Distribution costs	(20,000)	(16,000)	(14,000)
Administrative expenses	(40,000)	(32,000)	(28,000)
Contributions to retirement benefit plan (Exhibit 5)	(5,000)	Nil	Nil
Finance costs	(20,000)	(15,000)	(12,000)
Profit before tax	95,000	80,000	70,000
Income tax expense	(32,000)	(20,000)	(16,000)
Profit for the year	63,000	60,000	54,000
Other comprehensive income:			
Items that will not be reclassified to profit or loss			
Gain on property revaluation (Exhibit 6)	25,000	Nil	12,000
Total comprehensive income for the year	88,000	60,000	66,000

Exhibit 2 – Acquisition of Beta

Alpha purchased 80% of the equity shares of Beta a number of years ago, gaining control of Beta. Goodwill arising on the acquisition of Beta totalled $80 million. At the acquisition date, Beta had three cash-generating units and the goodwill on acquisition was allocated to the three units as follows:

- Unit 1 – 40%
- Unit 2 – 35%
- Unit 3 – 25%

No impairment of this goodwill had occurred in the years up to and including 31 March 20X3. However, in the year ended 31 March 20X4, despite making a profit overall, Beta suffered challenging trading conditions. Therefore, the directors of Alpha carried out an impairment review on the goodwill at 31 March 20X4 and obtained the following results:

Cash Generating Unit	Carrying amount of net assets (excluding goodwill) at 31 March 20X4	Recoverable amount at 31 March 20X4
	$'000	$'000
1	215,000	255,000
2	185,000	220,000
3	130,000	140,000
Total	530,000	615,000

None of the assets or liabilities of Beta which Alpha identified at acquisition remained in the statement of financial position of Beta at 31 March 20X3 or 20X4. Any impairment of goodwill should be charged to cost of sales.

Alpha measures all non-controlling interests at fair value at the date of acquisition.

Exhibit 3 – Acquisition of Gamma

On 1 July 20X3, Alpha acquired 60% of the equity capital of Gamma and gained control of Gamma from that date. The purchase consideration comprised:

- An issue of equity shares.

- A cash payment of $65.34 million due on 30 June 20X5. On 1 July 20X3, Alpha's borrowing rate was 10% per annum. No entry has yet been made in Alpha's financial statements regarding this future cash payment.

There was no significant difference between the carrying amounts of Gamma's net assets at 1 July 20X3 and their fair values at 31 March 20X3.

No impairment of the goodwill in Gamma is required at 31 March 20X4.

The profit of Gamma for the year ended 31 March 20X4 accrued evenly over the year. All other comprehensive income of Gamma arose after 1 July 20X3.

Exhibit 4 – Trading between Alpha and Beta

Alpha supplies a component to Beta which is used by Beta in its production process. Alpha marks up its cost of production by one-third in arriving at the selling price. In the year ended 31 March 20X4, the revenue of Alpha included $30 million in respect of the sale of these components. On 31 March 20X4, the inventory of Beta included $6 million of components purchased from Alpha. On 31 March 20X3, the inventory of Beta included $4.4 million in respect of identical components purchased from Alpha at the same mark up on cost.

Any consolidation adjustments which are necessary as a result of the information given in this Exhibit should be regarded as temporary differences for the purpose of computing deferred taxation. The rate of corporate income tax in the jurisdiction in which all three entities are located is 25%.

Exhibit 5 – Defined benefit pension plan

Certain senior executives of Alpha belong to a defined benefit pension plan. In the financial statements of Alpha, the contributions paid into this plan have been shown as an expense in the statement of profit or loss and other comprehensive income. You should assume that the contributions are paid in a lump sum on 31 March 20X4. Relevant information regarding this plan is as follows:

- The pension liability was $60 million at 31 March 20X3. This liability increased to $68 million by 31 March 20X4.

- The pension asset was $40 million at 31 March 20X3. This asset increased to $46 million by 31 March 20X4.

- The current service cost was $4.5 million.

- Alpha's borrowing rate at 31 March 20X4 was 9% per annum. On that date market yields on government bonds were 8% per annum.

The salary costs of the senior executives who belong to this plan are presented in administrative expenses. You should ignore any adjustment to deferred tax as a result of the information included in this Exhibit.

Exhibit 6 – Property revaluations

It is the policy of the Alpha group to measure property using the fair value model and all properties were revalued on 31 March 20X4. The gains shown in the financial statements of Alpha and Gamma do not take account of the deferred tax implications of the revaluations.

Requirement

Using the draft statements of profit or loss and other comprehensive income of Alpha and its subsidiaries Beta and Gamma for the year ended 31 March 20X4 in Exhibit 1, and the further information provided in Exhibits 2–6, prepare the consolidated statement of profit or loss and other comprehensive income of the Alpha Group for the year ended 31 March 20X4. **(Total = 25 marks)**

Question 2

You are the financial controller of Gamma. You report to the finance director. One of your key roles is to prepare the draft financial statements for approval by the directors. You are currently preparing the draft financial statements for the year ended 30 September 20X7.

Information related to Gamma is provided in the Exhibits:

Exhibit 1 – Commitment to purchase new machinery

On 1 July 20X7 Gamma entered into a contract with a foreign supplier. The terms of the contract were that the supplier would construct a machine for Gamma's use and deliver the machine to Gamma on 31 December 20X7. The agreed construction price of the machine was 20 million groats (the currency of the supplier). The invoice is due for payment on 31 January 20X8.

On 1 July 20X7 Gamma entered into an agreement for the forward purchase of 20 million groats. The settlement date for this forward purchase of foreign currency was 31 January 20X8. Gamma intends to use this forward purchase as a hedge of the expected cash outflows arising under the contract to pay for the machine on 31 January 20X8.

Gamma wishes to use hedge accounting for this arrangement if this is possible under International Financial Reporting Standards. Gamma has prepared all relevant documentation that is necessary to enable hedge accounting to be used if the qualifying conditions are met.

Data relevant to the contract and to the forward purchase of currency is as follows:

- Increase in expected cash flows arising under the contract due to market changes between 1 July 20X7 and 30 September 20X7 = $2,600,000.

- Positive fair value of forward currency purchase contract at 30 September 20X7 = $2,700,000.   **(9 marks)**

Exhibit 2 – Purchase of inventory from a foreign supplier

On 1 August 20X7 Gamma purchased some inventory from a supplier whose functional currency was the dinar. The total purchase price was 3.6 million dinars. The terms of the purchase were that Gamma would pay for the goods in two instalments. The first instalment payment of 1,260,000 dinars was due on 15 September 20X7 and the second payment of 2,340,000 dinars on 30 October 20X7. Both payments were made on the due dates. Gamma did not undertake any activities to hedge its currency exposure arising under this transaction. Gamma sold 60% of this inventory prior to 30 September 20X7 for a total sales price of $480,000. All sales proceeds were receivable in $. After 30 September 20X7 Gamma sold the remaining inventory for sales proceeds that were in excess of their cost.

Relevant exchange rates are as follows:

- 1 August 20X7 – 6.0 dinars to $1.
- 15 September 20X7 – 6.3 dinars to $1.
- 30 September 20X7 – 6.4 dinars to $1.   **(11 marks)**

Exhibit 3 – Ethical issue

The finance director has discussed the preparation of the financial statements for the year ended 30 September 20X7 with you. He has requested you measure the closing inventories of goods purchased in dinars (Exhibit 2) at their anticipated selling price. He suggests you may have to estimate an appropriate exchange rate.

He has stated that 'Gamma plans on paying a profit-related bonus to all employees for the year ended 30 September 20X7. I feel sure you agree with me that we need to report as healthy a profit as possible to ensure our efforts are rewarded with an appropriate bonus. I will be very pleased if you comply with my suggestion'.

Requirements

(a) Using the information in Exhibits 1 and 2, explain and show how the two events would be reported in the financial statements of Gamma for the year ended 30 September 20X7.

Notes:

- Marks will be awarded for BOTH figures AND explanations.
- The mark allocations for requirement (a) are indicated in each exhibit. **(20 marks)**

(b) Using the information in Exhibit 3 identify and explain the ethical issues confronting you as a result of your discussion with the finance director. **(5 marks)**

(Total = 25 marks)

Question 3

Delta, a company with a year end 30 September 20X7, applies IFRS 16 *Leases* to report lease transactions in the financial statements. Relevant information is provided in the Exhibits:

Exhibit 1 – Property lease

On 1 October 20X6 Delta began to lease a property on a 10 year lease (its useful life to Delta). The annual lease payments were $500,000, payable in arrears – the first payment being made on 30 September 20X7. Delta incurred initial direct costs of $60,000 in arranging this lease. The annual rate of interest implicit in the lease was 10%. When the annual discount rate is 10% the present value of $1 payable at the end of years 1–10 is $6.145.

Exhibit 2 – Sale and leaseback

On 1 April 20X7 Delta sold a property to a third party for proceeds of $4,500,000. The carrying amount of the property in the financial statements of Delta at 1 October 20X6 was $17,500,000 (depreciable component $12,000,000) and its estimated future useful life was 20 years.

On 1 April 20X7 Delta began a 10 year leaseback of the property from the third party. The annual rate of interest implicit in the lease was 10%. Annual rentals were $528,500, payable in arrears.

The sale of the property by Delta does not constitute the satisfaction of a relevant performance obligation under IFRS 15 *Revenue from Contracts with Customers*.

Requirements

1 (a) Explain how IFRS 16 *Leases* requires lessees to recognise and measure rights and obligations under leasing arrangements. **(4 marks)**

(b) Explain whether there are any exceptions to the usual requirements of IFRS 16.

Your answer should briefly describe the accounting treatment required in the case of such exceptions and, where appropriate, state examples of assets which these exceptions might apply to. **(4 marks)**

2 Explain and show how the transaction described in Exhibits 1 and 2 would be reported in the financial statements of Delta for the year ended 30 September 20X7. The marks are allocated as follows:

Exhibit 1 – Property lease **(8 marks)**
Exhibit 2 – Sale and leaseback **(9 marks)**

(Total = 25 marks)

Question 4

You work for Omega. Your managing director has raised a number of queries relating to the application of various IFRS Accounting Standards. Relevant information is provided in the Exhibits:

Exhibit 1 – Reporting by segment

I notice that the disclosures relating to operating segments in the consolidated financial statements appear to be based on the geographical location of the customers of the group. I am the non-executive director of another large listed entity and the segment disclosures in their consolidated financial statements are based on the type of products sold. Also some of our larger subsidiaries have customers located in more than one geographical region yet they provide no segment disclosures whatsoever in their individual financial statements. I would like to see segment disclosures given in the individual subsidiary accounts as well. I really don't understand these inconsistencies given that all these financial statements have been prepared using IFRS Accounting Standards. Please explain the reasons for these apparent inconsistencies.

Exhibit 2 – Accounting policies and accounting estimates

I have recently heard someone talking about accounting policies and accounting estimates. He said that when there's a change of these items sometimes the change is made retrospectively and sometimes it's made prospectively. Please explain the difference between an accounting policy and an accounting estimate and give me an example of each. Please also explain the difference between retrospective and prospective adjustments and how this applies to accounting policies and accounting estimates.

Exhibit 3 – New subsidiary

As you know, we recently acquired a new subsidiary, Temerity, which is a small company that specialises in the research and development of pharmaceutical products. The purchase consideration was by way of a share exchange and valued at $35 million. The fair value of Temerity's net assets was $15 million, excluding the patent and research described below.

The Temerity brand name is internally generated and is not recognised in Temerity's separate financial statements. A firm of specialist advisors has estimated the current value of the brand to be $10 million, however the company is awaiting the outcome of clinical trials, which would increase the value of the brand to $12 million if the trials are successful. Temerity is also engaged in a research project and has incurred costs of $2 million to date which it has recognised as an expense. It is not expected that the research project will lead to future developments.

I haven't included the brand or the research when calculating the goodwill on acquisition of Temerity, but one of the other directors has queried whether this is correct. Can you help me to understand how these intangibles should be accounted for on acquisition?

Exhibit 4 – Revaluation of property portfolio

When looking at the statement of comprehensive income I noticed that a gain of $64 million was included relating to the revaluation of our portfolio of properties. I looked in the notes to check that a corresponding amount of $64 million had been added to property, plant and equipment. However the note explaining movements in property, plant and equipment showed a revaluation increase of $80 million. There was a reference to tax in one of the notes I looked at but I don't see why this is relevant. I know our rate of tax is 20% and this would explain the difference but we won't pay any tax on this gain unless we sell the properties. We have no intention of selling any of them in the foreseeable future so what relevance does tax have? Please explain the difference between the $64 million gain in the statement of comprehensive income and the $80 million gain added to property, plant and equipment.

Requirements

Provide answers to the following questions raised by your managing director.

Reporting by segment (Exhibit 1)	**(6 marks)**
Policies and estimates (Exhibit 2)	**(7 marks)**

IFRS Accounting Standards – new subsidiary (Exhibit 3)   **(7 marks)**
Revaluation of property portfolio (Exhibit 4)   **(5 marks)**

(Total = 25 marks)

Your answers should refer to relevant provisions of IFRS Accounting Standards.

Answers

DO NOT TURN THIS PAGE UNTIL YOU HAVE
COMPLETED THE MOCK EXAM

Question 1

	Marks
Revenue	2
Cost of sales and gross profit	4½
Distribution	1
Administration	1½
Finance cost	4½
Tax	1½
Other comprehensive income	5
Allocation between NCI and owners of parent	5
Total	**25**

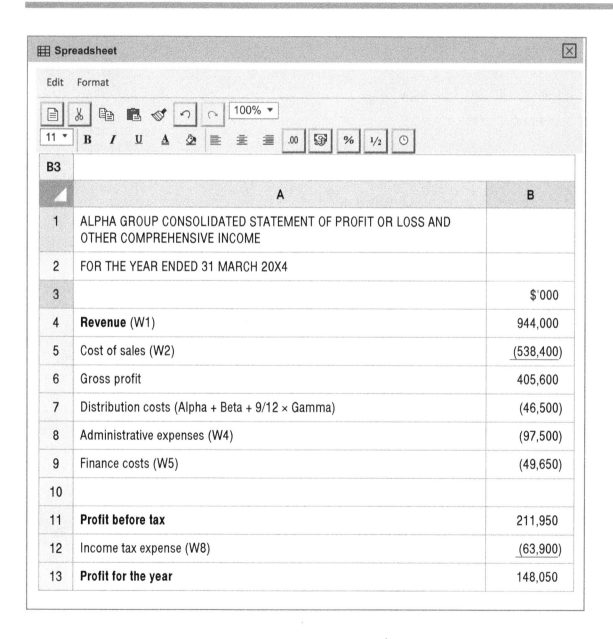

	Spreadsheet	
Edit Format		
B3		
	A	**B**
1	ALPHA GROUP CONSOLIDATED STATEMENT OF PROFIT OR LOSS AND OTHER COMPREHENSIVE INCOME	
2	FOR THE YEAR ENDED 31 MARCH 20X4	
3		$'000
4	**Revenue** (W1)	944,000
5	Cost of sales (W2)	(538,400)
6	Gross profit	405,600
7	Distribution costs (Alpha + Beta + 9/12 × Gamma)	(46,500)
8	Administrative expenses (W4)	(97,500)
9	Finance costs (W5)	(49,650)
10		
11	**Profit before tax**	211,950
12	Income tax expense (W8)	(63,900)
13	**Profit for the year**	148,050

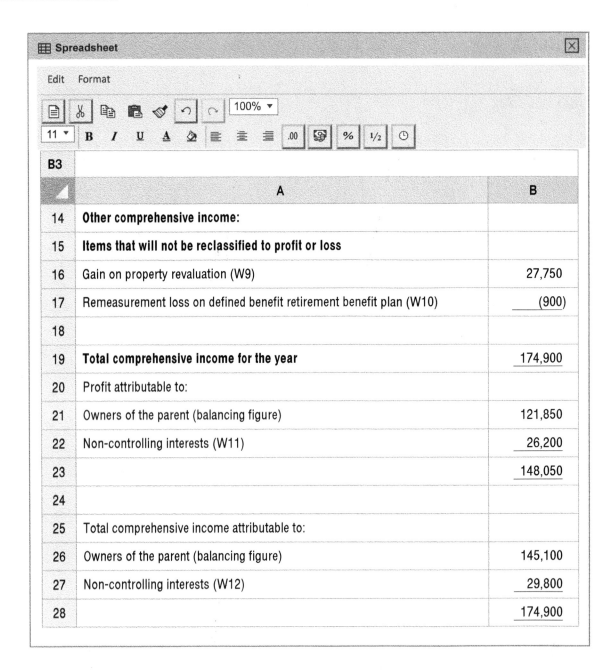

	A	B
14	**Other comprehensive income:**	
15	**Items that will not be reclassified to profit or loss**	
16	Gain on property revaluation (W9)	27,750
17	Remeasurement loss on defined benefit retirement benefit plan (W10)	(900)
18		
19	**Total comprehensive income for the year**	174,900
20	Profit attributable to:	
21	Owners of the parent (balancing figure)	121,850
22	Non-controlling interests (W11)	26,200
23		148,050
24		
25	Total comprehensive income attributable to:	
26	Owners of the parent (balancing figure)	145,100
27	Non-controlling interests (W12)	29,800
28		174,900

Tutorial note. The answer above has been presented in a spreadsheet to replicate how you might present your answer in the spreadsheet response option in your computer-based exam. It is important that you get familiar with the exam software and the features available within it. You can do this by accessing the past exams available in the DipIFR Study Support Resources section of the ACCA website.

Workings

1   *Revenue*

	$'000
Consolidate Alpha + Beta + 9/12 × Gamma	
Alpha + Beta + 9/12 × Gamma	974,000
Sales of components by Alpha to Beta	(30,000)
	944,000

2   *Cost of sales*

	$'000
Alpha + Beta + 9/12 × Gamma	558,000
Sales of components by Alpha to Beta	(30,000)
Movement in unrealised profit on sale of components:	
¼ (6,000 – 4,400)	400
Impairment of goodwill on acquisition of Beta (W3)	10,000
	538,400

3   *Impairment of Beta goodwill*

	Unit 1	Unit 2	Unit 3
	$'000	$'000	$'000
Carrying amount of net assets	215,000	185,000	130,000
Allocated goodwill	32,000	28,000	20,000
	247,000	213,000	150,000
Recoverable amount	255,000	220,000	140,000
So impairment equals	Nil	Nil	10,000

4   *Administrative expenses*

	$'000
Alpha + Beta + 9/12 × Gamma	93,000
Current service cost – defined benefit pension plan	4,500
	97,500

5   *Finance costs*

	$'000
Alpha + Beta + 9/12 × Gamma	44,000
Finance cost on deferred consideration (W6)	4,050
Net interest cost on defined benefit pension plan (W7)	1,600
	49,650

6   *Finance cost on deferred consideration*

	$'000
Present value of future payment ($65,340/(1.10)^2$)	54,000
Annual finance cost (10%)	5,400
Finance cost for nine month period (5,400 × 9/12)	4,050

7   *Net interest cost on defined benefit pension plan*

	$'000
Opening net liability (60,000 – 40,000)	20,000
Annual finance cost (8%)	1,600

8   *Income tax expense*

	$'000
Alpha + Beta + 9/12 × Gamma	64,000
Deferred tax consolidation adjustments:	
– PURP on components (25% × 400)	(100)
– Impairment of goodwill (outside scope)	Nil
	63,900

9   *Gain on property revaluation*

		$'000
Alpha + whole of Gamma (all post-acquisition)		37,000
Deferred tax on gain (25%)		(9,250)
		27,750

10   *Remeasurement loss on defined benefit retirement benefit plan*

	$'000
Opening net liability (60,000 – 40,000)	20,000
Current service cost	4,500
Finance cost on net liability (W7)	1,600
Contributions	(5,000)
	21,100
Closing net liability (68,000 – 46,000)	(22,000)
Remeasurement loss (balancing figure)	900

11   *Non-controlling interests in profit*

	$'000	$'000
Beta		
Profit for the year	60,000	
Impairment of goodwill	(10,000)	
	50,000	
NCI (20%)		10,000
Gamma		
9/12 × profit for the year	40,500	
NCI (40%)		16,200
		26,200

12   *Non-controlling interests in total comprehensive income*

	$'000
NCI in profit (W11)	26,200
NCI in Gamma's property revaluation	
(40% × (12,000 × 75% – the net of tax amount))	3,600
	29,800

Question 2

	Marks
Exhibit 1	
Hedge accounting is permitted (describe why)	2
Hedging instrument is a derivative that is recognised at fair value, with the gain recognised in the SOCI	2
Commitment to buy machinery not recognised in current accounting period	1
Gain on effective portion of hedging instrument recognised in OCI (with explanation)	3
Gain on ineffective portion recognised in P/L	1
	9
Exhibit 2	
Opening net liability	1
Current and past service cost	1½
Finance cost	1½
Settlement	1
Remeasurement gain/loss	1
Remeasurement gain/loss calculation	5
	11
Exhibit 3	
Objectivity discussion (up to)	2
Professional competence and due care (up to)	1½
Integrity discussion (up to)	1½
	5
Total	25

Exhibit 1 – Commitment to purchase new machinery

Under the principles of IFRS 9 *Financial Instruments* Gamma is permitted to use hedge accounting when reporting the hedging arrangement in its financial statements. This is because:

- The relevant documentation has been prepared.
- There is a clear economic relationship between the hedged cash flows and the hedging instrument.
- Gamma is entering into a forward purchase of exactly the required amount of foreign currency.

The hedging instrument is a derivative financial instrument. Derivatives are normally measured at fair value in the financial statements with changes in fair value being recognised in the statement of profit or loss.

On 30 September 20X7 Gamma would recognise the derivative as a current asset at its fair value of $2.7 million and the change in fair value recognised in the statement of comprehensive income.

The hedged item is designated to be the changes in the expected cash flows arising on the contact. For the year ended 30 September 20X7 changes in the expected cash flows arising from the contract would not be recognised since the contract is an executory contract (a contract made by two parties in which the terms are set to be fulfilled at a later date).

Since the hedging documentation indicates that the hedged item is the changes in the expected cash flows then cash flow hedge accounting is used. In this case this involves comparing the change in the value of the derivative (the recognised hedging instrument) with the (unrecognised) changes in the value of the expected cash flows arising under the contract.

To the extent that the change in the value of the derivative is less than or equal to the change in the value of the expected cash flows (the effective portion of the hedge) the change in value of the derivative is recognised in other comprehensive income rather than profit or loss.

However any over-hedging would result in any gains or losses arising on the hedging instrument that relate to the over-hedging (the ineffective portion of the hedge) being immediately being recognised in profit or loss.

In this case the overall gain in fair value of the derivative between 1 July 20X7 and 30 September 20X7 is $2.7 million. In that same period the change in the expected value of the cash flows arising under the contract is $2.6 million. Therefore $2.6 million of the gain on the derivative would be recognised in other comprehensive income with the balance of $100,000 being recognised in profit or loss

Exhibit 2 – Purchase of inventory from a foreign supplier

Under the principles of IAS 21 *The Effects of Changes in Foreign Exchange Rates*, the purchase of inventory on 1 August 20X7 would be recorded using the spot rate of exchange on that date. Therefore, Gamma would recognise a purchase and an associated payable of $600,000 (3.6 million dinars/6).

Gamma would recognise revenue of $480,000 in the statement of profit or loss because goods to the value of $480,000 were sold prior to 30 September 20X7. At the same time Gamma would recognise $360,000 ($600,000 × 60%) in cost of sales because the revenue of $480,000 is recognised.

The closing inventory of goods purchased from the foreign supplier would be $240,000 ($600,000 - $360,000) and would be recognised as a current asset. This would not be re-translated since inventory is a non-monetary asset. Under the principles of IAS 2 *Inventories* – the inventory would be measured at cost.

The payment of 1,260,000 dinars on 15 September 20X7 would be recorded using the spot rate of exchange on that date therefore the payment would be recorded at $200,000 (1,260,000 dinars/$6.3).

The closing payable of 2,340,000 dinars (3,600,000 dinars – 1,260,000 dinars) is a monetary item therefore would be translated at the rate of exchange in force at the year-end (6.4 dinars to $1). Therefore, the closing payable (recorded in current liabilities) would be $365,625 (2,340,000 dinars/$6.4).

The difference between the initially recognised payable ($600,000) and the subsequently recognised payment ($200,000) is $400,000. Since the closing payable is $365,625 (see above), Gamma has made an exchange gain of $34,375 ($400,000 – $365,625). This gain is recognised in the statement of profit or loss, either under other income category or as a reduction in cost of sales.

Exhibit 3 – Discussion with Finance Director (FD)

The Financial Controller (FC) is in danger of breaching the fundamental ethical principle of objectivity. As an employee who is due to receive a bonus based on reported profits the FC has a personal interest in reporting a favourable profit. The comment made by the FD (a superior) urging the FC to comply with this request is an intimidation threat meant to deter the FC from acting objectively and the FD is exercising undue influence.

The FC is also in danger of breaching the fundamental principle of professional competence and due care. Complying with the FD's request would mean that inventories were not being measured in accordance with the requirements of IAS 2 *Inventories*.

Finally the FC is in danger of breaching the fundamental principle of integrity. Deliberately overstating inventories in order to inflate reported profits is unethical behaviour.

Question 3

	Marks
Requirement 1 (a)	
Initial recognition and measurement of right of use asset and lease liability (up to)	2½
Subsequent treatment of above items (up to)	1½
	4
Requirement 1 (b)	
Exception re: short-term leases (up to)	2
Exception re: low value assets (up to)	2
	4
Requirement 2	
Exhibit 1	
Initial recognition of lease liability and right of use asset (up to)	2
Subsequent accounting for right of use asset (up to)	2
Computation of finance cost and closing lease liability (up to)	2
Split of closing lease liability into its current and non-current components	2
	8
Exhibit 2	
Explain treatment of 'sale'	3
Account for property	2
Account for financial liability	4
	9
Total	25

Requirement 1 – Questions relating to the requirements of IFRS 16 *Leases*

(a) IFRS 16 requires lessees to recognise a right of use asset and an associated liability at the inception of the lease. The initial measurement of the lease liability will be the present value of the future lease payments. The discount rate used to measure the present value of the future lease payments is the rate of interest implicit in the lease – essentially the rate of return earned by the lessor on the leased asset. (Note if this rate is not available to the lessee then a commercial rate of interest can be used instead). The right of use asset is initially measured as the amount of the initial lease liability plus any lease payments made at or before the commencement of the lease less any incentives received, plus any initial direct costs plus any dismantling or restoration costs. The right of use asset is subsequently depreciated over the shorter of the useful life of the asset and the lease term. The lease liability is subsequently amortised, using the rate of interest implicit in the lease as the effective interest rate.

(b) Exceptions to the usual requirements of IFRS 16 are available for short-term leases and leases of low value assets. A short-term lease is a lease that, at the date of commencement, has a term of 12 months or less. Lessees can elect to treat short-term leases by recognising the lease rentals as an expense over the lease term rather than recognising a 'right of use asset' and a lease liability. A similar election – *on a lease-by-lease basis* – can be made in respect of 'low value assets'. Examples of low-value underlying assets can include tablet and personal computers, small items of office furniture and telephones. (Note: any reasonable attempt to describe a 'low-value' asset would receive credit).

Requirement 2

Exhibit 1 – Property lease

The initial right of use asset and lease liability would be $3,072,500 (500,000 × 6.145). The initial direct costs of the lessee would then be added to the right of use asset to give a carrying amount of $3,132,500 ($3,072,500 + $60,000).

Depreciation would be charged over a ten-year period so the charge for the year ended 30 September 20X7 would be $313,250 ($3,132,500 × 1/10). The closing carrying amount of PPE in non-current assets would be $2,819,250 ($3,132,500 × 9/10).

Delta would recognise a finance cost in profit or loss of $307,250 ($3,072,500 × 10%). The closing lease liability would be $2,879,750($3,072,500 + $307,250 – $500,000). Next year's finance cost will be $287,975 ($2,879,750 × 10%) so the current liability at 30 September 20X7 will be $212,025 ($500,000 – $287,975). The balance of the liability of $2,667,725 ($2,879,750 – $212,025) will be non-current.

Exhibit 2 – Sale and leaseback

Because the 'sale' to a third party does not constitute the satisfaction of a relevant performance obligation under IFRS 15 *Revenue from Contracts with Customers* this is treated as a financing transaction rather than a sale. Therefore Delta will continue to recognise the property and depreciate it over its useful life. The 'sales proceeds' will be treated as a financial liability.

The depreciable component of the property is $12 million and so the depreciation on the property for the year ended 30 September 20X7 will be $600,000 ($12m × 1/20). This amount will be charged to profit or loss as an operating expense. The carrying amount of the property at 30 September 20X7 will be $16,900,000 ($17,500,000 – $600,000). This will be shown as a non-current asset in the statement of financial position.

The financial liability will have a carrying amount of $4,500,000 at 1 April 20X7. There will be a finance cost charged to profit or loss for the year ended 30 September 20X7 of $225,000 ($4,500,000 × 10% × 6/12). The closing financial liability at 30 September 20X7 will be $4,725,000 ($4,500,000 + $225,000).

The rental payment that will be made within 12 months of the reporting date will be the first payment of $732,300 due on 31 March 20X8. This payment will first be applied to the outstanding finance cost at 31 March 20X8. Any amounts over and above the outstanding finance cost will be applied to a reduction in the principal amount owing. The outstanding finance cost at 31 March 20X8 will be the finance cost of $225,000 for the six months to 30 September 20X7 (included in the year end liability) plus the finance cost for the six months from 1 October 20X7 to 31 March 20X8 (also $225,000 but not included in the year-end liability). Therefore, the amount of principal amount that will be discharged by the payment of $732,300 on 31 March 20X8 will be $282,300 ($732,300 – $225,000 –- $225,000). Therefore, the total current liability at 30 September 20X7 will be $507,300 (the $225,000 finance cost for the six months to 30 September 20X7 plus the $282,300 principal repayment). The non-current liability will be $4,217,700 ($4,725,000 – $507,300).

Additional explanation but not part of required answer – analysis of liability at 30 September 20X7 and 30 September 20X8

(1) Loan profile for the first two years of the loan

Year to 31 March	Balance b/fwd £	Finance cost (10%) £	Rental payment £	Balance c/fwd £
20X8	4,500,000	450,000	(732,300)	4,217,700
20X9	4,217,700	421,770	(732,300)	3,907,170

(2)   Analysis of total liability at <u>30 September 20X7 and 20X8</u>

Date	Accrued finance cost £	Outstanding principal (balancing figure) £	Total liability £
30 September 20X7	225,000 (450,000 × 6/12)	4,500,000	4,725,000 (4,500,000 + 225,000)
30 September 20X8	210,885 (421,770 × 6/12)	4,217,700	4,428,585 (4,217,700 + 6/12 × 421,770)

(3)   Analysis of impact of payment on 31 March 20X8 on liability at 30 September 20X7

- Payment of accrued finance cost £225,000. [A]
- Reduction in principal sum outstanding £282,300 (£4,500,000 – £4,217,700). [B]
- A + B = £507,300 (see above)

Note. Any reasonable attempt at splitting the liability into current and non-current will be awarded marks

Question 4

Marking guide

	Marks
Exhibit 1	
Discuss how operating segments are reported under IFRS 8 (up to)	4
Discuss query relating to publication of segmental information by individual subsidiaries (up to)	2
	6
Exhibit 2	
Definition of accounting policy (with example)	2½
Accounting treatment of changes in accounting policy	2
Definition of accounting estimate (with example)	1½
Accounting treatment of changes in accounting estimates	1
	7
Exhibit 3	
Explanation of intangible assets in a business combination (up to)	2
Explanation of brand (up to)	3
Explanation of research (up to)	2
	7
Exhibit 4	
Identify the differences are caused by deferred tax (up to)	2
Apply the given figures to explain the exact difference (up to)	3
	5
Total	25

Exhibit 1 – Reporting by segment

The relevant IFRS Accounting Standard that deals with operating segments is IFRS 8 *Operating Segments*. The definition of an operating segment in IFRS 8 is based around an entity's business model, which could be different from entity to entity and the disclosures focus on the information that management believes is important when running the business. IFRS 8 defines an operating segment as a component of an entity:

- That engages in business activities from which it may earn revenues and incur expenses;
- Whose operating results are regularly reviewed by the chief operating decision maker; and
- For which discrete financial information is available.

The 'chief operating decision maker' is a role rather than a title or it is a function and not necessarily a person. The role/function is defined around who monitors performance and allocates resources of the operating segments. IFRS 8 is only compulsory for listed entities. If we wanted to include information regarding the operating segments of individual subsidiaries then we could as IFRS 8 requires judgement in its application. However the information in the individual financial statements would either need to comply with IFRS 8 in all respects or the information cannot be described as 'segment information'.

Exhibit 2 – Accounting policies and accounting estimates

IAS 8 *Accounting Policies, Changes in Accounting Estimates and Errors* defines an accounting policy as 'the specific principles, bases, conventions, rules and practices applied by an entity in preparing and presenting financial statements'. An example of an accounting policy would be the decision to apply the cost model or the fair value model when measuring investment properties.

When an entity changes an accounting policy, the change is applied retrospectively. This means that the comparative figures are based on the new policy (rather than last year's actual figures). The opening balance of retained earnings is restated in the statement of changes in equity.

Accounting estimates are monetary amounts in financial statements that are subject to measurement uncertainty. They are made in order to implement accounting policies. An example of an accounting estimate would be (consistent with the above given example) the fair value of an investment property at the reporting date (where the fair value model was being applied).

Changes in accounting estimates are made prospectively. This means applying the new estimates in future financial statement preparation, without amending any previously published amounts.

Exhibit 3 – New subsidiary

Intangible assets acquired as part of a business combination are recognised at fair value provided that they can be valued separately from goodwill. The acquirer will recognise an intangible even if the asset had not been recognised previously. If an intangible cannot be valued, then it will be subsumed into goodwill.

Internally generated intangible assets can be recognised if they are acquired as part of a business combination. The Temerity brand name can be separate recognised in the business combination whereas an internally generated brand does not meet the recognition criteria. The brand should be recognised at its fair value at the date of acquisition of $10 million. The higher value of $12 million can't be used because it depends on the successful outcome of the clinical trials. The estimated useful life of the brand should be determined, and the brand should be amortised from the date of acquisition.

Research can be recognised on acquisition if it meets the definition of an asset and is identifiable. As it is not expected that the research will lead to future developments and therefore cannot be said to have the potential to produce economic benefits, it does not meet the definition of an asset and cannot be capitalised.

Exhibit 4 – Revaluation of property portfolio

The difference between the $64 million gain in the statement of comprehensive income and the $80 million gain included in property, plant and equipment is caused by deferred tax.

IAS 12 *Income Taxes* requires that deferred tax liabilities we recognised (with a very few exceptions) on all taxable temporary differences.

A taxable temporary difference arises when the carrying value of an asset increases but its 'tax base' does not.

When an asset is revalued the carrying value increases but the tax base stays the same (as the future tax deductions are unaffected).

Therefore a revaluation of $80 million causes a taxable temporary difference of $80 million and (when the tax rate is 20%) an additional deferred tax liability of $16 million ($80m × 20%).

This liability reduces the gain reported in the statement of comprehensive income to $64 million ($80m – $16m).

Tell us what you think

Got comments or feedback on this book? Let us know.
Use your QR code reader:

Or, visit:
https://bppgroup.fra1.qualtrics.com/jfe/form/SV_9TrxTtw8jSvO7Pv

Need to get in touch with customer service?

www.bpp.com/request-support

Spotted an error?

www.bpp.com/learningmedia/Errata